Family Mediation

Appropriate Dispute Resolution in a new family justice system

Second Edition

Family Mediation

Appropriate Dispute Resolution in a new family justice system

Second Edition

Lisa Parkinson

Neil Robinson, Editorial Consultant

Family Law

Published by Family Law
a publishing imprint of
Jordan Publishing Limited
21 St Thomas Street
Bristol BS1 6JS

British Library Cataloguing-in-Publication Data

A catalogue record for this book is available from the British Library.

ISBN 978 1 84661 274 9

Typeset by Letterpart Ltd, Reigate, Surrey

Printed in Great Britain by CPI Antony Rowe, Chippenham and Eastbourne

DEDICATION

This book is dedicated to mediators everywhere

FOREWORD

The first edition of this book was published in 1997. By then family mediation in Britain had for nearly twenty years been developing a limited public identity; and throughout that period Lisa Parkinson had been a central figure (arguably even the central figure) in its development.

The depth of the author's experience of family mediation even by then; the level of her intellectual energy; her way with words; her breadth of vision; but above all her skill in communicating with different sorts of people (and in communicating how to communicate): all these qualities were likely to make the book an immediate success. But few could have forecast the level of its success. Reviewers wrote that it fizzed with good ideas; was packed with nuggets, all gold; brimmed with sheer quality; and was the most fitting text for any aspiring mediator. In the light of its necessary relationship with the family law and procedure of England and Wales it is in a way astonishing that the book was nevertheless chosen for translation into Russian, Portuguese, Italian, Spanish and Slovenian.

But it was in part its nexus with our family law and procedure at that time which has rendered the first edition – still in print – seriously out of date. It had been published a year after the enactment of the Family Law Act 1996 and in the expectation that all of it would soon be brought into force. Both expressly and by necessary implication a greatly increased role for mediation was written across much of the Act. In the book Lisa Parkinson addressed it all at length but, with typical prescience, questioned whether the new path to divorce there laid would prove too long and tortuous. In the event, of course, neither Part I nor Part II was brought into force at all.

There was, however, one Part of the Act – Part III – which did come into force; which has survived in a replaced form; and which was to have important consequences for the role of family mediation. Section 29 required most applicants for public funding for proposed applications to the court in private family law matters first to have attended an assessment for suitability for mediation; and public funding was made available for a mediator to conduct the assessment. If, as quite often occurred, mediation then followed, further public funding was made available for it. But, even when it did not follow, the process of assessment brought the possibility of mediation to the attention of one if not both of the parties and, in that it was a mainstream procedure, it came over time to raise the profile of mediation with the general public.

Now, however, we have two dramatic developments; and the result is that the timing of this second edition could not be more apt.

The first is the threatened removal of public funding for almost all applications to the court in private family law. Most mediators, certainly including Lisa Parkinson, are as concerned as are we family lawyers about the effect of its threatened removal on the ability of the family courts to work efficiently and to deliver justice. The proposal however is that in principle public funding of mediation should remain. Although the terms under which the funding for it is to continue will require the closest scrutiny lest they erode its provision through the back door, a situation in which family mediation were to be funded but family litigation were not to be funded would of course transform the landscape in favour of mediation.

The second is the Practice Direction about to be issued by the President which will substantially extend the ambit of the procedure introduced by section 29 of the Act of 1996. Instead of being a prerequisite to the grant of public funding for the making of an application, evidence of attendance at an assessment for mediation will be expected to be filed upon issue of most private law applications, whether the applicant is acting in person or is represented by solicitors privately funded or (in the rare remaining situations) publicly funded. Absent such evidence, the court will at the first appointment consider whether to use its power under rule 3.3(1) of the new Family Procedure Rules 2010, which will come into force on 6 April 2011, to adjourn the proceedings in order to enable the parties to obtain advice about alternative dispute resolution.

For long mediators have been forecasting a breakthrough for family mediation. Today, at least, the forecast is solidly based. The subtitle introduced into this second edition is 'Appropriate Dispute Resolution in a new family justice system'. Yes, the system will be new in various respects. And, yes, mediation will no longer be outside it nor even running in parallel with the system. It will indeed be *in* the system. So, irrespective of whether we are already family mediators or whether (as I do one day) we aspire to be family mediators, all of us who work in the system need a comprehensive understanding of family mediation, the practice of which is far more complex and multi-faceted than the uninformed observer might assume. We will need a *vademecum*. It will be Lisa Parkinson's book.

Nicholas Wilson
Lord Justice of Appeal
President of the Family Mediators Association
31 January 2011

PREFACE

The 1st edition of this book, published by Sweet & Maxwell in 1997, was written when family mediation was on the verge of achieving its first recognition in legislation and limited provision for public funding through the legal aid system. This breakthrough came after nearly twenty years of vigorous campaigning by pioneer family mediation services. I am grateful to Jordans Publishing Ltd for giving me this opportunity for a 2nd edition (with Sweet & Maxwell's support), at a time when family mediation is reaching another critical turning point in its evolution. In 2011, with the new Family Procedure Rules coming into force in April and the prospect of further change following the Family Justice Review, family mediation faces new challenges and opportunities. Some of these changes may be controversial and mediators will be on their mettle to demonstrate that they are effective practitioners, not ideological dreamers. There are questions to be addressed, standards for training and practice to be further defined and regulated and new models to develop in collaborative, multi-disciplinary partnerships.

This edition sets out to be more than just an update of the first one. Until 1996, family mediation was outside the family justice system and seen by many as a fringe service for mainly middle class, middle income clients. Even after publicly funded mediation was made available in the legal aid sector from 1997 onwards, it continued to be a small side-stream alongside the main flow of private family law proceedings. Now mediation is entering the main stream, while retaining its identity as an independent and voluntary process of Appropriate Dispute Resolution. The role of family mediation is being strengthened not only to help family members resolve disputes outside the legal system, but also in a new system of family justice in which 'participative justice' is destined to play a much greater part. Participative justice enables people to maintain their autonomy in reaching legally informed agreements that can be made enforceable when necessary through an order of the Court. Family mediation, together with other forms of Appropriate Dispute Resolution including collaborative law and hybrid civil/family mediation, is part of an evolving system of family justice that may be shifting from a traditional adversarial system to one that is far more inquisitorial and participative.

This is therefore an opportune time to consider the role that family mediation can play, to reflect on experiences of mediation from mediators and clients over more than thirty years, to take note of research findings and to look to the future. There is now much greater recognition of the need to listen to children's views and feelings and to provide ways of communicating with children as well as adults in helping parents to reach agreements that incorporate understanding of the voice of the child. Over the last two decades, family mediation has developed in many European countries, as well as in the UK. Exchanges with mediators and researchers in other countries enrich our own developing practice. Having a particular love of languages and travel, I have benefited from wonderful experiences of training and co-training in other countries, from Russia and Lithuania to the French Antilles and the Indian Ocean. This international network is of great value in developing international cross-border family mediation in private law proceedings over children. The Hague Conference is developing a Guide to Good Practice for international family mediation, while the European Union is funding projects to develop specialised training in this emerging and complex field. These subjects were barely on family mediators' radar in 1997.

I hope this book will be of interest to family mediators both in training and with experience, and also to students in other disciplines and members of other professions who have an interest in mediation and ADR. It is very much a shared endeavour that has grown through continuously thought-provoking and enjoyable co-mediating and co-training with colleagues in England, Wales and Scotland, and in other countries. There are many innovative developments that lie beyond its scope and which need exploration by other writers. I hope that anyone who glances at the book will find something in it that may catch your attention, suggest different ways of looking at things and encourage you to express your own ideas. This is, after all, what mediators seek to do.

Lisa Parkinson

Bristol
February 2011

ACKNOWLEDGMENTS

First and foremost I should like to express my warm thanks to Neil Robinson, Editorial Consultant on this book, for his encouragement and support in preparing this new edition and for the benefit of his unique combination of expertise (both as a family lawyer and mediator), acuity of mind and creative imagination. Exchanges with Neil on many questions addressed in this book have been wonderfully stimulating and enjoyable and his input on specific aspects has been indispensable.

I should also like to express my warm thanks to other colleagues for giving me invaluable help, particularly Henry Brown, Robert Clerke, Robin ap Cynan, Sheila Gooderham and Beverley Sayers. Sheila Gooderham provided generous and valuable contributions to Chapter 9 (mediating on financial matters) and I should like to thank her organisation, The Mediation Specialists, for permission to include their format for the Open Financial Statement (Appendix C).

I am very grateful to the Family Mediation Council for permission to include the FMC Code of Practice for Family Mediators (Appendix A) and to the Family Mediators Association for permission to include the Agreement to Mediate (Appendix B) and the co-mediation file record (Appendix D). Bristol Family Mediators Association Ltd, of which I am a member, kindly agreed to my using the flowchart in Chapter 3, while The Mediation Centre in Stafford allowed me to include their Additional Ground-rules for court-referred mediation (Appendix E). I am also grateful to Family Mediation Manchester Ltd for their permission to include their Parental Consent Form for direct consultation with children (Appendix F). There are also individual mediators I wish to thank: Jane Staff of Salmons Mediation for her mediation example in Chapter 7, Terry Bastyan of Gilbert Stephens Mediation Service in Exeter for his example in Chapter 8 and, of course, the examples provided by Neil Robinson. All identifying details have been removed from these examples and names have been changed. Emma Turner, Manager of The Mediation Centre, Stafford, provided the stepping-stones metaphor in Chapter 6.

I also want to thank my friends and colleagues in other European countries who responded so readily to requests for 'updated snapshots' of developments in their jurisdictions. They include Pia Deleuran in

Denmark, Claudio Jacob in France, Sybille Kiesewetter, Christoph Paul and Jamie Walker (MiKK) in Germany, Dr Costanza Marzotto in Italy, Manuela Pliżga-Jonarska in Poland, Professor Juan Carlos Vezzulla in Portugal, Dr Tsisana Shamlikashvili in Russia, Professor Leticia Villaluenga in Spain, Bernt Wahlsten in Sweden. Beyond Europe, I should like to express my warm thanks to Dr Jenn McIntosh and Professor Lawrie Moloney in Australia, Jim Melamed at mediate.com, Stephan Auerbach at International Social Service (ISS) in Geneva and Dr Mohamed Keshavjee, formerly with the Aga Khan Foundation in Aiglemont, France. Verena Schlubach of ISS Berlin kindly provided the ecogram for cross-border family mediation in Chapter 14.

Thanks to the generosity of Jenn McIntosh, I have been able to include the 'voice of a child' in the very moving poem at the end of Chapter 7, 'Rachel's Poem'. I should also like to thank Pan Books for permission to include the extract from 'The Prophet' by Kahlil Gibran.

This edition of the book contains some material from my articles published previously in the journals, *Family Law* and *International Family Law*. Benjamin Johnson, my editor, has been very prompt and helpful and I thank him too.

Finally I should like to thank my husband, Tim, for his unfailing support over many years of immersion in mediation and especially for his expert computing skills in compiling tables and diagrams well beyond my limited competence.

Although so much is owed to other people, all omissions, errors and other failings in this book are entirely my own responsibility.

Lisa Parkinson
February 2011

CONTENTS

CHAPTER 1

MEDIATION AND THE MANAGEMENT OF CONFLICT

'So hope for a great sea-change
On the far side of revenge
Believe that a further shore
Is reachable from here'[1]

CONTENTS

1.1   THE NEED FOR PEACEFUL WAYS OF RESOLVING CONFLICT

Violent conflict and acts of mass destruction pose great threats to the survival of communities, to the environment and to humanity as a whole. Violent conflict arouses deep fear and brings suffering and death. As conflict is dangerous, there are instinctive, biological reactions among all animals, including humans, to conflict and aggression. Many reactions are

---

[1]   Seamus Heaney *The Cure at Troy.*

of a fight-or-flight nature. Some animals avoid direct conflict instinctively by surrendering to the individual or group they perceive as the stronger. Human societies have developed more sophisticated ways of dealing with conflict, including negotiation and mediation, but all too often they fail to use them. Reactions to conflict in so-called developed societies are often primitive.

'Conflict is everywhere, not only between human beings, but throughout nature, from quantum mechanical particles to dark energy'.[2] Conflict itself is neither positive nor negative: it is a natural force that is necessary for growth and change. Life without conflict would be static. What matters is how conflict is managed. If conflict is managed carefully, it need not be destructive. It need not destroy individuals, communities and relationships. The energy that is generated in conflict can be used constructively, instead of destructively. 'Resolving conflict is rarely about who is right. It is about acknowledgment and appreciation of differences'.[3] Resolving conflict involves changing perceptions and attitudes. When conflicts are resolved in an integrative way instead of through contest, relationships can be sustained and strengthened. With willingness on the part of disputants, perceptions and attitudes towards each other may change. The changed atmosphere of openness, listening and co-operation may then radiate out from them to other members of their family or community. From Buddhist teaching we can learn that:[4]

> 'most of our time is spent in analysing differences. Now concentrate on similarities, on what is common between ... antagonistic opposites ... Look for the higher thirds above all opposites ... look for this relationship, and you will be kinder to each of the pairs.'

Mediation offers a means of managing conflict and settling disputes. In mediation, the mediator holds a centred and balanced position between the participants. From this centred position, the mediator can help them to channel and combine their energies in working out solutions, instead of fighting, giving up or accepting an unsatisfactory compromise.

1.2   DEFINING MEDIATION

The word 'mediation' is derived from the Latin 'medius, medium', meaning 'in the middle'. The word mediation is used with only minor variations of spelling and pronunciation in many languages – English, French, German, Italian, Spanish and Portuguese. Mediation processes are used across the world, in Europe and North America, Australia and New Zealand, China and Japan and Ismaili communities. In the Spanish and Portuguese speaking countries of South America, the use of

---

[2]   Cloke 'Mediation and Meditation – the Deeper Middle Way' *Mediate.com Weekly* No 266 (March 2009).
[3]   Crum *The Magic of Conflict* (Touchstone, 1987), p 49.
[4]   Humphreys *Zen Buddhism* (Unwin Paperbacks, 1984), p 158.

mediation has grown rapidly. The word mediation is now in common usage, but still liable to be confused with similar-sounding words such as 'conciliation', 'reconciliation' and 'meditation'. In the 1990s mediation became a fashionable portmanteau word carrying various bundles of meanings and values that policy-makers and practitioners chose to pack into it. 'That's a great deal to make one word mean', Alice said in a thoughtful tone. 'When I make a word do a lot of work like that,' said Humpty Dumpty, 'I always pay it extra'.[5] Different disciplines (law, psychology, social work) sometimes battled like divorcing parents to win 'custody, care and control' of the mediation 'child'. As family mediation develops in many countries and across national borders it has become increasingly necessary to agree a universal definition, to develop harmonised training and standards of practice and to reduce ambiguities and areas of potential misunderstanding.

The Council of the European Union defines mediation as:[6]

> 'a structured process ... whereby two or more parties to a dispute attempt by themselves, on a voluntary basis, to reach an agreement on the settlement of their dispute with the assistance of a mediator. This process may be initiated by the parties or suggested or ordered by a court or prescribed by the law of a Member State.'

A mediator is defined as:[7]

> 'any third person who is asked to conduct a mediation in an effective, impartial and competent way, regardless of the denomination or profession of that third person in the Member State concerned and of the way in which the third person has been appointed or requested to conduct the mediation.'

In issuing its Directive on Mediation, the Council of the European Union stated that its objective was:[8]

> 'to promote the amicable settlement of disputes by encouraging the use of mediation and by ensuring a balanced relationship between mediation and judicial proceedings.'

Mediators assist the parties to explore options for settlement and to reach mutually agreed decisions. Participants are encouraged to reach their own voluntary and informed decisions, without threat or pressure from each other and without direction from the mediator. If the proposed settlement has legal and financial implications and needs to be made legally binding, parties need to take legal and other professional advice before confirming an agreement. Mediation is used in many spheres – civil and commercial,

---

5 Carroll *Through the Looking Glass* (First published 1872, Penguin Books, 1948), p 117.
6 European Directive on Mediation, 2008/52/EC of 21 May 2008, Art 3.
7 Ibid, Art 3b.
8 See n 6, Art 1.

neighbourhood and community, housing, divorce and other family disputes, health, education, employment, the criminal justice system and international cross-border disputes.

1.3   MEDIATION – ORIGINS AND DEVELOPMENT

Mediation is often seen as a new development, but it has a very long history in many different civilisations and cultures. In ancient China, Confucius urged people to use mediation instead of going to court. As early as the fifth-century BC, Confucius warned that litigation was liable to leave disputants embittered and unable to co-operate with each other. Confucius recommended that, instead of going to court, they should meet with a neutral peacemaker who would assist them to reach agreement. Peaceful resolution of conflicts in Ismaili Muslim communities is deeply embedded in Islamic religious traditions and rituals. In many countries across the world, from Canada to Kazakhstan, Ismaili Muslim communities have set up Conciliation Boards to encourage resolution of disputes with the help of trained mediators. These services are increasingly used by non-Ismailis.[9] There are many early examples of mediation in Europe and North America. In early industrial societies, the Quakers used mediation as their preferred means of settling marital and commercial disputes. The first Boards of Conciliation were set up in the 1860s to help resolve disputes in certain industries. There is also a long tradition of mediation in Jewish communities. The American Jewish community in New York set up the Jewish Conciliation Board in 1920 to encourage consensual settlement of disputes. In every sphere of life, mediation has been used in different ways to facilitate communication and assist disputants to reach consensual decisions. Anthropologists have described traditions in many African tribes to call a moot or meeting where respected senior tribesmen were asked to help settle disputes between individuals, families or villages. A Cheyenne Indian chief had a duty to act as peacemaker to settle any quarrels in the camp.

The use of mediation has become institutionalised in many fields – employment, industry and commerce, health and education and the criminal justice system, particularly in victim-offender reparation schemes. Community mediation is used to settle disputes between neighbours over boundaries, noise or shared facilities and in housing disputes between landlords and tenants. At international level, mediators may be brought in to help settle disputes between different countries and communities. Mediators helped to achieve a negotiated agreement between Israel and the Palestinians in January 1997 on the withdrawal of Israeli forces from the West bank city of Hebron. Although mediation has not brought peace to the Middle East, dialogue between Israel and the

---

9   Keshavjee *Family mediation in Ismaili Muslim communities throughout the world* Paper
      *given at the Council of Europe's 7th European Conference on Family Law – International
      Family Mediation* (Strasbourg, March 2009).

Arab world needs to be sustained with the utmost energy and determination. Nelson Mandela, the former president of South Africa, is probably the most acclaimed international mediator. In July 2000, Nelson Mandela used his mediation skills in the dispute within South Africa over the cause of AIDS, urging scientists and politicians to work together in the struggle against a disease which is devastating Africa. The Nobel Peace Prize for 2008 was awarded to Martti Ahtisaari, former President of Finland. The Norwegian Nobel Committee praised Mr Ahtisaari's achievements in resolving international conflicts:

> 'He is one of the most forward-looking of peace-makers. The world needs more like him. We wanted to focus on successful peace-makers because this world needs peace-makers.'

In some countries, mediation is the normal way of settling disputes and may be mandatory. Modern China, with over one billion people, has nearly a million mediators. Mediation is available nearly everywhere and disputes in the family, the community and the workplace are normally referred to mediation. Chinese and Japanese mediators have authority. They are expected to uphold moral values, to reproach one party's wrongdoing and to praise the other for acting correctly. Disputants are urged to resolve their differences in a responsible and peaceable manner for the good of the family and society as a whole. This paternalistic approach is accepted both in China and Japan, where its emphasis on moral precepts and persuasion seems to work well. In contrast, mediation is seen in other countries as a means of encouraging participants to work out their own decisions and agreements. Many countries have introduced legislation and procedures enabling the courts to refer cases to mediation and to encourage pre-court settlements. Australia was one of the first states to pass legislation promoting the use of mediation in family disputes.[10]

1.4 FAMILY MEDIATION – DEVELOPMENT IN ENGLAND AND WALES

The term 'family mediation' is used in Europe in preference to 'divorce mediation', the term commonly used in the United States. Divorce mediation is not relevant to cohabiting couples or those in civil partnerships. It also gives a one-sided message, by appearing to be pro-divorce and on the side of the partner initiating divorce. The emphasis on the word *family* is important for other reasons. First of all, families include children and secondly, there are many different kinds of disputes involving family members – such as adoption, care of the elderly, inheritance disputes – that do not involve separation or divorce. Family mediation is used mainly, however, by couples needing to settle any or all issues arising from their separation or divorce, including arrangements for

---

[10] Family Law Act of Australia 1975.

children and financial and property matters. Other family members, such as stepparents, grandparents and the children themselves may be included in the mediation process. It is a process for families in transition from one family structure to another. The aims are to facilitate communication, co-operative decision-making and the renegotiation of relationships.

Family mediation in the UK began as a grassroots initiative following the recommendations of the *Finer Report on One-Parent Families* (1974) for a new system of family courts in which *conciliation* (distinguished from *reconciliation* and defined in similar terms to *mediation*) would be the preferred means of settling any or all issues arising from separation and divorce. The first family mediation service was started in Bristol in 1978 as a local project run by a small group of social workers and family lawyers. This pilot scheme offered mediation out of court on child-related issues.[11] Independent, out-of-court mediation developed in parallel with court-directed conciliation schemes in which judges referred disputes over children to the divorce court welfare service (now Cafcass, the Children and Family Court Advisory and Support Service). Mediation at the pre-court stage facilitates early settlement of disputes and acts as a filter for disputes capable of being settled by the parties themselves. The aim of family mediation is not simply to reach quick agreements on limited issues. An important aim is to facilitate communication between family members, especially between parents during the stressful transitions of separation and divorce. The mediator facilitates a dialogue that helps them to reach joint decisions and focus on their children's needs and feelings. Independent family mediation services, funded mainly by charitable grants, spread across Britain during the 1980s and 90s. Initially, family mediators were mainly qualified social workers or marriage guidance counsellors and most of the early services had support from their local judges and some family lawyers. Twenty years of campaigning for family law reform and public funding for family mediation services finally led to the Family Law Act 1996. Parts I and II of the Family Law Act, introducing a major reform of divorce law, were abandoned as unworkable. Part III of the Act dealt with family mediation and these provisions were implemented. Section 13 (Resolution of Disputes) sets out directions with respect to mediation:

> '(1) After the court has received a statement, it may give a direction requiring each party to attend a meeting arranged in accordance with the direction for the purpose—
>
> (a) of enabling an explanation to be given of the facilities available to the parties for mediation in relation to disputes between them; and
>
> (b) of providing an opportunity for each party to agree to take advantage of those facilities.'

Section 29 dealt with mediation and civil legal aid:

---

[11] Parkinson 'Bristol Courts Family Conciliation Service' [1982] Fam Law 13–16.

'a person shall not be granted representation for the purpose of proceedings relating to family matters, unless he has attended a meeting with a mediator—

    (a)   to determine—

         (i)   whether mediation appears to be suitable to the dispute and the parties and all the circumstances, and

         (ii) in particular, whether mediation could take place without either party being influenced by fear of violence or other harm, and

    (b)   if mediation does appear suitable, to help the person applying for representation to decide whether instead to apply for mediation.'

Domestic violence and some other cases were exempted from the requirement to consider mediation before legal aid could be obtained. The requirement for legal aid applicants to attend a mediation information and assessment meeting in order to consider mediation as an alternative to court proceedings was subsequently re-enacted in the Access to Justice Act 1999, while the exemptions, including the domestic violence exemption, were reduced in 2007 and further in November 2010.

The Family Mediation Council (FMC) defines family mediation as:[12]

'a process in which those involved in family breakdown, whether or not they are a couple or other family members, appoint an impartial third person to assist them to communicate better with one another and reach their own agreed and informed decisions concerning some, or all, of the issues relating to separation, divorce, children, finance or property by negotiation.'

The FMC consists of representatives of the three main family mediation providers in England and Wales, known as 'Lead Bodies'. These are the Family Mediators Association (FMA), National Family Mediation (NFM, formerly the National Family Conciliation Council) and Resolution (formerly the Solicitors Family Law Association). Other members of the FMC represent the College of Mediators (formerly the UK College of Family Mediators), the ADR Group and the Law Society. The Law Society is not a key mediation provider but it represents solicitors and manages the Law Society's Family Mediation Panel for solicitor mediators, providing one of the routes to Legal Services Commission (LSC) recognition for conducting publicly funded family mediation.

Scotland has not followed England and Wales in requiring consideration of mediation before legal aid can be obtained for family proceedings. Family mediation in Scotland is provided by Family Mediation, now part of Relationships Scotland, and by CALM (Comprehensive Accredited Lawyer Mediators recognised by the Law Society of Scotland). The confidentiality of mediation provided by members of these two

---

[12]   FMC Code of Practice 2010, para 1.2; see further www.familymediationcouncil.org.uk.

organisations has the formal approval of the Lord President of the Court of Session. The Scottish Civil Courts Review, known as the 'Gill Review'[13] recommended a free mediation service for lower value claims to encourage out-of-court settlements, but did not propose measures to encourage greater or pre-court use of family mediation.

1.5 GOVERNMENT POLICY ON FAMILY MEDIATION

In contrast to current policy in Scotland, the Ministry of Justice in England and Wales is taking active steps to increase the use of mediation in family matters:[14]

> 'People can find themselves embroiled in court actions when their disagreements might be better resolved between themselves at a much earlier stage and with a more satisfactory outcome, rather than the "winner takes all" approach offered by litigation. There is already a range of alternatives to court that include mediation, conciliation and arbitration. As a government we want to encourage people in disputes to play a greater role in resolving them themselves, in both civil and family issues. The intervention of the court should only be sought when a genuine point of law exists or when people or businesses are at risk. Particularly in relation to family cases where decisions about contact and residency of children are being made, we must ask whether a court is the most appropriate setting. I firmly believe that we need to look at the role mediators can play, so that more families can sit down and come to agreements without the cost and disruption often caused by lengthy court cases. Our evidence shows that mediation can be quicker, cheaper and provide better outcomes than going to court.'

The Pre-Application Protocol on Family Mediation Information and Assessment Meetings, issued in February 2011 by the Ministry of Justice and Her Majesty's Courts Service[15] states that:[16]

> 'family mediation can help some people reach a resolution where there is a family dispute. It can help in private law disputes between parents relating to children, with such disputes often best resolved through discussion and agreement, where that can be managed safely and appropriately.'

1.6 MEDIATION AND LITIGATION

Comparisons between mediation and litigation tend to portray mediation as 'good' and court proceedings as 'bad'. These simple value judgments do not do justice to either system. Mediation is not always appropriate or possible and does not invariably produce agreement. Mediation has

---

[13] September 2009.

[14] Djanogly 'Going into mediation instead of going to court' *Government Gazette* (20 September 2010).

[15] See Chapter 3 at **3.7** below.

[16] See the Introduction to the Pre-Application Protocol on Family Mediation Information and Assessment Meetings (Feb 2011).

limitations and the outcomes vary. There are many cases in which the court process may be needed instead of, or as well as, mediation. Many courts now operate settlement-directed procedures. Nonetheless, disputants who risk becoming caught up in lengthy and adversarial court proceedings have a right to know the differences between litigation and mediation so that they can make an informed choice of process, recognising that litigation involves emotional as well as financial costs. A study by the Centre for Research on the Child and Family found that:[17]

> 'existing legal interventions have limited capacity to facilitate contact or reverse a downward spiral in contact relationships ... Resources should be directed towards more creative work to improve parental and parent-child relationships rather than repeated attempts at imposing a solution.'

Hunt found that:[18]

> 'court proceedings may be effective in restoring contact and increasing the extent of contact [but] do not appear ... to improve parental relationships and therefore their capacity to manage post-separation parenting.'

Family mediation is creative work that aims not only to settle disputes, especially where children are concerned, but also to encourage co-operation between separated parents and to maintain nurturing relationships between parents and their children.

> 'While mediation provides the chance for parents to repair their relationship sufficiently to be able to co-parent more positively in future, litigation in a real sense teaches couples to argue and to litigate, sometimes rather too well.'[19]

Adversarial litigation	Mediation
The parties are regarded as adversaries	Seeks mutual interests, common ground
Issues defined by lawyers in legal terms	Participants explain issues in their own words
Lawyers act as advocates for their client	Participants talk and listen to each other
Polarises, drives parties further apart	Narrows differences, bridges gaps
Formal legal rules govern the process	Informal, private and flexible

---

[17] Trinder, Beek and Connolly 'Making contact: How parents and children negotiate and experience contact after divorce' (2002) *Joseph Rowntree Foundation Findings* 092, p 4.

[18] Hunt *Parental Perspectives on the Family Justice System in England and Wales: a review of research* (Report for the Family Justice Council, December 2009), p 122.

[19] Harte and Howard 'Encouraging positive parental relationships' [2004] Fam Law 456.

Adversarial litigation	Mediation
Usually takes a long time, involves delay	Agreements can be reached quickly
Parties rely on their legal advisors	Participants reach their own, informed decisions
Focus on past grievances and wrongs	Looks for acceptable future arrangements
Conflict and stress usually prolonged	Resolves conflict and reduces stress
Possible options may not be explored	Explores all available options
High costs for disputants and the state	Legal costs may be avoided or reduced
Orders imposed by judicial authority	Participative decision-making
Imposed decisions are less likely to last	Consensual decisions more likely to last

1.7   ADR – APPROPRIATE DISPUTE RESOLUTION

Mediation is one of a number of settlement-seeking processes that include arbitration, conciliation, collaborative law and negotiation. These processes have been grouped together under the collective heading of 'Alternative Dispute Resolution' and its acronym, ADR. 'Alternative' in this context was generally understood to mean alternative to court proceedings. '*Appropriate* Dispute Resolution' is now considered preferable, because settlement-seeking processes may be used in conjunction with court proceedings, rather than as a substitute.

Mediation in family law proceedings does not fit well with an adversarial legal system that has subsisted in England and Wales for over eight hundred years. One of the changes that the Family Justice Review may recommend[20] is a shift to an inquisitorial system with which mediation could dovetail far more appropriately.

---

[20]   See **1.19** below.

1.7.1   Negotiation, arbitration, collaborative law, conciliation, mediation – how do they differ?

Direct Negotiation

Direct Negotiation is a bilateral process in which the parties negotiate directly with one another, without asking other people to manage or assist their negotiations. In separation and divorce, many couples work out their own arrangements to a large extent, but they may need to have their agreements ratified by the court or by an administrative authority.

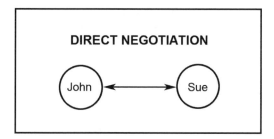

Indirect negotiation via representatives

It is difficult for parties to negotiate directly when their relationship has broken down. Communication often breaks down as well. The tendency is to turn to lawyers. A great many settlements are reached through negotiation by legal representatives. Experienced lawyers with good negotiation skills settle most of their cases by negotiation and rarely take cases to court. If, however, negotiations fail, legal advocates may be appointed to represent each party in court, to press their claims and defend their rights.

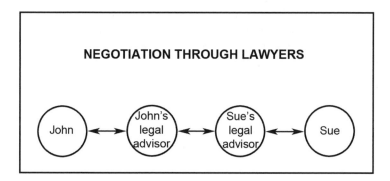

Arbitration

When parties in dispute go to arbitration, they ask an independent expert or panel to make or recommend a decision. The arbitrator's decision is usually binding but may be only advisory. The hearing is private and the parties may decide on aspects of its form, such as the recording of the proceedings. The parties usually have their legal representatives present at the arbitration hearing.

Collaborative law

This is a relatively new approach in which each party instructs a specially trained collaborative lawyer. The two collaborative lawyers and their clients work together co-operatively in order to resolve matters without going to court. The aim is to reach settlement in constructive, four-way meetings in which the collaborative lawyers provide legal advice and guidance to their clients and encourage them to negotiate with each other. If no settlement is reached, new lawyers in different firms have to be instructed for court proceedings.

1.8   CONCILIATION AND MEDIATION

The terms *conciliation* and *mediation* are often used interchangeably, but they need to be distinguished as two intrinsically different processes. 'Conciliation' usually takes place under the court's direction, whereas 'mediation' is an independent, settlement-seeking process that provides a resource for the courts in suitable cases. Both processes aim to facilitate settlement and increase co-operation, especially in cases concerning children, but there are significant differences between them in terms of process and outcomes. Conciliation often takes place in court, possibly at the first appointment, and the outcome is reportable to the court. In England and Wales, mediation generally takes place prior to court application, or court proceedings may be adjourned to allow time for mediation. Mediation meetings are held mainly out of court in the premises of private and independent family mediation services. The courts in England and Wales may make referrals to mediation and can order attendance at mediation information and assessment meetings as a way of dealing with disputes over child contact in private law cases. However, the courts cannot order mediation itself. The following table may help to clarify the roles of family mediators and conciliators in England and Wales.

Family Mediation	Conciliation
Mainly prior to court application, most clients referred by legal advisors/representatives, courts increasingly encouraged to refer.	Court referral to conciliation following court application on children issues.

Family Mediation	Conciliation
Essentially voluntary, but attendance at information and assessment meeting with recognised mediator is expected prior to court application. Court may make referral to mediation at any stage of proceedings, including appellate level, but cannot order parties to mediate.	Parties in private law disputes over children are expected to take part in conciliation on direction of the judge. Conciliation is thus imbued with the court's authority.
Private and independent, mainly out of court. In-court mediation schemes in some courts refer parties to a mediator available in court on the day. Following initial information and mediation, mediation may continue out of court if both parties willing.	Conciliation often takes place at court in the context of a court hearing.
Participants charged fees unless qualifying for legally aided mediation.	Free of charge.
All issues – children, family home, finance etc. Not only separation and divorce – grandparent contact and other proceedings over children.	Children issues only.
Independent, qualified mediators, do not report to the judge.	Family court social workers (Cafcass) are officers of the court.
Impartial and non-directive: parents encouraged to co-operate and take account of children's needs, reaching their own decisions and agreements, with legal advice from their solicitors.	Not neutral – welfare of child is paramount and conciliator may be directive in seeking settlement on residence and/or contact.
Confidential, with exceptions (both parties, with legal advice, may give joint written consent for terms of agreement set out in the mediation summary to be made available to the Court).	Conciliation by family court social worker is not privileged, outcome reportable to the court.
Facilitates dialogue, often extends over several sessions, seeks sufficiently flexible arrangements for children.	Usually a one-off meeting, 1 hour on average. Tends to produce standardised agreements.
Wide spectrum from co-operative to high conflict.	Difficult disputes over children.

Family Mediation	Conciliation
May change attitudes and perceptions and have longer term effects in improving relationships.	Unlikely to change attitudes or relationships (research by Trinder et al, 2002–07).
Agreements reached through mediation by the parties themselves (with court orders made with consent where needed) more likely to last over time.	Research by Trinder et al (2002–07) shows conciliated settlements more liable to break down, but some parents renegotiate contact arrangements.

1.9   THE AIMS AND OBJECTIVES OF FAMILY MEDIATION

The following aims and objectives are set out in the FMC Code of Practice 2010:

'2.1   Mediation aims to assist participants to reach the decisions they consider appropriate to their own particular circumstances.

2.2   Mediation also aims to assist participants to communicate with one another now and in the future and to reduce the scope or intensity of dispute and conflict within the family.

2.3   Where a marriage or relationship has irretrievably broken down, mediation has regard to the principles that the marriage or relationship should be brought to an end in a way that–
   •   minimises distress to the participants and to any children;
   •   promotes as good a relationship between the participants and any children as is possible;
   •   removes or diminishes any risk of abuse to any of the participants or children from the other participants; and
   •   avoids any unnecessary cost to participants.'

1.10   THE BOUNDARIES OF FAMILY MEDIATION

The boundaries of mediation preserve the integrity of the process and protect those who use it. These boundaries distinguish formal mediation processes undertaken by qualified mediators from informal kinds of mediation that may be undertaken by a mutual friend or trusted relative. Family mediation by qualified mediators provides the following boundaries:

•   neutral ground – meetings take place on neutral territory, not on territory belonging to a participant;

•   essential principles including privacy and confidentiality (see below);

•   safeguards – principles and ground-rules are designed to provide security for participants and their children;

- time boundaries – mediation is normally short-term and the length of each session is limited. Time boundaries help participants to focus on issues and concentrate on priorities. The use of time in each session needs to be planned and organised well.[21]

1.11   CORE PRINCIPLES OF FAMILY MEDIATION

The Family Justice Council (FJC) and the Family Mediation Council (FMC) have jointly issued a document for widespread circulation, endorsed by the President of the Family Division, entitled *Independent Mediation – Information for Judges, Magistrates and Legal Advisors* (2011). This document defines four core principles of mediation:

- It is a voluntary process;

- It is a confidential process;

- The mediator acts in an impartial way;

- Decision making rests with the participants to the mediation.

These principles are central to the delivery of an independent family mediation process and govern the way in which all recognised family mediators work. Mediators cannot dilute these principles which are embedded in Code/s of Practice applied by all mediation representatives and regulatory bodies and in documentation provided by mediators to clients.

The FMC Code of Practice 2010, reproduced in full in Appendix A, provides guidance on the application of the principles in mediators' practice.

1.11.1   Voluntary participation

'Participation in mediation is voluntary at all times and participants and the mediator are always free to withdraw. Where mediators consider that a participant is unable or unwilling to take part in the process freely and fully, they must raise the issue and possibly suspend or terminate the mediation.'[22]

The European Directive on Mediation of 21 May 2008 upholds the same principle of voluntary participation, stating that:[23]

'the mediation provided for in this Directive should be a voluntary process in the sense that the parties are themselves in charge of the process and may organise it as they wish and terminate it at any time.'

---

[21]   See Chapter 5 below.
[22]   FMC Code of Practice 2010, para 5.2.
[23]   Article 13.

Although mediation is mandatory in a few jurisdictions, notably Norway, mandatory mediation is generally seen as a contradiction in terms. In England and Wales, the requirement to receive information and consider mediation before application may be made to the court in family proceedings[24] is not mandatory mediation, because the mediator must explain to the parties, separately or together, that mediation is voluntary and ascertains whether both of them are willing to accept it and able to participate freely, without intimidation or risk of harm. Participants are free to withdraw from mediation at any stage and the mediator may terminate the process if it is no longer suitable, or if no progress can be made.

Some concerns have been raised as to whether the requirement to consider mediation before application may be made to the court is contrary to Article 6 of the European Convention for the Protection of Human Rights and Fundamental Freedoms 1950 – the right to access to justice. Would-be applicants must surely also have the right to receive information about different means of reaching settlement and the costs and time-scales involved, before embarking on one route without knowledge of others. Another concern is that the requirement to consider mediation causes delay. National statistics on the time lapse between referral to mediation and the information meeting are not available, but family mediation services in Bristol, Manchester and Stafford contact referred parties immediately to offer an initial meeting, usually within a week and even on the following day, if they respond quickly and are able to attend. There is no waiting list for appointments.

1.11.2   Confidentiality

The confidentiality of mediation is covered as follows in the FMC Code of Practice 2010:

> '5.5.1 Subject to paragraphs 5.5.3, 5.5.4 and 5.5.5 below mediators must not disclose any information about, or obtained in the course of, a mediation to anyone, including a court welfare officer or a court, without the express consent of each participant, an order of the court or where the law imposes an overriding obligation of disclosure on mediators.
>
> 5.5.2 Mediators must not discuss the mediation or correspond with any participant's legal advisor without the express consent of each participant. Nothing must be said or written to the legal advisor of one party regarding the content of the discussions in mediation which is not also said or written to the legal advisor(s) of the other.
>
> 5.5.3 Where it appears necessary so that a specific allegation that a child has suffered significant harm may be properly investigated or where mediators suspect that a child is suffering or is likely to suffer significant harm, mediators must ensure that the relevant Social Services department is notified.

---

[24]   See Chapter 3 below.

5.5.4 Mediators may notify the appropriate agency if they consider that other public policy considerations prevail, such as an adult suffering or likely to suffer significant harm.

5.5.5 Where mediators suspect that they may be required to make disclosure to the appropriate government authority under the Proceeds of Crime Act 2002 and/or relevant money laundering regulations, they must stop the mediation immediately without informing the clients of the reason.'

Mediators undertake in the Agreement to Mediate signed by both parties[25] that they will not disclose information to any other person or body without obtaining the written consent of all participants, except where there is an overriding obligation of disclosure. It must be made clear to participants that the confidentiality of mediation is not absolute. Where a child or adult is said or believed to be at risk of significant harm, the mediator must as far as practicable discuss with participants the immediate steps that they should take and must in any event immediately notify the appropriate child protection agency.[26]

Confidentiality in relation to the court

The document on *Independent Mediation – Information for Judges, Magistrates and Legal Advisors* (2011) states that:

> 'The confidentiality of any process of family mediation is covered by an existing precedent: *Re D (Minors) (Conciliation: Privilege) Disclosure of Information)* [1993] 1 FLR 932, which states that "parents would not achieve a compromise unless they approached conciliation openly and were prepared to give and take. They would not make admissions or conciliatory gestures unless they were confident that these could not be used against them. Any attempt at conciliation must be off the record but there were exceptions …" and further "the only exception would be in rare cases where a statement made during conciliation indicates that the maker has caused or is likely to cause serious harm to a child."
>
> Any client entering a mediation process is asked to sign an "Agreement to Mediate" – which sets out both the scope of and limitations to confidentiality in line with *Re D* (and in regard to legislation relating to abuse and harm and money laundering) – and further, participants to a mediation are asked not to call the mediator to provide evidence (either as notes or in person).
>
> Independent mediators are therefore not able to provide information to the court as to the content of any discussions held in mediation or the reasons why proposals were not reached and/or any view as to who may have not co-operated or declined to enter or continue with a mediated process.'

---

[25] See Appendix B below.

[26] See Chapter 3, mediation and child protection issues.

In English law, the legal privilege attaching to mediation is derived from case-law. A series of legal rulings have established that it is subject to three limitations:[27]

(1)   The privilege belongs to the parties jointly, not to the mediator or the process. The privilege can therefore be waived with the consent of both parties.

(2)   The privilege does not cover statements that are not sufficiently relevant to the dispute that is the subject of negotiation.

(3)   A binding agreement that results from privileged negotiations is not itself privileged. For this reason, the standard wording in the Memorandum of Understanding drawn up by a family mediator refers to 'proposals subject to legal advice' and avoids using the word 'agreement'.[28]

English courts have long supported the existence of a legal privilege attaching to statements and communications where parties enter into negotiation with the aim of achieving reconciliation.[29] The privilege rests on the principle that there is a public interest in allowing the possibility of reconciliation to be explored, without either party being disadvantaged in subsequent court proceedings as a result of attempting reconciliation. *Re D* established that the privilege covering mediation on children matters is based on a public interest principle. This privilege has been extended to mediation on other issues.

The European Directive (2008) states (in Article 7):

'Given that mediation is intended to take place in a manner which respects confidentiality, Member States shall ensure that, unless the parties agree otherwise, neither mediators nor those involved in the administration of the mediation process shall be compelled to give evidence arising out of or in connection with a mediation process, except:
(a)   where this is necessary for overriding considerations of public policy of the Member State concerned, in particular when required to ensure the protection of the best interests of children or to prevent harm to the physical or psychological integrity of a person; or
(b)   where disclosure of the content of the agreement resulting from mediation is necessary in order to implement or enforce that agreement.'

The question of privilege in civil and commercial mediation was addressed in the case of *Farm Assist v Defra*,[30] where the mediator applied

---

[27]   *Cross on Evidence* (Butterworths, 6th edn, 1985).
[28]   See Chapter 12 below.
[29]   See, for example, *McTaggart v McTaggart* [1948] 2 All ER 754; *Pais v Pais* [1970] 3 All ER 491.
[30]   [2009] EWHC 1102 (TCC).

to set aside a witness summons and asserted a mediation privilege. Her attempt to assert privilege was rejected. In his judgment Ramsay LJ stated that there are:

> 'exceptions which permit use or disclosure of privileged communications or information outside the conciliation where, after balancing the various interests, it is in the interests of justice that the communications or information should be used or disclosed.'

The privilege attaching to mediation belongs to the parties jointly and may be waived with their joint consent:[31]

> 'If participants do reach a consensus, they may request the mediator to draft a mediation summary to provide details of this. Such a summary is a "without prejudice" document which cannot be legally binding until the participants have had the opportunity to take legal advice upon it. Having had that opportunity they can then decide if they wish to enter into a binding agreement. (In "All-Issues" cases, where issues relating to finance, property as well as children have been considered, financial information is provided on an open basis and an open financial summary is prepared as a separate document.)
>
> Mediators can only provide further information to the court if both clients agree to waive their privilege. This is likely to be only in those cases where it would assist the participants to resolve their dispute for the court to be made aware of some information as to the progress or conclusion of the mediation. It would be appropriate and reasonable that clients should take legal advice before agreeing to waive their privilege.'

In the context of First Hearing Dispute Resolution Appointments, the Practice Direction of 1 April 2010 authorises:[32]

> 'arrangements for the mediator to ask the parties to waive privilege for the purpose of the first hearing where it seems to the mediator appropriate to do so in order to assist the work of the mediator and the outcome of the first hearing. In all cases it is important that such arrangements are put in place in a way that avoids any pressure being brought to bear in this connection on the parties that is inconsistent with general good mediation practice.'

1.11.3   Impartiality

The first principle in the FMC Code of Practice 2010 is that:[33]

> 'it is the duty of the mediator at all times to ensure that he or she acts with impartiality and that that impartiality is not compromised at any time by any conflict of interest, actual or capable of being perceived as such. Mediators must not have any personal interest in the outcome of the

---

[31]   *Independent Mediation – Information for Judges, Magistrates and Legal Advisors* (2011).

[32]   At paras 4.3.b and 4.3.c.

[33]   FMC Code of Practice 2010, para 5.1.

mediation, must not mediate in any case in which they have acquired or may acquire relevant information in any private or other professional capacity and must not act or continue to act if they or a member of their firm has acted for any of the parties in issues not relating to the mediation.'

Even if the parties themselves have no objection to a mediator who has advised or acted previously for one or both of them in a different capacity, or who has a colleague who has done so, they may not realise the potential influence in mediation of knowledge and rapport derived from a previous professional relationship. Mediators must decline to mediate if they have prior knowledge or experience of advising or working with either or both parties in another role or capacity.

'All information or correspondence provided by either participant should be shared openly and not withheld, except an address or telephone number or as the participants may agree otherwise.'[34]

Mediators need to be careful not to engage in separate telephone discussions, emails or correspondence with one party unless the basis for sharing the content of the communication with the other party has been agreed.

Mediators are sometimes described as 'neutral third parties', but neutrality is capable of different definitions. A mediator is neutral in the sense of being non-partisan and having no personal stake in the outcome of the mediation:[35]

'Mediators must remain neutral as to the outcome of a mediation at all times. Mediators must not seek to impose their preferred outcome on the participants or to influence them to adopt it, whether by attempting to predict the outcome of court proceedings or otherwise. However, if the participants consent, they may inform them that they consider that the resolutions they are considering might fall outside the parameters which a court might approve or order. They may inform participants of possible courses of action, their legal or other implications, and assist them to explore these, but must make it clear that they are not giving advice.'

Neutrality and impartiality in mediation also incorporate the concept of 'equidistance', meaning that the mediator gives equal attention to all participants and manages the process in a balanced and even-handed way. Some mediators prefer the term 'multi-partial'. However, mediators cannot be neutral in the sense of having no influence, because their professional and personal values and experience inevitably have some influence in the mediation process. A mediator may intervene in ways that reinforce certain values.[36] There are also questions concerning the provision of information in mediation and whether mediators should have

---

[34]   FMC Code of Practice 2010, para 5.6.3.
[35]   FMC Code of Practice 2010, para 5.3.
[36]   See Chapter 13 below.

a role as educators in encouraging parents to understand their children's needs in separation and divorce. A mediator who advises parents in a directive way or who expresses an opinion on what constitutes a fair settlement would be breaching the principles of mediation. There is however a continuum between passive facilitation and pro-active intervention, including the provision of information. Maintaining strict impartiality in mediation is not a simple matter (see Chapter 10 on managing power imbalances in mediation).

1.11.4 Party control of decisions

Participants retain control over their own decisions in mediation. Mediators do not have any decision-making power. They assist participants to reach their own, well-informed and considered decisions. The aim is to help them reach decisions that are acceptable to them both: they can also decide to disagree. In mediation jargon, this principle is sometimes termed 'empowerment'. Like neutrality, empowerment has a number of meanings. At one level, there is empowerment through the sharing of information. Mediators explain the need for full financial disclosure and in signing the Agreement to Mediate participants undertake to provide full information and necessary documentation. They are encouraged to take legal advice on the financial disclosure made in mediation and whether any further enquiry is needed. Mediation should be terminated if a participant refuses to provide information or provides information that appears to be deliberately incomplete or inaccurate.

Another aspect of empowerment is protection from intimidation or any form of pressure. Mediators should prevent pressure being put on one participant by the other and should not give advice or steer participants towards a particular outcome, for example by suggesting the kind of order the court might make. The Agreement to Mediate makes it clear that the outcome of mediation is not binding on participants. If there are legal and financial consequences, participants are encouraged to take independent legal advice before entering into an agreement that is intended to be legally binding. Mediators should also caution against a premature agreement that might prejudice one or both parties in relation to a final settlement. If, on the other hand, agreement is reached on a matter where there is no need for independent legal advice, such as details of contact arrangements, participants may decide to enter into their own agreements.[37]

1.12 FURTHER PRINCIPLES

The four core principles of voluntary participation, confidentiality, impartiality and party control of decision-making may need to be extended by further principles:

---

[37] See Chapter 12 below.

- Protecting personal safety;

- Respect for individuals and for cultural diversity;

- Focus on the present and future, rather than the past;

- Consideration of the views and needs of all concerned, including children;

- Mediator competence.

1.12.1   Personal safety and the suitability of mediation

The FMC Code of Practice 2010 states:[38]

> 'In all cases, mediators must seek to ensure that participants take part in the mediation willingly and without fear of violence or harm. They must seek to discover through a screening procedure whether or not there is fear of abuse or any other harm and whether or not it is alleged that any participant has been or is likely to be abusive towards another. Where abuse is alleged or suspected mediators must discuss whether a participant wishes to take part in mediation, and information about available support services should be provided.'

Individuals who have experienced domestic violence or abuse or who are in fear of it, may be reluctant to accept mediation, but they may also be so afraid of disclosing domestic violence that they accept mediation, especially if they fear repercussions if they refuse it. Family mediators are required to consider the suitability of mediation in all the circumstances and in particular to screen for domestic abuse and child protection issues. Mediators must be able to recognise when another form of assistance or court process is needed, rather than mediation. Each participant should be seen separately at the assessment meeting, even if they choose to come together, because an effective check cannot be done in the presence of a violent or potentially violent partner. There are at least five different categories of domestic abuse that have indications or contra-indications for mediation and other circumstances in which mediation would be unsuitable.[39] Screening with each participant separately is essential. Where there are any fears or risks of violence or harm, the mediator should consider very carefully whether mediation should take place at all and if so, with what safeguards and conditions. Appropriate arrangements should be made for separate waiting-areas and, if necessary, shuttle mediation.[40] If either party fears violence or further conflict, he or she should be able to arrive and leave at a different time from the other one, to reduce fears or any risk of being attacked or followed. Mediators

---

[38]   FMC Code of Practice 2010, para 5.8.2.
[39]   See Chapter 3 below.
[40]   See Chapter 5 below.

should be able to recognise different kinds of power imbalances that affect the mediation process and take appropriate steps to manage these imbalances, such as establishing ground-rules, sharing information and identifying a need for legal or other advice. If there are concerns about personal safety, a decision that mediation is not suitable in the circumstances should rest with the mediator, rather than leaving one party responsible for the decision and its consequences. If, in the course of mediation, power imbalances cannot be managed adequately or if there is intimidating or abusive language or behaviour, the mediator should suspend or terminate the mediation.[41]

1.12.2 Respect for individuals and cultural diversity

Mediators seek to ensure that all participants are treated with respect in mediation and that people from every race and culture are treated with equal respect. Mediation as a process should be available and accessible in accordance with equal opportunities policy and special needs should be catered for, such as access for the disabled and assistance for those with speech or hearing difficulties. Mediators need to take special care to respect cultural diversity and differences and may need additional resources for cross-cultural mediation.

1.12.3 Present and future focus

Litigation tends to focus on past wrongs and grievances. Mediation focuses on the present and the future, generally without going into past history. Many participants find it a relief to be encouraged to look forwards, rather than back. Some information about the past may be needed, however, in relation to decisions and future planning and to understand, at least to some extent, the sources of powerful emotions and entrenched conflict.

1.12.4 Consideration of children's needs, feelings and views

The need to consider with parents (or other family members) their children's needs, feelings and views is covered as follows in the FMC Code of Practice 2010:[42]

> '5.7.1 At all times mediators must have special regard to the welfare of any children of the family. They should encourage participants to focus on the needs and interests of the children as well as on their own.
>
> 5.7.2 Mediators must encourage participants to consider the children's wishes and feelings. If appropriate they may discuss with them whether and to what extent it is proper to consult the children directly in order to ascertain their wishes and feelings.

---

[41]   See Chapters 3 and 10 below.

[42]   At paras 5.7.1–5.7.3.

5.7.3 Where mediators and both participants agree that it is appropriate to consult any children directly, the consent of the children must first be obtained. Mediators consulting directly with any children must have been specifically trained to do so and have received specific enhanced clearance from the Criminal Records Bureau. Such mediators must provide appropriate facilities for direct consultation.'

Mediators' concern for children's well being and the right of the child to be consulted[43] does not mean that a mediator should act as advocate for a child or have responsibility to ensure the welfare of a child. Mediators should not advise parents as to what constitutes the best interests of a particular child. They can however offer general information, if parents are willing to receive it, about children's needs in separation and divorce and may suggest reading material, DVDs or other resources. Parents are encouraged to consider each child's position, needs and feelings in working out arrangements that will work as well as possible for the family as a whole. To a varying extent – and more so in some countries than in others – family mediators take on an educational role to help separated parents become more aware of children's needs in separation and divorce so that parents' decisions and arrangements incorporate this fuller understanding.[44] Family mediators are not child welfare officers and they should be careful not to be prescriptive. In posing questions rather than giving answers, mediators encourage parents to consider whether their children should have a say in arrangements that will affect their lives and whether parents can talk with their children at home or consider other ways of giving them opportunities to express their feelings and concerns.[45]

1.12.5   Mediator competence

The FMC Code of Practice 2010 includes the following requirements:

'3.1 Mediators must have successfully completed such training as is approved by a Member Organisation and accredited by the Council to qualify them to mediate upon those matters upon which they offer mediation.

3.2 Mediators must be a member of a Member Organisation and must therefore have successfully demonstrated personal aptitude for mediation and competence to mediate.

3.3 Mediators must satisfy their Member Organisation that they have made satisfactory arrangements for regular professional practice consultancy with a professional practice consultant who is a member of and approved for the purpose by a Member Organisation.

3.4 Mediators must agree to maintain and improve their skills through continuing professional development courses approved by a Member Organisation and/or the Council.'

---

[43]   See Chapter 8 below.
[44]   See Chapter 14 below.
[45]   See Chapter 8 below.

The government Green Paper *Support for All: the Families and Relationships Green Paper*[46] recognises the importance of participants' being able to trust the competence of the mediator:[47]

> 'Couples who attend mediation need to feel confident in the quality and professionalism of the mediator in whom they are placing their trust. To this end, the Government will work with the Family Mediation Council to build on accreditation schemes for mediators.'

Participants cannot be expected to take the competence of the mediator solely on trust. Following implementation of Part III of the Family Law Act 1996, the Legal Services Commission issued contracts to services meeting the 'Quality Mark Standard for Mediation'[48] to provide publicly funded mediation. Mediators working in these services became subject to regulation. Those wishing to be recognised by the Legal Services Commission to undertake publicly funded mediation information and assessment meetings and mediation are required not only to have taken recognised training: they must also undertake an Assessment of Competence. This involves submission of a portfolio explaining the mediator's practice and illustrating it with examples and documentation (with identifying details removed) from five completed mediation cases. The Legal Services Commission carries out audits on contracted mediation services and checks mediators' compliance with standards, including supervision, file reviews and continuing training. Assessment of mediator competence and regulation of practice uses an evidence-based system to examine mediators' application of principles and skills in practice, as well as academic qualifications.

Mediators should mediate on issues in which they are trained and competent to mediate. They need to consider the complexity of the issues and whether these lie within their competence as mediators. If the mediator does not have the necessary training and knowledge to mediate on the issues concerned, co-mediation with a more experienced or specialised mediator may be considered if available, or the mediation should be passed to a suitably qualified mediator.

1.13   DISTINGUISHING FAMILY MEDIATION FROM COUNSELLING AND THERAPY

Some family mediators have training and experience as counsellors, psychologists, social workers or family therapists. Knowledge and experience gained from the profession of origin are extremely valuable. It is essential, however, to distinguish the family mediator's role from other roles with which it might be confused. Divorce should not be seen as an

---

[46]   January 2010.
[47]   See para 4.37.
[48]   (1st edn, 2002).

illness needing treatment and a family mediator is neither a counsellor nor family therapist. The following comparisons may help to clarify the differences.

Differences between counsellors and family mediators

Counsellors	Family Mediators
May counsel one partner alone	Engage both partners from the outset
Reconciliation may be a goal	Decision to separate established/explored
Not linked to legal process	Complements legal processes
Often start without written contract	Normally start with written contract
May be long-term	Usually short-term
Explore personal and family history and past experience, as a key to the present	Focus on the present and the future rather than on the past
Focus on feelings, perceptions and troubled relationships	Focus more on practicalities, including finances, and on decision-making
Adult perspectives and needs are often the primary focus	Parent-child relationships and parenting plans often the central focus
Provide counselling-related information	Provide mediation-related information
Aim to increase personal insight	Aim to help participants reach agreement
May use psycho-analytic theory	Conflict theory and mediation theory
Mainly facilitating	May be more interventionist
Client-counsellor relationship may involve some dependency for a time	Seek to empower participants and to increase their autonomy
Often end without a written agreement	Prepare a Memorandum of Understanding

Differences between family therapists and family mediators

Family Therapists	Family Mediators
Help families with their problems	Help disputants to reach agreed decisions
Often work with 'intact families'	Work mainly in separation and divorce
Involve children from the outset	Children rarely involved at the outset
Usually work without a written contract	Start with a signed mediation contract
No links with the legal process	Links with the legal process
Communication not structured, observe how family members communicate	Facilitate communication in a structured way, to ensure balanced participation
Focus on family processes	Focus on interpersonal differences
Consider underlying problems	Focus on overt issues and open tasks
Give messages rather than information	Give 'neutral' information
Develop hypotheses to explain family functioning	If a hypothesis made, purpose is to assist participants to negotiate effectively
If a one-way screen is used, communication with consultants is not heard by the family	In co-mediation, the mediators work together and their communication is open
May give paradoxical instructions without explaining the reasons	Discuss and agree tasks with participants
Work strategically in ways that involve family members	Help parents to work out how they will talk and listen to their children
Often end without a written agreement	Draw up a Memorandum of Understanding

1.14 DISTINGUISHING FAMILY MEDIATION FROM ADVISING AS A LAWYER

The members of Resolution, now totalling around 5,700, are committed to the constructive resolution of family disputes. They follow a code of practice that promotes a non-confrontational approach and encourages clients to consider the needs of the whole family, particularly the best interests of children. However, even family lawyers with substantial experience and expertise in Resolution's settlement-seeking approach may not find it simple to move from the role of legal advisor to the different role of family mediator. The transition from 'Resolution lawyer' to Collaborative Family Lawyer (CFL) is probably a shorter step than from CFL to mediator. A mediator provides information, but not advice, in a non-directive way to assist participants with their decisions. Information provided in mediation is offered differently from the way in which lawyers provide it, because lawyers have a duty to advise and assist their own clients in reaching settlement and this may entail giving advice in a partisan way. Mediators provide general and verifiable legal information without indicating how legal principles would be applied in a particular case. They may need to translate legal terminology into everyday terms, or vice versa, and consider exactly what information is directly relevant to the questions under consideration and the timing and effects in giving it.

Legal Advisors	Family Mediators
Work within the discipline of the law	Multi-disciplinary
Advise individual clients	Impartial, balanced help to all participants
Often start with a history of the dispute	Participants are invited to explain their needs
Advise within a framework of legal rights	Focus on interests and mutual concerns
Financial information collected and exchanged between lawyers	Financial information gathered and shared within the mediation process
Use legal terminology	Use ordinary language as far as possible
Address clients' grievances where necessary	Focus on present and future arrangements
Not trained in psychological processes	Trained in conflict management and mediation
Rely on their own clients' account of events and their views of issues concerning children	Discussion with both parents jointly about their children. Children may be included directly.
Advise clients on best course of action	Explore options in a non directive way
Negotiate with 'the other side' mainly by correspondence	Participants negotiate in face-to-face meetings
Draft applications to the court	Do not draft legal documents

1.15   THE AIM OF MEDIATION – SETTLING DISPUTES OR RESOLVING CONFLICT?

Mediation needs a theory to provide a coherent framework for its practice. Mediation practice is rooted in fundamental beliefs and values about people and conflict. In 1973 a social psychologist, Morton Deutsch, published his theory on the nature of human conflict and the constructive use of a third party in conflict resolution.[49] Family mediators come from a variety of disciplines, particularly law and human sciences. Mediators from a legal background tend to see mediation as a contractual process of dispute settlement. Mediators from a psychology or therapy background are more likely to define it as a process of conflict management and put greater emphasis on improving communication. The words 'dispute' and 'conflict' are often used interchangeably, but they are not synonymous. Disputes are overt and in 'settling' their dispute, disputants may accept terms that involve a compromise or concessions. A settlement may be reached because both sides recognise it to be necessary, but their attitudes to each other may remain hostile and they may have no further communication with each other. 'Conflict', on the other hand, may be overt or hidden. Settlement is not necessarily looked for. Mediation aims to help parties reach consensual decisions and settle disputes. It may also help them to resolve their conflicts. But it is unrealistic to expect a brief process to resolve the deep anger and pain of a broken relationship. It can take years for a partner who feels abandoned and betrayed to come to terms emotionally with separation or divorce. Some never do so. Mediation does not offer counselling or psychotherapy. Yet the process of working towards a settlement on certain issues enables some couples to hear each other, perhaps for the first time. Some couples, in hearing and understanding each other, find that their perceptions and attitudes alter a great deal. At one end of the spectrum, a settlement can be reached without changing attitudes and without resolving anger. At the other end, some couples seem to experience a kind of catharsis in which they move from angry recriminations to a different relationship built on co-operation and trust. One of the differences, therefore, between different forms of ADR is whether the aim is to settle disputes by reaching a concrete agreement or whether there is a further aim to seek to help participants to resolve the psychological and emotional conflicts that underlie their disputes. These aims are not incompatible. Many mediators blend them in some way.[50] If agreement is seen simply as the opposite of dispute, this fails to recognise that there is a continuum between conflict and co-operation. Disputants are not only at different points on the continuum but may shift in either direction along it at different points in time. In cases where mediation does not lead to agreement, mediation has not necessarily 'failed': it may have opened a door to communication that is more important than getting an agreement.

---

[49]   Deutsch *The Resolution of Conflict* (Yale University Press, 1973).
[50]   See Chapter 2 below.

1.16 TURBULENCE, CHANGE AND MEDIATION WITH CHANGING FAMILIES

Mediation theory needs to explain the dynamics of the process, irrespective of its outcome. We need a theory to explain how mediation *actually* works, as opposed to how it *should* work. Turbulence and fluid dynamics offer a metaphor and a theory for the process of family mediation, irrespective of outcome. There is a story about the quantum theorist, Werner Heisenberg, on his deathbed. Heisenberg said he would have two questions to put to God: why relativity, and why turbulence. Apparently he added: 'I really think He may have an answer to the first question'.[51] Mediators who see the destructive effects of marital and family conflict may likewise be inclined to ask 'Why conflict?' Conflict in separation and divorce fits the scientific definition of turbulence remarkably well:[52]

> 'What is turbulence? It is a mess of disorder at all scales, small eddies within large ones. It is unstable. It is highly dissipative, meaning that turbulence drains energy and creates drag.'

Conflict in divorce drains energy and creates drag, just as turbulent airflow over the wing of an aeroplane creates drag and destroys lift. Conflict itself is not necessarily destructive. It can produce positive change and growth. But, scientifically speaking, a rough surface uses a lot of energy. Separating couples who are struggling for change or trying to maintain the status quo against the threat of change use a lot of energy. But the energy is often used wastefully and counter-productively – to attack, to threaten or to compete with each other. Mediators need to help couples conserve as much of their energy as possible, so that they achieve forward movement and 'lift'. Instead of draining their reserves of energy, separating couples need to find ways of using it that enable them to pull together in some areas while letting go in others. This is not at all an easy task. As those who work with separating and divorcing couples will know, the movement is typically fluctuating, up and down, backwards as well as forwards, sometimes purposeful but often chaotic. This reality of irregular rather than smooth movement, with sudden peaks and troughs, is familiar to most mediators.

Turbulence is caused by interactions between forces of stability and forces of instability. In the turbulence that occurs when a couple's relationship breaks down, there is often a struggle as the experience of increasing instability overwhelms efforts to maintain some stability. In this struggle, energy may be used up in generating even more turbulence or it may be directed towards controlling the turbulence. Mediators seek to help couples use their energy constructively instead of destructively, to *manage the dynamics of change*. When turbulence subsides, stability is regained.

---

[51] Gleick *Chaos – Making a New Science* (Abacus, 1993), p 121.
[52] Ibid, p 122.

Another characteristic of turbulence that is highly relevant to mediation is that turbulence produces unpredictable and highly variable results known to scientists as 'surface tension effects'. Surface tension effects are typically small, 'micro' effects (think of snowflakes, all of which are different) that scientists had assumed to be too small to be significant. However, the new ideas of chaos theory caused them to look again at surface tension effects and how they come about. To their surprise, they found that small changes in surface tension effects 'proved infinitely sensitive to the molecular structure of a solidifying substance'.[53] The significance of this finding for mediation is the realisation that even small changes in surface tension effects may influence the development of new family patterns and structures more profoundly than might have been expected. The changing structures of separating families may still be malleable. Relationships may still be ambivalent and flexible, if they have not yet solidified. A crisis in the family, when forces of instability interact most powerfully with forces of stability, creates unique opportunities for change and growth. The timing of the intervention is important: the stage at which mediators become involved affects the level and management of turbulence. Early interventions are usually more influential than later ones, when dysfunctional patterns or structures may be set or stuck and resistant to change.

1.17   CHAOS THEORY

Chaos theory offers some fresh insights for family mediators who wonder why, if they follow the same steps or procedures in working with separating couples, they get such different results. Chaos theory is a science of the global nature of systems. It has brought together thinkers from different fields that had previously been widely separated. The first chaos scientists had an eye for patterns, especially patterns that appeared on different scales at the same time. In the 1970s, scientists in the United States and Europe came increasingly to realise that although physicists had established certain principles to explain the laws of nature, they still had no understanding of the forces that produce disorderly weather patterns, turbulence in water and the oscillations of the heart and the brain. The irregular side of nature, its discontinuous and erratic side remained deeply puzzling. But in the 1970s a few scientists began to seek links between order and disorder. Edward Lorenz, a scientist at the Massachusetts Institute of Technology found in his study of weather patterns that there were familiar patterns over time, pressure rising and falling, airstreams swinging north or south. But the repetitions were never quite exact. The patterns showed wide and unpredictable variations. From almost the same starting point, two similar weather patterns could grow further and further apart until all resemblances disappeared. What caused these differences?

---

[53]   See n 51, p 311.

It was assumed that substances such as fluids that were more easily measurable than the atmosphere were well understood. However, this was not so. Gleick took the example of two bits of foam falling over a waterfall and bobbing side by side at the bottom:[54]

> 'What can you guess about how close they were at the top? Nothing. As far as standard physics was concerned, God might just as well have taken all those water molecules ... and shuffled them personally.'

Couples on the brink of divorce may be a long way apart, or they may be quite close to one another. Even if the varying distance between them could be measured, it would not be a reliable predictor of the distance that will exist between them at the end of the mediation process. There are many currents to navigate along the way that may alter each partner's course.

Scientists studying unpredictable variations gradually realised that very small differences in input could make a major difference to the final shape of things. In weather systems, Lorenz translated this idea into what is only half-jokingly known as the Butterfly Effect: the notion that a butterfly stirring the air today in Beijing could result in storm systems next month in New York. Had Lorenz stopped with the Butterfly Effect – an image of a tiny, fragile movement having far-reaching but entirely random results, he would not have helped much. But his work showed that a chain of events has critical turning points in which small interventions can be very influential. This new science of chaos theory evolved as 'a science of process rather than state, of becoming rather than being'.[55] Mediation, too, is a science of process rather than state, of becoming rather than being.

1.18 THE EVOLUTION OF FAMILY MEDIATION AS A NEW PROFESSIONAL DISCIPLINE

Family mediators work with families who are moving through major transitions. The evolution of mediation itself may be seen as a series of transitions in becoming established as a unified and independent professional discipline:[56]

> 'Mediation must be conducted as an independent professional activity and must be distinguished from any other professional role in which the mediator may practise.'

---

[54] See n 51, p 8.
[55] See n 51, p 5.
[56] FMC Code of Practice 2010, para 5.1.7.

The Australian National Alternative Dispute Resolution Advisory Council identified four phases in the development of mediation and ADR:[57]

(1) A period of pioneering work.

(2) Increasing use of ADR and training of mediators.

(3) Rivalry and power battles among mediation practitioners and organisations.

(4) Increasing co-ordination and collaboration.

Similar phases in the evolution of family mediation may be traced in many countries. Perhaps inevitably, and serving as indications of continuing growth, there are still tensions and struggles, but also many positive signs of increasing interdisciplinary co-ordination and collaboration, fostered in particular by the Family Mediation Council and the Family Justice Council. The movement through the four phases of development is more cyclical than linear. There was a considerable amount of collaboration and co-ordination among pioneering family mediation services in the 1980s. These independent services worked together to form a national association, producing a national code of practice and standards for family mediation training. The National Family Conciliation Council held its inaugural meeting in March 1983 with encouragement from judges and family lawyers who supported interdisciplinary co-working.[58] It is perhaps an indication of the dynamic and creative nature of mediation that it will always be going through 'a period of pioneering', if not chaos and turbulence! The 'dynamics of change' driving forward family mediation in the spring of 2011 arise from a confluence of forces flowing in the same direction, although with different goals – the Coalition government's drive to stem litigation and cut back public funding for family cases, the Ministry of Justice's initiative to create a protocol requiring pre-Court consideration of mediation and the determination among ADR practitioners to preserve the integrity of mediation while contributing to debates on a new system of family justice under consideration in the Family Justice Review.

1.19 FAMILY JUSTICE REVIEW

The Ministry of Justice, together with the Department for Education and the Welsh Assembly Government, launched a Family Justice Review in June 2010 by 'to examine the effectiveness of the family justice system and the outcomes it delivers, and to make recommendations for reform.'

---

[57] NADRAC 2001.
[58] Parker and Parkinson *Solicitors and Family Conciliation Services: A Basis for Professional Co-operation* [1985] Fam Law 270–274.

Recognising that 'long and complicated legal processes are emotionally and financially draining for parents and distressing for children', the aim is to produce a system:[59]

> 'which allows families to reach easy, simple and efficient agreements which are in the best interests of the children, whilst protecting children and vulnerable adults from risks of harm. Family mediation and similar support should be used as far as possible to support individuals themselves to reach agreements about arrangements, rather than having an arrangement imposed by the courts.'

In his evidence to the House of Commons' Justice Committee on 26 October 2010, the Lord Chief Justice, Lord Judge said that in ordinary private law cases he could not think that the adversarial system improved parents' relationship with each other and their relationship as mother and father of their children. Lord Judge went on to express his 'most serious reservations about whether the adversarial system is in any way to the advantage of the child'.[60] The views of the Lord Chief Justice have been conveyed to the Family Justice Review on behalf of the judiciary. The interim report of the Family Justice Review is due to be published in April 2011.

---

[59] Family Justice Review *Terms of Reference 2010*.
[60] [2010] Fam Law 1252.

CHAPTER 2

DIFFERENT APPROACHES TO MEDIATION

'One must make the skills one's own. Light your own torch from other's candles, but make the skills fit your person ... Try to be whole'[1]

CONTENTS

2.1 DIFFERENT APPROACHES TO MEDIATION

Researchers who have studied ADR processes all carrying the same label of 'mediation' have found significant variations between them in their approach to clients, theoretical frameworks and techniques used.[2] The best-known approaches are probably those referred to as Structured or Settlement-seeking, Transformative and Narrative. A fourth approach, particularly relevant for disputes in family proceedings and cross-border disputes over children is the ecosystemic or family-focused approach. There are also processes referred to in mediation literature as 'therapeutic family mediation'[3] and 'evaluative mediation'. These last two processes

---

[1]   Davis 'Special Education Mediation' in Kolb *When Talk Works – Profiles of Mediators* (Jossey-Bass, 1994).

[2]   Irving and Benjamin 'Research in Family Mediation – an Integrative Review' in Irving and Benjamin (eds) *Family Mediation – Contemporary Issues* (Sage, 1995); see also Chapter 13 below.

[3]   Ibid.

are controversial, as a mediator who seeks to act as therapist or evaluator would be breaching the core principles of mediation. As Robey[4] says:

> 'people in conflict do not want therapy. They all believe that there would not be a problem if only the other party were more reasonable and understood their point of view.'

Pre-mediation assessment of suitability of mediation and willingness to participate[5] should not be confused with evaluation during mediation and providing an evaluative report to the court, such as Cafcass conciliators may do, using their child welfare expertise. Under their Code of Practice, mediators may, however, with participants' consent, 'inform them that they consider that the resolutions they are considering might fall outside the parameters which a court might approve or order'.[6] However, evaluating whether a proposed settlement lies within parameters likely to be acceptable to the court falls far short of directive or evaluative forms of ADR such as arbitration or the hybrid process of 'med-arb', which are outside the scope of this book.

2.2   STRUCTURED MEDIATION

'The most powerful interests are basic human needs'.[7]

The structured or settlement-seeking approach to mediation is based on the system of *principled negotiation* developed in the Harvard Negotiation Project.[8] Fisher and Ury's thinking drew from the pioneering work of Mary Parker Follett[9] in the field of industrial relations. Mary Parker Follett advocated a 'mutual gains' approach to negotiations in place of the traditional system of 'distributive bargaining' that resulted in inflated initial demands and forced concessions. The application of structured, settlement-seeking mediation in resolving disputes in divorce was taken forward by Coogler[10] and Haynes,[11] whose writing and teaching were major influences in the development of family mediation in the UK and many other countries. Structured mediation is a staged model with procedures designed to ensure evenly balanced participation through rules and guidelines agreed in advance between the mediator and the participants. The structure provides physical and psychological bounda- ries that help to contain strong emotions and channel energies towards negotiation and problem-solving. Separate time with each participant may be included during the process, as well as at the outset. The

---

[4]   Robey 'Mediation and the Revised Private Law Programme' [2009] Fam Law 69.
[5]   See Chapter 3 below.
[6]   FMC Code of Practice 2010, para 5.3.
[7]   Fisher and Ury *Getting to Yes* (Penguin Books, 1983), p 49.
[8]   Fisher and Ury *Getting to Yes* (Penguin Books, 1983).
[9]   Metcalf and Urwick (eds) *Dynamic Administration: The Collected Papers of Mary Parker Follett* (Harper, 1942).
[10] Coogler *Structured Mediation in Divorce Settlement* (Lexington Books, 1978).
[11] Haynes *Divorce Mediation – A Practical Guide* (Springer Publishing, 1981).

mediator's role is clearly defined and distinguished from other roles. A Code of Conduct or Practice sets out the ethical values that underpin the model and provide safety for participants in terms of confidentiality and safeguards.

One of the main features of structured mediation is its focus on interests instead of on positions. A *position* is a statement of one party's preferred outcome. Stating a position usually involves strategic elements such as accusation, overstatement, insisting on one's rights and entitlements and denying that the other party has equal rights. In contrast, an *interest* is an underlying need or goal that needs to be met. Demanding a fixed proportion of capital assets is an example of a position, whereas needing sufficient money to provide adequate housing is an example of an interest. For example, a couple may be arguing over the amount of money each of them is entitled to receive. As parents, they may have a mutual interest in providing stability for their children and avoiding a change of school, if possible.

When mediation is directed towards settlement, the parties are first invited to put forward their respective positions. The mediator seeks to identify and understand the interests that underlie these positions and to help the parties recognise that they may have mutual interests and needs, despite being in conflict. Mutual needs are often concrete, such as the need for affordable housing, and there are also psychological needs such as maintaining respect and self-esteem. The mediator helps the parties to look for integrative or 'win-win' solutions which meet as many of these mutual needs as possible. In the well-known catchphrase, the mediator is 'soft with the people and tough with the problem'. Engaging the parties in a problem-solving approach enables them to work together towards agreement, instead of wasting time and energy in destructive competition. This problem-solving approach relies heavily on negotiation and bargaining techniques. The mediator is likely to use left-brain thinking, characterised as linear, logical, analytical, rational and task-oriented.

Using the techniques of principled negotiation, the mediator aims to:

- separate the people from the problem;

- focus on interests rather than on positions;

- create options for mutual gain;

- reach win/win outcomes instead of win/lose.

Structured mediation consists of a series of steps or stages. A basic four-stage model consists of the following stages:

1.	Defining the issues	Participants explain their positions
2.	Fact-finding	Gathering and sharing information
3.	Exploring options	Considering needs, concerns and consequences
4.	Reaching agreement	Negotiating a mutually acceptable outcome

This model may be expanded to twelve stages for family mediation.[12]

Haynes defines the final bargaining phase in the settlement-seeking model as one in which 'positions are modified, options traded, and the give-and-take of bargaining occurs'.[13] When the focus is on interests instead of positions, different ways of meeting these interests can be explored and areas of agreement may emerge. The process can work very well where there are mutual interests and motivation to reach agreement on concrete issues. Fisher and Ury[14] developed the concept of a BATNA – the Best Alternative to a Negotiated Agreement. The BATNA and its opposite, the WATNA – the Worst Alternative to a Negotiated Agreement – may be used as benchmarks against which a potential negotiated agreement may be measured. For structured mediation to be most effective, participants need to be:

- motivated to reach a settlement;

- capable of thinking rationally;

- reasonably clear about the issues they need to settle;

- able to explain and assert their positions;

- able to negotiate;

- able to recognise a fair or acceptable outcome.

Many mediators use structured mediation because the focus is on achieving concrete agreements and lawyer mediators, in particular, are accustomed to playing an active or even directive role in working towards settlement. In structured mediation, the mediator can exercise considerable power. If the mediator manages the process too strongly, there could be risks of disempowering participants instead of empowering them, while attempts to empower a weaker participant could prejudice the mediator's impartiality. There are also risks that mediators who are impatient to obtain a result may steer participants towards their own

---

12 See Chapter 5 below.
13 Haynes *Alternative Dispute Resolution – The Fundamentals of Divorce Mediation* (Old Bailey Press, 1993), p 4.
14 Fisher and Ury *Getting to Yes* (Penguin Books, 1983), ch 6.

preferred solution, rather than spending time building a mutually satisfactory settlement with both or all participants.[15] The aim of structured mediation is to achieve concrete results and practical solutions. These are indeed important goals, whereas improving relationships between participants may not be seen as a necessary or appropriate objective. Although participants may express strong feelings at the outset, a mediator using a tightly structured approach may expect them to put their emotions aside in working towards a concrete settlement. However, suppressing emotions or putting them aside may not be possible for many people, especially for couples during separation and divorce.

Structured mediation was not specifically designed for divorce and family disputes. It is commonly used in civil and commercial mediation and its principles and techniques are extremely useful in all forms of mediation. However, if participants' feelings are not acknowledged sufficiently and if insufficient time is given to renegotiating family relationships, a settlement may be reached that does not improve communication between separated parents or take sufficient account of children's needs.

2.3 TRANSFORMATIVE MEDIATION

> 'The heart of the transformative approach to mediation has been identified as human moral growth in two specific dimensions together: strength of self and relation to other.'[16]

In separation and divorce and in other kinds of intense family conflict, participants may not be able to negotiate in a calm and rational way. They may be overwhelmed by such strong emotions that they cannot think clearly. Some family mediators, especially those from psychotherapeutic backgrounds, found that the use of structured mediation in divorce disputes encouraged mediators to take too much control of the process and too much responsibility for solving problems. In the *transformative* approach promoted by Bush and Folger,[17] participants are encouraged to take the lead while the mediator follows, instead of the mediator giving a direction that participants follow. Transformative mediation seeks fresh vision through talking and listening. Fresh vision and understanding transform perceptions. Writing on the integration of meditation techniques with mediation, Cloke suggests that:[18]

> 'The deeper, transformational middle way can be accessed through skilful means, which include not only meditation techniques that assist us in becoming more centered, compassionate, and aware of ourselves and others, but mediation techniques that enable us to engage in authentic and

---

[15] See also Chapters 11 and 13 below.
[16] Bush and Folger *The Promise of Mediation* (Jossey-Bass, 1994), p 230.
[17] Bush and Folger *The Promise of Mediation* (Jossey-Bass, 1994).
[18] Cloke 'Mediation and Meditation – the Deeper Middle Way' *Mediate.com Weekly* No 266, March 2009.

committed listening, openhearted communication, empathetic dialogue,
creative problem solving, collaborative negotiation, genuine forgiveness and
reconciliation'.

The first premise of Bush and Folger's approach is that mediation has the
potential to generate transformative effects that are beneficial for the
parties and for society. The second premise is that mediation has potential
to generate these transformative effects only in so far as the mediator
brings a mind-set and methods of practice conducive to the realisation of
two key goals – *empowerment* and *recognition*. *Empowerment* encourages
self-determination and autonomy, increasing people's capacity to view
their situation clearly and to make decisions for themselves. *Recognition*
involves participants being able to recognise each other's feelings and
perspectives and being more responsive to each other's needs.
Empowerment and recognition are intrinsic elements of mediation.
Although not unique to the transformative approach, they have much
greater emphasis here than in the structured model. Empowerment and
recognition help participants to gain mutual understanding so that they
can acknowledge each other's needs with more empathy.

Folger and Bush[19] identify ten hallmarks of transformative mediation:

(1)   Commitment to empowerment and recognition as the main aim of
      the process and the main features of the mediator's role.

(2)   Leaving responsibility for the outcome with the parties – 'it's their
      choice'.

(3)   Consciously refusing to be judgmental about the parties' views and
      decisions – 'the parties know best'.

(4)   Taking an optimistic view of the parties' competence and motives.
      Transformative mediators take a positive view of the parties' good
      faith and decency, whatever the appearances may be. Instead of
      labelling people as inherently uncaring, weak or manipulative, the
      mediator sees the parties even in their worst moments as temporarily
      weakened, defensive or self-absorbed.

(5)   Allowing and responding to the expression of emotions – not just
      allowing the parties a few moments to vent their feelings so that the
      feelings can be put aside in moving on to the 'real issues'.
      Transformative mediators encourage the parties to describe their
      emotions and the events that gave rise to them, in order to promote
      understanding and shared perspectives.

---

[19]   Folger and Bush 'Transformative Mediation and Third-Party Intervention' (1996) 13(4)
       Mediation Quarterly.

(6) Allowing for and exploring the parties' uncertainty – their lack of clarity should be seen as positive, rather than negative. If mediators assume that they understand the situation and each party's needs at an early stage of the mediation they may block an important stage of fluidity and ambivalence. Rather than developing a hypothesis which leads in a particular direction, it is preferable for mediators to retain a healthy sense of uncertainty, so that they continue to ask questions instead of drawing conclusions.

(7) Remaining focused in the here and now of the conflict interaction – 'the action is in the room'. Instead of trying to solve problems, the mediator focuses on specific statements as they are made, trying to spot the precise points where the parties are unclear, feel misunderstood or may have misunderstood each other. When mediators spot such points, they slow down the discussion and spend time on clarification, communication and recognition.

(8) Being responsive to the parties' statements about past events – 'discussing the past has value to the present'. Mediators generally encourage parties to focus on the future, not the past. In contrast, Folger and Bush argue that if the history of the conflict is seen as an evil that must not be dwelt on, important opportunities for empowerment and recognition will be missed. Reviewing the past can reveal choices that were made, options that were available and key turning-points. Reviewing the past can lead to a reassessment of the present.

(9) Viewing an intervention as one point in a larger sequence of conflict interaction. Conflict often goes in cycles, as the parties struggle with doubts and uncertainties. If mediators expect a cycle of moving towards and then away from agreement, they are less likely to panic when progress towards agreement stops or stalls. Transformative mediators may even welcome these cycles as part of the natural ebb and flow of the mediation process.

(10) Feeling a sense of success when empowerment and recognition occur, even in small degrees. 'Small steps count'. Mediation is always challenging and often difficult. Allowing ourselves to perceive and enjoy small successes is very important in sustaining our energy and motivation. Instead of defining success solely in terms of the final agreement reached, transformative mediators value each small step that contributes to personal strength and interpersonal understanding and compassion.

Folger and Bush believe that their transformative approach should be preferred over settlement-seeking. However, people come to mediation because they have problems to solve. They are not necessarily seeking 'transformation'. The term 'transformative mediation' may suggest that mediators are miracle workers who transform people or their conflicts in the course of a relatively brief process. Even long-term therapy may not produce fundamental change. Folger and Bush do not explain sufficiently whether the aim is to transform people and their relationship, or their perceptions of their conflict. A conflict has the potential to be transformed, if it is understood and managed differently. Transforming individuals is well outside the mediator's role and a potentially dangerous aim. People do not come to mediation to be transformed and mediators should not impose a process of their own – however creative and visionary – on people who do not want it. If participants want help in reaching a concrete agreement without being expected to change their negative views of each other, they are entitled to receive the kind of help they have asked for.

Mediators who feel they have a mission to transform their clients might operate outside the ethical boundaries of mediation. Yet there is evidence that taking part in mediation can be a cathartic experience for some people, leading to changes in their relationship and even in their self-perception. If this catharsis happens without being forced by the mediator, the mediator's role is genuinely transformative. Mediation can have therapeutic effects without being therapy. Folger and Bush's contribution is to emphasise the empathising, visionary and human aspects of mediation, in contrast to the structured approach which can be too cold, logical and limited in dealing with interpersonal relations.

2.4   NARRATIVE MEDIATION

> 'The potential to awaken the curiosity of each individual to listen to the narrative of the other and to inspire the courage necessary to hear what one would prefer not to.'[20]

Narrative mediation is based on the idea that mediators and disputants exercise a continuing reciprocal influence on each other throughout their dialogue. Writers with a narrative perspective on mediation[21] conceive it as a story-telling process in which participants are invited to tell their story, with the dual purpose of involving them equally while also helping them towards a shared understanding. Recognising the continuous reciprocal influence that mediators and disputants exercise on each other is seen by Cobb[22] and others as a challenge to the settlement-directed model of mediation in which disputants are guided by the mediator as a

---

[20]   Barenboim *Everything is Connected – The Power of Music* (Weidenfeld and Nicolson, 2008), p 73.

[21]   See Burrell, Donahue and Allen 'The impact of disputants' expectations on mediation' (1990) 17 *Human Communication Research* 104–139; and Cobb and Rifkin 'Neutrality as a discursive practice' (1991) in Sarat and Silbey (eds) *Studies in law, politics and society* (JAI Press, USA).

[22]   Cobb 'Narrative Perspective on Mediation' in Folger and Jones (eds) *New Directions in Mediation – Communication Research and Perspectives* (Sage Publications, 1994).

series of steps or stages. Stage models provide a useful structure for the mediation process, but they do not explain the dynamics or utilise a wide range of communication strategies.

Central to the narrative or communication model of mediation is Bateson's concept of *framing*.[23] Bateson defined a frame as a psychological means of delineating messages. Frames operate by including certain messages and excluding others, just as a picture frame contains the picture to be viewed and excludes subjects outside the frame. Frames also suggest how the message within the frame is to be interpreted. For example, a negative message can be given a positive frame, or vice versa. However, the notion of a frame is static, whereas mediation has taken over the more process-oriented term *reframing* to represent an interactive exchange of messages. *Reframing* is widely seen as one of the main tools by which mediators help participants move towards settlement. In much of the literature on mediation, reframing is seen as a unilateral function carried out by the mediator as a planned strategy. In contrast, communication models emphasise the joint influence or 'co-construction of frames'[24] in which all the participants frame and reframe for each other continuously. The influence traditionally attributed to the mediator is fundamentally altered by this perception, with its implications for mediators' shaping or sculpting the mediation process in response to each participant's moves and countermoves.

Bodtker and Jameson[25] offer the metaphor of a kaleidoscope to depict the complexity of interacting frames. Each participant (at least three, if there are two parties and one mediator) brings a frame to the process, like a disk that fits the end of the kaleidoscope. We need a conceptual tool to help us understand the relationship between these three kaleidoscopes during the mutual influence process. What features does the mediator pick out from the disputants' frames as more significant than others, and for what reasons? Greatbatch and Dingwall[26] investigated mediators' intervention shifts in relation to different responses from the parties – verbal resistance, verbal compliance and silence. Their study illustrates the reciprocal influences of the mediation process. Cobb and Rifkin,[27] in a narrative analysis of mediation sessions, suggest that the sequence of frame bids is important. They report that the party who tells his or her story first has an advantage, because the second party's story is then seen as a reaction or challenge to the first story, instead of a story in its own

---

[23] Bateson *Steps to an Ecology of Mind* (Chandler, 1972). See also references to Neuro-Linguistic Programming (NLP) in Chapters 6 and 11 below.

[24] Bodtker and Jameson 'Mediation as mutual influence: re-examining the use of framing and reframing' (1997) 14(3) *Mediation Quarterly*.

[25] Ibid.

[26] Greatbatch and Dingwall 'The Interactive Construction of Interventions by Divorce Mediators' in Folger and Jones (eds) *New Directions in Mediation – Communication Research and Perspectives* (Sage, 1994).

[27] Cobb and Rifkin 'Neutrality as a discursive practice' (1991) in Sarat and Silbey (eds) *Studies in law, politics and society* (JAI Press, USA).

right. The second story becomes a subplot, unless it is skilfully woven into the first story by the mediator. This raises further questions as to whether the mediator invites the parties to decide who is going to speak first, as in the Coogler model,[28] or whether the mediator makes the choice as to which party will speak first, having formed a hypothesis about their power relationship or other factors.

Cobb[29] describes conflict stories as 'notoriously rigid, readily re-enacted and recalcitrant to change.' The character roles in each disputant's story are contested and reformulated in the opposing version and the values upheld in one story are denigrated in the other. The kaleidoscope picture is fixed. Haynes[30] describes mediation as opening couples' stories to new interpretations. Cobb[31] argues that all three features of a post-structural perspective on narrative – narrative coherence, narrative closure and narrative interdependence – function collectively to challenge traditional views of mediation. Story telling in mediation is thus more than a metaphor. Understanding the reciprocal influence of frames and reframing by all participants in the process provides us with a new analytic frame for understanding interventions. It also leads to the development of new techniques for mediators, whether they are seeking to *transform* disputants' stories or simply encourage greater congruence.

2.5   ECOSYSTEMIC, FAMILY-FOCUSED MEDIATION

> 'The family justice system is a network of organisations and individuals from many different professions all working co-operatively and collaboratively so that the system achieves its ends.'[32]

An 'ecosystemic' approach complements other approaches and may be combined with them. In one sense, mediators mediate between the private system of family decision-making and public systems of law, adjudication and child protection. Mediators work at the interface between these systems, enabling some of the cogs to turn more freely. All those who work in the family justice system need to understand the complementary roles of judges, legal advisors, conciliators and mediators. Mediators need knowledge and understanding of the ways in which these systems function and interact with each other. Ecosystemic mediation does not operate in a vacuum: it relates to other systems and has links with them. Structured and transformative mediation could take place in an imaginary space-capsule where mediators and participants are insulated from other influences and intrusions. Ecosystemic mediation also provides privacy

---

[28]   Coogler *Structured Mediation in Divorce Settlement* (Lexington Books, 1978).
[29]   Cobb 'Narrative Perspective on Mediation' in Folger and Jones (eds) *New Directions in Mediation – Communication Research and Perspectives* (Sage Publications, 1994), p 54.
[30]   Haynes *Alternative Dispute Resolution – the Fundamentals of Divorce Mediation* (Old Bailey Press, 1993).
[31]   See Cobb at n 29 above, p 61.
[32]   Ministry of Justice *Family Justice Review: Terms of Reference 2010*.

and confidentiality, but there are windows in the ecosystemic space capsule giving outlooks on the surrounding landscape and allowing light to come in from outside.

The main theoretical framework for ecosystemic mediation is systems theory. In general systems theory, the concepts of first order and second order learning provide ways of looking at how social systems change:[33]

> 'Orderly and creative transformation of social systems... depends on a capacity for second order learning, which requires a willingness and capacity for challenging assumptions.'

Rapoport, a systems theorist, considers that:[34]

> 'the critical issue of peace and the need to convert conflict to co-operation demand incorporation of second order learning in social systems, *and the most effective way to produce social learning is through a participative design process.*'

Family systems theory offers a means of conceptualising and understanding individual experience and life events in the context of social and family processes. It offers helpful ways of understanding family structures, relationships and patterns of behaviour. Fragmented or dysfunctional communications between family members may become coherent and can be seen to have a positive function if these communications are understood in the context in which they occur. Looking at interactions and patterns of communication helps mediators move away from linear cause-and-effect explanations that encourage blaming and tunnel vision. When couples coming to mediation are seen as interconnected and interacting, rather than as detached individuals moving in different directions, the difficulties they bring to mediation are easier to understand. A systems perspective helps mediators to take account of social and legal factors that are relevant to a particular situation. As Roberts[35] points out:

> 'an understanding of the impact of the legal, economic, political, social, gender, cultural, ethnic, family and psychological environment of any dispute between individuals, particularly one involving children, is fundamental to the discussions that occur in mediation.'

If negotiations take place in mediation without reference to influences and consequences outside mediation, power imbalances may be accentuated.

---

[33] Ramsbotham, Woodhouse and Miall *Contemporary Conflict Resolution* (Polity Press, 2nd edn, 2005), p 46.
[34] Rapoport *The Origins of Violence* (Paragon House, 1989), p 442 [emphasis added].
[35] Roberts *Mediation in Family Disputes* (Ashgate, 2nd edn, 1997), p 16.

Much of the literature on different approaches to mediation – structured, transformative and narrative – focuses on adult perspectives and adult needs. Children are scarcely mentioned. Even where there are child-related issues, the child may be regarded as an object of care or competition, rather than as the subject of rights who may need to be consulted and given a voice in the decision-making process. The ecosystemic model is well suited to family mediation because parents are encouraged to consider children's perspectives as well as their own, to manage change in ways that take account of children's needs and wishes and to maintain child-parent relationships that nurture and support children. This approach is particularly relevant to cross-cultural, cross-border and inter-generational disputes. Unlike other models that may be undertaken by a mediator from a legal or psycho-social background, the ecosystemic approach is essentially multidisciplinary and interdisciplinary. This has important implications for family mediators' training and practice.

Before looking at an ecosystemic approach to family matters, we need to ask ourselves: 'Who, these days, counts as family?' The definition of 'family' as a biologically related group consisting primarily of two parents and their children – the traditional nuclear family – is largely obsolete. Families in Europe are a blend of many different cultures and traditions. There are infinite varieties of living patterns and child-rearing arrangements. For many people, 'family' means a pattern of relationships rather than a biological group. Children who were asked about their concept of 'family' define it mainly in terms of relationships with people who are not necessarily blood-related. Younger children when asked who belongs to their family very commonly include neighbours and close friends as part of their family, although children as young as six may also be clear about the difference between biological and non-biological relationships. Enabling children to maintain their attachments to grandparents, aunts and uncles and special friends may be crucial for their well-being and psychological security, especially when their life is in turmoil and they are pulled between two warring parents. A research study with children aged between eight and fourteen found that, from the children's perspectives, the key defining characteristics of 'family' were love, care, mutual support and respect (Morrow, 1998). Children shared this concept of 'family' irrespective of differences in their gender, ethnic background and where they lived. Older children were less likely than younger ones to define family in terms of formal relationships and more likely to see the nature or quality of relationships as the defining feature. Tara, a 13-year-old, thought a family was:[36]

> 'a group of people which all care about each other. They can all cry together, laugh together, argue together, and go through all the emotions together. Some live together as well. Families are for helping each other through life.'

---

[36] Quoted in Morrow 'Children's Perspectives on Families' (1998) *Rowntree Research Findings* 798.

Ecosystemic mediation seeks to help couples, especially parents – and, if appropriate, other family members (children, grandparents, stepparents, adult children) – to work out arrangements that help families to manage change. Family members are helped to communicate with each other and to reach agreed decisions during a critical period of transition and readjustment. The changes that have to be coped with in moving from a two-parent household to two single-parent households – or to other family arrangements involving new partners and children from other relationships – involve multiple psychological and practical adjustments for adults and for children. There are many dimensions in which these adjustments need to be made – emotional, psychological, legal, economic and social. Each family is unique and all these dimensions of change need to be understood and addressed in considering the needs of the particular family concerned.

Saposnek pointed out that:[37]

> 'child custody disputes are typically created out of a complex of interactional dynamics ... By viewing custody disputes from a family systems perspective, the mediator is able to understand these contributory elements and utilize interventions to achieve effective resolution ... The children's behaviour may ... have the effect of further increasing the polarization of each parent's position, because each parent may interpret the children's behaviour as evidence that it is both valid and necessary to assert their own position in order to ensure the well-being of the children.'

If the dispute is viewed in a systemic frame, it may be evident that the actions of each family member, including the children, influence the actions and reactions of the other family members, in a reciprocal way. Therefore to work solely with the adults involved, without taking account of the needs, feelings and reactions of their children, may be ineffective. Children can block arrangements with which they are profoundly unhappy. The ecosystemic model of mediation[38] focuses on the family as a whole. Children and other family members are brought into the frame, indirectly and possibly directly. The mediator maintains equidistance by helping participants to consider the needs of the family as a whole, rather than focusing solely on the dyad of two conflicted parents. Most family mediators meet only with parents and rarely involve children directly. However, account needs to be taken of the child's right and need to be consulted on matters that will have a profound impact on the child's life.[39] In cross-border child abduction cases, consultation with the child may be a legal requirement.[40]

---

[37] Saposnek *Mediating Child Custody Disputes* (Jossey-Bass, 1983).
[38] Bérubé *Workshop at International Family Mediation Trainers Conference* (Edinburgh, April 2002); Parkinson 'A family systems approach to mediation with families in transition' *Context, the magazine for family therapy and systemic practice* (October 2002).
[39] See Chapter 8 below.
[40] See Chapter 14 below.

2.6   MEDIATING WITH FAMILIES IN TRANSITION

> 'My family just *is*. It's different from other people's families but I don't
> mind, because who says what a family should be like?'[41]

In some ethnic groups, children may be brought up by members of the
extended family, rather than by their parents. Grandmothers and aunts
may be the main carers of loosely formed groups of siblings, half-siblings
and cousins. Other children live in single-parent households and some of
these children may never have experienced life in a two-parent family.
Many different carers may come and go – their parent, the parent's new
partner or a succession of different partners, childminders and teachers.
Mediators should be careful not to assume that the mother is, or should
be, the sole or principal carer. Many mothers work full-time and more
fathers, stepmothers and stepfathers take an active part in shared
childcare. Single-parent households headed by fathers are more common
than they used to be. Occasionally, siblings are split between their parents,
sometimes for the parents' convenience and sometimes because of
children's wishes, or the wishes attributed to them. Siblings who are split
between two warring camps may be drawn into the conflict, yet
desperately need their parents to present a united front.

Family mediators are presented with complex relationships in dramatically – often traumatically – changing family structures. In practical
terms, childcare is often an issue for parents in stable relationships trying
to juggle family and work commitments. Many couples who co-parented
their children when they lived together continue to co-parent after they
separate. Other separated couples do their parenting in parallel, rather
than jointly. Parallel parenting needs basic agreements between parents
who may have different parenting styles and routines and who may not
communicate much with each other, except over essentials. But there are
many other separated parents who battle over parenting rights and
wrongs and over the amount of time the children should spend with each
parent, now that they live apart. There may also be conflict over the
children's contact with other family members, such as grandparents, and
over the involvement of new partners on either side. Stepfamilies have
multiple adjustments to make and there can be tensions and disputes
between the 'old' and 'new' family, especially where a stepfamily includes
'his' children, 'her' children and 'their' children. When parents and
stepparents all manage to co-operate together, the children thrive.

> 'In my family I have five parents – my mum and my step-mum, then my dad
> and my other step-mum, and then my half-sister's dad, and my brothers and
> sisters and then there's all the pets of course'.[42]

---

[41]   Hope, aged 14, quoted in Neale and Wade *Parent Problems – children's views on life when
parents split up* (Young Voice, 2000), p 6.
[42]   Sonya aged 9, quoted in Neale and Wade ibid, p 21.

2.7 ECOGRAMS

Family mediators need to understand who is living in each household, whether new partners are seen as part of the family, and if so, by whom. One of the family mediator's first tasks, after welcoming both parents and helping them to understand and engage in mediation, is to draw a 'map', verbally or literally, of the immediate family, as seen by each parent. Questions need to be put to each parent. This may be facilitated by drawing an 'ecogram' on the flipchart. The ecogram is a modified version of a geneogram, a classic tool in family therapy that is used differently in family mediation and for different purposes. Geneograms are by definition diagrams that show family structures, generations and relationships on vertical, generational lines. The term 'ecogram' is used instead of 'geneogram'[43] to depict the 'ecology' of families in transition. When separated parents acquire new partners, the family grows outwards on a horizontal axis, not just downwards. To understand the ecology of the evolving family structure and system, mediators use ecograms to depict the family's *landscape* (using computer terminology here to mean a wider picture) rather than the family in *portrait* format (ie a narrower, linear format). Another helpful feature of an ecogram is to show two horizontal lines connecting the parents, instead of the usual single line. The top line represents the marital or living-together relationship that is ending in separation or divorce. The lower line represents the *co-parenting relationship* that usually needs to continue, for the benefit of the children and the parents themselves. It is extremely difficult for parents to deal with the ending of their marital relationship, while still continuing to co-parent. The threads often become entangled. Separating them out visually may help parents to be aware of the need to disentangle the marital threads that pull them back into the breakdown of their relationship from the parenting threads that connect them as parents, in the present and the future.

Some family mediators draw an ecogram on the flipchart at the start of the mediation, as a means of gathering information from both parents as the picture of their family emerges. This needs to include information about employment, income and each parent's most urgent issues and priorities. Mediators may also draw an ecogram in their case notes as a quickly read record. It is also a way of thinking about the family structure and functioning, possibly for discussion with a consultant or supervisor. Ecograms are particularly helpful when the wider family system includes children from previous relationships, stepparents, stepchildren, grandparents and stepgrandparents. They are also very helpful in cross-cultural and cross-border cases.

---

[43]   Bérubé *Workshop at International Family Mediation Trainers Conference* (Edinburgh, April 2002); Parkinson 'A family systems approach to mediation with families in transition' *Context, the magazine for family therapy and systemic practice* (October 2002).

The ecogram should show by means of dotted lines (ie permeable boundaries) who lives in each household and who is in contact with whom. It provides a visual focus for parents that may make it easier for them to talk about their children's relationships and contacts with other family members.

In the ecogram below, Carol and Hugh have come to family mediation to work out arrangements for their children, following their separation four months ago. Hugh is now living with his new partner, Pam, and with her daughter, Meg. Pam divorced five years ago and Meg spends time with her father, Keith, on a regular basis. Keith's new partner has children as well, but the mediation with Carol and Hugh focuses on their concerns and disputes concerning their children, Ian aged 12 and Jess aged 10. An immediate problem is that Ian is saying he does not want to see his father.

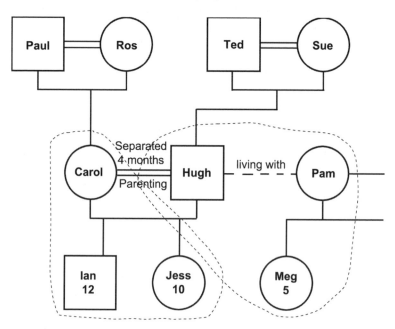

Hugh blames Carol for turning Ian against him and for not giving him the 'emotional permission' he needs from his mum to visit his dad. Carol accuses Hugh of abandoning her and the children and going off with another woman. She says Ian feels his father has let him down and he is very angry. A visual portrayal of the family in an ecogram, whether this is considered with Carol and Hugh in mediation or only as an aid for the mediator's own reflection, may suggest other possibilities that are worth exploring. For example, what does Ian like doing at weekends? Does he really want to spend weekends away from his mates, in the company of two small girls aged 10 and 5? How boring! If Hugh phoned Ian and suggested going to a football match with him (or whatever would be attractive to Ian), how might Ian respond? An ecogram can help mediators and parents to look at the sharing of parental responsibilities, the continuity of parent-child relationships and communications and interactions between 'old' and 'new' family systems in graphic and helpful ways.

2.8 MAIN PRINCIPLES OF AN ECOSYSTEMIC APPROACH TO FAMILY MEDIATION

- The ecosystemic approach offers an holistic view of families in transition: good communication between family members is of key importance.

- The aim is to help family members to manage change and reach agreed decisions for the future during a critical period of transition and readjustment.

- A separated family is still a family: the needs of family members are interrelated and they may need help to communicate with and listen to each other.

- Participants are helped to work out practical and workable arrangements in relation to parenting of children, housing, financial support and division of assets and beyond these practical arrangements, to value each other's continuing co-operation and support.

- An interdisciplinary approach is needed because mediation takes place within cultural, social and legal contexts. Family mediators need interdisciplinary knowledge and understanding of interrelated contexts.

- Ecosystemic mediation relates to the family justice system while maintaining its identity and confidentiality. Mediation takes place 'in the shadow of the law',[44] helping participants to move out of the shadow of the court in reaching their own agreed decisions.

- Children are individuals with rights of their own, including the right to maintain family relationships that are nurturing and sustaining.

- Children and young people need to understand the changes in their lives. If both parents agree that this would be appropriate, children and young people may be involved directly in mediation, as well as indirectly. Family mediators need further training on the inclusion of children in mediation.

---

[44] Mnookin and Kornhauser 'Bargaining in the shadow of the law: the case of divorce' (1979) 88 *Yale Law Journal* 950–997.

Each family is unique: their culture, particular needs, circumstances and relationships are variables needing outcomes that are individually designed *by* that family, rather than *for* that family – outcomes that are likely to differ from the kind of order a court would make. The approach draws from conflict theory and negotiation theory, as well as from family systems theory and attachment theory. It takes account of relevant cultural, social and legal factors. If negotiations take place in mediation without addressing legal aspects or the influence of important family members who remain outside the mediation, power imbalances may be accentuated. The eco-systemic model of mediation is a system of participative decision-making in which family members – mainly parents – seek to reach agreed decisions on matters that have psychological, social, economic and legal implications and consequences. It may lead to concrete agreements, as in settlement-oriented mediation, and it may incorporate elements of enhancing communication. It differs from settlement-seeking and transformative mediation in the way it fuses interdisciplinary knowledge, understanding and conflict management.

> 'Decision-making is a ... process rooted in the past, carried on in the present, shaping the future ... a deliberate and conscious act of selecting from between at least two alternatives or melding several alternatives into a course of action.'[45]

2.9   CONNECTIONS BETWEEN FAMILY SYSTEMS AND OTHER SYSTEMS

At another level, the ecosystemic model makes connections between private family processes and public systems, including the legal system, employment and economic systems and social support services for families. Family members are helped to work out their ongoing relationships arrangements and practical arrangements and to formalise these in legal terms, if they need to. An interdisciplinary approach facilitates agreement on issues that neither lawyers nor therapists would be able to deal with on their own.

> 'A legal resolution that ignores the client's psychological needs is as inappropriate as a psychological resolution that conflicts with the client's legal needs.'[46]

In the 1980s the Family Mediators Association (FMA) was formed in England and Wales to develop the model of interdisciplinary co-mediation in which a mediator who is a qualified and experienced family lawyer co-mediates with a mediator qualified in social work or therapeutic work with families.[47] Both need to have training in order to

---

[45]   Paolucci *Family Decision-Making – an Ecosystem Approach* (Wiley, 1977), p 5.
[46]   Steinberg 'Towards an Interdisciplinary Commitment' (1980) *Journal of Marital and Family Therapy* 261.
[47]   Parkinson 'Co-mediation with a lawyer mediator' [1989] Fam Law 48–49, 135–139.

make the transition from their profession of origin to family mediation. Interdisciplinary co-mediation offers a number of benefits,[48] including a wider range of knowledge and expertise. A gender balance of male-female co-mediators is particularly helpful in managing power imbalances in mediation. Interdisciplinary co-mediation is also used in international cross-border mediation.[49]

The style, experience and values of the mediator or co-mediators constitute a significant part of the 'mediation system' in an ecosystemic approach. Mediators bring their own personal history and experience, cultural conditioning, views, values and beliefs to the mediation process. It is very important to be aware of these influences so that they do not impact on the way they mediate, consciously or unconsciously. Co-mediation provides additional safeguards in terms of increasing awareness and management of each mediator's input and reactions. The skills needed by family mediators are complex and extensive. Self-awareness, reflection on practice and supervision are very important. Supervision and continuing mediation training are requirements for recognised family mediators in the UK.

The use of systems theory in mediation must be clearly distinguished from its use in family therapy, where there are connotations of pathology and treatment. Many writers on family mediation have sought to distinguish mediation from family therapy.[50] A systems perspective in mediation is a conceptual tool, not a form of treatment involving family members. Therapy is a form of treatment, whereas the application of systems theory in industry and other contexts does not have a treatment function.[51] The use of techniques in family mediation that are also used in counselling and family therapy can cause confusion and a blurring of roles. Reframing is often given as an example. Reframing is a communication and conflict management skill which mediators use differently from therapists and for different purposes.[52] Reframing in mediation typically involves re-stating positions or concerns in a different way that enables them to be heard and understood. Underlying aims are picked up and made explicit for both parties. Reframing does not mean imposing the mediator's views or values on participants. This would be neither reframing nor mediation. Reframing and circular questioning are invaluable techniques in mediation, where they are used differently from the ways in which a therapist would use them. These techniques are very helpful at a 'micro' level in working with a particular family system. At a 'macro' level, an ecosystemic approach makes connections between families, processes and outcomes.

---

[48] See Chapter 4 below.

[49] See Chapter 14 below.

[50] See, for example, Folberg and Taylor *Mediation* (Jossey-Bass, 1984); Walker and Robinson 'Conciliation and Family Therapy' in Fisher (ed) *Family Conciliation within the UK* (Family Law, 1990), pp 61–66.

[51] Emery *Systems Thinking: Selected Readings* (Penguin Education, 1969), Vol 1.

[52] See Chapter 6 at **6.21** and **6.22** below.

2.10   ATTACHMENT AND LOSS

The theory of attachment and loss provides a means of understanding the multiple losses of separation and divorce and the importance of providing an anchor or buttress for family members during this painful period in their lives.

> 'The dimensions of meaning and belonging are at the core of the experience of separation and divorce; they form the arc of relatedness to others, the bonds we all need to live. Divorce transforms and shifts these bonds. Each person feels its meaning differently; belonging is an issue for each. Links within the family, and connections to the broader social realm, can only be recreated over a long period of time. The family needs temporary buttressing while new foundations are laid, new beams put in place.'[53]

Mediation may provide a temporary anchor or buttress for couples facing immediate loss and fearing further loss. It can help them by offering:

- pre-transition help: opportunities to consider and prepare for a transition that will allow continuity in some areas (co-parenting of children) and changes in other areas;

- mid-transition help, working out 'holding arrangements', managing crisis;

- post-transition help, to review arrangements and assist with further adjustment.

Understanding the importance of attachment in human relationships may be a key to understanding what is happening below the surface, even where the surface issues are financial. It is clearly relevant where children are involved. The non-resident parent often fears losing relationships and contact with the children, especially if they fear being replaced by a stepparent. For children, the sudden loss of a loved parent may be devastating. If they do not receive enough love and 'buttressing' to cope with this loss, their future development and capacity to form relationships may be affected.

Family mediators who work with couples and, indirectly or directly, with children, need to understand the importance of attachment and the effects of losing a person to whom one is deeply attached. Although Bowlby's ideas on infant-mother attachment were questioned, his later work[54] and other studies[55] are supported by evidence from clinical

---

[53]   Hancock 'The dimensions of meaning and belonging in the process of divorce' (1980) 50(1) *American Journal of Orthopsychiatry* 27.

[54]   Bowlby 'Loss: Sadness and Depression, Vol 3' in *Attachment and Loss* (Hogarth Press, 1980).

[55]   Ainsworth 'Attachment: Retrospect and Prospect' in Murray Parkes and Stevenson-Hinde (eds) *The Place of Attachment in Human Behaviour* (Tavistock, 1982), pp 3–30.

research. This evidence shows the importance of secure attachments for children's healthy development and suggests that the quality of parenting a person receives in childhood may affect the quality of care he or she later gives as a parent.[56] Those who experienced insecure attachments to their own parents or who lost a parent through death or divorce may have greater difficulty providing the solid base on which their children in turn rely in becoming securely attached to them. Thus a cycle may be formed in which an insecure pattern of attachment may be passed on from one generation to the next.

Bowlby[57] suggested that attachment to parents has now become even more crucial for children, because other family members are often more scattered or occupied than they used to be. Grandparents and other relatives may be working and less available to the children. Attachment to parents gives children a secure base from which to begin exploring the world around them. As they get older, children show progressively less attachment behaviour and more exploring behaviour. Two types of behaviour indicative of insecure attachment in infancy are avoidance behaviour and clinging. Clinging may seem the opposite of avoidance, but it is also evidence of insecure attachment.[58] Clinging children have learnt to use frequent and intense attachment behaviour to keep reassuring themselves of their mother's (or father's) availability.

Clinical studies suggest that both clinging and avoidance behaviour is liable to persist in adolescence and adulthood. Whereas these patterns may have served a useful function in childhood, they can have the opposite effect in adult life. The excessively clinging partner may find that being very possessive of the other partner may result in rejection – the very result that the clinging was intended to prevent. Fear of rejection intensifies the clinging and thus the cycle of clinging/rejection/tighter clinging is repeated. One partner's inability to let go of the other, long after their relationship has effectively ended, is often a feature of a very difficult divorce. In contrast, an independent person who appears not to want close attachments may be left in isolation, because other people interpret the lack of signs of affection as indifference. Over-dependence and careful avoidance of dependence may be learnt responses to insecure attachments in childhood. When these behavioural patterns continue in adult life, they impair a person's ability to cope with further loss and change. Problems in coping with loss and change have been found to be precipitating factors in a number of mental illnesses. For example, losing one's mother before the age of eleven is associated with increased vulnerability to depression following other critical life events.[59]

---

[56] Murray Parkes *Bereavement* (Tavistock, 1972).

[57] See n 54 above.

[58] See n 55 above.

[59] Brown 'Early Loss and Depression' in Murray Parkes and Stevenson-Hinde (eds) *The Place of Attachment in Human Behaviour* (Tavistock, 1982), pp 232–268.

One reason for the particularly traumatic effect of losing a deeply loved partner or parent is that this person is often the very attachment figure to whom the bereaved one would normally turn for support in a time of crisis. A bereaved person often feels that the whole sense or meaning of life has been lost as well: 'My whole world has been turned upside down.' Those whose early relationships were relatively secure tend, after a period of grieving, to be able to resume normal life and can form new attachments, whereas those who had insecure or permanently broken early relationships are more likely to show pathological reactions to loss. They may find it very difficult to form and maintain lasting attachments that allow both intimacy and space within the relationship.

Essential elements in helping people to cope with loss and avoid pathological or chronic grieving are recognition of the psychological need to grieve and giving reassurance to grieving people that their overwhelming and fluctuating emotions are normal, not abnormal. Acknowledging the normality of these feelings helps parents to cope with their own and their children's reactions, recognising that they may need to give extra reassurance to a child who is anxiously clinging and demanding extra attention, or to comfort a child who seems detached and remote. One of the most widely known theories of grief is Kübler-Ross's[60] model of the stages of grieving that a bereaved person traverses: denial, anger, bargaining, depression and acceptance. As Emery et al[61] point out, a key difference between losing one's partner through death and losing the partner through separation and divorce is that instead of moving through the stages from denial to acceptance in a linear way, a recently separated individual tends to swing between them, sometimes uncontrollably. This *cyclical model of grief* is unpredictable. In the course of one mediation session, both partners may swing between all these stages in rapid and exhausting succession. Some get stuck at one stage, with the needle of their emotional compass pointing only in one direction, while others have outbursts of anger and distress, yet manage to reset their compass to bargaining and acceptance before they finish the session.[62]

Mediators need to understand the importance of attachment and loss even though they are not providing counselling or therapy. They need to be aware of and able to acknowledge the pain that may be expressed. Mediators also need to consider when there may be need for individual counselling or therapy. More positively, understanding the harmful effects of loss is helpful in working with parents to prevent unnecessary losses that they do not want to happen. Cycles do not repeat themselves inexorably. People may alter their perceptions and expectations of each other and of themselves. Learnt behaviour and communication patterns

---

[60]   Kübler-Ross *On Death and Dying* (Macmillan, 1969).
[61]   Emery, Margola, Gennari and Cigoli 'Emotionally Informed Mediation: processing grief and setting boundaries in divorce' in Cigoli and Gennari (eds) *Close relationships and community psychology: an international perspective* (FrancoAngeli, 2010).
[62]   See also Chapter 11 at **11.9.1**.

may change. It is possible to manage a painful loss with increased strength and to go on to form new and lasting relationships. Mediators need optimism, as well as understanding, in providing a temporary buttress to parents who are dealing with loss, so that they can support their children and avoid unnecessary loss for their children. The techniques used in family-focused mediation in working on these difficult tasks are discussed and illustrated in more detail in later chapters.

2.11 CROSS-CULTURAL MEDIATION

North American and West European models of mediation need to be adapted to meet the diverse needs of different cultures, communities and legal systems.[63] In some cultures and communities, a dispute between a married couple cannot be resolved effectively without considering the concerns, ethical beliefs and influences of the wider family, religious leaders, employers and employees.

> 'A Western, individualistic, problem-solving model of mediation suitable for a Western context [is] not totally suitable for a communitarian culture to which most of the Ismaili communities belong.'[64]

Afro-Caribbean communities, like Ismaili communities, have strong societal and family ties. Some concepts applicable in Western societies do not have the same importance for them. A core of universal values needs to be based on best mediation practices in the context of 'diversity in unity'.[65] An ecosystemic approach is helpful in cross-cultural and cross-border mediation because it takes account of different cultural, legal and family systems and their interactions. There may be intergenerational issues involving members of the extended family. Family members and in some cases community leaders may need to be involved in the mediation, directly or indirectly. It is important to clarify at the outset who holds power to take the decisions and whether other third parties need to be involved, directly or indirectly, so that if agreements can be reached, they will be accepted and not sabotaged. Cross-cultural and cross-border mediators need to be not just impartial, but multi-partial.

2.12 MEDIATION – SCIENCE OR ART?

Mediation is increasingly accepted as a discipline in its own right, with its own body of theoretical and practical knowledge, principles and ground-rules. Like other branches of science, mediation has accumulated

---

[63] See Chapter 14 below.
[64] Keshavjee 'Family mediation in Ismaili Muslim communities throughout the world' *Paper given at the Council of Europe's 7th European Conference on Family Law – International Family Mediation* (Strasbourg, March 2009).
[65] Fiadjoe 'Family mediation in the Caribbean' *Paper given at the Council of Europe's 7th European Conference on Family Law – International Family Mediation* (Strasbourg, March 2009).

a body of knowledge based on case studies, classification of cases and analysis of outcomes. Mediators and researchers have tended to approach mediation in a linear way, dividing mediation into a series of steps or stages with outcomes classified as successful, partially successful or unsuccessful, according to whether participants are able to reach agreement, partial agreement or no agreement. This approach to mediation uses 'left-brain thinking' which may be characterised as logical, analytical and task-oriented.

When family mediation is seen as a science, emphasis is put on the need for:

(i)   an intellectual grasp of mediation as a rational process consisting of a sequence of steps in which facts are gathered, differences are clarified, available options identified and proposals for settlement worked out;

(ii)   knowledge, including knowledge of the law and financial knowledge including tax, pensions and welfare benefits; knowledge of the experience and impact of divorce for adults and for children; knowledge of child and adult development and family dynamics, availability of support services;

(iii)   numeracy and the ability to analyse financial data;

(iv)   knowledge and experience of negotiated and litigated divorce settlements: structuring of settlements, trends, current issues;

(v)   negotiation and bargaining techniques involving logic and reasoned thinking;

(vi)   training in the discipline of mediation, knowledge of research studies on mediation.

Mediation is a complex process that cannot be understood or evaluated only by studying outcomes and counting agreements. Human behaviour is highly variable and unpredictable, especially in the turmoil of separation and divorce. Separating and divorcing couples show a range of reactions and patterns that vary over time, although some patterns are highly resistant to change. In family mediation, the volatile dynamics of separating couples may be calmed in varying ways and degrees by the presence and active interventions of the mediator. This process involves a complex series of interactions: it is not an automatic conveyor belt to agreement. Mediators are also recognising that while they need the logical, systematic approach of 'left-brain thinking' they also need to use 'right-brain thinking' which encourages creativity and intuition. 'Right-brain thinking' seeks to make connections in a more holistic way. It works on different levels and can make connections or intuitive leaps between them. It looks at patterns and at relationships in circular rather than linear ways.

When family mediation is recognised as an art, emphasis is put on the need for:

(i)   empathy, intuitive understanding and ability to engage with people;

(ii)   maturity and life experience, not just textbook knowledge;

(iii) skills in responding to the emotional as well as practical needs of separating couples, including skills in crisis management where irrational reactions from participants may heighten and prolong their disputes;

(iv) a personal and flexible style of working which enables the structure and pace of the process to be varied according to the dynamics of the couple or family;

(v)   concern for the family as a whole, in which good relationships and co-operation between family members are valued more highly than agreements per se;

(vi) communication skills – use of language, ability to translate and interpret.

Family mediation is both a science and an art. Family mediators need a blend of knowledge, human understanding and special skills to help couples facing separation or divorce to engage in dialogue together and to work out ways of settling future arrangements for themselves and their children. To use French phraseology, mediators need *savoir, savoir-faire* and *savoir-être.* In May 2000 thirty family mediation trainers from eleven countries met for two days in a Family Mediation Trainers Exchange Forum held near London. It was an enriching and inspiring experience. In seeking to capture the values of mediation, it was agreed that family mediators seek:

•   to listen in a certain spirit which comes from the heart and not only from the head;

•   to respect the individuality of each person;

•   to show humility, compassion and tolerance;

•   to maintain an appropriate distance;

- to facilitate communication in ways that convey human warmth and understanding;

- to create hope for the future;

- to develop the ability to see and sense things which are not always capable of being expressed in words.

2.13   DIFFERENT FACETS OF THE MEDIATOR'S ROLE

Mediation is evolving and mediators need to be creative in exploring new methods and ideas. Using an eclectic approach, models can be designed that offer the best 'fit' for the particular couple or family, rather than expecting the same off-the-peg model to suit everyone equally. Families and conflicts come in many forms and mediators need imagination and creativity, as well as expertise and experience. Mediators have multiple roles including the following:

- **The catalyst:** The mediator is a catalyst who initiates a dialogue between participants. Communication has often broken down and in some cases participants have had no direct discussion for a considerable time.

- **The manager:** The mediator manages the mediation process and provides a structure for negotiations. Participants are helped to define their issues, agree an agenda and move from one stage to the next.

- **The referee:** The mediator sets and maintains the ground-rules, giving time for each participant to speak, controlling interruptions and aggressive behaviour.

- **The facilitator:** The mediator helps participants to communicate better and to explain their concerns. The anger that is expressed is sometimes a cover for hurt and fear. Mediators also need to be sensitive to feelings that remain unspoken. Humour may be used, when appropriate, to relieve tension.

- **The interpreter:** The mediator helps couples to listen to each other and to look at issues in new ways, often by reframing negative statements as positive objectives and concerns. Mediators look for common interests and shared commitment – particularly to children – that transcend parents' differences.

- **The information-giver:** Mediators help participants collect and consider relevant information. Mediators are also a resource to both parties, explaining relevant legal or other information. Good communication skills are needed to give legal or other information to both parties jointly, in a sensitive, balanced and clear way.

- **The bridge to new family structures:** Mediators provide a bridge to support families – parents and children – in transitions from one kind of family structure to another. Separating parents often need short-term support to help them maintain or rebuild good parental relationships while ending their marital relationship.

- **The reality tester:** Mediators explore possible options, raise questions and check the viability of proposals. Sometimes one party makes demands or puts a proposal based on wishful thinking or inadequate knowledge. Exploring how proposals would work in practice helps people look at their real situation.

- **The conductor:** A mediator is a conductor in verbal, musical and scientific terms: verbal in the sense that the mediator helps people convey to each other what they need to say and musical in the sense that the mediator orchestrates different voices and blends them from discord into harmony. The noise of warring couples is discordant and clashing. Mediators need to control the sound so that each voice can be heard, keeping a balance between them and orchestrating the tempo during stages or movements in the process. This involves 'punctuating' or closing each phase, to help signal the next movement. Orchestrating the voices can produce a new form of harmony. Mediators are also conductors of energy. The energy people bring to mediation is often negative – being angry uses up a lot of energy. Mediators try to switch the current from negative to positive so that the energy can be used constructively.

- **The synthesiser:** Mediators need summarising and drafting skills to blend disparate statements and to summarise mediation outcomes in a way that assists both participants and their legal advisors. Mutually acceptable proposals need to be clearly drafted, to provide a basis for legally binding agreements. If there are no proposals for settlement, the mediation summary needs to clarify outstanding issues and the parties' positions, to assist further negotiations via lawyers or, if necessary, litigation. The language of mediation is important in building a synthesis out of discordant parts.

- **The juggler:** Skilled mediators are rather like jugglers in their ability to catch ideas and toss them so that different surfaces catch the light. The juggler's skills are open and visible, unlike the magic tricks of a conjuror. Although not trying to emulate a juggler's dazzling speed, mediators need balance, dexterity of movement and intellectual suppleness to keep information and ideas circulating freely. Entertaining an idea or throwing a suggestion into the air need not trivialise the difficulties.

The word 'trickster' has negative connotations but Benjamin, an American mediator, has compared the mediator's role to that of 'a folkloric trickster' who may 'confront the harsh, jagged reality of conflict' in seeking to turn things on their heads, transforming settled views and perceptions.[66] Mediators question conventional thinking and assumptions, not to lead people away from directions they wish to take, but to encourage innovative ideas and a fresh vision when they are unclear or stuck. If mediation is heavy going, like wading through treacle, people are more likely to want to extricate themselves from it. There need to be ways of lifting the spirits – moments when couples who are sad or angry find themselves able to laugh again. If being in mediation gives them a lift, rather than casting them down, they are more likely to retain what was said and consider it afterwards, perhaps together. Mediators need to take others seriously and themselves lightly.

---

[66]   Benjamin 'The Constructive Use of Deception: Skills, Strategies and Techniques of the Folkloric Trickster Figure and their Application by Mediators' (1995) 13(1) *Mediation Quarterly* 17.

CHAPTER 3

CONSIDERING FAMILY MEDIATION

'I was much further out than you thought
And not waving but drowning'[1]

CONTENTS

3.1   THE PARADOX OF FAMILY MEDIATION

Paradoxically, more may be expected from separating and divorcing couples at an extremely difficult time in their lives than would be expected from married couples. It would be unreasonable to ask a married couple in the midst of a bereavement to obtain valuations of their property and exchange contracts with a would-be buyer. Yet in mediation, an individual may be expected to agree arrangements with a partner who has just left to live with someone else. Although the couple may not have seen or spoken to each other since they parted, they are expected to sit down together to agree arrangements for their children and settlement of financial and

---

[1]   Stevie Smith (1957).

property matters. There are expectations of reasonableness when reason may be swamped by anger and grief. Many people faced with relationship breakdown feel like screaming at their partner or weeping, rather than sitting down together to negotiate over finances. Discussions about future arrangements make the ending of the relationship more real and painful. Agreements may be looked for to finalise a divorce that one partner does not want at all. Holmes and Rahe[2] developed a scale of 43 stressful life events and asked four hundred people to rate the level of stress they associated with each event. Divorce scored the second highest score, next in level of stress to the death of the spouse. Redundancy, imprisonment, or a close friend's death were rated as less stressful than divorce. Mediators need to be aware of the trauma and degree of adjustment faced by separating couples in every area of their lives. The emotional impact and psychological processes are profound and far-reaching. Divorce should not be seen as an illness from which people suffer and then recover. It is an extremely difficult and painful process involving the restructuring of identity and reintegration of personal experience, adjusting to changes in relationships and new living arrangements. Many couples seek help with these adjustments from relatives, friends and professional advisors. The point at which they seek and accept outside help may be a critical factor in the way they surmount the crisis of separation and navigate their way through different stages of separation and divorce.

3.2   IS EARLY MEDIATION INADVISABLE?

It is sometimes questioned whether mediation should be used in the early stages of separation or divorce, when individuals may be in turmoil and emotionally ill-prepared to take decisions. The decision to separate is rarely a joint decision. More often, one partner initiates the separation unilaterally, sometimes after a long period of withdrawing from the relationship. In other situations, the breakdown may be precipitated by a critical event. Some couples accept they have grown apart and take a mutual decision to separate in a calm and reflective way. But they are not the norm. More often, there is an initiator and a recipient of the decision to end the relationship. The gulf between these positions and the feelings that accompany them may be so wide that communication breaks down completely. If one partner discovers that the other has a new relationship, or if a divorce petition arrives without warning, the shock may be extreme. Emotional and psychological adjustment begins earlier for the leaver than for the left partner. A partner who is abandoned is left behind emotionally, as well as physically. Acute feelings of shock, rejection and betrayal often spill over on to children and financial issues. Many individuals come to mediation in a fragile state and are expected to negotiate over arrangements for children and financial matters in a reasonable way, at a time when the ability to think rationally may be

---

2   Holmes and Rahe 'The social readjustment rating scale' (1967) 11 *Journal of Psychosomatic Research.*

temporarily diminished. When decisions are needed on many different issues simultaneously, it is hardly surprising that many people feel overwhelmed. Outrage and anger can quickly spread from one issue to another. On the other hand, co-operation and agreement in one area help to maintain trust and increase co-operation in other areas.

3.3 MEDIATING IN CRISIS SITUATIONS

The Chinese ideogram for 'crisis' combines two characters, one meaning 'danger' and the other 'opportunity'. Separation is generally a period of acute crisis for both partners and for the family as a whole. Emotions run high and physical violence may occur for the first time in a way that is out of character for the couple's relationship. In these volatile situations, major decisions should not be hurried or imposed by the initiating partner on a shell-shocked one. On the other hand, there may be urgent questions over the non-residential parent's contact with the children and the payment of household bills. Such matters are not helped by delay. At an early stage when everything is in a state of flux, there are usually more options and more scope for change. The highest level of crisis is usually during separation, rather than the legal divorce. Individuals are more ready to accept outside intervention in the early stages of crisis. Help 'purposefully focused at a strategic time is more effective than more extensive help given at a period of less emotional accessibility'.[3] As time goes by, the range of options narrows, positions become entrenched and attitudes harden. If contact with children has broken down or has not even started, the longer the break continues, the harder it becomes to renew contact and rebuild damaged relationships.

A dialogue is needed, but many separating or separated couples find this dialogue very hard to manage on their own. Couples involved in relationship breakdown may be divided into three broad categories: those who are able to talk and work things out, those who argue and fight, and those who cannot talk at all. Couples from all three categories come to mediation and may belong at different times to more than one category. Mediators need to adapt their approach to different levels of conflict and the varying stages each partner may be at in the emotional and psychological divorce. The diagram below illustrates the phases of emotional and psychological separation and divorce, starting with an initial crisis in which one partner leaves the other or announces the intention of doing so. The leaver is more able to cope with a break up that has been pondered over, whereas the unprepared recipient may be inclined, at first, to deny that it is happening. Denial may be followed by anger or depression and this phase may be prolonged. If there is not

---

3   Rapoport 'The state of crisis – some theoretical considerations' in Parad *Crisis Intervention* (Family Service Association of America, 1965), p 30.

enough help and support, the partner who feels abandoned can slip from depression into despair. David Lodge describes despair as:[4]

> 'a downward spiral movement – like an aeroplane that loses a wing and falls through the air like a leaf, twisting and turning as the pilot struggles helplessly with the controls, the engine note rising to a high-pitched scream, the altimeter needle spinning round and round the dial towards zero.'

When one partner is spiralling downwards and the other partner who can still fly is impatient to move on, the challenge for mediators is how to help them both equally and prevent the gap between them from widening still further.

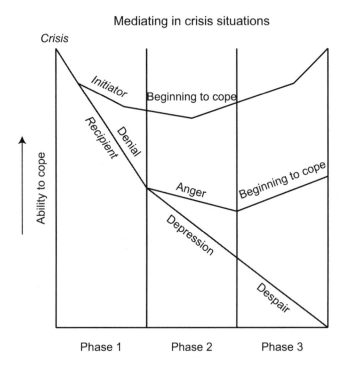

Mediating in crisis situations

Mediation at an early stage does not need to be hurried. Intervals between sessions allow time to reflect on what has been said and opportunities to take advice and prepare for the next meeting. Separated parents often return saying they have talked together since the last meeting. There are, however, understandable concerns that premature decisions might be taken under pressure. Skilled mediators should be aware of these risks and able to help couples work out interim or holding arrangements without pressure to take long-term decisions. Independent legal advice is needed alongside mediation to make sure that both partners understand their legal position and possible disadvantages if the status quo should be prolonged. Time management is important in planning an agenda that

---

4   Lodge *Therapy* (Penguin Books, 1996), p 63.

incorporates both partners' needs. A staged process can give the recipient some time to catch up and engage in decision-making, instead of remaining on the receiving end. Entrenched positions may ease when couples find they can agree certain matters and not deal with everything at once.

A family mediation centre may be the only place where a recently separated couple can meet and talk together on any or all of the issues that need to be resolved, with impartial third party support. Public awareness remains low, however. When parents in one study were asked what kind of help they needed during separation and divorce, many suggested mediation or a mediation-type service, unaware that such services already exist. Separating couples are at a crossroads. They need to consider what path they want to take. There are different routes to settlement, some of them longer and more costly than others and none providing certain outcomes. Mediators can give information about these pathways in the context of individual circumstances, to help couples consider whether they can tentatively try the mediation route or whether the circumstances require a different course. Various models and pilots have been tried to assist clients' choice of process in an impartial and constructive way, including Family Information Pilots and the FAINs scheme, but none so successfully as to lead to nationwide implementation. Leaflets are available explaining the options available. Resolution's '*Divorce and Separation: Choosing the right process for you*' is probably the best of these. A leaflet on family mediation, '*Independent Mediation – Information for Judges, Magistrates and Legal Advisors*' has been sent to family courts.

3.4 AMBIVALENCE ABOUT ENDING RELATIONSHIPS

The FMC Code of Practice 2010 states that 'throughout the mediation, mediators must keep the possibility of reconciliation of the participants under review'.[5] Even where both partners seem certain of their need to separate or divorce, mediators may enquire whether counselling was sought at any stage and if so, for how long. By the time they come to mediation, most couples say that it is too late for them to go to counselling to resolve problems in their marriage or relationship. Some say that they have already been to counselling. Ambivalence about ending a close relationship is very common, however. Mixed feelings may be concealed under a defensive shell of anger. If communication and relationships improve following initial information meetings or in the course of mediation, some couples have second thoughts about separating and decide to stay or get back together. Mediators need to be sensitive to signs of ambivalence or a need for counselling to help one or both partners understand and come to terms with the breakdown of their relationship. Counselling may be suggested where there is need to explore

---

[5]   At para 6.3. See Appendix A below.

feelings in more depth and have support over a longer period. Although one partner may seem more in need of counselling than the other, the suggestion of counselling should be put to both of them as something they may wish to consider, if they have not already done so. The mediator should have leaflets about local counselling services and lists of accredited private counsellors.

Although uncommon, it is not unknown for a couple to go through a complete mediation process culminating with a Memorandum of Understanding and then decide to get back together and not divorce after all. Mediation does not provide counselling or marital therapy, but it can lead to increased insight and understanding. Sometimes the reconciliation does not last and the couple may re-refer themselves to mediation, but individual follow-up in some cases has shown that other reconciled couples have stayed together and forged a stronger relationship than they had previously.

3.5   TRIANGULATION

The partner who makes the first contact with a mediation service often predicts that the other partner will refuse to take part. Although this pessimism may be well founded, the other partner should have an equal opportunity to consider mediation. The first partner may be trying to gain the upper hand, hoping to secure any available help for their sole benefit. A family therapist has referred to the Battle for Initiative and the Battle for Structure.[6] Mediators are aware of the battle for control that take place when one partner seeks to win the mediator's support before the other can do so. When couples are ending a relationship, they commonly look for allies, experts or other third parties who may become triangulated in their conflict. Mediators need to be aware of the risks of triangulation, especially if they mediate alone.

Couples in conflict often embark on a series of moves and counter-moves in which increasing numbers of third parties are liable to become involved. These moves are strategic. As the supporting army of relatives, friends and advisors grows on each side, other people's vested interests may escalate and obscure the original dispute. Mediators need to understand the strategic moves that may be made, so that they can respond with impartial yet engaging strategies of their own. Even at an early stage there may be moves to take control of the mediation process and its outcome. There may be moves by one partner to take control of the new territory in which the 'game' is to be played. The first move might be called 'Seize the Initiative'. The partner proposing mediation finds out about it first and puts the other partner at a disadvantage by knowing

---

[6]   Whitaker 'Process Techniques of Family Therapy' (1977) 1 *Family Process.*

more about mediation, claiming the higher moral ground of 'wanting mediation' and stating that they have already been offered an initial meeting with a mediator.

The second move may be called 'Let me explain the problem'. One partner may try to influence the mediator and take control of the mediation process by saying 'Let me explain the problem' or 'Here is the correspondence to give you the background'. Mediators need to be reassuring and firm in explaining the ground-rules of mediation and adhering to them from the outset, without alienating either party. It is easy to underestimate the skills and time involved in engaging both participants in mediation. It is worth taking this time and trouble because adequate information and careful assessment increase the likelihood of mediation taking place when the circumstances are suitable.

3.6   FAMILY MEDIATION AND CULTURAL DIVERSITY

Britain is 'a rainbow nation' whose population includes children born in 185 out of the world's 192 countries.[7] Mixed-race relationships and marriages are increasingly common. Many children have a multicultural heritage from mixed-race parents whose families originate from countries the children may have never visited. For family mediation to be acceptable to multi-cultural and ethnic minority couples, mediators need to appreciate and respect cultural diversity and recognise the limitations of a mono-cultural perspective. In some communities, the interests of the wider family take priority over individual concerns and needs. Family members have strong obligations to each other and in times of crisis it may be normal for children to stay with relatives or for a dependent relative to be taken in by other family members. This kind of family system is very cohesive when extended families live in close proximity. But some are isolated and fragmented. A separated parent may be cut off from relatives in their country of origin and may be rejected by their community for religious or social reasons. Mediators need to be aware of cultural factors and norms that influence a couple's ability to negotiate in mediation. In traditional Asian marriages, the husband is dominant and the wife submissive. Divorce is discouraged because it brings social stigma and upsets the harmony of the family. Culturally specific mediation literature is needed to identify variables that influence the mediation process. Mediators need to be open to understanding different cultural and ethnic traditions so that their approach is not dominated by their own social traditions and values. Even where a mediator has the same ethnicity as the participants, the mediator needs to appreciate the uniqueness of each family's history, traditions, values and ways of functioning. Cross-cultural mediation needs the same openness from the mediator as any mediation.

---

[7]   (2010) *The Times*, 13 April.

3.7   CONSIDERATION OF MEDIATION PRIOR TO FAMILY LAW PROCEEDINGS

Since implementation of section 29 of the Family Law Act 1996, legal aid applicants have been required, with certain exemptions, to attend a mediation information and assessment meeting with an LSC competence-assessed mediator before legal aid can be obtained for court proceedings in family matters. Under the subsequently introduced 'Willingness Test', an applicant for legal aid is not required to attend a meeting if the other party declines to attend a meeting or consider mediation. From 6 April 2011, potential applicants for and respondents to a court order in most family proceedings, whether publicly funded or otherwise, will be expected to have followed the steps set out in the Pre-Application Protocol for family mediation information and assessment contained in Practice Direction 3A, issued by the President of the Family Division as a supplement to Part 3 of the Family Procedure Rules 2010:[8]

> 'This requires a potential applicant, except in certain specified circumstances, to consider with a mediator whether the dispute may be capable of being resolved through mediation. The court will expect all applicants to have complied with the Protocol before commencing proceedings and (except where exceptional circumstances apply) will expect any respondent to have attended a Mediation Information and Assessment Meeting, if invited to do so. If court proceedings are taken, the court will wish to know at the first hearing whether mediation has been considered by the parties. In considering the conduct of any relevant family proceedings, the court will take into account any failure to comply with the Protocol and may refer the parties to a meeting with a mediator before the proceedings continue further.'

The new protocol 'does not affect the operation of the private law programme, now set out in Practice Direction 12B, or the role of the court at the first hearing in any relevant family proceedings'.[9] The purpose is:

> 'to help the public access information and advice earlier about mediation … so that those wishing to make an application to court, whether publicly funded or otherwise, will have to first consider, as appropriate, alternative means of resolving their disputes.'

The Family Justice Council has produced an explanatory leaflet[10] giving further guidance. This leaflet has been circulated to all family courts for distribution to court staff, potential applicants and enquirers. It explains that attendance at a mediation information and assessment meeting is not compulsory mediation, since mediation is voluntary and attendance at such a meeting does not prevent the filing of a divorce petition or making

---

[8]   See the Guidance section of the Pre-Application Protocol.
[9]   Ibid.
[10] *The Family Court Guide to Family Applications and Mediation Information and Assessment Meetings* (FJC, February 2011).

an emergency application. At the information and assessment meeting, which may be attended jointly or separately, the mediator explains different routes to settlement and the benefits of reaching agreements at an early stage, without litigation. To comply with the Practice Direction, applications to the court, whether in person or through a solicitor, will need in most cases to be accompanied by Family Mediation Information Form (FM1), completed and signed by a recognised mediator stating that mediation is not suitable to the dispute because another party to the dispute is unwilling to attend a Mediation Information and Assessment Meeting and consider mediation, or that their whereabouts are unknown, or the mediator considers, after meeting with the applicant and/or the respondent, that the dispute, the parties and all the circumstances are not suitable for mediation. Annex C of the Protocol sets out circumstances in which attendance at a mediation information and assessment meeting is not required. These circumstances include the urgency of a prospective application ('meaning that there is a risk to the life, liberty or physical safety of the applicant or his or her family'[11]), or the unwillingness of another party to attend a meeting to consider mediation, or situations where a mediator has found mediation to be unsuitable in an assessment made at any time within the previous four months, or:[12]

> 'where any party has, to the applicant's knowledge, made an allegation of domestic violence against another party and this has resulted in a police investigation or the issuing of civil proceedings for the protection of any party within the last 12 months.'

Another category of exemption is where:[13]

> 'there is current social services involvement as a result of child protection concerns in respect of any child who would be the subject of the application.'

The Protocol, whatever its failings, and despite the claims that it has been brought in at speed on the back of savage public spending cuts, is in reality the logical extension to all potential litigants of the *opportunity* offered to publicly funded clients since 1997, representing a climate change in ways of resolving family disputes that proponents of ADR have long been awaiting. It is the next step in the development of Appropriate Dispute Resolution and should be seen in the context of other changes and potential changes brought about by the Family Procedure Rules 2010 and the Family Justice Review.

---

[11]   See Annex C, para 10.
[12]   See Annex C, para 4.
[13]   Ibid, para 11.

3.8   MEDIATION AND LEGAL AID

The threatened removal of legal aid in many family cases, including divorce, private law children and family proceedings and ancillary relief proceedings[14] is highly controversial. One of the government's stated intentions is to encourage the use of Appropriate Dispute Resolution rather than litigation. However, there are many situations in addition to those listed in Annex C of the Pre-Application Protocol where legal aid for an application to the court is needed to protect the rights and needs of a vulnerable party and/or children. If legal aid for many family proceedings is no longer available to those on low incomes or dependent on welfare benefits, the 'power imbalance' would be heavily weighted in favour of a party who is able to pay privately for court proceedings, with legal representation, thus increasing pressure to settle in mediation on another party who is unable to afford to go to court. A further concern is the reduced availability of lawyers able to do family legal aid work in the few areas where legal aid remains. For these reasons, mediators' responses to the Green Paper have been as vociferously against the proposals as those from family lawyers. Since most of the growth in mediation in the last thirteen years has resulted from referrals from solicitors in the legal aid sector, there is a real risk that cuts in legal aid would have the opposite effect of reducing use of mediation, despite the effect of the Pre-Application Protocol. The Green Paper states that legal aid would be retained for family mediation in private law family cases and for a limited amount of legal advice and assistance from solicitors in conjunction with mediation and the implementation of mediated agreements. Consultation is taking place on these proposals and they will also be considered in the wider deliberations of the Family Justice Review.

3.9   SCOPE OF FAMILY MEDIATION

The FMC Code of Practice 2010 states that:[15]

> '4.1   Mediation may cover any or all of the following matters
> > 4.1.1 options for maintaining or ending the marital or other relationship between the adult participants and the consequences of doing so;
> > 4.1.2 arrangements for dependant children: – with whom they are to live; what contact they are to have with each parent and other family members; any other aspect of parental responsibility such as, but not exhaustively, schooling, holidays, religious education;
> > 4.1.3 the future of the family home and any other property or assets, including pensions, belonging to the adult participants; issues of child maintenance and spousal maintenance; issues relating to debts;

---

[14]   Green Paper *Proposals for the Reform of Legal Aid in England and Wales* (November 2010).

[15]   See para 4: set out in Appendix A below.

4.1.4 how adjustments to these arrangements are to be decided upon in the future;

4.2 Participants and mediators may agree that mediation will cover any other matters which it would be helpful to resolve in connection with relationship breakdown between the participants and which the mediators consider suitable for mediation.'

It is increasingly recognised that family mediation can be of assistance in a much wider range of family disputes[16] and also in international cross-border disputes over children.[17] Early mediation research in the UK[18] found that those who went to mediation often had difficulty explaining the issues they needed to settle. Many said they needed 'to sort everything out.' Arrangements for children, property and financial issues are often tied up in a tangled knot of unsettled questions. Teasing out the knotted threads is an essential part of mediation. Mediation can involve turning the knot around and seeing which threads can be loosened first. The knot may begin to unravel if the threads are teased out gently, whereas tugging at them tightens the knot.

3.10 MEDIATION INFORMATION AND ASSESSMENT MEETINGS

On receiving a referral from the parties or their lawyers, the mediation service normally contacts both parties to offer an initial information and assessment meeting, unless there are concerns about personal safety. Whereas under the Funding Code the first party has not been required to attend a meeting if the second party declines the appointment or fails to reply within ten days, the Pre-Application Protocol appears to impose an expectation on all parties that they should have considered mediation before participating in litigation. If there are particular concerns such as risks of violence or other kinds of harm, an individual can attend the mediation information and assessment meeting alone or with support, without their ex-partner being present or informed of the appointment. If both partners come together, the mediator must see them separately during the initial meeting so that screening for the suitability of mediation can be done with each of them alone. Individuals referred to mediation information and assessment meetings may be on the verge of court proceedings or already involved in proceedings. They may be strongly disinclined to meet face-to-face with an ex-partner with whom they are no longer on speaking terms. Yet they may also fear the financial costs, delays and emotional stress of litigation. Family mediation services must have separate waiting areas available. When mediation is suitable and accepted by both parties, those who qualify financially are eligible for mediation free of charge. They may also obtain public funding for legal

---

[16] See Chapter 4 below.

[17] See Chapter 14 below.

[18] Walker, McCarthy and Timms *Mediation: the Making and Remaking of Co-operative Relationships* (Relate Centre for Family Studies, University of Newcastle, 1994).

advice and assistance from legal advisors on proposed agreements reached in mediation, before entering into a legally binding agreement. Those not eligible for public funding are charged at an hourly rate or per session.

The specialist task of the mediator/assessor, whether under the Pre-Application Protocol or the Funding Code, has developed considerably from the way it was envisaged in the Family Law Act 1996. Many potential applicants and respondents already appreciate that the mediation information and assessment meeting is not just another obstacle to be negotiated on their way to court. Those who are hostile to the idea of mediation, and object to paying for it, may need considerable information and empathetic listening before they can begin to understand it and contemplate taking part. To undertake the assessment process effectively, mediator/assessors have developed skills and expertise that may require additional training. It also follows that the separate activity of information giving and assessment, leading to acceptance of mediation or the signing of Form FM1, must be charged for at an economic rate and can no longer be a loss leader.

The flowchart below, produced by Bristol Family Mediators Association, illustrates how referral for mediation information and assessment currently works in practice under the Funding Code.

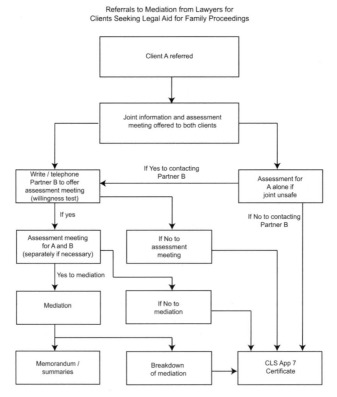

Referrals to Mediation from Lawyers for
Clients Seeking Legal Aid for Family Proceedings

Reproduced courtesy of Bristol FMA Ltd 2010

Mediation information and assessment meetings under the Pre-Application Protocol may develop in a somewhat different way. Judges may need to consider whether a respondent has justification for refusing to attend an information and assessment meeting to consider mediation. If court proceedings are delayed because the court directs a respondent to attend a mediation information and information meeting, despite a previous refusal to do so, the delay could have disadvantages for the applicant and for children. There is a delicate balance to maintain between upholding the principle of voluntary participation in mediation, while not giving undue scope for deliberately obstructive people to play the court system to their advantage, without considering different routes available and the costs involved.

The interdisciplinary professional knowledge and skills required by mediators for information and assessment meetings are extensive and challenging. They include:

(i) Interpersonal skills to engage with angry and distressed individuals who may be referred at different stages of separation, divorce or other family matters, often in high conflict. Ex-partners are usually at different emotional stages in accepting the ending of their relationship. Some divorcing couples have been married for many years, while some parents in residence and contact disputes have never lived together at all.

(ii) Communication skills to understand each partner's issues and to explain mediation in a clear and helpful way as a possible means of resolving their issues, provided the circumstances are suitable and both parties willing to take part. Information needs to be tailored to the needs of each person receiving it, not a standardised discourse from a disengaged assessor.

(iii) Assessment skills to screen for domestic violence or abuse, child protection concerns or any other circumstances that would make mediation unsuitable. Parties to cases involving allegations or concerns about domestic violence are no longer automatically exempt from the requirement to attend an information and assessment meeting. Any risk for an adult or child needs to be assessed by the mediator, with immediate referral where necessary to other services and agencies. Screening for domestic abuse and child protection issues needs awareness, empathy and the use of carefully graduated questions. Individuals may find it very hard to disclose domestic violence and may fear reprisals if they do so. Confidentiality is an important issue that needs to be handled extremely carefully when assessing suitability and potential risks. For some people, violence means physical violence, whereas unremitting verbal and psychological abuse is a form of violence that may be even more destructive of morale. Mediation may be suitable in certain circumstances with appropriate conditions and safeguards and only if both parties are willing, whereas it would be strongly contra-indicated in other categories.[19]

(iv)   Assessment of financial eligibility for public funding. As well as having communication skills, mediators need to be sufficiently numerate to calculate average monthly income from a range of sources paid at different intervals (eg variable weekly earnings, fortnightly tax credits, child benefit paid four weekly and child support received calendar monthly). Evidence of income must be provided and scrutinised. Income from self-employment is particularly difficult to assess and bank statements are needed, but some income may be 'cash in hand' and hard to determine. Eligibility assessment is not compulsory for those who already know they are not eligible for public funding and who are willing to pay privately for mediation. In accepting mediation, they accept that full financial disclosure will be needed, with supporting documents, for mediation on financial and property matters. Lawyer mediators with experience of civil legal aid work are accustomed to financial assessments, whereas mediators from social work and counselling backgrounds need to develop competence in assessing financial eligibility as an additional responsibility.

3.11   ASSESSING THE SUITABILITY OF MEDIATION

When one partner or a couple is referred to mediation, the way forward is like a crossroads with a set of traffic lights. Before going ahead, it is essential to slow down and consider whether the lights are green, amber or red and whether they are steady or flashing. If red lights show in situations such as the following, mediation is unlikely to suitable:

•   certain categories of domestic violence or abuse (see below), especially where there are continuing risks;

•   child safety and protection issues;

•   intimidation, threats, extreme power imbalances;

•   mental illness;

•   mental disability;

•   substance misuse;

•   evidence of deceit and false information;

---

[19]   See **3.11–3.16** below.

- refusal or inability to accept ground-rules in mediation.

3.12 DEFINING DOMESTIC VIOLENCE AND ABUSE

Although domestic violence and abuse occur in all societies and social classes, perceptions of what constitutes violence and abuse are not universally the same. Behaviour that is accepted as normal in some cultures or communities may be condemned in others, yet perpetrated in secret. Definitions and value judgments vary among those providing help, as well as among those needing help. Researchers in Bristol found a tendency among professionals to look for circumstances that fitted their personal views and theories, without making careful assessments to check whether accounts and experiences of abuse supported their assumptions.[20] The government definition of domestic violence was agreed in 2004 and is as follows:[21]

> 'any incident of threatening behaviour, violence or abuse (psychological, physical, sexual, financial or emotional) between adults who are or have been intimate partners or family members, regardless of gender or sexuality.'

Psychological, emotional and verbal abuse and threats may be even more damaging and destructive than physical violence. A majority of respondents in a research study in Australia on experience of abuse reported that verbal, psychological and emotional abuse occurred daily and was more devastating and long lasting in its negative impact than physical attacks.[22] Understanding the impact of abusive behaviour on the abused person and on children who witness or overhear it is a key factor in assessment. An abused person may experience fear and humiliation to an extent that impairs their ability to assess the risks they continue to face.

> 'Domestic violence is behaviour that seeks to secure power and control for the abuser and to undermine the safety, security, self-esteem and autonomy of the abused person.'[23]

The British Crime Survey 2009/10 (3.4) reported that 29% of women and 16% of men have experienced domestic violence or abuse. Women who have separated have the highest risk (22.3%), compared with other groups.[24] Just over half (54%) of 94 female homicide victims in 2009/10 had been killed by their partner, ex-partner or lover. When divorce mediation developed in the United States during the 1980s, there was opposition from women's rights groups and feminists. The strongest objections were to mandatory mediation, where women who had been

---

[20] Borkowski, Murch and Walker *Marital Violence* (Tavistock, 1983).
[21] Mills 'Effects of Domestic Violence on Children' [2008] Fam Law 166.
[22] Bagshaw *Disclosure of Domestic Violence in Family Law Disputes: Issues for Family and Child Mediators* (Conflict Management Research Group, University of South Australia, 2001).
[23] National Family Mediation (1996).
[24] See para 3.4 of the British Crime Survey 2009/10.

victims of violence were required to take part in mediation with a partner who had been violent. Critics of mediation objected that physical safety could not be ensured and that risks of further violence would be increased through face-to-face meetings with an abusing partner. Victims of violence were thought to be at greatest risk immediately after a mediation meeting, on leaving the building at the same time as a partner who might have become enraged. There has been large-scale debate on these issues, involving many different organisations and professions. Legislation was enacted in many states in the USA exempting women who had been victims of violence from mandatory mediation. Women's groups tend to oppose mediation whenever violence is an issue, yet women themselves may choose mediation because they need an opportunity to talk to their partner or ex-partner in the presence of an impartial, competent and trustworthy third party.[25]

3.13   LINKS BETWEEN DOMESTIC VIOLENCE AND CHILD ABUSE

Children are liable to have suffered physical abuse themselves in as many as 40–60% of domestic violence cases.[26] 750,000 children annually are reported to have witnessed domestic violence and in 90% of incidents, children were in the same or an adjoining room.[27] Children have described their terror of the violence they could hear taking place: 'I used to hide myself in the smallest part of my bedroom'.[28] The impact on children of witnessing or experiencing violence and fearing further violence is likely to be devastating. In the longer term, it may have deeply damaging effects. Domestic violence features in the lives of 37% of children who are receiving social work interventions and 60% of those on the child protection register.[29] English law recognises that a child witnessing or hearing domestic violence is a child protection issue. The meaning of harm to a child has been amended in the Adoption and Children Act 2002 to include 'impairment suffered through seeing or hearing the ill treatment of another'. When there is domestic violence, questions need to be asked about child abuse and when there is child abuse, questions need to be asked about domestic violence. Many children remain in contact after separation with an allegedly violent parent and some continue to live with one.

In February 2006, Wall LJ, now President of the Family Division, presented a report to the then President on thirteen cases in which

---

[25]   Herrnstein 'Women and mediation: a chance to speak and to be heard' (1996) 13(3) *Mediation Quarterly* 229–241.

[26]   Hester and Radford *Domestic Violence and Child Contact in England and Denmark* (Polity Press, 1996).

[27]   Mills 'Effects of Domestic Violence on Children' [2008] Fam Law 165–171.

[28]   Cockett and Tripp *The Exeter Family Study: Family Breakdown and its impact on children* (University of Exeter Press, 1994), p 46.

[29]   Children in Need Census 2001.

twenty-nine children from thirteen different families had been murdered by their fathers during contact visits approved by the court.[30] This report led to a shift from the judicial view that contact is nearly always in the best interests of the child to judicial recognition that contact needs to be safe and positive for the child.[31] However, 'swings of the pendulum' persist. A further recommendation that Judges should always hold findings of fact hearings to establish the realities of risk has now been superseded by 2010 guidance[32] that such hearings are taking up 'a disproportionate amount of the court's time and resources.' When courts refer disputes concerning children to mediation, Cafcass will have already carried out safety checks before mediation takes place.[33] Screening by mediators for risks of violence or abuse to children and adults is not a substitute for those safety checks or for judicial findings of fact. Mediators have an important complementary role in undertaking detailed and skilled explorations of fears, risks and histories of violence and abuse, combined with the ability to take account of very recent incidents reported by one party at the information and assessment meeting.[34] The mediator needs to screen properly for risks of violence or abuse to children and adults, while providing opportunities for child-centred discussions that may be a more effective safeguarding intervention for the child than a lengthy fact-finding process.

3.14 SCREENING FOR DOMESTIC ABUSE AND CHILD PROTECTION ISSUES

Requirement F.4 of the Legal Services Commission *Quality Mark Standard for Mediation*[35] states that Family Mediation Services must:

> 'ensure that the relevant systems are in place to protect any children who might be at risk, and to consider the views of any children directly involved in the mediation process.'

Research studies on mediation and domestic abuse show the importance of skilled screening procedures. A person who feels threatened may fear that disclosing violence would put her at greater risk. The word 'violent' should be avoided unless the client uses it, because behaviour seen by some as violent may be seen by others as normal. Initial questions can be ordinary ones, such as: 'When you are/were together, are/were there many arguments? ... What usually happens/happened when you argue?'

---

[30] Wall LJ [2006] Report on the publication by the Women's Aid Federation of England entitled *Twenty-nine Child Homicides: Lessons still to be learnt on domestic violence and child protection*.

[31] Craig 'Everybody's Business: Application for contact orders with consent' [2007] Fam Law 261.

[32] President's Guidance in relation to split hearings [2010] Fam Law 752.

[33] See **3.18.2** below.

[34] See example at **3.14.4** below.

[35] (2nd edn, September 2009).

Mediators need to phrase their questions sensitively and respond to body language suggesting nervousness or fear. In screening for domestic violence, intimidation and child protection issues, mediators need to show awareness and empathy and use carefully graded questions. If an individual refers openly to domestic violence, the mediator needs to ask whether the police were called or social services involved, whether medical treatment was necessary and whether there are, or have been, court injunctions, care orders or personal protection orders. A screening form should be used to gather and record information. Individuals needing legal advice and urgent help should be given information about other services and helped to access them. Although no measures can guarantee full protection, the extended circumstances in which restraining orders can be made in the criminal courts[36] offer longer protection to a wider group of people, some of whom might not seek protection through the civil courts. Twelve-month pilot schemes are also being introduced giving powers to the police to protect women by removing violent partners from the family home, initially for 48 hours, to give the woman the opportunity to obtain advice and support.

The level of fear needs to be understood and assessed as part of the screening process. Degrees of fear and risk need careful assessment, since an abused person is liable to underestimate the impact of their experience and the risk of continuing and even more severe violence. It is helpful to ask individuals if they can say what level of fear they are experiencing on a scale of 1–10. Johnston and Campbell[37] identified five categories of domestic violence and abuse. Mediation may be used with great caution in some of these categories, whereas it would be strongly contra-indicated in others. Mediators need to recognise and distinguish between different categories in assessing forms of violence and abuse, the impact on abused adults and children and current levels of risk.

3.14.1   Ongoing severe battering by the male partner

This kind of battering is liable to increase in severity over time and these cases are not suitable for mediation. It is the possibility of couples in this category being referred to mediation that causes the greatest concern. If a victim of this type of violence is referred to mediation, the greatest care must be taken to help her obtain advice and help, without putting her at further risk. In England and Wales, information given by one partner in a separate intake meeting is confidential and may not be given to the other partner, even if he subsequently attends an intake meeting with the same mediator.

---

[36]   See Domestic Violence, Crime and Victims Act 2004, s 12.
[37]   Johnston and Campbell 'A clinical typology of interparental violence in disputed custody divorces' (1993) 63(2) *American Journal of Orthopsychiatry* 190–199.

3.14.2 Violence associated with psychotic and paranoid reactions

In a minority of cases, the disordered thinking and distortions of reality that occur in psychotic illness may generate violence. This violence is unpredictable, there is usually little build-up to the attack and the victim does not provoke it. The level of violence ranges from moderate to severe. Separation triggers an acute phase of danger. Such cases should be screened out of mediation and referred to other services.

3.14.3 Interactive violence used to provoke reactions and gain control

Johnston and Campbell suggest that couples who have an established pattern of provoking each other verbally and exchanging insults often end up having a physical struggle. Either partner may start provoking the other but the overriding response by the man is to assert control by physically dominating and overpowering the woman. The man does not batter her and does not normally use more force than is necessary to obtain her submission.

3.14.4 Violence by women against men

Around a fifth of domestic violence cases involve violence by women against men.[38] Women who kill a violent partner have usually endured years of being battered by him. In some cases, both partners admit that they have been violent to the other. Typically, women who resort to violence are infuriated by their partner's passivity or failure to meet their expectations. They may throw things or hit him, but rarely use a weapon. Serious physical injury inflicted by women is uncommon, but it does occur. A young father came to a mediation information and assessment meeting with his arm in plaster. He explained that he had sole care of four small children and the previous day his former partner, who had abandoned the family, came back and tried to wrest the baby out of the father's arms. In the ensuing struggle, the mother closed a door on the father's arm and broke it. Neighbours called the police, who arrested the mother and called Social Services but gave a wrong address for the father, so Social Services had not visited him or seen the children. With the father's ready consent, a phone call to Social Services put the child protection system into action. This incident had occurred in an interval of two or three days between the father's solicitor referring him to the mediation service and his attendance at an information and assessment meeting.

---

[38] British Crime Survey 2001/02.

3.14.5   Abuse associated with separation

There can be incidents of physical violence associated with separation that are uncharacteristic of the couple's relationship and previous behaviour towards each other. This kind of violence typically occurs for the first time when one partner announces the intention of leaving the other. Johnston and Campbell suggest that mediation may be helpful to couples in this category and that they should not be denied the opportunity, if they both accept mediation. Often, these couples are loath to admit to an outsider that an argument between them has escalated into violence, because they feel humiliated. A mediator who senses this may need to comment how easily a crisis situation can get out of control, when stress levels are very high. If the couple then acknowledge that they have lost or fear losing control, it is important to ask each partner about their fears, to establish whether there has been any physical injury, and whether medical attention and legal advice have been sought. If there has not been previous violence and both partners are anxious to work together to regain control of their situation, mediation may be appropriate and may enable them to regain control. There may be need for shuttle mediation and/or different arrival and departure times. Arrangements for child contact need to minimise risks by defining precise boundaries (place and/or time) or, if the couple still live together, agreements to avoid talking at home about a subject that triggers anger. Couples who still live together may agree that disputed matters should not be discussed at home: they should be brought to mediation. Safeguards for both partners need to be considered. They need to know the legal or other action that could be taken if rules agreed between them are not kept.

3.15   THE NEED FOR SAFEGUARDS

Experience of providing mediation and consumer studies indicate that mediation may be appropriate where previous incidents of violence or abuse occurred a long time ago and there is no fear of recurrence, or where there has been a single, atypical incident possibly involving both partners to some extent. A written policy and code of practice should be adhered to, with procedures and safeguards to ensure that:

(i)   Screening takes place at the outset, with a full explanation of the process, the safeguards available and the ground-rules that would be applied.

(ii) Both partners agree to participate on an informed and voluntary basis. Mediators must continue to check during mediation that neither partner is participating under pressure and/or in fear.

(iii) Separate waiting-areas are available, so that neither partner need fear having to wait in the same area as the other while tension mounts between them.

(iv) Where one party is afraid of arriving or leaving the building at the same time as the other, prior arrangements are made to enable them to arrive and leave separately.

(v) Mediators have sufficient awareness of domestic abuse, other services available and the protection orders the courts can make.

(vi) Mediators have received training and continue to receive training in screening and recognising non-verbal signals, so that they can respond and refer appropriately to other forms of help.

(vii) Mediation services provide adequate working conditions and safeguards, including not allowing a mediator to work alone in part of a building at any time. There should be an emergency call system or panic button.

(viii) If one party's address and phone number is held in confidence, mediators and mediation services must protect confidential addresses and telephone numbers with the utmost care.

(ix) Where one party alleges violence by the other, an essential condition for offering or continuing mediation is that the alleged abuser does not deny the basic *facts*. Although views and explanations of causes and reasons are likely to differ, the basic fact that an assault or violent incident took place must be recognised by both parties.

3.16 OTHER CIRCUMSTANCES NEEDING CAREFUL CONSIDERATION OF SUITABILITY

Other circumstances needing careful consideration of suitability, where the lights for mediation may be orange, rather than red or green, include:

- Indications that counselling, therapy or other form of help may be needed.

- Power imbalances appear too extreme for mediation.[39]

- High levels of hostility and mistrust.

- Depression – chronic or reactive (many people going through separation show some degree of depression).

---

[39] See Chapter 10 below on power imbalances.

- Acute distress needing medical or therapeutic help.

- Complex finances where collaborative law may be more appropriate than mediation.

- Language difficulties, illiteracy, deafness.

- Indications that one party wants to use mediation to prolong the status quo, without motivation to settle.

The suitability of mediation in these and similarly difficult or complex circumstances needs fuller discussion than there is room for here. Some difficulties, such as a language or hearing problem, may be addressed by bringing in specialist help, but this may be hard to access and it brings its own complications. An additional person who is invited to join the mediation must be acceptable to all participants and should have a good understanding of the mediation process. Mediation where one or both parties are deaf may be possible with the help of a worker for the deaf. There must be prior consultation to ensure that both parties would feel comfortable with the proposed worker. If the worker is already known to one party but not to both, there could be an actual or perceived bias and the other party might not accept the worker as impartial. Mediators and participants need to be able to trust the integrity and professionalism of a specialist worker who joins in the mediation process. If a worker for the deaf signs the mediator's words for one or both parties, the mediator cannot check the accuracy of the translation. The same applies when an interpreter is used to translate to and from another language. Apart from the accuracy of the translation, it can be difficult to convey nuances of language and feeling from one language to another.[40]

3.17 'CONVERSION' FROM INFORMATION AND ASSESSMENT MEETINGS TO MEDIATION

The information and assessment meeting should help people to decide on their next steps. If they accept mediation, they should understand its principles and aims and feel sufficiently reassured about the way in which the process will be conducted. When the initial sole or joint meeting does not lead to mediation, it should not be assumed to be a failure or a waste of time. In some cases, couples begin to realise that they are capable (allowed, even) to settle matters between themselves. Some phone after the initial meeting to say that they do not need mediation because they have reached agreements between themselves that their solicitors are drafting in a consent order. When circumstances are unsuitable for mediation, the information meeting might be seen as a waste of time, but experience does not bear this out. Individuals who are stressed and often confused value being listened to and understood. They may also need

---

[40] See Chapter 6 below.

information about other services offering the kind of help they need. Naturally, there are cases in which one partner wants mediation and the other is not contactable or does not respond. Sometimes the second party ignores or declines the offer of an information meeting, but accepts a couple of months later, following further legal advice. The conversion rate from sole/joint initial meetings to mediation needs to be sophisticated enough to record positive outcomes from non-conversion. When mediation is not taken up, contested court proceedings do not always follow. The information and assessment meeting is a skilled process which has the dual purpose of assisting participants to make an informed choice of process, while also making the assessment of suitability for mediation that is needed by legal advisors, the Legal Services Commission and in some cases, the court.

3.18 REFERRAL TO MEDIATION AT ANY STAGE OF LEGAL PROCEEDINGS

3.18.1 Prior to court application

Information about mediation should be provided by court staff and on court application forms. In some areas, a letter from the Designated Family Judge makes clear the court's expectation that ADR will have been tried before court proceedings are embarked on. The Revised Private Law Programme implemented by a Practice Direction of 1 April 2010:[41]

> 'is designed to assist parties to reach safe agreements where possible, to provide a forum in which to find the best way to resolve issues in each individual case and to promote outcomes that are sustainable, that are in the best interests of children and that take account of their perspectives ... The detailed arrangements for the participation of mediators will be arranged locally.'

The Pre-Application Protocol annexed to Practice Direction 3A[42] is likely to result in greater use of mediation prior to court application, especially if legal aid is no longer available.

3.18.2 Court referral to mediation, prior to court hearing

The Good Practice Guidelines for court-referred mediation recommend a triage system similar to the one at Milton Keynes County Court, where the district judge allocates applications to mediation or non-mediation lists. Plymouth County Court sends out C100s simultaneously to Cafcass and the rota'd local mediation service. Safeguarding checks are carried out quickly in Plymouth, unlike the six to eight weeks' delay experienced in some regions. Information meetings are arranged without delay, but

---

[41] [2010] Fam Law 539–544 at para 4.3.
[42] See **3.7** above.

mediation out of court does not start until after safeguarding checks have been done. The effectiveness of the Plymouth scheme demonstrates the benefits of co-operation between the judiciary, court staff, Cafcass and mediators, working together with an agreed protocol and respecting each other's role. Family courts such as Stoke on Trent also use a triage system for referring cases out to mediation services, with the expectation of receiving limited feedback on the take-up and outcome of mediation, and find this preferable to mediation assessment or mediation taking place at court. The key element is clarity of roles: mediators are not officers of the court or assistants to overworked Cafcass officers: they work in conjunction with legal processes while maintaining their identity and working principles.[43] Local services vary, but a consistent national approach is needed so that the courts, Cafcass and mediation services work together in an integrated system. Good partnerships maximise opportunities for settlement and reduce Cafcass and court waiting lists.

The Revised Private Law Programme referred to above provides for a first hearing dispute resolution appointment (FHDRA), at which the judge, legal advisors or magistrates, accompanied by an officer from Cafcass, discuss with parties whether their dispute could be resolved by mediation, or in some other alternative way, and provide information about services which may be available to assist them. The document 'Independent Mediation – Information for Judges, Magistrates and Legal Advisors' is being made available to all court staff.

3.18.3   Adjournment of proceedings for referral to mediation

The Family Procedure Rules 2010 state:

> **'3.2 Court's duty to consider alternative dispute resolution**
>
> The court must consider, at every stage in proceedings, whether alternative dispute resolution is appropriate.
>
> **3.3 When the court will adjourn proceedings or a hearing in proceedings**
>
> (1) If the court considers that alternative dispute resolution is appropriate, the court may direct that the proceedings, or a hearing in the proceedings, be adjourned for such specified period as it considers appropriate—
>
> > (a)   to enable the parties to obtain information and advice about alternative dispute resolution; and
> >
> > (b)   where the parties agree, to enable alternative dispute resolution to take place ...
>
> (3) Where the court directs an adjournment under this rule, it will give directions about the timing and method by which the parties must tell the court if any of the issues in the proceedings have been resolved.'

---

[43]   Robinson 'Developing Family Mediation' [2009] Fam Law 734–744.

This accords with Article 13 of the European Directive on Mediation of 21 May 2008 that:

> 'it should be possible under national law for the courts to set time limits for a mediation process. Moreover, the courts should be able to draw the parties' attention to the possibility of mediation whenever this is appropriate.'

Even at Court of Appeal level, referral may be made to mediation. In one such case, the presiding judge observed that 'This case supports our conviction that there is no case, however conflicted, which is not open to successful mediation, even if mediation has not been attempted or has failed during the trial process'.[44] Mediation in entrenched disputes is difficult, but it should still be considered. Litigation fatigue may have set in, motivating some litigants to work things out themselves. Mediation can provide much-needed opportunities to speak and be heard in ways that the courts do not offer. An impasse on children issues may turn out to be rooted in other family issues that need to be spoken about. Making connections in mediation is not therapy, but it can have therapeutic effects. Experienced mediators offer cross-disciplinary knowledge in difficult disputes over children, not only legal knowledge, and they have a wide range of skills. Mediation in long-running disputes over children is not a new role. It needs careful assessment of suitability and time limits set by the court. Rules on privilege and confidentiality need to be adhered to or varied with informed consent. Co-mediation, if available, may be the model of choice (see below). There is scope for further development in referring entrenched disputes to mediation and in the range of mediation models available.

3.18.4 Mediation following court proceedings

Although final orders on financial matters in divorce cannot be renegotiated, arrangements for children often need to be modified as they grow up and as circumstances change. Children themselves may have wishes that need to be listened to, especially as they get older. A child may wish to alter a contact schedule or even move from one parent to the other. Second marriages and child-parent relationships are liable to break down if children feel they are not being heard or forced to go on contact visits that conflict with other relationships and activities. Children and parents may want to discuss possible changes in a private forum and not in court. The guide for children and young people proposed in the Green Paper *Support for All*,[45] should include information on family mediation and a designated Helpline where children can seek help and find information about family mediation to give to their parents. A note of caution is needed, however:[46]

---

[44] Thorpe LJ in *Al-Khatib v Masry* [2005] 1 FLR 381, CA.
[45] (2010), para 4.23.
[46] Neil Robinson, personal communication.

'The growing tendency to use mediation at the end of public law children proceedings is potentially problematic in expecting parents to engage voluntarily in mediation following highly directive Court proceedings. Mediation should not be treated as a 'dumping ground' for unresolved issues of which other professionals have grown tired!'

The aim of the Pre-Application Protocol 2011 is to promote consideration of mediation at an early stage, with gateways to mediation also open at later stages of family law proceedings to encourage settlement and avoid further litigation.[47] In a well-articulated family justice system, the judiciary, lawyers, Cafcass and family mediators work alongside each other, without combining or blurring their different responsibilities and functions. The Midland Courts Judges' document, *What the Family Courts expect from parents*, explains that 'experience suggests that court-imposed orders work less well than agreements made between you as parents'.[48] At all stages – before, during and following family law proceedings – the Courts are encouraging people to try mediation before they embark on or pursue proceedings. There can be no guarantee, however, of mediation leading to full agreement on all issues. Mediation offers opportunities, not a magic wand.

---

[47] Robinson 'Developing Family Mediation' [2008] Fam Law 926–928; Parkinson 'Gateways to Mediation' [2010] Fam Law 867–871.
[48] (Judiciary of England and Wales, 2010).

CHAPTER 4

DESIGNING MEDIATION MODELS

'Partnership and co-operation is not a choice: it is the only way to advance our common humanity.'[1]

CONTENTS

4.1   SOME GENERAL CONSIDERATIONS

The basic principles of mediation need to be maintained consistently in designing and developing a range of models that can be adapted for different stages of dispute resolution, varying levels of conflict and different circumstances. As Brown and Marriott propose, ADR practitioners:[2]

> 'can devise a permutation of procedures and approaches which fit all the nuances of the parties' needs and circumstances without being constrained by prescribed rules.'

---

[1]   Barack Obama, Berlin, 24 July 2008.
[2]   Brown and Marriott *ADR Principles and Practice* (Sweet & Maxwell, 1993), p 19.

In his series of articles on innovative approaches to ADR, Neil Robinson[3] considered:[4]

> 'creative options for dealing with an ever greater variety of family conflicts … [through] modifying the model and working in partnership.'

It is beyond the scope of this chapter, and indeed of this book, to examine all these creative options in detail. They are covered more fully and expertly elsewhere, particularly in the work of Henry Brown and Neil Robinson. As Robinson cautions,[5] ADR practitioners may modify the model, but they should not 'break the mould'. Mediators can work collaboratively with Judges, Cafcass and local authority social workers, provided they maintain the integrity and boundaries of the mediation process, especially where confidentiality is concerned. Neil Robinson has suggested analogies between mediation, mathematics and jazz as 'spontaneous invention within a theoretical framework'.[6] In a similar way, Daniel Barenboim, pianist, conductor and co-founder of the West-Eastern Divan orchestra, describes variations on a musical theme as a 'process of transformation'.[7] However, before venturing into new territory, there are some basic questions to consider, such as physical arrangements for mediation, the use of one mediator or two, shuttle mediation and caucusing and possibilities of mediating with family members in other kinds of dispute and at different stages during the 'family life-cycle'.

4.2   SETTING AND FACILITIES

First of all, both the setting and the time-scale for mediation need careful consideration. Mediation needs to be conducted in a private setting away from the court, with sessions arranged at intervals to suit the needs of participants. Court-referred mediation is usually less flexible. When proceedings are adjourned to allow mediation to take place, the court is likely to set a date for the outcome to be reported back to the court by the parties or their lawyers. The setting for family mediation needs to be considered carefully. Mediators need a private environment for discussions, free from disturbance and providing suitable facilities. The general ambiance should be pleasant and welcoming. Careful consideration should be given to the suitability of premises, waiting-areas, mediation rooms and facilities. The court is seldom a suitable location even for initial information meetings.

---

[3]   Robinson 'Developing Family Mediation' [2008] Fam Law 926–928; 'Developing Family Mediation: Innovative Approaches to ADR' [2008] Fam Law 1048–1053; 'Developing Family Mediation' [2009] Fam Law 734–744.
[4]   Robinson 'Developing Family Mediation' [2008] Fam Law 926.
[5]   Ibid, p 928.
[6]   See n 4, p 927.
[7]   Barenboim *Everything is Connected – The Power of Music* (Weidenfeld and Nicolson, 2008), p 32.

The Legal Services Commission's requirements for contracted family mediation services[8]

(i)   Reception areas with facilities for clients to wait in separate waiting areas.

(ii)   A minimum of two suitable rooms to enable clients to be seen separately, or separated if necessary.

(iii) Privacy for clients.

(iv)   Easy access for disabled clients.

(v)   Facilities for children.

(vi)   Identification of the mediation service as separate from any other service provided on the same premises.

4.3   THE MEDIATION ROOM AND SEATING ARRANGEMENTS

Mediators generally prefer to use a round or oval table. Chairs should be placed at a comfortable distance from each other and in the mediator's line of vision, so that the mediator can keep eye contact equally with participants, without turning from one to the other like an umpire at a tennis match. Participants should not face each other because this is too confrontational. They need to be able to look at each other and at the mediator, without sitting side by side or facing each other.

Sole Mediator

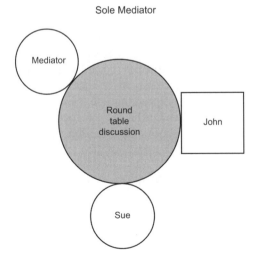

4.4 GENDER ISSUES

With a sole mediator, there is inevitably a gender imbalance in the room. Gender issues run through family mediation like an electric current. Mediators have to be careful not to make assumptions, such as assuming that the children live, or should live, with their mother. They may be living with their father and his application for sole or shared residence may be the main issue. Any gender-based assumptions by a mediator indicating bias would destroy trust in the mediator's impartiality. Gender issues are highly relevant to power imbalances in mediation and mediators need to be aware of feedback from mediation clients on these issues.[9]

The partner who is the same sex as the mediator does not necessarily see this as an advantage. Quite often, there are fears of the mediator being 'seduced' by the other party. The same-sex partner may make a remark such as 'Richard has a way with him, you know. People always believe what he says'. Or 'Laura is very persuasive'. If these remarks are made pointedly, implying that the other party is dishonest, the mediator must respond straightaway to the mistrust. Full financial disclosure with supporting documentation is discussed in Chapter 9. If the mistrust is more general, it is usually possible to make a normalising comment, such as:

> 'I think trust usually breaks down, when a relationship has broken down ... separated parents need to be able to trust each other where the children are concerned. Shall we come back to these concerns later and see what assurances you would be looking for?'

4.5 CO-MEDIATION

The old adage, 'two heads are better than one', is particularly apt in mediation. Provided they work well together and enhance each other's strengths, co-mediators working together as a team have greater capacity to manage difficult and stressful conflicts. Some mediation services are fortunate in having a balance of male and female mediators, but in general, female mediators predominate. In co-mediation, gender imbalances are compounded by the use of two same-sex mediators. In practice, two female co-mediators often co-mediate, but this may create perceptions of imbalance, however skilled the mediators are. Most mediators consider an all-male mediator team unacceptable in family mediation. Any imbalance of 3:1 in the room needs careful consideration and re-checking at intervals with the participants. If co-mediation is offered with two mediators of the same sex, participants should be asked beforehand whether this would be acceptable to them. Male-female

---

9   See Chapters 10 and 13 below.

co-mediation offers considerable advantages in addressing gender issues and power imbalances, but it may be a Rolls Royce when the only transport available is a Smart car.

Co-mediation may be used for different purposes:

(i)   training – helping an inexperienced mediator to learn from a more experienced partner;

(ii)   gender and/or cultural balance – essential in some situations;

(iii)   balance and support to manage major power imbalances between participants;

(iv)   increasing the range of knowledge and skills available within the mediation;

(v)   changing the dynamics of the process;

(vi)   allocating different roles to each mediator to maximise effectiveness;

(vii)   providing scope for different strategies.

4.5.1   Advantages of co-mediation

Provided essential conditions are met, co-mediation offers many advantages. Family members at different stages of relationship breakdown bring discordant views, conflicting needs and a complex mix of issues – marital, parental, financial and legal. Co-mediators may be more able than a sole mediator to contain conflicting needs and feelings in mediation.

Balance

A four-legged structure is more stable than a two-legged one. Co-mediators can provide physical and psychological balance:[10]

> 'It probably sets you more at ease to have two. Otherwise it is like having someone in charge, whereas with two it is not a case of being in charge.'

---

[10]   Mediation client quoted by Walker, McCarthy and Timms *Mediation: the Making and Remaking of Co-operative Relationships* (Relate Centre for Family Studies, University of Newcastle, 1994), p 128.

Scope for wider perspectives and different points of view

> 'It was also useful having two people there because you could perhaps get two slightly different views on something which certainly helped both of us to have an option.'[11]

Dynamics

A sole mediator may put questions to each party in turn, gathering information from each of them and making sure they have equal opportunities to respond. This question-answer dynamic might be described as linear, whereas co-mediators facilitate round-table discussion – a circular dynamic. Co-mediators encourage discussion and debate without giving the impression of one person taking control.

Support for mediators

Co-mediating provides support for mediators, as well as for participants. Mediation is stressful work that demands a high level of concentration. There is a great deal of information to absorb. A sole mediator has to address questions which may be intellectually demanding and emotionally draining. The presence of a co-mediator is supportive and reassuring. Responsibilities can be shared and tasks divided. Provided the co-mediators work comfortably together, the stresses and strains are much lower than when mediating alone.

Complementary styles and skills

Co-mediators bring different personal qualities, styles of working and different skills. Different personalities and styles are appreciated by participants who may recognise that it is unrealistic to expect one person to have all the qualities and skills they are looking for. Some co-mediators offer bicultural or bilingual expertise and address issues of cultural diversity that a sole mediator, with experience confined to a single culture, might miss.

Gender balance

Male-female co-mediators provide gender balance in the room and a model for power balancing. Some research has suggested that male-female mediation teams may facilitate fairer and more balanced agreements.

Cross-cultural balance

In cross-cultural mediation, the co-mediator team may usefully include a mediator who is knowledgeable about the participants' cultural traditions

---

[11] Ibid, p 125.

and needs and who possibly belongs to the same culture. Cultural diversity is overtly respected and understood. The specialist mediator is an educator for the co-mediator and can monitor for any ethnically-based assumptions or stereotypes.

Modelling

Co-mediators provide models of constructive debate when they have different points of view. It is not necessary to agree all the time, provided they offer different perspectives in a constructive way. It is of course important to avoid contradicting each other, becoming allied with one participant or getting into an argument that competes with the couple's argument (see ground-rules for co-mediation, below). When co-mediators discuss differences in a friendly dialogue, this demonstrates that there are different ways of seeing things and positive ways of exploring differences. This helps participants discuss their differences instead of fighting over them.

Maintaining good practice

The presence of a co-mediator helps to guard against oversights and omissions. A sole mediator's practice cannot be monitored closely, unless a supervisor is present or the sessions are recorded on audiotape or video. A mediator working alone may step outside the role, develop inappropriate ways of working or miss important points, without anyone realising that this is happening. Co-mediators learn from each other and provide informal monitoring of each other's practice. If either has cause for concern or discomfort, this needs to be raised and explored between the two mediators and may need discussion with a peer group or a supervisor.

4.5.2 Potential disadvantages of co-mediation

Cost

Some services consider that the choice to provide a co-mediator should be a choice of process made by the mediator and that additional cost should not be passed on to a private paying client. Other services consider that, especially in cases of high assets or financial complexity, co-mediation should be an option offered to privately paying clients at a higher charging rate. Publicly funded co-mediation is paid at a higher rate, but the need must be justified clearly in the case file. The Legal Services Commission *Family Mediation Specification* (December 2009) states in relation to co-mediation that:[12]

---

[12] Legal Services Commission *Family Mediation Specification* (December 2009), para 2.23.

'whilst you do not need our prior authority to use Co-Mediation, any decision to use Co-mediation will need to be recorded on the file including, where appropriate:

- reasons as to the complexity, legal, psychological or otherwise of the case;
- a risk assessment for the participants and/or Mediator;
- any reasons as to the requirement of specialist and/or expert skills;
- any management issues for the Mediation.'

There is evidence that LSC auditors are raising audit queries where services undertake a significant proportion of co-mediated cases. It is therefore critical to record the justification properly, using a pro-forma such as the one devised by the Family Mediators Association.[13] Mediation services need to demonstrate to the LSC that litigation can be reduced or avoided if co-mediators are able to encompass the full range of issues in more complex cases and resolve a significant proportion of entrenched disputes over children.

Logistics

It is more difficult to schedule sessions with two mediators than one. If one mediator is unwell or unavoidably held up in a traffic jam, does the other mediator carry on alone or offer another appointment? Postponing a session is problematic for couples in crisis and re-arranging it may involve considerable delay.

Time

As well as the time needed to set up co-mediation meetings, time is needed for consultation and planning beforehand and for discussion and feedback afterwards. Mediation summaries should be checked by both mediators and signed by them both.

Competition or confusion

If each co-mediator is eager to have a say and/or pursuing issues in different directions, the resulting confusion may endanger the mediation. These problems are more likely to occur if co-mediators have not had the same training, with practice in training placements.

Becoming split, taking sides

There are risks of co-mediators being split by a warring couple, consciously or unconsciously. Participants often try to persuade mediators to take sides. If co-mediators do not understand each other well, the couple's conflict could be projected on to them and used to split

---

[13] See Appendix E below.

them. Trying to resolve matters with co-mediators who are working at cross-purposes would not be a good experience for couples in crisis.

Combined pressure

The combination of two assured and knowledgeable mediators may be overpowering for a nervous client. Mediators who constantly confirm each other's statements make it difficult for participants to express views that diverge from the mediators' joint view. Well-trained mediators should not allow this to happen, however.

4.6   INTERDISCIPLINARY CO-MEDIATION

When co-mediators come from different professional backgrounds, they can jointly provide greater expertise, experience and confidence in mediating in high-conflict disputes and on interrelated issues involving children, finance and property. Co-mediators from family law and psychosocial backgrounds complement each other in very valuable ways.[14] This interdisciplinary model was developed in a pilot project, Solicitors in Mediation, and in the national association that developed from it, the Family Mediators Association.[15] Initially, the Law Society permitted solicitors to act as mediators only in a separate form of professional practice, outside their legal practice.[16] Subsequently, both the Law Society and the General Council of the Bar modified their professional practice rules to enable solicitors and barristers to act as mediators within their legal practice, in accordance with a code of practice for mediation.[17] The home page of the Family Mediators Association website[18] confirms continuing commitment to this 'uniquely robust and flexible model of Appropriate Dispute Resolution based on an interdisciplinary community of family mediators'.[19]

Interdisciplinary co-mediation offers:

4.6.1   A wider range of expertise

The combination of a family law mediator working with a second family mediator from a psychosocial discipline (counsellor, therapist, social worker, psychologist) offers wider expertise and experience than a sole mediator could provide, even those few who are cross-trained in law and counselling. This wider range of knowledge and skills is particularly helpful in dealing with inter-related children and financial issues, where

---

[14]   Parkinson *Conciliation in Separation and Divorce* (Croom Helm, 1986).
[15]   Parkinson *Family Mediation* (Sweet and Maxwell, 1997).
[16]   Brown and Marriott *ADR Principles and Practice* (Sweet & Maxwell, 1993), pp 332–337.
[17]   See, for example Law Society Family Mediation Code of Practice 1997.
[18]   www.thefma.co.uk.
[19]   FMA 2011.

expertise in addressing emotional and family issues can be combined with expertise on legal and financial aspects.

Co-mediators should not be restricted, however, to their established area of expertise. FMA training is designed to integrate and blend interdisciplinary knowledge and skills through interactive forms of training, including role-play. When co-mediators can mediate flexibly on a full range of family issues, without inhibitions about entering into each other's specialist territory, the benefits of co-mediating are greatly increased.

4.6.2   Mediating on inter-related issues

When there are power imbalances, as there usually are, co-mediators can help maintain a balance in the unfolding process of emotional, family, financial and legal divorce. A sole mediator may find it hard to keep all these different dimensions in simultaneous focus. At a practical level, one mediator can concentrate on working with figures while the other mediator concentrates on the dynamics in the room.

4.6.3   Greater creativity

This is possible in the generation of options and ideas. Brainstorming is more effective where co-mediators bring complementary experience and ways of thinking – analytical or intuitive. They can spark ideas off each other and help couples to generate their own ideas.

4.7   DIFFERENT MODELS OF CO-MEDIATION

4.7.1   Co-pilots

Both mediators operate the controls and can take over from each other at any stage of the flight (process). They provide balance and support, especially in managing power imbalances. But there can be duplication in the sharing of controls and tasks. There could also be confusing changes of direction, if one co-pilot cuts across the other.

4.7.2   Pilot and Navigator

The pilot operates the controls so that the craft moves forward, steering through headwinds or strong currents. The navigator studies the map and tracks the course. The navigator may notice particular landmarks or see a new route opening up. The navigator may intervene less often than the pilot and focuses on dynamics, rather than on content. The navigator has more time to observe body language and to think about underlying issues, while the pilot keeps the process in movement. The pilot/navigator roles may alternate, as in the co-pilot model, but the allocation of tasks is planned beforehand and more clearly delineated. For example, if one mediator leads the discussion while the other records key points or figures on the flipchart, the pilot flies the plane while the navigator records the flight-path.

4.7.3   Pilot and Apprentice

Opportunities to observe, learn on the job and gain confidence.

4.7.4   Pilot and Controller (Advanced Flying Test!)

This may be used for supervision or in testing competence. Differences in seniority and experience between co-mediators may need to be explained to participants. It may be possible for the Controller to take a back seat and provide support, allowing the pilot to fly independently, unless there is risk of crashing!

4.7.5   Strategies and skills in co-mediation

Consulting openly

Eg 'Do you think we should talk about x first, or y?' The process becomes a conversation between four people, instead of one mediator addressing participants in turn.

Picking up on non-verbal signals and pre-empting

One mediator may miss signs of a participant's bewilderment, distress, frustration or mounting tension. The co-mediator may notice these signs and respond.

Giving information

It may be difficult for a sole mediator to volunteer information without seeming like an expert, whereas a co-mediator can give a prompt: 'Do you think it would be useful to discuss ...?' Relevant information may be provided impartially, reducing the need for couples to go backwards and forwards between mediation and legal advisors.

Strategic debates

Mediators from different backgrounds tend to have different perspectives and approach questions from different angles. These debates may be used strategically to reduce power imbalances. Provided co-mediators are comfortable in discussing dilemmas and do not undermine each other, they may question or challenge each other in helpful ways. The reduction of tension in the room is often palpable. Participants who feel different needs or views are heard may feel validated and better understood. Constructive disagreements between co-mediators can be used to model positive conflict management and as an impasse strategy.[20] It is important that neither mediator undermines the other or puts the other down. The tone should be reflective and friendly and may involve some humour, if appropriate.

Using humour to reduce tension

Co-mediators often use humour in commenting on their own differences of approach, as a way of lightening the atmosphere. Provided there is sensitivity to all those present and sufficient mutual respect and trust, a teasing remark between co-mediators may ease the couple's tensions. Timing is important and awareness of the feelings in the room. Humour alters the dynamics and often encourages participants to use humour too.

Brainstorming

Co-mediators can generate options that draw on different knowledge and perspectives. They can play hard/soft negotiator and use a range of impasse strategies.

Drafting written summaries

A blend of skills is needed in preparing the Memorandum of Understanding (MOU). Drafting and 'mutualising' skills need to be combined. The preparation of a MOU is a good learning experience for mediators from different professional backgrounds.

4.8   PRE-REQUISITES FOR EFFECTIVE CO-MEDIATION

4.8.1   Trust your co-mediator

Co-mediators need confidence in each other's integrity and competence and need to be able to trust each other. A partnership built on mutual trust and respect provides a strong anchorage in working with stormy couples.

4.8.2   Consider professional and practice issues

Including premises, facilities, model of practice, charging and professional indemnity cover. Co-mediators need to be clear about their joint or separate accountability and the basis on which fees are being charged. They also need to consider 'what if?' questions, such as what one mediator would do if the other mediator were unwell at the last moment,

---

[20]   See Chapter 11 below.

leaving insufficient time to rearrange the appointment. Would clients who have come a long distance be seen briefly, or not at all?

4.8.3 Training for co-mediation

Co-mediators should have trained together, if possible, as this develops joint understanding and skills and provides opportunities to practise co-mediating in role-play. If co-mediators have not trained together, they should check the consistency of their approach, including the documentation used.

4.8.4 Agree roles and tasks

Co-mediators need to consider how to allocate responsibility for different tasks or parts of the process. The mediators may alternate in taking the lead at different stages. Will both mediators take notes and maintain duplicate sets of records?

4.8.5 Agree whether both mediators are equally in charge, or whether one is apprenticed to the other

One mediator may be more experienced than the other. Mediation often takes place in one mediator's premises and the other mediator may be a guest on the other's territory. It is important for co-mediators to discuss questions of seniority and status and to make sure that both feel at ease. Power imbalances between mediators could have an unfortunate impact in mediation.

4.8.6 Give each other openings to join in discussion

It is not necessary for both mediators to have equal input and unhelpful if they feel a need to compete. A mediator who listens and observes has a very important role that can be explained to the parties as a listening role. However, when one mediator is leading, it is important to provide openings for the other one to come in:

'Is there anything you would like to add?'

'Shall we move on to ...?'

'What do you think about ...?'

Regular consultation avoids the second mediator feeling superfluous or frozen out. Seating arrangements should enable co-mediators to keep eye contact with each other.

4.8.7   Understand each other's views and values

Co-mediators need to understand each other's views and values, especially where they differ. Mediation may involve highly controversial issues, such as whether children should live with a lesbian mother or visit a transvestite father. Co-mediators need to be able to accommodate each other's view and values and be skilled in reading signals from each other. They need to manage differences in ways that enhance their complementary roles.

4.8.8   Mutual support

Co-mediators do not need to agree on every point but must give support to each other and be ready to rescue each other from a difficulty. When they disagree, they should be careful not to contradict or undermine each other.

4.8.9   Speak the same language

Mediators from different backgrounds need to speak the same language, avoiding jargon from their own professional fields. One mediator may need to clarify or amplify what the other mediator has said.

4.8.10   Preparation and debriefing

Co-mediators need to prepare for mediation sessions and debrief afterwards. This means allowing additional time for each session. Planning and debriefing, when thinking is shared and tension offloaded, are both important. Co-mediators need to give each other positive feedback as well as questioning each other, if necessary. Once a good working relationship has been built up, most co-mediators develop an intuitive understanding that enables them to work together creatively.

4.8.11   Have a fallback plan

Preparation may go out of the window when couples come in with an unexpected turn of events or change of direction. Co-mediators need to be able to alter course easily, when the situation requires. Familiarity with each other and ability to read signals reduces the need for lengthy discussion.

4.8.12   A good sense of humour

It is difficult to imagine co-mediation working well if co-mediators lack a sense of humour, or if they are unable to use humour sensitively.

4.8.13 Consider practical details

Seating arrangements should facilitate discussion, maximise eye contact and avoid alignments.

4.8.14 Use a consultant or supervisor

Regular case discussions with a consultant or supervisor and continuing mediation training develop skills and new ideas.

4.9 THE SYNERGY OF CO-MEDIATION

Co-mediation should be an essential component of mediation training. It provides on-the spot learning, builds confidence and allows mediators to see what does or does not work. Newly trained mediators welcome the safety net provided by an experienced mediator and their fresh vision may encourage experienced mediators to think differently about the way they work. Although potentially costly in its use of resources, co-mediation enables more issues to be tackled more efficiently, because co-mediators can work in tandem more flexibly. The process can be structured in different ways to suit different needs and circumstances. To borrow from a jazz musician, co-mediation allows 'contrapuntal interplay' (no sexual innuendoes here!). The mobility of co-mediation helps to maintain momentum. Co-mediators who enjoy working together create a lighter atmosphere that helps clients to regain their own strength and creativity. Co-mediation provides synergy – combined energy and ideas – while maintaining equilibrium. Co-mediators need to hold the destructive forces of polarity within a contained emotional, psychological and physical space, while possible changes are explored and negotiated.

A balance needs to be kept between stability – *homeostasis* – and change – *morphogenesis*. There are many pressures in mediation that threaten this balance. The stresses on a single mediator can be very heavy. Co-mediators have greater resources for managing stress, because they can support each other, offload together and stimulate fresh thinking. Together, they offer a well of resources. Clients can draw from this well to replenish their own depleted energy and limited resources. Mediators also need to replenish their energies when they feel drained. Co-mediation offers many benefits for participants – for the mediators as much as for the mediated.

> 'There is now a greater readiness among mediators to explore different ways of working, to adapt accepted processes and models, and to work with other professionals.'[21]

---

[21] Robinson 'Developing Family Mediation' [2008] Fam Law 926.

4.10   SHUTTLE MEDIATION AND CAUCUSING

Although the aim is to encourage direct communication and negotiation, face-to-face mediation meetings can inflame couples who have highly confrontational conflict styles. Shuttle mediation and caucusing, using co-mediators if possible, enable options to be explored more calmly. In shuttle mediation and caucusing, the mediator meets separately with one party in the absence of the other.

Shuttle mediation is commonly used in civil and commercial mediation. The parties and their lawyers remain in separate rooms while the mediator 'shuttles' between them, conveying clarifications, proposals or counter-proposals. Shuttle mediation is rarely used in family mediation because the aim is to facilitate direct communication between family members. Separated parents need to be able to talk directly with each other about their children after mediation ends. If they are seen separately, they do not listen to each other and may be unable to communicate directly either before or after mediation. However, in cases involving domestic violence or other form of abuse, shuttle mediation may be the only appropriate model. In situations where it would be unsafe for ex-partners to meet face-to-face, or where one of them refuses to do so, shuttle mediation may provide a way of settling issues such as division of joint assets or responsibility for debts. If public funding is authorised for shuttle mediation when necessary, it would be a possible option in domestic violence cases involving some degree of continuing risk or fear. Attendance at a joint meeting could be negotiated later, if any further risk or fear has been clearly overcome and if both partners are willing to meet face-to-face.

Caucusing differs from shuttle mediation in combining one or more short separate meetings with or within joint meetings. The word *caucus* is derived from an Algonquian Indian word for tribal leader and its original transcription from the Algonquian language – *cawcawwassoughes* – suggests interminable and repetitive discussions! Caucusing can be structured in various ways. If a participant appears extremely emotional at the information and assessment meeting, but there are no concerns about domestic violence or abuse, it may be helpful to suggest that the first mediation meeting could begin with a short initial caucus with each partner separately, with the expectation that they will then be able to move into a joint meeting for the remainder of the session. A brief initial caucus can reduce high levels of tension at the outset and provide reassurance to each partner about the other one's mood and willingness to discuss matters in a contained and constructive way. This builds a stronger bridge for both participants to meet face-to-face. Alternatively, a mediation meeting may begin with a joint meeting, followed in situations of particular difficulty by a short caucus with each partner on their own and then a continuation of the joint meeting. Participants feel freer to disclose an underlying fear or to put forward a tentative proposal, without the other party being present. The mediator can give one-to-one support and encouragement, but must be careful not to give any impression of forming an alliance.

Caucusing is very useful as a fallback strategy, rather than as the model of choice. If mediation is on the verge of breaking down, proposing a short caucus can prevent a 'walk-out' and allow recovery time when emotions are running high. Caucusing should be used with care and takes time, but it enables more mediations to be 'held'. Some mediators are opposed to caucusing because it interferes with the transparency of the mediation process and may blur the mediator's role. Confidentiality needs to be clarified with participants before caucusing or shuttle mediation take place.

4.11   CONFIDENTIALITY IN SHUTTLE MEDIATION AND CAUCUSING

In civil/commercial mediation, the content of separate meetings is confidential and the mediator may carry only authorised information from one party to the other. A civil/commercial mediator may therefore know, on a confidential basis, the terms on which each party would be willing to settle. The mediator uses this knowledge to bargain, negotiate and look for leverage, without revealing either party's position to the other party. Holding information in confidence is also used in 'hybrid' cases such as inheritance disputes whose subject matter straddles the family and civil jurisdictions.[22] In family mediation, however, the mediator generally establishes a 'no secrets' ground-rule at the outset, to avoid problems of holding information in confidence from one party or disclosing what they believed they had said in confidence. A family mediator cannot continue to mediate while holding confidences such as: 'Don't tell Jim that I am planning to marry Charlie as soon as the divorce is through.' A family mediator should therefore establish that no information provided by either partner in a caucus meeting, or in mediation as a whole, may be held in confidence from the other. Both of them must accept that the mediator is able to share the content of separate discussions with both of them. This does not mean that the mediator repeats each word that was said during a caucus, exactly as it was said. The mediator's feedback from caucus meetings is given to both participants together and both of them are asked to confirm the accuracy of the feedback from their perspective. This confirmation by the participants acts to curb selective or slanted feedback by the mediator.

---

[22]   See **4.16** and Chapter 9.

4.12   CONSIDERING WHETHER TO CAUCUS

Before offering shuttle mediation or caucusing, it is important to consider possible benefits and disadvantages. How might it affect each participant and the process? Would it help them to feel safer? Might it draw them further apart, while drawing the mediator into a supportive, counselling role? The partner who feels left out when the other one is being seen may become very anxious and wonder what is going on. There may be suspicions and fantasies about what one party has said behind the other one's back. If the mediator misreports something to one party by mistake, the other party is not present to correct the error. Caucusing may be useful as a crisis strategy, however, when one partner is distraught or the discussion so heated that a participant is about to rush from the room. A stormy departure can be anticipated and pre-empted, if possible. Offering a short time with each participant alone may be helpful if the couple can no longer remain in the room together. It may allow a very distressed person some recovery time. It is easier to do this in co-mediation, because one mediator can spend a short time with one partner while the co-mediator talks with the other partner. Before caucusing, the ground-rules on impartiality and open communication must be clarified and accepted. There may also be gender issues to consider, such as whether it is preferable for the male mediator to meet with the male partner, and the female mediator with the female partner, or whether the reverse would avoid an impression of gender alliances. If the caucus needs to be repeated on a second occasion, any such arrangement can be reversed. After caucusing, it is often possible for the joint meeting with both participants to be resumed immediately. Co-mediators do not need to withdraw and confer privately: they can summarise key points and proposals and encourage participants to elaborate on them. A short caucus may enable mediation to continue with a lower level of conflict and a more clearly defined focus.

Haynes[23] gives reasons for caucusing similar to those mentioned above, suggesting that it is useful 'when the level of hostility is so high that it prevents rational discussion', or when 'continual ventilation of grievances by one person impedes the progress of the negotiations.' However as caucusing involves major variations in the standard family mediation model, possibly altering it fundamentally, there should be careful consideration of its potential benefits and disadvantages.

4.12.1   Potential benefits

- Increases possible use or continuation of mediation in high conflict or other difficult circumstances.

---

[23]   Haynes *Alternative Dispute Resolution – the Fundamentals of Divorce Mediation* (Old Bailey Press, 1993).

- Helps to manage extreme power imbalances or very volatile emotions.

- Greater flexibility and choice – helps participants to feel considered and empowered.

- Provides greater safety and protection in domestic abuse cases.

- Builds trust in the mediator – increases rapport with very nervous people.

- May be needed where a participant becomes overwhelmed with distress.

- Avoids or curtails destructive and harmful confrontations.

- Calms inflamed situations – gives opportunities to acknowledge, reassure and refocus.

- Helps to pre-empt a walk-out and breakdown of the mediation.

- Screens out blaming, accusations, aggressive body language etc.

- Helps mediator to gain fuller understanding of each partner's position and needs.

- Enables mediator to explore sensitive areas, such as an underlying wish for reconciliation, and to test hypotheses.

- Gives the other partner time to cool down and reflect while waiting their turn (unless there is simultaneous caucusing by co-mediators).

- Reality-testing – raising doubts – exploring blocks to settlement.

- Increases mediator control of process (but see disadvantages also).

- Avoids loss of time through interruptions, sidetracking etc.

- Helps to maintain future focus, positive ways forward, promotes agreement.

- Overcoming impasses – exploring scope for compromise.

- Special needs – illness, disability, need for an interpreter.

- Geographical distance – liaison with other mediation services, may be needed in cross-border cases.

4.12.2   Potential disadvantages

- Risk of mediator losing impartiality or being perceived as taking sides.

- Participants may lose trust in the mediator and become suspicious.

- Fantasies of what is being said 'behind one's back' – feelings of abandonment.

- Difficulties of carrying negative messages between parties ('shoot the messenger').

- Additional resources – two rooms needed – may take more time.

- May be time-consuming, demanding and stressful for the mediator.

- Confidentiality problems, if a client seen alone is permitted to give information to the mediator that is not to be disclosed to the other partner.

- Mediator selects the information that is conveyed – risk of distortion, inaccuracy etc.

- Gives the mediator great influence – empowers the mediator but may disempower participants.

- Who decides who is seen first? Disadvantages for the second partner in responding to first partner's position or proposals, without the same opportunity to put their position or proposals first of all.

- The mediator might be directive and manipulative – no check on the mediator by both parties.

- Enables couples to avoid direct communication.

- Enables couples to opt out and let the mediator do the work.

- May prolong mediation to no avail.

- If a client who is deeply distressed is seen alone, the boundaries of mediation could become blurred with counselling or therapy.

- Inclusion of a third party in a caucus, such as a grandparent or new partner, could cause problems of imbalance and confidentiality.

High-conflict couples may reach pragmatic settlements through caucusing, without changing their relationship or their views of each other. Stirum has reported[24] that shuttle mediation and caucusing work well for high conflict parents. As well as settling arrangements for children, ground rules for ongoing communication also need to be agreed between parents that will be less likely to re-ignite their conflict.

4.13 SHUTTLING AT A DISTANCE

How far apart in time and space can participants be? This is an area of some controversy. For example where use of the telephone is considered, might this enhance or dilute the process of resolving the dispute. Like shuttling itself, undertaking assessment or mediation by telephone can never be a satisfactory method of communication compared with face-to-face meetings, but what if it is the only way? If it is to be used, how should it be funded, particularly in publicly funded cases? These are difficult questions that need to be tackled, both in specific cases and in mediation policy, in the spirit of exploration and creativity that imbues the best mediation practice. In circumstances where distance precludes face-to-face dialogue between participants and the mediator, the use of the telephone raises important issues over boundaries and clarity, but the benefits may outweigh the risks. An example was the use of the telephone in a mediation undertaken by The Mediation Centre in Stafford. The couple, Lorissa and Zack, had been married for 30 years and until their separation nine months earlier they had lived together in the family home owned in Zack's sole name. Their son Joel (aged 25) suffered from Asperger's Syndrome and was unable to live independently. Lorissa was housebound and the council property where she and Joel were living had been equipped for her needs. Neither Lorissa nor Zack was in employment. Lorissa and Zack were not in communication with each other (although co-operating to support Joel) and they both wanted to use mediation as a constructive and cost effective way of working things out. The common ground was their joint concern to protect Joel's interests. Mediation proceeded by way of:

(1) Separate assessment with Lorissa on the telephone.

(2) Separate assessment with Zack.

(3) A detailed letter to solicitors, approved by Lorissa and Zack, raising issues about lifetime and estate planning for the whole family.

(4) Mediation meetings firstly at Lorissa's house with Zack on the telephone and then with Zack at the mediation centre, with Lorissa on the telephone, followed by a joint session with solicitors with both clients on the telephone, and finally, face-to-face meetings with Zack and Lorissa separately, to go through their draft Memorandum of Understanding.

---

[24] Stirum 'ADR Professional' [2010] Fam Law 1228–1230.

The use of emails in family mediation raises further questions that need careful consideration. Possibilities for mediation online are discussed further in Chapter 14 at **14.16**.

4.14   WIDENING THE SCOPE OF FAMILY MEDIATION

Family mediation still takes place mainly with separating/divorcing couples, but increasingly its scope is widening to embrace all family conflicts. Separating cohabitants have issues that readily lend themselves to co-operative resolution. Whereas the legal basis for the dissolution of same-sex relationships is now similar to that of married partners, for separating heterosexual cohabitants the unsatisfactory state of the law is an invitation to mediation.[25] Another growing area is the arrangement of finances where there may be no dispute, but rather a series of competing interests, such as estate planning or pre-nuptial arrangements for subsequent relationships, particularly where there are children.[26] Mediation can also be applied in many domains to help family members reach agreements on matters that can give rise to disputes in families, including care of the elderly, adoption and post-adoption support, children in care, people with disabilities and inheritance disputes. Whilst many of these issues are litigated within the civil jurisdiction, there is much to be said for them to be mediated by dual-trained family mediators, using a hybrid model[27] that also gives participants scope for further advice, reflection and other steps between meetings.

4.14.1   Mediation with extended families

> 'My family is my brother, step-dad, half-brother, mum and dad and my dad's fiancée. I've got two homes. My dad, brother and I live here and my mum's side live fifteen miles away.'[28]

Most family mediations involve two parties – mainly, separating or separated couples. However, many separated parents have new partners and many new partners, stepparents and grandparents provide practical and emotional support in looking after children. The role and co-operation of other family members may be crucial if arrangements agreed between parents are to work in practice. If key family members feel excluded from decisions reached in mediation, they may sabotage the agreements. Yet if a new partner or grandparent is involved on one side but not the other, bringing a third party into the mediation would unbalance the process unacceptably. Sometimes both parents are living with new partners. Are foursomes fearsome and to be avoided at all costs? If planned carefully with all concerned, it may be helpful in some

---

[25]   See **9.18** below.
[26]   See **9.17** and **9.19** below.
[27]   See **4.16** below.
[28]   Sally, aged 12, quoted by Neale and Wade *Parent Problems – children's views on life when parents split up* (Young Voice, 2000), p 7.

circumstances to invite the former couple and their new partners to take part in a four-way mediation meeting. In some circumstances, some form of shuttle mediation or caucusing might be more appropriate. Careful assessment is needed to consider the inclusion of other adult family members (for child-inclusive mediation, see chapter 8) and their actual or potential influence, both within and outside the mediation. Mediators need to assess possible benefits and risks in involving them directly. Different ways of structuring meetings need to be explored and pre-conditions agreed, before involving other family members and adapting the model of mediation. Co-mediators are likely to be needed for mediation with a larger family group.

In disputes involving stepparents, mediation can help those involved to understand the options available – such as shared residence, stepparent adoption or other form of agreement – so that they can consider the needs of the child concerned and the objectives and potential consequences of each option. Negotiated agreements provide a better basis for working out future parenting responsibilities than a court order imposed without agreement, while arrangements are more likely to work in practice where there is agreement and co-operation over what constitutes the best interests of the child. Those with parenting responsibilities may also be helped to consider appropriate consultation with and explanations to the child.

4.14.2 Intergenerational mediation

Consensual decisions on future care are often needed in relation to the care of the elderly. Medical advice may be needed on the elderly person's mental capacity, functioning and ability to represent their own interests in any negotiations. Decisions about the residential care of an elderly relative can cause deep rifts in families. Mediators could help family members to consider the options available, facilitating family meetings and decision-making with professional advice. When elderly parents are clearly unable to manage their own affairs and enduring powers of attorney have been granted, mediation can assist adult children to negotiate and reach agreement over their parents' property and management of their assets. One mediation involved an estranged elderly couple living in different residential homes who were not competent to mediate themselves. The husband had been married previously and the wife had had two previous marriages. The daughter of the husband's first marriage and the daughter of the mother's second marriage took part in mediation as their parents' legally appointed representatives. They reached agreement on the sale of their parents' former matrimonial home and on factors affecting the division of the sale proceeds. The agreement enabled the costs of their parents' residential care to be covered more comfortably and also settled some minor disputes over family possessions.

4.14.3   Mediation concerning children in care

Previously, it was considered that children cases involving a public interest
were unsuitable for referral to independent family mediation services.
Current thinking is rather different. As so many childcare cases involve
the placement of a child back with his/her own parents or with another
family member, rebuilding relationships is a priority. In recognition of
this, the model of Family Group Conferences has been developed and is
proving highly successful, with good outcomes reported by family
members and social workers.

It is important to recognise that the role of mediator is not compatible
with holding statutory authority and responsibility, such as the duty to
prepare reports for the court. Lawyers and social workers involved in
childcare cases cannot act as mediators if they have a statutory duty to
report to a public authority with decision-making power. They may
however apply mediation skills in relation to:

- engaging with all the parties involved;

- clarifying the issues;

- understanding different priorities and points of view;

- facilitating dialogue and negotiations;

- exploring options and objectives;

- drawing up written agreements.

The Children's Solicitor and Guardian are in a good position to mediate,
since they have an independent role within the proceedings, provided they
have mediation skills and understanding. The reduction of public funding
may however bring an end to this intervention. More childcare cases may
need the help of a fully independent mediator who can gain the trust and
co-operation of all concerned precisely because a mediator has no power
to influence the outcome. Again, a fundamental principle is working in
partnership. Social workers involved in child protection cases may not be
perceived as impartial by both parents. Their efforts to form a
co-operative relationship with the parents may be hampered by the
parents seeing them as agents of social control. Social work reports may
be critical of the parents and strenuously opposed by them. It is very
difficult for social workers to use their authority to protect the child, while
at the same time forming a supportive and co-operative relationship with
the child's parents. The primary concern must be the protection of the
child and the child's immediate safety must be assured before mediation
can be considered. In the longer term, the aim may be to help parents

cope with stress and cease abusive or neglectful behaviour, but the family may be at war with the statutory child protection system.

Family members and social services may therefore see family mediators as having a potentially useful, independent and supportive role in mediating on an agenda agreed between social services and the family. This use of mediation may be an effective way of reaching mutually agreed decisions that promote a child's well being. Social workers do not need to participate directly if they support the referral to mediation and if the Agreement to Mediate is modified to allow the outcome of the mediation to be reportable to social services. Nevertheless, mediators may need some background information from social services in order to carry out mediation with full information and awareness of child protection issues. Some mediation services may therefore require, subject to the participants' agreement, to see either the initial or final Social Work statement. In a self-referral to mediation encouraged by Social Services, background information was not required. The foster-parents came to mediation with their 18-year foster daughter who had just left care and moved into her own flat a few streets away. Cara, the 18-year-old, had a 4-year-old daughter, Molly, who was continuing to live with the foster-parents. Cara had a close and trusting relationship with her foster-parents and as she was not yet settled and fully independent, there was consensus between them that Molly's residence should continue to be with her foster-grandparents, with Cara visiting her every day, whenever she wanted. Social services supported this agreement.

The Public Law Outline (2008/2010)[29] envisages greater use of mediation and other forms of ADR before, during and after care proceedings. Active case management under paragraph 3.20 includes:

> '(14) where it is demonstrated to be in the interests of the child, encouraging the parties to use an alternative dispute resolution procedure, if the court considers such a procedure to be appropriate and facilitating the use of such procedure.'

Whilst power imbalances are inevitable in mediations involving family members and a public authority and these need to be taken into account, if mediation on certain issues is suitable and accepted, mediators can use a range of interventions that help to empower families and promote children's well being.[30] A growing area is the use of mediation at the end of care proceedings to support the move of a child in foster care to a family member under Special Guardianship. In this way, supportive relationships between the prospective carers and the parents can be encouraged. There is a risk, however, that mediators could become unwilling participants in the local authority relinquishing its responsibilities at too early a stage. Mediators will no doubt be keen to embrace the

---

[29]   Practice Direction of 26 March 2010 [2010] All ER 275.
[30]   Barsky *Conflict Resolution for the Helping Professions* (Wadsworth, 2000).

challenges of new models to meet the competing interests involved in these cases. In a case referred to The Mediation Centre in Stafford, where a one-year-old child had been found to have been injured non-accidentally by his father in circumstances denied by both the young father and mother, mediation was used to rebuild fractured relationships between the maternal grandparents who became the child's Special Guardians, the separated parents, and the estranged paternal grandmother, all of whom had taken competing positions concerning the child.

4.14.4   Mediation in adoption and post-adoption support

Mediation may also be needed on the question of continuing contact between an adopted child and the natural parents. Although it may not be possible to bring natural and adoptive parents together for face-to-face meetings, mediation skills can be used in separate meetings to explore the principle and frequency of contact visits and to work out practical details. As 'Open Adoption' becomes more common, mediation can facilitate communication between natural and adoptive parents and between the child and both sets of parents. Agreed arrangements for contact can be recorded in a written agreement provided to all concerned, including the child, and formalised as necessary. There should be provision for reviewing the agreement and modifying it as circumstances change and as the child gets older. This is again an area for 'working in partnership', since many local authorities have excellent practice in relation to post-adoption support.

4.14.5   Mediation involving people with disabilities

A more controversial use of mediation is in relation to complaints involving discrimination against people with physical and mental disabilities. Some disability advocacy groups have been alarmed by this development, fearing that hard-won battles for legal rights could be lost if disabled people are not represented adequately. One of the concerns about mediation involving people with certain forms of disability is their ability to communicate and negotiate fully. As Maida[31] has pointed out, there is the problem of ensuring informed participation and secondly, the problem of power balancing. Effective communication in mediation requires adequate mental capacity and techniques that allow everyone to participate fully. Many people question the use of mediation with someone who does not have full mental capacity or only intermittent capacity. Mediators have an obligation to ensure that individuals are able to participate fully and that their interests are adequately represented. There are a number of strategies that may be used to level the playing-field and manage actual or potential power imbalances. Medical

---

[31]   Maida 'Mediating disputes involving people with disabilities', ch 12 in Kruk (ed) *Mediation and Conflict Resolution in Social Work and the Human Services* (Nelson-Hall, 1997).

advice may be needed in the first instance on the suitability of mediation. If mediation is suitable, the disabled person may need someone to provide additional physical and emotional support in the mediation process. The role of supporters and the extent to which they speak on behalf of the disabled person need careful consideration. Systems theory provides a helpful framework for mediators in understanding the tangled web of facts, perceptions, communications and feelings that may need unravelling in order to settle a specific dispute or work out a consensual decision on future care. (An example of mediation involving a disabled, housebound mother with an adult son diagnosed with Asperger's Syndrome is given at **4.13** above).

4.14.6   Mediation in inheritance disputes

See Chapter 9 at **9.21** below.

4.15   LEGAL ADVISORS AND MEDIATION

> 'Lawyers need to be encouraged to invest in the process in which their clients are engaged.'[32]

Brown and Marriott[33] devote a chapter of their book to considering the role of lawyers who advise and assist clients who are taking part in different forms of ADR. Lawyers often object that mediators 'take work away' from them, but mediators are also a source of referrals to lawyers. Many individuals come to mediation without having taken legal advice. Mediators encourage them to take legal advice during mediation, as well as at the end. The roles of lawyers and mediators are different and complementary. Although mediation should reduce litigation, questions frequently arise in mediation on which participants need independent legal and financial advice before making proposals for settlement.

In civil/commercial mediation, the parties' lawyers attend with their clients and advise them during the process. This is not general practice in family mediation, but in some cases it may be worthwhile to consider it.[34] The logistics are more difficult in family mediation than in civil/commercial mediation that may take a whole day and be concluded on the same day, whereas family mediation normally takes place over several sessions held at intervals of weeks or even months. In some American states it is common for lawyers to attend family mediation sessions, whereas in Britain and other European countries this is uncommon. Lawyers who take part without understanding the mediation process might try to take control and inhibit their clients from talking

---

[32]   Robinson 'Developing Family Mediation: Innovative Approaches to ADR' [2008] Fam Law 1049.

[33]   Brown and Marriott *ADR Principles and Practice* (Sweet & Maxwell, 1993), pp 299–310.

[34]   Loram 'Solicitors in the Mediation Room March' [2008] Fam Law 262–266.

with each other. If lawyers seek to use mediation as an opportunity for advocacy, the nature of the process would change fundamentally. In a survey in Florida, well over half the lawyers said that over the previous twelve months they had attended family mediation sessions with their clients in 75% of their family law cases. The majority said their reason for attending was to facilitate agreements being reached. Another reason given by many of them was the need to protect their client. A lawyer's presence can certainly give support to an anxious and vulnerable client who might otherwise refuse to take part in mediation.

Some lawyers admitted that they attended mediation in order to learn about the mediation process and the mediator's abilities. Once they were satisfied that the mediators were competent and knowledgeable, they were more comfortable to allow their clients to participate. The survey showed that after first-hand experience of attending mediation sessions, lawyers recognised that the benefits of mediation far outweigh any potential disadvantages. One of the advantages of having lawyers present is that there can be a break during the mediation session in which the parties withdraw with their own lawyer for a short separate meeting or caucus. When legal advice can be given on the spot, a great deal of delay is avoided. Lawyers can advise their client privately, if they perceive that the client is being obstructive, for example by explaining that their position is unrealistic or unhelpful. Mediators cannot spell things out in this way. Lawyers can also be very helpful in assisting negotiations and finalising a settlement.

Before legal advisors are invited to attend a mediation meeting, it is important that some ground-rules are established with them so that the lawyers understand and respect the mediation process. The Agreement to Mediate needs to be adapted for lawyers and they should be asked to sign it so that the confidentiality of the mediation process is not breached in subsequent litigation. A number of other aspects also need to be clarified with lawyers. They need to know whether they are being invited to as passive observers, whether they are invited to contribute actively and whether there will be opportunities for them to withdraw with their client at intervals to give further advice. Roles and structure need to be agreed and it also needs to be established that the mediator is not responsible for paying the costs of lawyers who attend mediation with their clients. Effective mediation:[35]

> 'in complex and entrenched cases is likely to involve working in partnership with other professional colleagues and the court process – a far more evolved multi-disciplinary approach than we have previously embraced.'

---

[35]   Robinson 'Developing Family Mediation' [2008] Fam Law 927.

4.16 MERGED FAMILY/CIVIL MEDIATION

Brown and Marriott[36] considered ways in which ADR practitioners may combine different ADR processes, or different fields of ADR, such as civil and family, to create a merged process, 'epitomised by the practitioner's ability to create a bespoke hybrid format for an individual case'.[37] The permutations of such models are beyond the scope of this book. Some mediators who are cross-trained in family and civil mediation are well equipped to mediate in family and civil cases that have potential for lengthy and costly litigation in different courts. Robinson[38] has given examples of the use of mediation in such cases. He has quoted a case involving intergenerational litigation over interests in a family farm, involving both Chancery and family proceedings. The final hearing in Chancery proceedings was stayed pending mediation between four parties, two of whom were divorcing spouses involved in ancillary relief proceedings. The ancillary relief proceedings had been stayed pending the outcome of the Chancery proceedings. The total costs to the parties over the four years of these proceedings had already climbed to over £30,000. A merged family/civil mediation was set up and attended by the four parties and their solicitors or counsel. The mediation lasted one day and culminated with a Memorandum of Understanding produced in respect of the ancillary relief proceedings and a *Tomlin Order* in the Chancery proceedings. The cost of the mediation to the four parties averaged less than £500 each.

Merged mediation models in complex cases involving civil as well as family proceedings, or in care proceedings alongside family proceedings, require mediators to have the necessary expertise and to be creative in designing models of mediation that are suited to particular needs and contexts. Barenboim reminds us, however, that 'spontaneous realisation' is only possible with 'all the repetitions and the familiarity resulting from intense study'.[39]

4.17 A MODEL FOR DESIGNING THE MEDIATION PROCESS

As Neil Robinson has written (personal communication), the examples above show how dynamically mediation models are evolving, and how essential it is to find new processes to deal with complexities and entrenchment. An assessment of suitability of mediation therefore needs to include an assessment with regard to the most appropriate model of ADR. In order to make sure that a specifically designed model would be a

---

[36] Brown and Marriott *ADR Principles and Practice* (Sweet & Maxwell, 1993).
[37] Ibid, p 273.
[38] [2009] Fam Law 253.
[39] Barenboim *Everything is Connected – The Power of Music* (Weidenfeld and Nicolson, 2008), p 58.

positive enhancement rather than a dilution of mediation principles, Robinson proposes an assessment tool to include the following:

(1)   Identify the needs, expectations and commitment of the parties.

(2)   Identify the issues in dispute.

(3)   Consider the level of entrenchment and/or complexity.

(4)   Assess possible risks, abuse and power.

(5)   Identify the aims and objectives of the ADR process.

(6)   Identify the stage reached in court proceedings and whether – and if so, how – any information is to be shared. Also whether other third parties need to be actively involved.

(7)   Design and define the tailor-made model.

(8)   Discuss process options with parties and any representatives.

(9)   If the ADR process offered is accepted, modify the Agreement to Mediate as necessary and agree any additional ground rules.

(10) Discuss and continue to liaise with the mediator's professional practice consultant (PPC).

It seems fitting to end this chapter with another quotation from President Barak Obama:[40]

> 'No one is exempt from the call to find common ground.'

---

[40]   Obama *The Audacity of Hope* (Canongate, 2008), p 68.

CHAPTER 5

STAGES AND SKILLS IN MEDIATION

'Begin at the beginning', the King said gravely, 'and go on till you come to the end: then stop'[1]

CONTENTS

5.1   DIFFERENT DIMENSIONS OF SEPARATION AND DIVORCE

Family mediation helps separating and divorcing couples to resolve issues and manage difficult transitions from one family structure to another. Separation is usually a very stressful period involving change at every level. Bohannan[2] identified six dimensions of adjustment in separation and divorce: emotional, psychological, legal, economic, parental and community. How many of us could cope with major adjustments in all these areas at once? Mediation provides a forum for issues in parental, economic and legal dimensions of separation and divorce. Interrelated issues may be closely entwined: it may not be possible to work out arrangements for children without considering related property and financial issues. In mediation, interrelated issues can be considered in conjunction with each other, whereas the court would consider them in separate proceedings, or possibly not at all. Emotional and psychological dimensions need to be understood and acknowledged, although they are not the main focus. Ignoring their force and impact is likely to make mediation on specific issues unworkable. A stage-by-stage mediation

---

[1]   Lewis Carroll *Alice in Wonderland*, p 107.
[2]   Bohannan *Divorce and After* (Doubleday, 1970).

process helps to contain powerful emotions, maintain commitment to mediation and keep up the momentum at a pace both partners can manage. Explaining the stages of the process reduces anxieties and encourages couples to continue. Whether mediation consists of a one-off meeting or a series of meetings spaced over a period of time, there is a beginning, middle and end. Even where there is high conflict and no possibility of agreement, the mediator is responsible for managing the beginning and the end in a clear and constructive way.

5.2   STAGES OF FAMILY MEDIATION

The basic four-stage model referred to in Chapter 2 may be expanded to twelve stages for family mediation. Although based on the structured mediation model, each step in a staged approach to family mediation needs the empathy and skills associated with transformative and family-focused approaches. In this twelve-stage model, the sequence from stage 5 onwards can be varied to meet the needs of participants, rather than imposing an inflexible structure on them that may not correspond to their priorities:

(1)   Explaining mediation and assessing suitability.

(2)   Gaining voluntary and informed acceptance.

(3)   Defining and clarifying the issues.

(4)   Agreeing the agenda for mediation.

(5)   Prioritising and planning.

(6)   Gathering and sharing information.

(7)   Exploring needs and options.

(8)   Indirect/direct consultation with children.

(9)   Negotiating on preferred options.

(10) Working out terms of agreement.

(11) Drafting Memorandum of Understanding.

(12) Concluding mediation.

5.2.1   Stages 1 and 2: Engaging people in mediation

The first two stages are discussed in Chapter 3. Unless the Agreement to Mediate has already been signed at the joint information and assessment meeting, the first stage in the first mediation session, after greeting and welcoming, is the Agreement to Mediate. People need to understand and accept the terms and conditions on which mediation takes place and accept them fully, before the process gets underway. These terms and conditions should have been explained at the initial information and assessment meeting. They are set out in writing in the Agreement to Mediate that participants are asked to sign before mediation can proceed. This document should explain in clear language the purpose of mediation and the mediator's role, the commitment to making full and open financial disclosure, the nature and limits of the confidentiality provided, the need to take independent legal advice and charging arrangements. Having made sure that participants understand the terms and conditions and that they are both willing to sign the Agreement to Mediate, the mediator invites them to sign it and keeps a copy signed by them both. This signed copy would be needed in the event of a breach of confidentiality or of complaint being made against the mediator. The FMA Agreement to Mediate is included in Appendix B.

5.2.2   Stage 3: Defining and clarifying issues for mediation

The issues for mediation should have been identified and clarified to some extent at the initial information and assessment meeting. These need to be established or re-established with both partners together at the first mediation meeting, especially as circumstances may have changed since the initial information meeting.

> 'So would you like to explain what you think needs to be settled?'

Mediators may begin by inviting each partner to explain what they want to work out in mediation. The theory is that giving them an opportunity to speak and explain their positions will help them to feel heard, release bottled-up feelings and enable the mediator to understand the issues from each partner's perspective. Unfortunately it does not always work out in this way. If the mediator says in her warmest mediation manner:

> 'So, Maureen, would you like to explain what you want to work out in mediation and then I'll ask you the same question, Chris ....'

Maureen may seize the opportunity to explain that the whole problem is that Chris has gone off with Sharon – that slut down the road – and he isn't giving her any money and she can't pay the rent and the children are so upset they don't want to see him and only last week he said ... and then she said. Maureen may need to get things off her chest, but if she is allowed to rant at Chris and he feels harangued, he will become increasingly angry and likely to walk out. This could be the end of the mediation when it has barely begun.

Rather than letting one partner take the floor, a series of focused questions may be put to each participant in turn. Focused questions help to gather basic information on matters that need to be settled, while clarifying the degree of urgency or priority on each question. Couples are often so preoccupied by their disagreements that they forget how much they agree. It is important to go through the main questions or issues systematically, checking those that are agreed while noting those that are not agreed.

5.2.3   Who speaks first?

The sequence in which questions are put to each participant needs to alternate, so that neither of them is invariably in the position of responding to what the other has said. At the beginning, it may be useful to put a question first to the more hesitant or reluctant party, rather than to the one who seems dominant or more confident. In the example given above, the mediator notices that Maureen is keen to do most of the talking, while Chris seems sullen and withdrawn. Chris might therefore be asked first about the main issues that he thinks need to be settled. Then Maureen might be asked to say what the issues are from her point of view – possibly suggesting that the main headings should be given first. Putting questions to each partner in turn in alternating order is very important in maintaining the mediator's impartiality and control of the process.

5.2.4   Acknowledging feelings and concerns

Empathy is one of the most important qualities needed by mediators and acknowledging participants' feelings and concerns is one of the mediator's most important skills. Feelings should be acknowledged as far as possible in a mutualising way.

> 'So you are both feeling very stressed ... concerned ....'

Strong emotions need to be named:

> 'I can see that you are both feeling very angry at the moment ... I can see that you are both extremely stressed ... It's very difficult to cope with the children's distress, as well as your own ....'

It takes a big effort to come to mediation and it may be very difficult to reach joint decisions. Recognising that partners have difficulties communicating with one another or that communication has broken down completely may be stating the obvious, yet it can have a calming effect, because the acknowledgment is accurate, non-judgmental and empathetic. Acknowledgments need to be phrased as 'I can see that' or 'I am hearing that' and not as 'I understand ...', because a mediator who claims to understand may be sharply rebuked, whereas not having heard accurately may be forgiven.

The ways in which questions are phrased by the mediator influence the answers that are given.[3] It is very important, especially in the opening stages, for mediators to ask appropriate questions and to phrase them with care. It is often possible to acknowledge that both partners want to settle issues rather than fighting over them, although they see them from different angles and have different points of view:

> 'You both say your main concerns are to work out contact and financial arrangements, so that the children can benefit from co-operation between you. Your objectives fit very well with the aims of mediation.'

Mediators need to acknowledge feelings of anger, stress and insecurity but do not usually explore the causes. The main focus is on the present and the future, rather than on the past. The mediator needs to keep eye contact with both partners in talking with them both in a calm and friendly way.

5.2.5   Stages 4 and 5: Agreeing the agenda, prioritising and planning

The agenda may be agreed quickly if both partners bring the same issues, but they do not necessarily have the same priorities. A mother living with the children in the family home may have urgent issues over maintenance, whereas the father's priority is contact with his children. If there are competing priorities that each parent needs time for in the first meeting, the time to be allotted to each issue can be divided equally, leaving time for summarising and planning the next steps and tasks to be undertaken. Alternatively, it may be agreed to discuss certain issues at the first meeting and others at the following meeting, when further financial information will be available. Unproductive arguments can be pre-empted by saying:

> 'With regard to child support, I can give you some information about this, but I think that some further details of your incomes and average monthly outgoings would help to show how each of you is managing. Then we can look at how the family income can be used for the support of the children.'

It may be helpful to list the main issues on a flipchart,[4] to show participants that they have been heard and to provide a common focus. Sometimes the list of matters that are already agreed is longer than those that are not yet agreed. This helps to put disagreements into a broader

---

[3]   See Chapter 6 below.
[4]   See Chapter 9 below.

perspective. The level of urgency or priority needs to be considered. If a flipchart is used, different colours or asterisks can be used to highlight issues and show urgency.

Stages from 6 onwards, gathering and sharing financial information, considering children's needs, exploring options and negotiating towards agreement, are considered in later chapters.

5.2.6   Should ground-rules be set at the outset?

Mediators do not always set ground-rules at the outset. Initial impressions formed at information and assessment meetings give indications of the need to set ground-rules at the beginning of the first meeting. Most participants appreciate knowing that there are certain ground-rules, such as:

- Each participant will be invited to explain their position and concerns: questions will be put to each of them.

- Each person is asked to listen to the other, without interrupting, even if they disagree.

- The mediator will discourage fault finding and accounts of what has gone wrong in the past: the focus is on making things better.

- Although participants are asked not to interrupt each other, the mediator may interrupt them if necessary, to keep discussions on track. There may be a way of saying this that can raise a smile:

    'I know it seems unfair that you are asked not to interrupt each other, but I am allowed to interrupt you! If I do interrupt at all – and I may not need to – it would be to help us keep on track and to use time as well as possible. Time runs away fast, so may we move on to ...?'

Ground-rules are discussed further in Chapter 6 at **6.17** and in Chapter 10 at **10.8**, while additional ground-rules for court-referred mediation are suggested in Appendix E.

5.3   CONFLICT MANAGEMENT

Couples may come to mediation determined to score points over each other.

    'We are so patterned in our lives to think of conflict as a contest that life becomes a big scoreboard.'[5]

---

[5]   Crum *The Magic of Conflict* (Touchstone, 1987), p 37.

Point-scoring tactics test the mediator's ability to be firm. It may be necessary to propose some ground-rules in order to keep discussions under control. These rules are often accepted with relief. It is the mediator's responsibility to make sure that rules that have been agreed are then adhered to. If rapport is established with both participants as early as possible, this makes it easier for the mediator to intervene when an angry outburst shows signs of turning into a long tirade. The mediator should intervene in a friendly but firm way, so that ground-rules are kept and each participant has a chance to speak, knowing that the mediator will control attacks and interruptions. Point scoring and verbal attacks need to be curtailed (see Chapter 10 on verbal goading and one-upmanship tactics in mediation). Mediators also need to be firm in prohibiting offensive or inflammatory language.

> 'Look, sorry, Barry/Brenda, I don't think I'm going to be able to help you unless we all agree that certain language cannot be used here – is that OK?'

What happens when one is angry? Physically, there is an increase in adrenalin, the heart rate quickens and blood pressure rises. Breathing quickens and muscles are tensed. It is hard to listen, when one is angry. People may need to express some of their anger before they are able to listen. Mediators should acknowledge their anger explicitly, rather than trying to stifle it:

> 'I understand that you are both feeling very raw and angry at the moment.'

It also helps to observe that feeling very angry in these situations is entirely natural and normal. Acknowledging anger and referring to it in a normalising way may make it less necessary for couples to show their anger in aggressive statements and loud voices. If progress is to be made, the mediator needs to calm people down after an angry outburst so that they can begin to move on, in spite of their anger:

> 'I know it's very difficult to talk about the house being sold, when it's your home and the children's home too, and you are both feeling so stressed. But can we look at what options there may be and how they would work?'

Conflict management does not mean suppressing negative outbursts. More importantly, it involves picking up positive statements and repeating them, to give them more emphasis.[6]

> 'So, Julie, you think it's important that the children see their father regularly? … So, Steve, you are saying you appreciate that Julie has always supported your relationship with the children?'

---

6   See Chapter 6 for discussion of the technique of reframing.

Conflict is stressful and is usually seen as destructive, so it may help to reframe it in positive terms. A couple who are arguing fiercely about the children may be quite surprised if the mediator says to them:

> 'Look, I can see you are both extremely upset and angry, but what comes across to me is how much both of you *care* about the children. Neither of you is walking away ... The saddest thing is when one parent gives up trying to keep in contact with the children. You both care a lot about what you think is best for them, even though you don't agree at the moment about what that is.'

Parents who are fighting with each other may be surprised to be praised and may feel encouraged by the praise, providing it sounds spontaneous and not patronising. A reframe of this kind can be used to help change the current of feeling from mutual anger as a separated couple to joint concerns as parents.

Although it can help people to let off steam, mediators need to control arguments that are bound to be unproductive because relevant information is not yet available. Participants are usually prepared to hold back to some extent, if they understand when and how their conflicting views will be addressed. When priorities have been identified and the next steps agreed, participants should be able to leave the first meeting feeling that they are working on a track that makes sense to them. They ought not to leave feeling frustrated and confused.

5.4 PATTERNS OF COMMUNICATION AND CONFLICT

Communication problems are often both cause and effect of relationship breakdown. How couples deal with disagreements is critical. Researchers at the Centre for Marital and Family Studies at the University of Denver, Colorado, have suggested[7] that it is not *whether* couples argue that matters, it is *how* they argue. Disagreements are normal and a relationship without any disagreement would be abnormal. Each situation of breakdown is unique, but some patterns are discernible. It is useful for mediators to recognise patterns, not to put couples into categories or to give them prescriptions, but as guidelines to the approach that is likely to be most helpful to the couple concerned. The pattern may change over time and one partner may show features of one pattern, while the other partner shows features of another. The question is how mediators can help them both at the same time. Mediators are not clinicians making a diagnosis or formulating hypotheses as a prelude to treatment. The process of mediation should be tailored to fit participants' needs and the emphasis should be on flexibility, not diagnostic skills. The mediator's interventions affect surface tensions[8] and the choice of technique at a particular moment is like using a cabinet-maker's box of tools. Using a

---

[7] Markman, Stanley and Blumbers *Fighting For Your Marriage* (Prentice Hall, 1996).
[8] See Chapter 1 above.

spirit-level to check for balance is frequently necessary and more helpful than applying a screw-driver to get at the facts.

Researchers have proposed typologies identifying different patterns of reaction and interaction between separating and divorcing couples. Kressel and colleagues[9] described four patterns: 'disengaged', 'direct conflict', 'autistic (non-communicating) and 'enmeshed'. Ahrons distinguished between 'perfect pals', 'co-operative colleagues', 'dissolved duos', 'angry associates' and 'fiery foes'.[10] The following typology suggests some further patterns drawn from mediation experience. Mediators need to vary their responses to fit in with different dynamics.

(i)   Co-operative couples.

(ii)   Conflict avoiders.

(iii)   Angry couples.

(iv)   Business managers.

(v)   Projected conflict.

(vi)   Semi-detached couples.

(vii)   Sea anemones and limpets.

(viii) Feuding couples.

5.4.1   Co-operative couples

Co-operative couples may seek mediation without being in dispute, because they want to resolve issues by agreement and maintain their co-operation. If there are financial issues, they want to draw on the mediator's expertise in working out a financial settlement, with only a minimum of correspondence between legal advisors. Co-operative couples move relatively easily from one stage of mediation to the next, dealing with questions and needs, gathering information and working out arrangements. Reality testing by the mediator is important, however, because financial plans that seem to have been agreed might not actually be viable. Sometimes the consequences have not been clearly understood. Mediation with co-operative couples is usually low-key and may be quite relaxed, but mediators need to be ready for sudden outbursts of anger and signs of emotional pain.

---

[9]   Kressel, Jaffee, Tuchman, Watson and Deutsch *Typology of Divorcing Couples* (1980) 19(2) *Family Process* 101–116.
[10]   Ahrons *The Good Divorce* (Bloomsbury, 1994).

The introduction of a new partner on one side often upsets the previous good level of co-operation. Mediators can help to anticipate difficulties by putting hypothetical questions,[11] such as asking when one partner would tell the other about a new relationship that could affect their arrangements. The couple might agree that they would return to mediation, if a new relationship on either side resulted in a need to review their arrangements. It may also be helpful to mention to co-operative couples who are separating or living apart that although they are clearly helping their children by working together so well, children can be confused by the very amicableness they see between their parents. Children may misinterpret friendliness as a sign that their parents are getting back together again. Younger children, especially, may find it very hard to understand why there is any need for divorce, if their parents get on so well. Even where parents are in agreement over the children, they may want to discuss how they are going to talk with the children. Parents often avoid talking to the children about their separation or divorce when they are unsure what to say to them.[12]

5.4.2   Conflict avoiders

In this common pattern, one partner may have withdrawn from the other over a period of time, often seeking compensation in work, leisure activities or a new relationship – or all of these. Communication may be very limited and may have ceased altogether. Some couples continue to live under the same roof but withdraw into a shell, sometimes not talking to each other for years. They retreat emotionally and often literally behind closed doors. Their silence conveys hurt, anger and feelings of mutual rejection. There may also be unspoken feelings of affection and attachment and great fear of being abandoned. Typical reactions are avoidance, retreat, non-communication and fear of confrontation.

If one parent leaves without any discussion, the children are often not told by the remaining parent if, when or how they will see the parent who has left. The pattern of avoiding discussion and conflict may be passed on to the next generation. Emotional and practical issues may remain unresolved and new partnerships may be formed, without the old ties being unknotted.

Sometimes both partners avoid discussing the breakdown in their relationship. At other times, one seeks discussion and is frustrated by the other's retreat into a closed shell. This shell may remain closed for years. If one partner leaves without having given any clear warning, the abandoned partner may experience profound shock, followed by disbelief, distress, anger or an unmanageable mixture of emotions. The leaver often insists that they tried to talk, but felt constantly rebuffed. The gulf of blocked communication may be so wide that it may be difficult to conceive of any

---

[11]   See Chapter 6 below.
[12]   See Chapter 8 at **8.5** on parents talking with their children.

bridge capable of spanning it. Counselling could help the partners understand what has happened and why it happened, but they may not be willing. Some couples who have avoided talking to each other may be able to talk in mediation, if there is understanding and support. The pace may need to be slow, especially to start with. Mediators need to be very attentive to body language, able to pick up unspoken feelings and aware of the dynamics of rejection, counter-rejection and ambivalence. Good listening and communication skills are important, especially in the phrasing and focusing of questions.

Example

Bill and Glenda sat down at their first mediation meeting without looking at each another. Both were silent. In response to a question from the mediator, Glenda said: 'Well, we've separated. So what do we do now?' Sensing a frozen atmosphere, the mediator asked if it would help to begin by explaining different ways of structuring a separation or divorce to see whether any of these ways would be helpful for them. Both nodded. The mediator explained different ways of structuring a separation or divorce, starting with the least formal and final way and moving on to ways of reaching a formal and final settlement in divorce. Getting back together was also mentioned, but without giving it special emphasis. Headings were put on the flipchart and questions arising from these headings were used to encourage dialogue between Bill and Glenda. In the course of explanations and discussions they became visibly less strained. By the end of the session, they had identified and discussed a number of specific issues. At the following session, they were helped to explore further questions together, taking one step at a time.

5.4.3 Angry couples

There is a stark contrast in mediating between conflict avoiders and mediating between raging couples. Raging couples need more rule-setting, quicker interventions by the mediator and careful structuring of sessions. When anger is expressed openly and directly, arguments can escalate very quickly. Mediators need to be quick and confident in their use of conflict management skills, including positive but firm control, reframing, acknowledging and mutualising anger. The aim is to channel the energy generated by the couple's anger – which may be valid and rational anger – into solving the problems, instead of prolonging the battle. Couples who fight over the spoils of the marriage may find these dwindling away, the more they fight over who gets what. Mediators need to shift the focus from individual rights and wrongs to mutual concerns and interests. Disagreements can be reframed as valid concerns, with a range of possible options to consider.[13] Pragmatic questions such as 'So, what do you think might help?' can elicit a simple suggestion that has not been put forward

---

[13] See Chapter 11 below.

before because the couple were too angry to think about anything else. When the separation is recent and feelings very raw, anger levels may be very high and have the positive function of galvanising energy and warding off depression. Couples may hit explosive levels of rage that present high risks but have a cathartic effect (danger and opportunity). If they have sufficient motivation and maturity, they may be able to move on with encouragement from the mediator.

5.4.4   Business managers

In contrast, there are dual-career couples whose relationship seems to have been based on mutual convenience and friendship, without deep feelings on either side. The relationship may be a short one and there may never have been a strong attachment. These couples are unlikely to have children. When a career move for one partner precipitates a decision to separate, the couple may treat the separation rather like a business deal. Practicalities are addressed briskly and there may be no mention of feelings at all. Mediators are expected to be highly efficient on technical matters and any enquiry into emotions may be seen as intrusive and brushed aside. Couples who treat a separation or divorce as a piece of business to get through as quickly as possible are entitled to receive efficiently managed mediation. Mediators should, however, have their antennae well tuned to pick up signs of pain and distress that are well concealed beneath a cool exterior.

Example – disagreement over possessions

Howard and Caitlin had lived together for two years and then got married. They owned a large and expensively furnished flat in London. They did not have children. Both of them worked long hours and Howard, who worked for an international telecommunications company, travelled a great deal. He paid the mortgage from his salary and Caitlin paid the housekeeping bills. They had rarely discussed financial matters as they had separate bank accounts and were largely independent financially. Once their various assets and income had been listed in mediation and values agreed, there was ready agreement to divide everything on a 50/50 basis – until it came to the candlesticks. These were a valuable pair of silver candlesticks that had more than monetary value. Howard and Caitlin acknowledged that the candlesticks had symbolic value and that the occasion on which they bought them had invested them with special meaning. Having previously seemed quite cold and detached towards each other, they then spoke with sadness about the ending of their relationship. Both were close to tears. Had the mediator attended only to questions of financial equality, Howard and Caitlin would have left mediation with a financial settlement, but the sadness they both felt would have remained unspoken.

Business managers may include older couples whose feelings for each other have withered away. Sometimes they have both formed new relationships and come to mediation ready to dissolve a marriage that is no more than an empty shell. If financial issues are relatively straightforward and there is no anger or resentment on either side, mediation may be swift and effective.

5.4.5 Semi-detached – apart, but not fully detached

Semi-detached couples are often ambivalent about separation or divorce. They may demonstrate this by preferring to leave some questions in the air. Mediation may help them clarify their arrangements and explore options on matters they have not yet resolved. In the process they may be able to express their uncertainties, insecurity and mixed feelings. It may be helpful to these couples to work out clearer boundaries concerning their separation and amount of contact with each other. A partner who makes frequent visits – 'just passing the house and thought I would drop in' – may justify this as keeping in touch with the children. But unplanned visits may be disruptive and can be an excuse for checking up on what is happening at home. It may help both partners to work out how much contact they actually need or want with each other and whether this should take place only by prior arrangement. When contact has been planned, it enables all those involved, including children, to prepare for it emotionally. Mixed feelings of pleasure and pain, when a missing partner or parent reappears for a contact visit, are often complicated by the unresolved anger of parents and children. The knot of tangled feelings is easier to cope with, if the contact visit has been planned carefully.

Many semi-detached couples are able to talk on their own to some extent, but they may need the mediator's help to tackle difficult questions that they otherwise avoid or shelve. Some admit that, while wanting to be fair and reasonable, they have an urge to hit back at a partner who has caused hurt. Mediators can help them address matters that they shy away from but need to resolve.

Example

Stephen and Rhoda had been to Relate for counselling the previous year. When they decided to go to mediation they had been living apart under the same roof for over a year and both accepted that their fifteen-year marriage (no children) had broken down irretrievably. They were detached from each other to a considerable extent but still had emotional, financial and legal ties to unravel. Although fully prepared to split assets on a 50/50 basis, Stephen did not see why he should share his pension with Rhoda. Rhoda was concerned about her long-term security, as she had a much lower income and much smaller pension. Stephen felt she could increase both. They had both consulted solicitors. Rhoda's solicitor suggested mediation and Stephen agreed to take part.

Rhoda was more able to tackle difficult issues than Stephen, who had a tendency to avoid emotional areas. They both responded well to a structured process of mediation in which issues were addressed systematically and concerns acknowledged. A careful use of humour proved a helpful way of reaching both of them, so that the discussions became lighter and freer. Three mediation sessions were spent defining issues, gathering and clarifying financial facts and circumstances and exploring possible options and time-scales for settlement. Stephen and Rhoda were encouraged to take legal advice on their proposals for a settlement in two stages. Their settlement was approved in a Consent Order.

5.4.6 Projected conflict

Whereas some couples fight openly on overt issues, others avoid fighting openly but are aware of unresolved conflicts lying below the surface. Disputes over child support or contact may be a vehicle for conflict that has been suppressed and driven underground. Attempts to settle the surface dispute may make little progress, if the underlying conflict is not addressed. Contact with children is often blocked because the decision to end the marriage was not a mutual decision. One of the strongest arguments for all issues mediation is that it enables emotional and practical links between issues to be understood and worked on.

Conflicts over children in divorce only occasionally have their roots in child-related issues. Much more often, conflict stems from unresolved marital issues. The conflict tends to boil up when one parent acquires a new partner. Disputes over children may be due to real concern about the children but are often a channel for anger about 'the other woman' or 'that bloke you're seeing'. A claim for residence may be a strategy to oust the partner and secure occupation and sole ownership of the family home. Children can be used as weapons and a means of retaliation. Some parents who come to mediation admit that they have been fighting each other through the children. In realising how this affects the children, they may become motivated to sort out the issues between them.

Example

David and Alison were referred to mediation because of problems over David's contact with the children. David was by this time living with a new partner called Lynne. Alison was struggling to make ends meet and deeply resented David and Lynne's higher standard of living. Alison felt David was wanting to have everything all his own way, with the children as well.

David reacted by accusing Alison of punishing him through the children and trying to turn them against him. His anger was to some extent a defence against his guilt feelings about leaving Alison for Lynne. It was necessary to let David and Alison express some of their anger, to acknowledge that they were both hurt and angry and accept their anger as normal and understandable. This acknowledgment of their feelings was combined with encouragement to start looking at ways forward. Before focusing on contact specifically, the mediator also enquired about other areas of agreement or disagreement. Asking these questions was important, because it enabled suppressed anger on other issues to come to the surface. Alison complained that David was not paying adequate child support. The links between contact and financial issues then became clearer. Another issue was Lynne's role in relation to the children when they visited their father. Mediation involved discussion on these interrelated issues, with acknowledgment of feelings and a focus on arrangements to help the parents give the children as much priority as possible.

5.4.7 Sea anemones and limpets

The most painful and prolonged source of emotional anger in divorce stems from one partner's continuing intense need for the other. It is not only children who harbour fantasies of reconciliation. When a continuing strong attachment on one side is not reciprocated, the abandoned partner's feelings of grief and anger may make rational discussion impossible. The emotionally desperate partner may embroil the other in prolonged disputes as a way of clinging on and maintaining involvement – like a limpet that cannot be prised off. The 'sea anemone' may react by closing its tentacles and withdrawing into a solid lump of impregnable jelly. If the 'limpet' refuses to discuss separation or divorce at all, mediation will be impossible. Referral to counselling may be needed, but the 'sea anemone' may refuse it. Legal advice is also needed when one partner pursues a separation or divorce that is strongly resisted by the other.

It is important to recognise with both partners that they are at different stages and that they are looking in different directions. It may also be helpful to acknowledge that ending a marriage involves more than the loss of the partner. Dreams for the future and the sense of security in an intact family are lost as well. Enforced changes of lifestyle, usually involving a lower standard of living, may intensify bitterness. One partner may accuse the other of failed promises and commitments. Disillusionment fuels more anger. Although anger over failed hopes and dreams may be mutual, the partner who is seen as responsible for ending the marriage is expected to carry the blame. Blaming the other partner enables the 'innocent partner' to take the role of victim and avoid responsibility for a share in the failed relationship.

Mediators do not explore one partner's reasons for blaming the other and do not offer therapy to help people work through acute grief and anger. They can, however, make some negotiation possible by acknowledging and legitimising anger over failed dreams and disappointments. The great difficulties, and in some cases impossibility, of mediating where one partner is unable to let go of the other are discussed further in Chapter 11 on deadlocks and impasse strategies. Mediation can recognise irreconcilable needs and look at hypothetical options, whether agreement can be reached or not. It may be possible to work out interim arrangements. 'Holding arrangements', meaning interim contact or financial arrangements, recognise the reality of a separation without looking for final decisions. Some issues can be left open, at least for a time. Although time does not always bring acceptance, the space between mediation meetings may be helpful. Gradually, the partner who was terrified of letting go may realise that some support is still there and find it possible to contemplate a future beyond the broken relationship.

5.4.8 Feuding couples

Every relationship is likely to consist of two sets of experiences and perceptions. In separation and divorce, partners often recount and reinterpret the history of their relationship in a way that serves to bolster their self-esteem while enlisting other people's support and sympathy. For some people, the experience of loss and the fear of further loss trigger a psychological defence mechanism known as 'splitting', in which what is perceived as 'bad' in a relationship or in the self is split off from the 'good' part. All the 'bad' part is then projected on to the other partner.

Where this splitting leads to reciprocal accusations and counter-accusations, couples can get locked into permanent war. Each partner's self-image and perceptions of the other comes under mutual attack.[14] These couples seem to have a deep emotional need to keep their fight going, despite the destruction it causes. Couples addicted to fighting seem to need the adrenalin they get from fighting and may sabotage any agreement in order to prolong their battles. They want war more than they want settlement. Kressel and colleagues[15] described these couples as 'enmeshed'. Although the potential for settlement may be low in such cases, it is worth exploring, as mediations outcomes are not always predictable. The couple may have reached a stage where they are tiring of the fight and ready to put it behind them. Their anger about the past can be acknowledged and their needs for the future clarified. If there are children involved, their position and feelings need to be discussed. If the parents seem bent on fighting, they can be asked how they see the future for the children, if their battles continue. It may be appropriate to consider involving children or teenagers who have been drawn into their parents' fight and who may be used as a means of perpetuating it.[16]

---

[14] Johnston and Campbell *Impasses of Divorce – the Dynamics and Resolution of Family Conflict* (Free Press, 1988).

[15] Kressel, Jaffee, Tuchman, Watson and Deutsch *Typology of Divorcing Couples* (1980) 19(2) *Family Process* 101–116.

[16] See Chapter 8 below.

Various kinds of impasse strategy can be tried with 'enmeshed' couples before mediation is abandoned.[17] Some of them need an outside person to recognise their intensely mixed feelings of anger and sadness. Being able to say that they wish the other one were dead can be a cathartic experience, especially if they realise the wish is mutual. Some couples who have a very intense relationship show a disconcerting ability to switch suddenly from seething fury to hilarity. If the mediator begins to understand the dynamics of their relationship and the kind of humour that works well for them, humour may be more effective than reasoning and common sense. But when nothing works, it may be necessary for these couples, as well as for the mediator, to recognise that they have come to mediation without actually wanting to agree anything. When this is the case, mediators should not struggle on indefinitely. They must be able to decide when 'enough is enough' and terminate a mediation where no progress can be made or where progress is immediately sabotaged by one or both parties, in an almost triumphant way. Legal advisors can spell things out to battling clients in a way the mediator is unable to do. Referring clients back to their legal advisors is not a sign of failure on the mediator's part. Paradoxically, it can result in them returning to mediation with greater readiness to negotiate.

5.5 TIME MANAGEMENT

'The speed of a harmonic progression, just like the speed of a political process, can determine its effectiveness and ultimately the reality it seeks to influence.'[18]

Barenboim suggests that the Oslo peace process in the conflict between Israel and Palestine was doomed to fail, because of faulty time management. The preparation was much too hasty and the process itself much too slow and frequently interrupted. Mediators need to be very conscious of time and tempo in conducting mediation sessions. They need a clock in their line of vision and may need to draw attention to the passing of time:

'I see we are already halfway through the time for today's appointment. Do you think we should move on to talking about ...?'

Or:

'I'm aware we are running out of time for today's meeting, so shall we use the last quarter of an hour to recap where we have got to and to discuss whether you would like to arrange another meeting?'

---

[17] See Chapter 11 below.
[18] Barenboim *Everything is Connected – The Power of Music* (Weidenfeld and Nicolson, 2008), p 15.

Sessions of an hour and a half are the norm: an hour is usually too short, while two hours of taxing discussions are too long for most separating couples. It is important not to assume that participants want to continue the mediation. If they are doubtful, a provisional appointment can be made with a request to phone by a certain date to confirm or cancel it. It is unwise to ask in the last five minutes: 'Is there anything else either of you wanted to discuss today?' Participants need to know that the time scheduled for the meeting will be kept. Extending the time should be resisted because time boundaries have symbolic as well as practical importance. There are usually unresolved issues to come back to. The mediator may say:

> 'Yes, it really is important that you've mentioned that and it does sound as though it needs full discussion, but unfortunately there isn't enough time left today. Shall we start with this issue next time, if you both think it should have priority?'

Or:

> 'I realise we haven't had time today to cover everything that is concerning you. If there are things you haven't had time to raise yet, or which occur to you when you get home, could you make a note of them, so that you can raise them next time we meet?'

This helps to reduce frustration at the end of a session and encourages participants to reflect between sessions. Many couples come to the second meeting having reflected further: some have met and talked together. The atmosphere in the second session is often strikingly different from the first. The date and time of the following session should be agreed with both participants before they leave. If there is substantial financial information to collect, an interval of a month may be needed. But if the couple is in crisis and the level of conflict is high, it may help to contain the crisis if a meeting is arranged for the following week.

5.6 TASKS AND SKILLS IN THE OPENING STAGES OF MEDIATION

Tasks	Example of use	Aims
Creating a forum and positive atmosphere	Friendly welcome	To put people at ease, enable them to engage in dialogue
Explaining, informing	'Shall I explain how I can help you both deal with this question?'	To help people reach informed decisions and avoid being pressurised into agreement

Tasks	Example of use	Aims
Questioning	Choice of question form, how? what if? etc	To understand the issues better, focus on ways forward
Listening	Mediator's eye contact, facial expression, posture, tone of voice	To show full attention is being given to what is being said
Acknowledging	'I can see that you are finding it hard to ..."	To help people feel heard and understood
Clarifying	'Could you say more about ... explain what you mean by ...'	To check understanding and encourage fuller explanation
Managing conflict without suppressing it	'Could you just let Tony finish and then I'll ask ...'	Controlling interruptions, balancing the discussion
Prioritising	'Which is the most important issue for you at the moment?'	To focus on immediate issues, agree the ordering of issues
Balancing	Putting questions to each participant in turn	To manage power imbalances, maintain impartiality
Building trust	'Could you reassure Sally that you will ...'	To restore or maintain sufficient trust that the other party can be relied on
Managing pace	'Should we spend more time on the question you raised about ...?'	To work at a pace both parties can cope with
Summarising	'Shall we recap on the things you are each going to find out before our next meeting?'	To be clear about the next steps and encourage participants to take charge themselves

5.7 LIMITATIONS OF STAGED MODELS

Although working stage by stage is very useful, it can also have limitations:

- It may be necessary to go back to a previous stage, for example where there is reluctance or hesitation to move forwards.

- Sometimes a couple will benefit from 'fast forwarding', where they both want to run through an outline agreement before considering other possible options.

- Agreement may not be the couple's main goal. There can be other more important goals, such as establishing or re-establishing communication. Kelly found that a substantial proportion of mediation users were pleased with the process although they did not reach agreement, because it brought other benefits.[19]

- Mediators may identify the more concrete or substantive issues and avoid identifying the more difficult emotional or relationship issues which act as blocks to progress.

- A mediator who works too rigidly in stages may drive a couple forward in a direction that neither of them wants. Participants may have needs that they find it hard to express if the mediator moves briskly from one stage to the next.

- Going part of the way is enough for some couples. They may not be ready to go any further. This does not make it a 'failed mediation'.

5.8   CIRCULAR MOVEMENT IN MEDIATION

Some couples move steadily forwards in mediation towards a mutually satisfactory outcome. Others seem more inclined to remain in the past or even to move backwards. They may be so stuck in their failed relationship that they need to keep going over the hurts and wrongs they have suffered. These couples are much harder to work with and they need more skills from the mediator. If they achieve a few steps forward, a real or imagined threat or accusation may be all it takes to throw them backwards again. If the mediator has listed their priorities or objectives on the flipchart at the start of the meeting, the flipchart may be a helpful reminder of where they were hoping to get to: 'Do you think this ties in with what you were wanting for the children, Sam?' or 'Would it help if we have another look at the information you have provided, Naomi, before ruling out that option?'

Forward and backward movements in mediation are very common. These movements are not just linear – very often they are circular, following a familiar – in both senses – circular path. Discussions or accusations may go round and round without getting anywhere – the gerbil wheel problem. Mediators try to help participants to get off their particular gerbil wheel, when they are willing to do so. If the mediator puts a question to each participant in turn, they tend to respond to the mediator, without talking

---

[19]   Kelly 'Mediated and Adversarial Divorce: Respondents' Perceptions of their Processes and Outcomes' (1989) 24 *Mediation Quarterly* 71–88.

to each other. Mediators encourage couples to talk to each other –
sometimes for the first time after a long period of not talking. One way of
facilitating their communication is to ask one of them to explain a
particular concern to the other, rather than to the mediator:

'Philip, it might help if you could explain to Margaret how you see ....'

This approach enables discussions to *converge*, instead of *polarising*. In
the diagram below, the mediator's linear approach shows communication
between the mediator and each partner separately, but not between the
couple themselves. In the converging, circular approach, communication
moves more freely between the participants and the mediator.

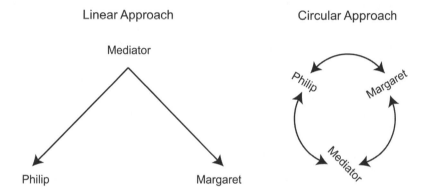

5.9 COMBINING PROCESS MANAGEMENT, INTERPERSONAL AND PROBLEM-SOLVING SKILLS

The table below lists skills that mediators need to combine and use
selectively, depending on the dynamics and level of conflict. Mediators
have different personal styles, as well as different ways of working. Many
mediators are efficient problem-solvers who maintain the pace from one
stage to the next. They may however lose participants if they do not
provide enough warmth and acknowledgement of feelings. Mediators
who have strong interpersonal skills may be less comfortable gathering
financial information and analysing figures. Effective mediators need to
be able to integrate process management, interpersonal and problem-
solving skills and vary the blend for each couple at critical points, to help
manage the 'surface tension effects' referred to in the opening chapter.

Process Skills	Interpersonal Skills	Problem-Solving Skills
Intake assessment	Engaging with participants	Defining issues
Setting up the first session	Active listening	Questioning and exploring
Explaining process and aims	Acknowledging feelings	Prioritising
The Agreement to Mediate	Mutualising concerns	Gathering, giving information
Structuring the process	Managing conflict	Analysing financial information
Maintaining ground-rules	Easing communication	Exploring options
Time management	Focusing on children	Future focus
Referral for professional advice	Managing power imbalances	Brain-storming
Managing pace of negotiations	Reframing	Narrowing gaps and negotiating
Producing written summaries	Reality testing	Anticipating and pre-empting
Concluding process	Ending with care, leaving the door open for re-referral	Seeking proposals for interim/final settlement

CHAPTER 6

LANGUAGE AND COMMUNICATION

'That is not what I meant at all. That is not it, at all'[1]

CONTENTS

6.1   COMMUNICATION

The essence of mediation is communication. Different means of communication therefore need special attention in mediation. There can be language without communication and communication without language. Our perceptions of other people and the outside world are determined by a number of filters, including experience, beliefs and

---

[1]   TS Eliot *The Love Song of J Alfred Prufrock.*

language. Depending on the meanings that are conveyed and the ways in which they are interpreted, language has great power to arouse feelings and evoke images. Words can confuse or clarify, infuriate or soothe. The words we use have layers of associations – personal, cultural, conscious and unconscious. These associations influence the way we see the world around us and condition our responses to people and events. We convey ideas through language and use it to organise our thoughts and shape them into messages. Dysfunctional communication erodes relationships. It is both a cause and effect of relationship breakdown. Couples who come to mediation have frequently become stuck in dysfunctional patterns of communication. They often cannot sustain a dialogue on their own because their arguments are too heavily freighted with emotions and accusations. Simply observing that they have problems communicating with one other can bring a measure of relief for several reasons. First, the mediator's observation shows understanding and empathy, secondly, both partners generally agree with it and thirdly, it recognises a shared problem without implying responsibility or blame. Exchanges between couples in mediation are often part of a familiar script in their personal drama. Both partners know the words of their script and a cue from one of them triggers the replay of an angry scene with the mediator providing a new audience whose sympathy each of them hopes to engage. Mediators need to be good listeners as well as good communicators. They need to listen sensitively with what John Haynes called a 'third ear' to pick up unspoken messages. Timely interventions from the mediator can help to shift the script in a different direction. With the mediator's involvement the dialogue becomes a 'trialogue' in which the mediator elicits responses from both participants and organises their communications in more manageable ways.

6.2   ACTIVE LISTENING AND CENTRED POSTURE

Mediators show that they are listening actively through their posture, facial expression and eye contact, as well as through their words. The mediator's posture needs to convey ease and attentiveness, neither leaning forward intrusively nor too relaxed. The Japanese martial art of Aikido, which is concerned with responding to aggression rather than instigating attack, emphasises the importance of a stable and well balanced posture in dealing with conflict and stress. A well-balanced and centred body position enables the mind to move freely. A mediator who is well centred can keep eye contact with both partners, glancing from one to the other to see how each is reacting and noting their posture and body language. Some mediators make non-committal noises of the 'mm' or 'yes, I see' variety. Others prefer to listen quietly. It is essential to show equal attention and empathy and to avoid giving more attention to one participant than another. Barenboim stresses the importance of listening:[2]

---

[2]   Barenboim 'Everything is Connected – The Power of Music' (Weidenfeld and Nicolson, 2008), p 37.

'Listening is hearing with thought, much in the same way as feeling is emotion with thought.'

6.3 NON-VERBAL COMMUNICATION

Verbal communication may be considered the core of mediation, but non-verbal communication is very significant too. Early research on non-verbal communication found that in a presentation before a group of people, 55% of the impact was determined by body language (posture, gestures and eye contact), 38% by tone of voice and only 7% by the content of the presentation.[3] Mediators need to be alert to participants' body language and aware of non-verbal messages passing between them. Some kinds of body language in mediation need a response from the mediator, whereas others do not need any comment. The mediator's own body language – eye contact, facial expression, gestures, seating position – also conveys messages to participants that the mediator needs to be aware of giving. Hands can be used to emphasise even-handedness and balance, but too much hand movement may be distracting. A warm smile to both participants at an opportune time can help them to feel welcome and more relaxed, whereas a mediator who shows no warmth of expression and only fleeting eye contact is likely to increase the tension in the room. Smiling invites a smile in response. Rapport is created more through body language and tone of voice than by words.

6.4 SILENCE

Silences are common in mediation. Feelings of sadness and understanding are often shared silently between separated couples. Silence is a form of communication and the mediator should not hasten to fill an emotionally charged silence. The silence may be thoughtful or highly emotional. If the atmosphere is thoughtful, more time may be needed for reflection. But if the silence feels threatening, the tension needs to be acknowledged and words found to release it, in order to avoid a damaging explosion during the mediation session or afterwards.

6.5 TENSION, STRESS, SUPPRESSED ANGER

When a mediator notices someone's hands gripping papers tightly or a foot jigging up and down, it is important to acknowledge that experiencing separation is extremely stressful and that mediation seeks to reduce stress, often by taking one step at a time. Arms folded across the chest, hands clenched, legs tightly crossed – these may be defensive positions indicating vulnerability, fear of attack, or suppressed anger. Participants may keep their eyes down and avoid looking at each other.

---

[3] Mehrabian and Ferris 'Inference of Attitudes from Nonverbal Communication in Two Channels' (1967) 31 *Journal of Counselling Psychology* 248–52.

They often turn away from each other. Mediators can help them to feel safer by seeking mutual reassurances that may not be offered spontaneously. If a participant avoids eye contact, constantly looking down at the floor or out of the window, this is a signal that something needs to be done to make the person feel safer or more involved. It is important to ask a question that re-engages the person who has withdrawn and invites eye contact. A sprawling posture, leaning back in the chair with legs stretched, may indicate feelings of superiority, yet mediators should be cautious in interpreting body language. A participant who closes their eyes may be avoiding confrontation, but the closed eyes may mask hidden fears or suppressed anger. Frowning, fierce looks, a pursed or quivering mouth, a hand kept over the face – these expressions need to be noted and responded to, in some way.

6.6   COUPLES WHO ARGUE WITHOUT LISTENING

When couples separate, their arguments are often fast and furious rather than quiet and reflective. Neither may hear what the other is saying, like two humming tops spinning away from each other in a whirl of words. Mediators need to slow them down, providing a structure in which each person can speak and be heard. The whirl of words may be an outlet for energies that the mediator needs to catch and channel more constructively. Many people have difficulty putting feelings into words. It is frequently necessary to seek information and clarify meanings. Words can accumulate layers of meaning that overlay their original significance. Mediators frequently need to seek clarification. When a parent raises a general objection to children having contact with the other parent, it may be helpful to ask for an example:

> 'To help me understand the difficulties when Dave picks up the children, could you give an example of what happened last time he called to pick them up ....'

It is useful to repeat what each partner says, especially when they are upset and angry:

> 'So you are worried that ... and Dave is worried that ....'

Reflecting each participant's position back to them as accurately as possible helps to calm them because it shows they have been heard. These techniques are essential ingredients of mediation. They help to slow the pace of fast-firing arguments. In high conflict situations, the mediator's use of language is particularly important. Strong words need to be used to acknowledge strong feelings, without implying judgments. Unacceptable *behaviour* can be distinguished from the *person* responsible for the behaviour.

6.7   CONFLICTING VERSIONS OF 'THE TRUTH'

Separating couples often become locked in circular arguments about what happened when and who did or said what to whom and who is now giving the 'right' account. Accounts of events are inevitably subjective, clouded by feelings and coloured by values about what is right or wrong, acceptable or unacceptable. Events, experience and perceptions are woven into a kind of tapestry that makes up our picture of the world. An important need in talking with others is to recount experiences in a way that confirms our perceptions and self-image. The very process of recounting experiences alters the way they are relived in the mind and engrained in the memory. With each retelling, the speaker becomes more convinced that the event took place in the way described. When separated couples argue over conflicting versions of the same event, this is more deeply threatening to them than mere differences of recollection. Each partner has an internalised picture that they seek to present to the outside world, but in face-to-face encounters it is confronted and affronted by the other partner's picture. If the confrontation is stark and one picture shatters into fragments, its owner may feel as though their whole self is falling apart. Mediators need to be aware of the extreme vulnerability of people who are struggling to hold on to a fragile sense of identity. Although mediators are not counsellors or therapists, they need to show understanding by acknowledging fears and stress in strong and warm terms. The power of acknowledgement is considerable. It is important, however, not to acknowledge distress in a way that may increase or expose one party's vulnerability to the other.

6.8   ASKING QUESTIONS

Mediators spend a lot of time asking questions. The questions need to be balanced, well focused and sensitively put, neither interrogating people nor asking the kind of questions that a therapist might ask. Researchers[4] found that good questioning by mediators was associated with positive outcomes, whereas mediations that broke down were associated with inadequate questioning techniques. Asking useful questions is a very important skill in mediation. Asking questions helps mediators to avoid making statements, offering opinions or giving answers. It is important for mediators to continue to ask questions, even when they think they know the answer. The same question should be put to both partners in turn as they are likely to give different answers. The order in which each partner is asked a question should alternate. 'Open' questions invite a free-ranging response, but may risk opening the floodgates. 'Closed' and focused questions help mediators to obtain specific information and contain high

---

[4]   Kressel, Butler-DeFreitas, Forlenza and Wilcox 'Research in Contested Custody Mediations' (1989) 24 *Mediation Quarterly* 55–70.

conflict. Unlike Aristotle, mediators do not normally begin by asking 'Why?' Enquiring about causes invites blaming and self-justifying answers that can be very upsetting.

Focused questions help to maintain structure and manage conflict. Many people are extremely nervous when they first come to mediation. An open question, such as 'Could you explain your current situation?' invites them to speak freely. However, it can also put them in the dilemma of not knowing where to begin or end. If one partner launches into a long tirade directed against the other partner, the latter may fear not getting a chance to speak and may lose confidence in the mediator. People are very afraid of losing control and of getting hurt. Some also fear inflicting hurt on each other. Many people find it easier and safer to answer focused questions such as 'Where are you living at the moment?' or 'Was the decision to separate a joint decision?' (rather than 'Why did you split up?), or 'At what time would you like to pick up the children next Saturday?' In this way, the mediator can gather information and identify issues in a systematic way that couples may find less stressful.

Kressel and colleagues[5] found that skilled mediators tended to use an identifiable structure in the type of questions they used and the timing of each question. The structure was rather like a pyramid, with broader information-gathering questions gradually tapering to finely tuned questions, as the mediation progressed. The following examples show how questions can be used to structure the mediation process and to focus attention on the present, the future or the past. Many couples have become locked in the past and need future-focused questions to help them to look forwards instead of backwards. Counsellors and therapists generally believe that some understanding of the past is necessary before beginning to help people to deal with the present and future. Mediators tend to focus on the present and the future, without asking when and how the couple's relationship began to unravel. Quite often, couples refer spontaneously to what each of them sees as the cause of the breakdown, but the mediator's role is not to explore it or make value judgments about what went wrong. Questions that help couples to look forward, rather than backward, are more helpful: 'So, what do you think needs to happen?' 'What would work better?' Future-oriented questions help people to put grievances behind them and to look at how they want the future to be.

6.8.1   Present-focused questions

It is usually necessary to ask about current arrangements in order to understand the present situation. If parents are already separated 'How often are you seeing the children at the moment?' 'What is the usual pattern?' 'How does each of you feel it is working?' It is also important to

---

5   Ibid.

ask about children's relationships with siblings ('How do they get on?' 'Who is closest to whom?') and with other family members. Grandparents often provide a haven of security for children when parents are splitting up. 'Are there other relatives living in the same area?' 'Is there anyone else who is especially important to a child?' The ways in which parents reply to these questions, as well as the content of their answers, shows the mediator how they communicate and whether they listen to each other. It is important to discover whether parents see their children as individuals and whether they are able to separate their children's needs from their own. This is particularly difficult where there is only one child. Sometimes a parent's professed concern about the children is part of a hidden agenda, such as maintaining occupation of the family home. Mediators need to use all their observations – verbal and non-verbal – in formulating further questions.

6.8.2   Past-focused questions

Information about how parenting was managed in the past may be directly relevant to working out parenting arrangements for the present and the future. Although mediators focus forwards, it is helpful in discussing arrangements to understand how children were looked after before their parents separated and to what extent the parents shared parenting tasks and responsibilities.

6.8.3   Examples of past-focused questions

'When you lived together, who looked after the children most of the time?'

'Who usually put the children to bed and got up to see to them during the night?'

'When they started school or nursery, who took and collected them?'

[If both parents were working] 'Who stayed at home when a child was ill?'

'Who took the children to the doctor or dentist?'

'Did you agree about how to discipline the children?'

'Who went to meetings with teachers, helped with homework?'

'Who bought the children's clothes, toys and birthday presents?'

'Was religion an important aspect of bringing up the children?'

'Were decisions about the children generally discussed and agreed, or were they mostly taken by one parent alone? Did you argue over these decisions?'

'Did the children get on well with each other, before you separated? Do they get on well now, most of the time?'

Asking these kinds of questions helps to understand previous patterns of parenting and relationships. It should not be assumed, however, that what worked or did not work before the separation should automatically form the basis for what will work in future. The purpose is to explore whether shared parenting was possible previously so that realistic plans can be made now. It is useful to ask parents whether they have been able to take joint decisions about the children's education, health and religion, distinguishing these major areas of parental responsibility from day-to-day care and the way children's time is shared between parents.

6.9   DIFFERENT TYPES OF QUESTIONS

Type of question	Purpose	Example
Open	Invites a general or free-ranging response	'So what are your main concerns in coming to mediation?'
Closed	Restricts the information that can be given in response. Keeps control of the process	'What type of mortgage do you have?'
Non-directed	Allows either participant to answer	'Could you tell me the present arrangements?'
Directed	Addressed to one party, usually to each in turn	'Have you looked at house prices, Anne ... John, have you had a look yet ...?'
Past-oriented	Gathers information about the past when necessary	'Did you put the money from the flat into buying the house?'
Present-oriented	Clarifies current arrangements	'So how often do you see the children at the moment?'
Future-oriented	Focuses attention forwards	'How would you like this to work next year?'

6.9.1   Thinking about the function of questions

It is important to think about the function of your questions. Mediators may be challenged to explain an apparently irrelevant question – 'Why are you asking that?' Some examples of different types of questions, which may be directed or non-directed, open or closed, include:

Opening questions

To build rapport and clarify each participant's main concerns and aims:

'Could you say what you would like to achieve through coming to mediation?'

Information-seeking questions

'How often do you see the children at the moment?'

'You are explaining that this is a savings account which is earmarked for tax purposes. When do you expect to get the next tax demand?'

Negotiating questions

'What could you do to make it easier ...?'

'What would be workable for you?'

Reality-testing questions

'What would happen if ...?'

'Who will provide the transport each weekend?'

Option development questions

'Are there any other possibilities that either of you can see?'

'Have you considered ...?'

Questions to clarify priorities and facilitate communication

'What is your main priority right now?'

'Could you explain what you want Bill to understand better ...?'

Reflective questions

Put slowly and reflectively, they may open a window that has not been opened before and which may offer a fresh view:

'I wonder what you will both say to the children in x years' time, when they are teenagers and ask you what happened when you split up?'

'If Luisa decides to get married when she is grown up, do you think she would want both of you to be at her wedding?'

If these are useful questions, one can see the response in people's eyes and almost see the thought bubbles above their heads. Sometimes they are a turning point in the mediation.

Hypothetical questions

Hypothetical questions help people to imagine a possible scenario, without being committed to it or feeling trapped. These questions can free people from their current situation, helping them to project themselves into the future and view possibilities, like running a film forwards. They can be asked about the changes they are looking for and then asked about the conditions that would make such changes possible to achieve. Suggestions from the mediator may be 'embedded' in a question, provided they are not put forward as recommended solutions. Hypothetical questions are very useful in exploring options and negotiating towards settlement.

Circular questions

Circular questions are a means of gathering and clarifying information derived from systems theory. It is a technique used in family therapy that may be used in mediation, but not for diagnosis and treatment. Circular questions explore perceptions, relationships and communications between couples and between family members. It is a mode of enquiry designed to make a person pause and think about another person's feelings and needs. Circular questions focus on communications and interactions *between* participants in mediation and *between* them and their children. They broaden the focus of enquiry beyond linear, two-way communications from each participant to the mediator. Circular questions explore *connectedness*, rather than differences between the parties' own views and positions. They are useful because they disrupt habitual cause-and-effect explanations that encourage blaming. Questions that invite someone to explain how they think *another* person – who may or may not be present – may be thinking or feeling about an issue, instead of asking those questioned to say how they *themselves* feel about it, encourage shifts of perspective which can lead to a different understanding or a fresh view. This technique is particularly useful in helping parents consider their children's needs and feelings. If both parents respond by describing a child's feelings or needs in similar terms, the mediator can mutualise their concerns and move on to exploring options or arrangements. If, however, they disagree, further circular questions can be asked about how a child may be showing different feelings to each parent, at different times. Each parent may be asked what they think their child, or children, would say, if they were asked about their feelings, or what they are most anxious about, at the moment.

Circular questions often invite some kind of comparison, such as a before/after comparison or asking what might make something better – or worse – for children. Parents are asked to put themselves in a child's place and see their children as individuals who have feelings and needs of their own, rather than as extensions of each parent. They are helped to compare their perceptions of their children's feelings and reactions, without either parent being seen as right or wrong. Circular questions help participants to look through someone else's eyes – especially, through their children's eyes – and perhaps see things in a different light.

The following table offers examples of the functions of different types of questions. It does not set out to provide a complete list of different questions and their functions.

6.10 FUNCTIONS OF DIFFERENT KINDS OF QUESTIONS

Type of question	Purpose	Example
Clarifying	Seeks more information, encourages a fuller reply	'Could you say a bit more about ...?'
Reality testing	Helps people to explain their proposals in concrete terms	'How would you see this working in practice ...?'
Summarising	Punctuates, gives a focus	'So have I understood that the main question for you now is ...?'
Strategic	To change direction or side-step an argument	'Is it possible to put this on one side for a moment and look at ...?'
Reflective	To encourage thought, to offer another perspective	'I wonder whether it would be useful to talk about ...'
Hypothetical	Allows exploration without asking people to commit themselves	'Jane, if you decided to work full time, would you need more help with childcare?'
Circular	Helps understand perceptions and relationships in families	'If Billy were here and you asked him what his main concern is at the moment, what would Billy say?'

6.11 FILTERING OUT NEGATIVES

Couples often talk at cross-purposes – sometimes at very cross-purposes – and often denigrate each other: 'Trevor is useless ... Judy can't be trusted'. As Fisher and Ury emphasise, it is important to separate the people from the problem.[6] Mediators need to show respect and empathy, using positive language as far as possible. Asking one partner to give a recent example to explain a particular difficulty seeks specific information about the problem, instead of a global judgment of the person. A specific incident can illustrate the problem in concrete terms. The other partner can then fill in further details ('but what I actually meant was ...'). Explanations often change perceptions of a particular incident and may begin to question the image of the other person.

When couples are in conflict, it is helpful to use positive language in talking about 'your plans (or arrangements) for the future' instead of repeating words like 'dispute' and 'disagree'. A verbal message can defuse or heighten conflict. Separating parents are very sensitive to language. For example, it helps to talk about *their concerns for their children*, rather than *disagreements over the children*, and about *child support*, rather than *maintenance*. Mediators should avoid using the term 'absent parent' because it can imply that a parent has chosen to abandon the family. Similarly, the term 'one-parent family' is judgmental and hurtful, because it implies that there is only one parent. Mediators include both parents by saying 'both of you, as parents ...', 'the family as a whole', 'to help both of you and the children', 'to make things easier for all of you', to show that they are concerned to help children *and* parents. Family mediation is not confined to helping adults settle adult issues. It may be stating the obvious but nonetheless worthwhile to observe that 'the separation [divorce] ends your relationship [marriage], but you are still parents. The family may be changing but it still exists'. It is helpful for parents to realise that there are many positive aspects of family life and relationships that need to continue after they separate. The questions are about what needs to continue, as well as about what needs to end.

Mediators tend to filter out accusatory words and judgmental labels. For example, if a mother says about the father 'He doesn't care what the children eat', a mediator would avoid repeating the words 'doesn't care' in asking 'So is the kind of food the children eat when they are with their father one of the things you would like to discuss here today?' Sometimes mediators risk giving offence because they neutralise too much. People can feel unheard or devalued if a mediator rephrases a powerful emotional statement so weakly that it loses its force. Mediators need to use strong words in a non-judgmental way. If a mother says: 'I get mad when he (the father) does whatever his mother tells him to do', she is likely to get more angry if the mediator says: 'So you feel a bit annoyed', because 'annoyed' is not an adequate substitute for 'getting mad'. At the other end of the scale of emotions, the word 'happy' may be used insensitively. In training role-plays, mediators often say: 'So you would be happy with Len having the children every other weekend?' Couples who are separating may experience relief, but they are hardly ever happy. It is

---

6   Fisher and Ury *Getting to Yes* (Penguin Books, 1983).

more acceptable for the mediator to ask: 'So you are saying that it would be all right with you for the children to go to Len every other weekend?'

6.12 USING STRAIGHTFORWARD LANGUAGE

When people are stressed, their ability to absorb information is limited. Plain language is easier to understand. We all have habitual ways of expressing ourselves and we need to listen to ourselves in order to hear how we sound to other people. People who are angry and distressed are easily confused by long sentences or specialist terminology from law or psychology. The way we talk is influenced by our family background, education, friends and leisure activities, as well as by the work we do. Speech varies according to cultural background and social class. People from different regions or social backgrounds may find it difficult to understand professional language and manner of speech. Mediators should watch out for bemused expressions on people's faces.

Couples in mediation may not be from the same culture as the mediator. English may be their second language or a language they use with difficulty. Using ordinary language helps them to understand and to feel that they are being treated as equals. There is usually no need to use legal terminology. When legal terms are necessary, some explanation or commentary is often very helpful. Mediation, like other disciplines, tends to develop its own specialist vocabulary. Mediators talk about 'caucusing', 'empowering' and 'mutualising'. This kind of jargon can mystify a process that should be transparent. We should be able to explain mediation clearly enough for a child of five to understand what it means.

6.13 LANGUAGE OR HEARING DIFFICULTIES

Participants who have a different first language may need a mediator who speaks their own language. However, multi-lingual mediators are scarce. Similarly, where one or both partners have hearing problems, they may need a mediator who can sign for them or a specialist worker with the deaf. Interpreters and specialists who join in mediation need to be equally acceptable to all participants and need a good understanding of the mediation process. There should be prior consultation to ensure that all participants will feel comfortable with the proposed specialist helper. If this person is already known to one of them, there may be an actual or perceived bias and the other partner may not trust their impartiality. It is also difficult when the mediator cannot check the accuracy of the translation. An interpreter may fail to convey the mediator's exact words, or nuances of language and feeling. An interpreter would need briefing on the mediation process, confidentiality and the tasks involved. The same applies if a specialist in signing for the deaf is needed or because of some other kind of language disability. It is essential to address questions of balance and impartiality, the specialist role of helpers and their effect on the process and its outcome.

6.14   GENDER CONDITIONING IN THE USE OF LANGUAGE

Although gender stereotypes oversimplify differences and may be misleading, linguistic studies suggest that men and women tend to use different modes or styles of speech because of cultural conditioning.[7] When feelings between a couple are running high, it is easy for one partner to misinterpret what the other partner is saying or to be annoyed by the way it is said. Many arguments are based on misunderstandings or different perceptions, rather than on actual disagreements. Men may be more comfortable talking about activities and practicalities and may find it hard to talk about feelings. Women, on the other hand, often discuss relationships and share their feelings more readily with each other. Men who find emotions too intense to deal with may withdraw. The more one partner withdraws, the more agitated the other one is likely to become and frustration can boil over. Mediators may be able to draw off some of the steam by commenting on the pattern they have just observed in a way that is empathetic to both partners:

> 'When it is hard to talk, it makes everything harder for both of you. May I check that I have understood the main concerns for each of you? Sandra, you were saying that … and Gordon, you were saying that ….'

Some couples have got into a habit of talking loudly whenever they disagree. They may have got used to shouting at each other, or there may be a pattern in which one partner turns up the volume and the other one switches off. Mediators see these patterns in action. When one partner seems to be blocking out while the other one is shouting with increasing desperation, the mediator may pick up the message and repeat it in a quiet, unthreatening tone. The blocking partner may be receptive to the mediator's quiet voice. The louder partner, seeing this, may turn down the volume.

6.15   ONE-UPMANSHIP

There may be problems in mediation when one partner has more knowledge than the other or more familiarity with professional or technical terms that are relevant to the mediation. The other partner who does not know these terms tends to feel inadequate and left out. A wife who has not had a career of her own may feel disadvantaged when the mediator asks the husband about his financial affairs. Although the wife realises that these questions need to be asked, she may not understand the

---

[7]   Tannen *That's Not What I Meant* (Virago, 1992).

questions or the answers. She may be afraid of losing face, if she reveals her ignorance. This can happen equally in reverse, where the wife manages the family finances or has a more high-powered career than her husband. When one partner uses technical terms to impress the mediator, the mediator needs to recognise the power game that is being played, continue to use plain language and make sure the other partner feels involved in the discussion.[8]

6.16 ENCOURAGING PEOPLE TO SPEAK FOR THEMSELVES

Angry couples sometimes talk about each other in the third person, even when the other one is present in the room: 'The problem with Jemima/Jeremy is that she/he ...' Or they may even refer to each other in a distant and patronising way as 'Mr Smith' or 'Mrs Smith', as though the other person had been married to someone else. Mediators seek to change these unhelpful tendencies by encouraging participants to speak for themselves and explain what they need, using the first person 'What I am looking for ... I would really like it if ...', instead of telling the other person what he or she ought to do, using the third person.

6.17 ACTING AS REFEREE, KEEPING THE GROUND-RULES

Couples in conflict often try to score points against each other. If one party is taking all the air space, the mediator may need to interrupt, as constructively as possible:

> 'George, let me stop you there. If I've understood you, you are saying that ... and Celia, you said just before that ...?'

The mediator needs to show that both parties are getting equal attention and that neither will be allowed to dominate the discussion. Balancing and rebalancing can be done through maintaining equal eye contact, giving time to each party, proposing and enforcing ground-rules. If one party uses offensive or threatening language, the mediator needs to be firm and confident enough to make it clear that this has to stop, if the mediation is to continue.

6.18 REPEATING AND SUMMARISING

Repeating what each person has said, using the words they have used, is important in mediation for several reasons:

---

[8] See also Chapter 10.

- It shows that you are listening carefully and that you want to understand.

- It gives each person an opportunity to confirm or to correct you, if necessary.

- It slows things down, if the argument is running too fast.

- Although words are repeated, the mediator's tone of voice may change the climate.

- A different tone of voice may enable the other party to hear.

- Repeating can give strong reinforcement to a positive statement or joint concern.

- A short summary helps to take stock and plan the next step.

Mediators may need to rephrase rather than repeat, because repeating an accusation might suggest that the mediator agrees with it.

6.19   THE MEDIATOR AS INTERPRETER

A separated wife wrote on her referral form before the first mediation meeting:

> 'Matthew and I need to rebuild our lives. There are bound to be parts we disagree on. We sometimes don't speak the same language and a third party may be able to interpret what one or both of us are saying to each other.'

An interpreter seeks to translate as accurately as possible to convey the essential meaning of what has been said. Mediators may translate for couples who have difficulty understanding each other. The same message spoken by a third person who is not emotionally involved can be heard differently. As well as repeating statements, the mediator may need to rephrase them so that the speaker feels heard and understood. At the same time, the mediator is helping the other party to listen and understand. The listener may then respond positively, instead of aggressively. When the mediator substitutes different words, it is important to check with the original speaker that the meaning or message is being conveyed accurately.

6.20   FRAMING AND REFRAMING

We construct our reality out of a mixture of perceptions, beliefs, interpretations of past experience, hopes and fears for the future. It is not surprising that separating couples present inconsistent and contradictory pictures of the same situation or same incident. Each of them has constructed a 'frame', a kind of filter through which they perceive their world as they see it. These 'frames' are used to define reactions and responses, even when they produce self-defeating results. Neither 'frame' is right or wrong: each has its own validity. But as long as separating couples argue about whose view is right or wrong, they will fail to make progress in working towards agreed solutions. In listening, clarifying and summarising, mediators show that they are interested in and accept these contradictory pictures, without preferring one picture over another or making judgments about them. In the early stages of mediation, each participant often portrays the other in a negative light. Explanations may be given in blaming or accusatory terms. The challenge for mediators is to re-phrase accusatory statements in a way that fits the picture, yet puts another frame around it so that it may be seen from a different perspective. (For further discussion of 'frames' and their use in Neuro Linguistic Programming (NLP) and mediation, see Chapter 11 at **11.2**).

Offering a different perspective may enable a view to be seen in a different light. Thus, when a mediator re-frames a perspective, this can help to modify attitudes without the mediator being directive or judgmental. Reframing involves rephrasing statements or ideas to offer a different way of understanding them, without substituting a new meaning belonging to the mediator. It can be used to shift the focus from one parent's opinion of the other parent to their joint concerns for their children. Regular reframing keeps the children in the forefront of the parents' attention. It is not uncommon for parents then to repeat the language and expressions the mediator has used. Reframing requires sensitivity and skills. It may involve changes of words and syntax, to help switch the energy flow from negative to positive. Timing is important, with careful attention to the impact on both parties.

6.21 HOW DOES POSITIVE REFRAMING WORK?

(1) It puts a word or statement in a different way: a particular facet is turned to catch a different light. The intention is to clarify and ease the communication between the two parties, not to impose the mediator's own personal view. One way to do this is to ask a question instead of making a comment, to check that the speaker's underlying concern or objective has been understood. If this is not so, their correction provides clarification. If, on the other hand, the re-frame is accurate and sensitive, there is an affirmative response, usually in the form of an appreciative nod and eye contact.

(2) If negative words and phrases are repeated, the repetition gives them added weight and reinforcement. A positive reframe does not blame, accuse or denigrate anyone.

(3)   Positive reframing assumes good motives. People can be given the benefit of the doubt, until they provide further evidence of having only destructive motives. Offering a positive explanation for a negative position helps people feel better. They are often aware of behaving badly. Being offered some form of validation helps restore the self-esteem that is often extremely low during the process of separation and divorce.

A positive reframe picks up underlying concerns that may be hidden underneath angry or defensive reactions. If the mediator expresses these as mutual concerns, shared by both parents, common ground between them can be opened up and explored.

(4)   A reframe addressed to one party needs to be balanced by a parallel re-frame or acknowledgment to the other. It is very important to balance and mutualise – to identify common ground and common concerns, even when focusing on one party's statements.

(5)   Especially when there is a high level of emotion or tension, reframing in a calm, reflective way lowers the emotional temperature. Active listening becomes easier. Reframing may be used as a step towards other questions that need to be explored.

6.21.1   The pace and timing of reframing

Inexperienced mediators tend to miss cues for reframing and lose valuable opportunities to intervene at a critical moment. If these opportunities are missed repeatedly, conflict may escalate and both parties may lose confidence in the mediator's ability to contain it. On the other hand, a reframe that is slid in too quickly and glibly may not help. It must not come across in a patronising way, nor diminish the importance of the speaker's original statement. Reframing is not a technique used in isolation: it is part of a process in which each intervention by the mediator must be made with care and lead to the next step.

6.22   MESSAGES AND METAMESSAGES

Some couples do not fight openly. They give each other coded messages. Mediators need to develop the skill of 'third ear listening' to pick up and decode these coded messages. A 'metamessage' is an underlying message conveying information about feelings, relationships and attitudes. The underlying message may contradict what is being said overtly. Coded messages or 'metamessages' may be subtle and more wounding than an outright attack, especially if they undermine the other partner through sarcasm or ridicule. Coded messages may be attempts to draw the mediator into an alliance, sometimes using apparently innocuous words to convey a message that the other party is unreasonable, stupid or ridiculous.

6.23 PUNCTUATION

Mediators need to orchestrate discussions and manage the tempo. It is useful to have a concept of 'punctuation' – underlining, putting a full stop, beginning a new paragraph. Structure can be maintained by marking the end of each step before going on to the next one. The mediator needs to be pro-active – not just reactive – in managing structure and pace.

Punctuation helps to:

• keep participants on track;

• draw a line under a particular discussion;

• emphasise progress and reinforce co-operation;

• mark stages of the process;

• plan the next stage or steps.

Punctuation is usually verbal, but the flipchart can be used as a visual tool to structure discussions and to help participants draw a temporary line under one issue and move on to the next one.

6.24 IMAGES AND METAPHORS

Arguments are often repetitive and the same words are used over and over again. A metaphor may change the pattern and convey in a vivid way something that might otherwise involve lengthy explanation. Metaphors catch the imagination and increase awareness. But there are also dangers: an inappropriate metaphor can be patronising, insensitive or just ridiculous. It is useful for mediators to think about the particular metaphors or images they can use naturally in the course of discussions. The following suggestions include some obvious metaphors that come into the category of overworked clichés. Others may prompt mediators to invent metaphors of their own. An unexpected metaphor may sow the seeds of an idea that takes root gradually.

6.24.1 Territory, middle ground

Mediation is often described as 'finding the middle ground'. Mediation meetings take place on neutral territory and mediators help participants find common ground that is firm and safe to build on. Mediators often talk about establishing some ground on which separated parents feel able to work together, or about building foundations for future co-operation, or about defining the boundaries for difficult discussions or the practical limits of contact or financial arrangements.

6.24.2 Journeys

There are likewise many obvious metaphors about roads and pathways, travelling forwards, choice of route, roads leading in different directions, crossroads, roadblocks and the need for signposts. Different options may be presented pictorially on the flipchart as different ways forward involving decisions that can be taken at different stages. Some situations seem to have no way out, but identifying all available routes and brainstorming possible options may open up a way forward. Are both partners aiming to reach an ultimate destination or a short-term one?

6.24.3 Bridges

Even burnt bridges may continue to exist in the mind. Mediation is a bridge which participants approach from either side. It can require great effort, and some hope for the future, to venture on to the bridge at all. Some people move on to it readily without needing much support, whereas others need encouragement and support before they can venture on to the bridge and trust it enough to take a few steps. In engineering terms, a cantilevered bridge rests on foundations built from each bank. People using the mediation bridge want to know if there is adequate support. The mediator is responsible for seeing that the bridge is adequately constructed, with sound supports both in emotional and practical terms. Those who are reluctant to let go of the past may be helped in mediation to take some steps on this bridge, towards a future that may feel very uncertain. In concrete terms, the bridge may consist of a period of financial support. Metaphorically, mediation discussions are a bridge that spans a gulf between conflicting views and needs. Bridges are needed between parents and children, as well as between the parents themselves. A parent who has lost all contact with a child or adolescent may feel completely rejected and cut off. This parent may need encouragement to go more than halfway across the bridge – writing or phoning regularly, even where there is no response. The child needs to see the parent's commitment to keeping the bridge in place, possibly over a long time, and may eventually feel able to respond. In stuck situations where a child is refusing to see the other parent, it may help to talk about keeping the bridge open and letting the child know that the bridge is still open.

The administrator at The Mediation Centre in Stafford uses the metaphor of stepping-stones to encourage doubtful people to come to an information meeting and try mediation:

> 'You can take just the first step and see if the next one looks safe enough. If it doesn't, you can always step back again.'

6.24.4   Elastic

Mundane objects can also be used as metaphors. Everyone knows how useful elastic is. It stretches and gives and retains its shape. But if elastic is stretched too hard or for too long, it begins to sag. A child's resilience is like elastic. Some children maintain their resilience and normal development, despite being pulled between conflicting feelings or forces. Others become vulnerable to pressures that are so great or prolonged that they lose their resilience and capacity to adapt. Parents may become more understanding of a child who is struggling to cope with major changes if they think of the child like a piece of elastic that has great resilience, provided it is not stretched too hard or for too long. Elastic is constructed from a number of small threads that are bound together. When several threads give way, there is little elasticity left. In the same way, most parents and children rely on a number of special bonds with other people. If these bonds (with a partner, parent, grandparents or friends) are suddenly cut, the whole structure may collapse. It is then very important to consider how additional supports can be provided, even temporarily, to maintain existing bonds.

The psychiatrist, Michael Rutter (1985) emphasised that stress is normal and that learning to cope with stressful situations can be strengthening.[9] Resilience is not achieved by avoiding stress, but by dealing with it in a way that increases self-confidence and competence. This may involve taking responsibility for one's own reactions to a stressful situation, instead of blaming others for causing it. Resilience is influenced by many factors, including temperament, personal strengths, early life experiences, events in later childhood and adolescence, 'buffering factors' such as family support and the ability to form close relationships. None of these alone determines the response to a major life change but, woven together, they can create a fabric that is elastic, rather than brittle.

6.24.5   Jigsaw puzzles

Arrangements for children and related financial and housing matters are like interlocking pieces of a jigsaw puzzle. Jigsaw puzzles are a useful source of metaphors when mediating with separated couples on all issues – children, finance and property. It is important to acknowledge that many people feel overwhelmed in trying to deal with so much at once, especially when they are extremely stressed. Comparing the complexity of their problems to doing a jigsaw puzzle might be insensitive and appear to trivialise the profound seriousness of their situation, if such a comparison were made without sufficient empathy and understanding. However, recognition that different elements of family re-organisation need to fit together, if they are to work in practice, can help to reduce anxiety. The

---

9   Rutter 'Resilience in the Face of Adversity' (1985) 147 *British Journal of Psychiatry* 598–611.

mediator can point out that just as a puzzle cannot be completed until missing pieces are to hand, in the same way it is necessary to collect further financial information and valuations. Independent financial advice may be needed. Participants are helped to prioritise in planning a step-by-step approach in which missing pieces are identified and gradually slotted into the picture. Doing a jigsaw puzzle involves picking up pieces that look as though they might fit together. If they do not fit, they have to be put aside while the search continues for the right piece. This is like exploring options in mediation:

> 'Working out a settlement has different parts that need to fit together – the children and the home and money. It's a bit like doing a jigsaw. If there are pieces that don't fit, we need to look for other ways.'

Some people like to start a jigsaw by doing one corner, while others prefer to do the outside edges before filling in the centre:

> 'Where would you like to start – by discussing the outline of what you are looking for, or is there one particular area that is a priority for you?'

A seemingly impossible situation may appear more manageable, if it is approached bit by bit. Jigsaw puzzles provide a homely and reassuring metaphor for a step-by-step approach, rather than expecting an immediate global solution.

6.24.6 Doors and keys

Finding the key to a problem is a common metaphor. Overworked though it is, the image of a key may help people shift into a problem-solving mode. When they are asked what they see as a key to solving the problem, it is surprising how often they come up with a useful suggestion. Could there be more than one key that would fit the lock?

6.24.7 Trees

Mediators who respond to a dispute about property by talking about trees risk rapid dismissal. Metaphors need to be appropriate and used with care. The concept of a sheltered place, protected from the hurly-burly of everyday life, is, however, fundamental in mediation. In the Camp David talks, Jimmy Carter invited President Sadat of Egypt and Prime Minister Begin of Israel to meet with him in a garden, away from the press and the outside world. He described the garden as:[10]

> 'sheltered by a thick growth of stately oak, poplar, ash, locust, hickory and maple trees ... [in] an atmosphere of both isolation and intimacy, conducive to easing tension and encouraging informality.'

---

[10]   Carter *Keeping Faith: Memoirs of a President* (Bantam Books, 1982), p 324.

At Camp David, Jimmy Carter mediated a peace agreement between Egypt and Israel.

6.24.8 Water and rivers

Metaphors about water offer an abundance of images. Water symbolises movement and change. It can flow fast or gently, or it can be still. Still water may stagnate, but sudden change is like a tide that sweeps people along on currents they feel unable to control. Being swept along is a very frightening experience. Mediators can help make the currents more manageable, recognising the fear of being swept along and noticing when, where and how the current flows fastest. Even those who seem in relatively calm waters can hit rocks or rapids. Asking participants if they foresee some rocks further downstream may help them anticipate and steer clear of future difficulties. The image may also help to strengthen their confidence in their joint ability to steer and keep control.

The process of mediation itself can be compared to water. Water can penetrate small crannies and trickle down. A trickle of water seems insignificant, yet it has the power to crack a block of stone. New ideas, proposals and changes often need to be absorbed gradually, rather than being injected by force. Encouraging people to consider and accept changes by degrees, rather than all at once, is a useful approach in facilitating children's adjustment to change, as well as the adjustments adults need to make. Water reflects light. Reflecting means thinking. Thinking may throw some light on a dark area, whereas the inability to see ahead in darkness causes panic. Although light does not necessarily provide answers to problems, light, like water, can filter through narrow chinks. It can illuminate the process of exploring problems. Reflections may be projected – thrown forwards – from one surface or angle to another and be seen in a different light.

Capacity to change is affected by the ambient temperature. Cold or frozen materials are very brittle. They snap under pressure. Water frozen into ice splinters and cracks, whereas boiling water is too hot to touch and evaporates as steam. Mediators need to register temperature, like a thermometer. If the temperature is too hot, it needs to be cooled in a careful and considerate way, before changes are looked at and discussed. When it seems very cold or frozen, mediators need to offer warmth and understanding, acknowledging fears and easing painful discussion. Warmth makes feel people more comfortable. It also increases pliancy and flexibility.

The importance of language, imagery and non-verbal communication in mediation cannot be overestimated. Even small differences in the angling of a question or the tone of a reflection may affect surface tensions. Managing surface tensions can facilitate change at a deeper level. The language/s that mediators use, verbally and non-verbally, and their tone and pace may have a significant influence in the process of mediation and its outcome.

'When the imagination sleeps, words are emptied of their meaning.'[11]

---

[11]   Camus *Resistance, Rebellion and Death* (1960).

CHAPTER 7

CHILD-FOCUSED MEDIATION

'I think when parents get divorced, they both have special responsibility towards their children'[1]

'Families have to care for each other or it doesn't work'[2]

CONTENTS

7.1   CHILDREN AND SEPARATION

On current trends, at least one in four children under the age of sixteen will experience their parents' divorce. Most children go through a period of unhappiness and insecurity when their parents separate, but provided they receive enough support and reassurance, the majority are able to settle back into a normal pattern of development.[3] Lund's study of thirty families two years after separation found that they fell into three groups: co-operative co-parent families, conflicted two-parent families and

---

[1]   Lulu, aged 8, quoted by Krementz *How It Feels When Parents Divorce* (Gollancz, 1985).
[2]   Rosie, aged 9, quoted by Neale and Wade *Parent Problems – children's views on life when parents split up* (Young Voice, 2000).
[3]   Rodgers and Prior *Divorce and separation: the outcomes for children* (Joseph Rowntree Foundation, 1998); and Dunn and Deater-Deckard 'Children's Views of their Changing Families' (2001) *Joseph Rowntree Research Findings* 931.

absent-father (or mother) families.[4] Many studies[5] have shown that when separated parents are able to co-operate with each other in continued joint parenting, children's adjustment is greatly eased. 70% of non-resident fathers in one study were found to be in contact with their children,[6] but the remaining 30% are likely to lose contact within two years of separation.[7] The Exeter study[8] found that half the children without reliable contact did not know where their non-resident parent was living. Parental separation is a process rather than an event, beginning before one parent actually leaves the home and continuing long afterwards. Children may feel the impact of separation throughout their childhood, but their experiences and reactions vary greatly. The quality of the child's relationship with each parent and the parents' relationship with each other are major influences in the child's adjustment.[9] A review of over two hundred research studies found that although the absence of a parent-figure is not the most influential factor in a child's development, two key factors in the child's adjustment to parental separation are continuing contact and good communication between the child and both parents.[10]

Strong and reliable attachments buttress a child's ability to cope with change. It cannot be assumed, however, that all children are alike and that they all need or want the same things. Smart and Neale found that in some families, boys were happy with arrangements that did not suit their sisters, while some older siblings were unhappy with arrangements that worked well for younger siblings.[11] Multiple factors play a part, including the resilience of the individual child. Following parental separation, a minority of children do not fare well. Some of them experience lasting problems that continue into adulthood. Factors associated with increased risk of poor outcomes for children are high levels of parental distress, financial hardship and multiple changes in family structure. In the Exeter study,[12] children who had experienced separation and divorce were more

---

[4]   Lund 'Research on divorce and children' [1984] 14 Fam Law 198–201.

[5]   See, for example, Wallerstein and Kelly *Surviving the Break-up – how children and parents cope with divorce* (Grant McIntyre, 1980); Johnston and Campbell *Impasses of Divorce – the Dynamics and Resolution of Family Conflict* (Free Press, 1988); Hetherington and Clingempel 'Coping with Marital Transitions – A Family Systems Perspective' (1992) 227 *Society for Research in Child Development* 57.

[6]   Lewis, Papacosta and Warin 'Cohabitation, separation and fatherhood' (2002) *Joseph Rowntree Foundation Findings* 552.

[7]   Trinder, Beek and Connolly 'Making contact: How parents and children negotiate and experience contact after divorce' (2002) *Joseph Rowntree Foundation Findings* 092.

[8]   Cockett and Tripp *The Exeter Family Study: Family Breakdown and its impact on children* (University of Exeter Press, 1994).

[9]   Hawthorne, Jessop, Pryor and Richards 'Supporting children through family change' (2003) *Joseph Rowntree Foundation Findings* 323.

[10] Rodgers and Prior *Divorce and separation: the outcomes for children* (Joseph Rowntree Foundation, 1998).

[11] Smart and Neale 'It's My Life Too – Children's Perspectives on Post-Divorce Parenting' [2000] Fam Law 163–169.

[12] Cockett and Tripp *The Exeter Family Study: Family Breakdown and its impact on children* (University of Exeter Press, 1994).

likely than children in 'intact' families to have health problems (especially psychosomatic disorders), to need extra help at school, to lack friends and to suffer from low self-esteem. The most significant factor seemed to be the amount of physical and emotional upheaval they experienced. Those who experienced three or more different family structures were likely to describe themselves as 'often unhappy' or 'miserable'. Divorced parents who took part in the Exeter study admitted that they had known little about the process of divorce and how to organise post-divorce parenting. Many were aware of their reduced ability to communicate with each other and to make sensible decisions in the early stages of separation, when they were under particular stress. In response to a widely felt need for information and advice, the provision of Parenting Information Programmes (PIPs) has been welcomed by many separated parents struggling to make arrangements for their children.

7.2 PARENTING INFORMATION PROGRAMMES (PIPS)

Under a section of the Children and Adoption Act 2006 brought into effect on 8 December 2008, the court may embody a direction or condition in a contact order that the parents should attend a Parenting Information Programme (PIP). Very little resistance has been met from parents when it is explained to them that it is not their parenting that will be addressed, but their relationship with the other parent as 'parents apart'.[13] Some courts with high referral rates to PIPs are finding high levels of satisfaction even among parents who had been engaged in 'trench warfare'. In New Zealand, attendance at a PIP is a mandatory pre-requirement before court proceedings. For the 10% of divorcing parents who take disputes over children's residence or contact to court, the combination of referral to a PIP with mediation information and assessment meetings could help them to agree arrangements for their children and avoid litigation. Parents have reported that attendance at a PIP had changed their behaviour or that of their ex-partner in a variety of ways, including listening more to their children and jointly attempting to avoid conflict and confrontation in front of them.[14]

7.3 PARENTAL CONFLICT AND CHILDREN'S ADJUSTMENT

Continuing parental conflict seems to be a consistent predictor of increased psychological difficulties for children of separated – as well as cohabiting – parents. Continuing high conflict between parents shows significant associations with children's behaviour problems, somatic and

---

[13] Dancey 'Contact Activities: Parenting Information Programmes' [2010] Fam Law 1101–1105.

[14] [2010] Fam Law 1238.

psychosomatic symptoms, underachievement at school and low self-esteem.[15] Conflict is a normal part of family life. What matters is how parents deal with it. American researchers found that children whose father was verbally aggressive towards their mother showed more behavioural problems and had lower self-esteem.[16] Mothers who were verbally aggressive towards the father tended to have poorer relationships with their children. These children were often solitary and played alone. When parents were able to co-operate, the children showed better psychological adjustment and lower levels of aggression. Conflict generally diminishes within a few years of separation but when parents remain in high conflict, life for their children 'often continues to be lived in the middle of a war zone'.[17]

Adults often underestimate children's capacity to understand feelings and relationships. Parents who think a child is too young to understand what is happening may be seeking to protect themselves, rather than the child. Although children's reactions to separation do not necessarily correspond to their chronological age, it is important for those working with parents to have knowledge of child and adolescent development. It is equally important to seek to understand the individual personality of each child and the family's culture, history and circumstances. When children are struggling and not getting enough support, they often show their distress in behaviour, rather than words. The way they show their feelings may cause further difficulties, because the parents tend to interpret the behaviour differently and give different meanings to it. Each parent then blames the other for causing the problems. The following summary lists reactions among children in a study of sixty families in California who were going through divorce.[18] There were 131 children in the study group and the follow-up continued over a five-year period. The group was not representative of divorcing families generally and the findings should not be generalised to all children experiencing parental divorce. However, where parents continue to be very distressed and/or caught up in prolonged disputes, their children are more likely to show negative reactions and these are the parents and children most likely to need professional help. Contrary to widely held views, boys are not more

[15] Emery *The Truth about Children and Divorce* (Viking, 2004); Johnston and Roseby *In the Name of the Child: a developmental approach to understanding and helping children of conflicted and violent divorce* (Free Press, 1997).
[16] Camara and Resnick 'Marital and parental sub-systems in mother-custody, father-custody and two-parent households: effects on children's social development' (1987) in J Vincent (ed) *Advances in family assessment, intervention and research* (Greenwich), Vol 4, 165–196.
[17] Trinder 'Conciliation, the Private Law Programme and Children's Well-being' [2008] Fam Law 338 at 341.
[18] Wallerstein and Kelly *Surviving the Break-up – how children and parents cope with divorce* (Grant McIntyre, 1980).

adversely affected than girls and the age at which children experience separation is not in itself important.[19]

7.4   POSSIBLE REACTIONS AT DIFFERENT AGES

7.4.1   Pre-school children (2–5 years)

• Confusion, anxiety and fear – young children may be very confused about the changes in their family life, if parents are unable to explain the changes to children of this age.

• Strong reconciliation fantasies – children cling to hopes that their parents will get back together again. They may make up fantasies to comfort themselves.

• Increased aggression – the children's anger often stems from their feelings of loss and rejection. Their sense of loss when one parent disappears from their lives, often unaccountably, may lead to aggressive behaviour towards siblings, parents and in school. The remaining parent may be so preoccupied that the child receives less attention from this parent as well, increasing the sense of loss and rejection.

• Guilt feelings – young children may imagine that they are to blame for their parents not getting on together. They may assume that their own naughtiness was the reason for a parent leaving them.

• Regression – children may demonstrate their anxiety and insecurity by lapses in toilet training, reverting to bed-wetting, showing increased clinging behaviour.

• Increased fears – of the dark, for example – or developing feeding problems. Parents who are already strained may find these behaviour problems very hard to understand and tolerate.

7.4.2   Primary school age (5–7 years)

• Pervasive sadness and grieving – this may be related to the level of turmoil in the home, but many children feel intensely sad even when the parent they live with is not sad.

• Yearning for an absent parent – similar to grieving for a dead parent, but with greater feelings of rejection.

---

[19] Rodgers and Prior *Divorce and separation: the outcomes for children* (Joseph Rowntree Foundation, 1998).

- Feelings of abandonment and fear – there are often fears of being forgotten and of losing the remaining parent as well.

- Anger – children often direct their anger at the parent they hold responsible for the breakdown.

- Conflicts of loyalty – a child who feels pulled between parents often does not know how to be loyal to both of them.

- Worry about parents' ability to cope – the more the child experiences a parent's problems in coping with separation, the more the child fears that the parent is no longer going to be able to care for them.

- Reconciliation fantasies.

7.4.3   Middle school (8–12 years)

- Children at this stage are more aware of the causes and consequences of separation and more likely to take sides in parental conflicts.

- May have profound feelings of loss, rejection, helplessness and loneliness.

- May feel shame, moral indignation and outrage at their parents' behaviour.

- May show extreme anger, temper tantrums, demanding behaviour, or fears, phobias and denial.

- Increased psychosomatic complaints – headaches, stomachaches, sleep disorders.

- Making judgments: identifying one parent as the good parent and the other parent as the bad parent; rejecting the 'bad parent'.

- Forming an alliance with one parent – not necessarily with the one to whom they feel closest.

- Reduced self-esteem – the child may have difficulty concentrating at school and under-perform at school.

- Acting out – some children, especially boys, are more likely to act out their distress and may become involved in delinquent behaviour.

7.4.4   Adolescents (13–18 years)

- Loss of childhood – older children may be burdened by increased responsibility for younger siblings and by the demands of an emotionally dependent parent.

- Pressure to make choices – some parents expect older children to make their own decisions about visiting the other parent or which parent they want to live with.

- Conflict between wanting to see an absent parent and wanting to keep up with peer group activities.

- Worry about money – resentful that they may receive less than their friends, pressure on parents to compensate for the divorce by giving them more materially.

- Heightened awareness and embarrassment about their parents' sexual behaviour and parents' involvement with new partners.

- Jealousy of a parent's new partner.

- Fears about forming long-term relationships and putting trust in people.

- Depression – withdrawal, refusal to communicate.

- Delinquency – stealing, drug-taking.

7.4.5   Young adults (18 upwards)

Young adults are often left out of discussions, on the grounds that they are financially independent and less affected by their parents' break-up than younger children would be. Both these assumptions may be wrong. Students in higher education still need a home to come back to and they may be dependent on financial support from parents. Equally importantly, many grown-up children worry a great deal about their parents and some are very involved emotionally in their parents' troubles. Some parents depend heavily on older children – as well as on younger ones – for emotional support and practical help. Parenting roles are sometimes reversed. A child may consciously accept responsibility for looking after a parent who is unwell or unable to function properly. Taking care of an emotionally dependent parent is a great burden for a child. It can be very difficult for sensitive and conscientious children to free themselves from this burden and get on with their own lives.

7.5   CHILDREN'S ADJUSTMENT TO PARENTAL SEPARATION

Children have complex psychological tasks in adjusting to their parents' separation and divorce. Wallerstein defined these tasks as:[20]

(1)   Recognising the breakdown in their parents' relationship.

(2)   Disengaging from their parents' conflict and distress and resuming their own customary activities.

(3)   Coping with loss.

(4)   Resolving their own feelings of anger and self-blame.

(5)   Accepting the permanence of the separation or divorce.

(6)   Achieving realistic hope regarding trustworthy relationships.

Children need to:

- Understand what is happening, with appropriate explanations according to their age and understanding and reassurance that they will continue to be loved and cared for.

- Keep attachments and relationships with both parents and with other important people in their lives. Wider kin networks, especially grandparents, can play an important part in supporting children and grandchildren around the time of separation.

- Feel reassured that they are in no way responsible for the break-up.

- Have emotional permission from each parent to go on loving the other parent.

- Have regular and reliable contact with the parent who leaves home, including overnight stays and holidays, unless there are contra-indications involving harm or continuing distress to the child.

- Stay in familiar surroundings, if possible. Although a move may be inevitable and sometimes welcomed, most children are attached to their home as well as to their parents. The disruption of moving home and changing schools adds to their confusion and stress and compounds the loss they experience.

---

[20]   Wallerstein 'Children of Divorce – the psychological tasks of the child' (1983) 53(2) *American Journal of Orthopsychiatry* 230–243.

- Maintain their daily routine as far as possible – at school and at home. When their familiar world is changing, children benefit from extra attention and nurturing, especially at bedtime.

- Be supported financially, so that they do not experience a sudden sharp drop in living standards.

- Have parents who can make thoughtful decisions and arrangements without involving the children too much or using the children for emotional support.

- Know that each parent can manage, even if they no longer live together.

- Enjoy having parents who can still play and have fun with them.

7.6 THE CHILDREN ACT 1989 AND CONTINUING PARENTAL RESPONSIBILITY

The Children Act 1989 (England and Wales) and the Children (Scotland) Act (1995) abolished the term 'custody' in private child law and introduced the term 'parental responsibility', emphasising that divorce does not end parental responsibility and that divorcing parents should be encouraged to agree their own arrangements for their children, rather than handing this responsibility to the court. This philosophy of non-intervention by the court, except where parents are unable to agree or where there are questions about the welfare of a child, is entirely in harmony with the aim of family mediation to help parents work out agreed arrangements for their children.

The principles of the Children Act 1989 are that:

- The welfare of the child is paramount.

- Parents have responsibilities towards their children, rather than rights over them.

- Parental responsibility does not end on divorce – it continues.

- Parents should agree their own arrangements for their children as far as possible.

- The court should make an order in respect of a child only if the court considers that doing so would be better for the child than making no order at all.

- The orders that the court may make are limited. There are five kinds of order that can be made: residence orders, contact orders, specific issues orders, prohibited steps orders and family assistance orders.

- When making an order in respect of a child, the court must have particular regard to a list of factors ('the checklist'). The first factor is 'the ascertainable wishes and feelings of the child concerned (considered in the light of his age and understanding).'

Ten years after the implementation of the Children Act, researchers at the Centre for Research on the Child and Family at the University of East Anglia (Trinder et al. 2002) found that the 'no order' principle of the Children Act was working well:[21]

> 'I always think, no matter what I feel or how hurt I am, that he is the children's father and this is going to be it for the rest of their lives and so we have to get on.'

However, the Judicial and Court Statistics 2009 showed an increase of 14% in the numbers of children involved in private law applications in 2009 (137,480), compared with 2008 (120,500). Applications for contact orders showed an increase of 23%, applications for prohibited steps orders an increase of 15% and applications for residence orders an increase of 11%. In his article in the *Government Gazette*,[22] Jonathan Djanogly MP, Parliamentary Under Secretary of State, Ministry of Justice asked:

> 'At a time when we must spend with the utmost care and when services are already straining to keep up with increased demand, how will we bring about change? First we must ask some fundamental questions about the way we, as a society, use our civil justice system and the role each of us plays in taking responsibility to resolve our own problems where possible. This is where other dispute resolution options other than court have an important, possibly revolutionary role to play.'

7.7   PARENTING PATTERNS AND CULTURAL DIVERSITY

Although research findings concur on the importance of parental co-operation and continuing contact after separation, it is important not to impose expectations of co-parenting on all separated parents, irrespective of their culture and circumstances. In some societies, children are brought up by the extended family rather than by their parents. Some children growing up in a single-parent household may not know their biological father and may have never experienced living in a two-parent

---

[21]   Mother, quoted by Trinder, Beek and Connolly 'Making contact: How parents and children negotiate and experience contact after divorce' (2002) *Joseph Rowntree Foundation Findings* 092.

[22]   'Going into Mediation instead of Going to Court' (September 2010).

family. They may be used to different carers coming and going – in addition to one parent, there may be a parent's new partner or a succession of partners or childminders. Single-parent households headed by fathers are more common than they used to be and many fathers play an active part in caring for their children. Although mothers still carry the major share of household and childcare responsibilities, parents in dual-earner households commonly report that childcare is shared equally.[23] Mothers are more likely to work part-time or shorter hours to fit in with looking after the children. With the rise in unemployment, many households contain two or more unemployed adults. However, unemployment does not automatically result in fathers doing more in the home.[24] Fathers who let the mother do most of the childrearing, because of longer working hours or other reasons, may find it difficult to become an active and involved parent after leaving the family home, especially if the mother tries to block their involvement.

7.8 MAINTAINING CHILDREN'S ATTACHMENTS

Wallerstein and Kelly found that:[25]

> 'the relationship between visiting father and child is at its most malleable immediately after the father has moved out of the household and as the visiting pattern emerges. The foundations of the new visiting relationship are laid down during the immediate post-separation period. The visiting parent and child also have a second chance at this critical juncture to break out of past unhappy relations and establish a new bond.'

The parent who leaves often fears losing contact with the children and is very concerned to spend significant amounts of time with them on a regular basis. However, unless there is co-operation from the resident parent – usually, the mother – the father may be confined to a minor role in the children's lives or may possibly be deprived of any role at all. Maintaining contact between the children and the non-resident parent requires sustained effort by both parents. Parents with care need to facilitate contact actively, even if their own relationship with their former partner is not amicable, while non-resident parents need to adjust to having 'contact' with their own children and to what appears to them – and may be – reduced status in their children's lives.[26] Some parents find this extremely hard, because their unresolved feelings and issues get in the way. In mediation, one father expressed his extremely bitter feelings towards his wife for having abandoned her children, as he saw it. The mother said she had left because the marriage had become deeply

[23] Lewis, Papacosta and Warin 'Cohabitation, separation and fatherhood' (2002) *Joseph Rowntree Foundation Findings* 552.
[24] Ferri and Smith *Parenting in the 1990s* (Family Policy Studies Centre, 1996).
[25] Wallerstein and Kelly *Surviving the Break-up – how children and parents cope with divorce* (Grant McIntyre, 1980), p 131.
[26] Trinder, Beek and Connolly 'Making contact: How parents and children negotiate and experience contact after divorce' (2002) *Joseph Rowntree Foundation Findings* 092.

unhappy and she felt that the very strained atmosphere in the family home was affecting the three children. As the father would not leave, she decided to leave herself and move into rented accommodation in the same area. Initially, the parents could only agree a rigid schedule for the children to visit their mother regularly. This schedule became more relaxed and flexible in conjunction with terms of settlement being reached in mediation on financial and property matters. In another situation, grandparents sought mediation because they had lost contact with their grandchildren. Following the breakdown of their daughter's marriage, they had supported their son-in-law against their daughter. Tragically, the son-in-law died in an accident and as the grandparents and their daughter were no longer on speaking terms, their contact with their grandchildren was broken off. Mediation did not rebuild the relationship between the children's mother and her parents, but arrangements were agreed for the children to visit their grandparents and other relatives.

The following account of mediation concerning contact with a small child comes from a family mediator in Staffordshire:[27]

'A referral was made by the court under the Private Law Programme to assist the parents with their contact arrangements for their son, Bobby (not his real name), aged eighteen months. On the day of the mediation meeting there was snow, ice and sub-zero temperatures. However, amidst reports of airports closing down and four hundred stationary lorries on the M25, both parents and the mediator managed to get to the meeting. It had been agreed that Mum would drop Bobby off at his nursery beforehand and Dad would collect him later. Because of the weather, after dropping Bobby off at nursery, Mum had gone to buy him his first pair of wellington boots. She brought the boots with her to the meeting so that Dad would have them when he collected Bobby later from nursery. So that she would not forget about the boots, Mum took them out of her bag and placed them on the table. And this is where they remained, in the middle of the mediation table, throughout the whole session. These were not any old wellington boots. They were tiny (baby size 5) wellies in shiny plastic camouflage greens and browns with sparkly soles. So there, in the middle of the table, was a reminder of what was important:
- Talking about a tiny vulnerable child whose feet were so small as to fit into these little boots.
- The army camouflage imitated toughness, but with these little boots any semblance of toughness was deceptive. Their small wearer needed care and protection.
- The boots were made of flimsy plastic and not substantial. Dad was going to add thick woolly socks.
- The boots would fit Bobby now and keep his feet dry, but he would soon grow out of them. His parents would need to think about his changing needs, as he grew up.
Neither of the parents nor the mediator attempted to move the boots from their prominent position in the middle of the table. The mediation had "a successful outcome".'

---

[27]   Jane Staff *Salmons Mediation* (December 2010).

7.9 PARENTAL DISPUTES AND AGREEMENTS

Trinder identified three related, but different, forms of conflict.[28] The first of these is the legal dispute, the second is conflict over the principle and/or practice of contact and the third, embedded conflict, defined as 'the broader context of the parents' relationship, including inter-parental distrust, anger, hurt etc.'[29] Some parents need a legally binding agreement or undertaking from the other parent before they will agree to contact taking place. If one parent has left recently to live with a new partner, the residential parent may stipulate that the children should have a period of 'one-to-one time with their dad' before sharing time with his new partner as well. If the father agrees, an undertaking to spend time with the children alone for a defined period may be recorded in a MOU followed by an 'open' agreement confirmed in an exchange of letters between solicitors. Many fathers recognise that children need time to adjust to a major change in their lives, without having to deal with too many changes at once. There can also be practical difficulties when the father has irregular working hours and inadequate accommodation for the children to stay overnight. Mothers often want to be reassured about sleeping arrangements and bedtime routines when the children are going to stay with their father for the first time. A father who has never put a young child to bed on his own may need to know the child's routine, while fathers of older children may willingly undertake to help them with their homework over a weekend visit, if the children bring their books with them. Both parents need to ensure that the children take their books with them and bring them back again. In general, the majority of parents agree about their children's basic needs, even if they disagree about aspects of their care and contact arrangements. Mediators may look first for the main principles and areas of agreement. Differences can then be addressed in a more positive context. Most parents agree that children need:

- to be loved;

- to be taken care of, physically and emotionally;

- to be reassured that they have parents who will look after them, even if the parents no longer live together;

- to be able to enjoy good relationships with both parents, without experiencing conflicts of loyalty;

- to maintain relationships with other family members and key people in their lives;

---

[28] Trinder 'Conciliation, the Private Law Programme and Children's Well-being' [2008] Fam Law 338–342.

[29] Ibid at p 338.

- to have as much stability as possible;

- to have parents who can take decisions and provide safe boundaries, even if the rules in each parent's home are not the same;

- to have parents who are actively involved and show interest;

- to have opportunities to expand their ideas and develop new interests;

- to develop as individuals, without being burdened by worries about their parents.

7.10 HELPING PARENTS TO WORK OUT PARENTING PLANS IN MEDIATION

Family mediation provides a forum in which parents can discuss their children's needs in constructive ways and work out arrangements either in broad terms or in precise detail. Family mediators assist parents by:

- emphasising positives ('What you said then about Pete being a good father was really important ...');

- helping parents to focus on each child individually;

- increasing co-operation and reducing conflict over children;

- encouraging parents to accept each other's continuing role in the children's lives;

- helping them to consider different areas of parental responsibility and how far these can be shared jointly or entrusted to one parent;

- helping parents to work out arrangements that free the children from conflicts of loyalty or other pressures;

- helping parents to work out child support payments and commitment to supporting the children financially;

- discussing with parents how they will talk with the children and explain new arrangements to them;

- helping parents to be more aware of what their children may be experiencing;

- considering with parents whether children should be directly involved in mediation if appropriate, so that account can be taken of their views and feelings, but without giving them responsibility for decisions.

Separated parents need to agree the extent to which day-to-day parenting will be shared between them or carried out mainly by one parent, with back up from the other parent or other family members. A commitment to continued joint parenting provides the foundation for post-separation arrangements. Many parents agree their own arrangements and do not need to discuss them in mediation. Other parents may need mediation to work out detailed aspects including decisions concerning:

- health care, care during illness;

- education – choice of school, school subjects, homework, school meetings and events;

- religious upbringing;

- holidays, festivals and birthdays – presents, parties, outings;

- sport and leisure activities;

- communication – passing on information about the children, reviewing and changing arrangements;

- contact with other family members;

- discipline – rules and boundaries, respecting the other parent's rules, agreeing whether anyone else has any responsibility for disciplining the child;

- responsibility for the child's security and development – sex education, teaching about drugs;

- emergencies – contacting the other parent.

Separated parents have not always thought about or discussed all these aspects. They may welcome a check-list and some prompting from the mediator, such as 'Have you thought about?' or 'What happens when …?' The mediator may also help them by clarifying boundaries in a very literal way. For example, when the non-resident parent collects the child or brings the child back from a visit, will the child be handed over at the door or walk alone to or from the car? If parents have agreed how to ease the children's transfer between them, they can give them more emotional support and avoid angry scenes in front of the children. In one case, the mother was willing for Grace, aged 3, to go out with her father every

Saturday but only if the handover took place in a public place, because at the time of the parents' separation there had been a single incident involving some physical violence. The police had been called and the father arrested, but released without charge. The fight had arisen in an argument over ownership of a car. This issue was resolved in mediation, but the mother was not willing for the father to come to her home in case there was another argument. They had tried handing Grace over to each other in the high street and were distressed that Grace went silently from one parent to the other with tears rolling down her cheeks. The parents decided in mediation that they could make the hand-over easier for Grace by meeting in a café where she could be partially distracted with a drink or snack and her father could then leave her gently, reassuring her that she would see him again very soon. Arrangements for Grace's birthday and holidays were also worked out.

7.10.1   Building step-by-step agreements

Parents with disputes over their children may accept short-term, trial or step-by-step arrangements for defined periods of time. Interim arrangements may be accepted on the basis that they are not permanent and that the parents will review the arrangements in mediation and discuss modifications as necessary. Mediators need to be careful, however, about enabling one parent to establish a status quo or allowing a parent to use delay to gain a personal advantage. Particularly for infants and very young children, step-by-step arrangements can work very well, as the parents can agree to extend the period the child spends away from the primary carer by degrees, in line with the child's psychological and physical development and capacity to manage change.

7.11   SHARED RESIDENCE

Research studies have shown that from an early age a child is able to form close bonds with more than one person.[30] When children are able to develop a number of secure relationships, this ability increases their emotional confidence and flexibility. Understanding the central function of emotional bonds is very important in appreciating the psychological consequences for a child of a close bond being broken, especially if this happens without explanation. The continuing involvement of both parents is very important. For many children, having two homes can work very well, provided there is good practical management and communication. But there can be difficulties.

> 'The only drawback is that we forget things we want – like toys and music stuff. It takes a lot of doing, getting it from the other house.' (Fred, aged 10).

---

[30]   Schaffer *Making Decisions about Children – Psychological Questions and Answers* (Blackwell, 1990).

'It didn't work for me having two bases because you've got like two bedrooms and two of everything and I was getting mixed up who I was.' (Caroline, aged 17)[31]

When parents live some distance apart, children may spend longer periods away from their familiar environment and friends. The child's age, views and emotional resilience need to be considered carefully, if the child is to manage frequent moves between different homes and environments. If children are shuttled to and fro too frequently, they may not have time to settle down and maintain their own activities and the friendships that become increasingly important to them, as they get older.

Some parents want their child's time to be divided equally between two equal homes. Trinder has pointed out that the term 'shared residence' or shared care covers a very broad range of timeshare arrangements and rarely means a child spending equal time with each parent on a 50/50 basis.[32] Mostyn J stated in his judgment in *Re AR (A Child: Relocation)*[33] that joint and shared residence orders are 'nowadays the rule rather than the exception, even where the quantum of care is decidedly unequal'. Grand DJ suggests that in contested proceedings over residence, a shared residence order now carries the meaning previously vested in a joint custody order:[34]

'The label which is attached to the result has assumed huge importance again, taking us away from the welfare of the child towards the welfare of the parents' egos.'

Sometimes, however, a sole residence order may be needed to clarify eligibility for child and housing benefits. Grand DJ suggests that 'parental time orders' would enable courts and parents to concentrate on child-parent relationships, rather than on labels that carry 'psychological baggage'.[35] Helping parents to focus together on each child's needs, views and relationships is precisely what mediators seek to do. Only a minority of parents who take part in mediation apply to court or go back to court for orders defining 'residence' or 'contact'. Clear – and also flexible – arrangements for children's time to be shared with each parent is an area of parental responsibility that parents need to consider carefully, along with all the other areas.

---

[31] Both children quoted by Neale and Wade *Parent Problems – children's views on life when parents split up* (Young Voice 2000), pp 12–13.

[32] Trinder *Shared Residence: A Review of Recent Research Evidence* [2010] Fam Law 1192–1197.

[33] [2010] EWHC 1346 (Fam), [2010] 2 FLR 1577.

[34] Grand 'Disputes between Parents: Time for a New Order?' [2011] Fam Law 75.

[35] [2011] Fam Law 75 (Mostyn J).

An Australian study[36] found that different groups of parents established different types of shared care that were in turn associated with different longer-term outcomes. The three groups identified were:

(1)   Co-operative parents, who were more likely to have higher income and education levels. These parents had good parent-parent and father-child relationships at mediation intake and sustained positive relationships over the four years of the study.

(2)   A rigid 'shared care' group with fixed arrangements that lacked flexibility. This group started and continued with higher levels of conflict, higher rates of litigation and lower levels of fathers' regard for mothers' parenting.

(3)   A 'formerly-shared care' group, where shared care was tried following mediation but broke down and reverted to primary mother care. This group also had high rates of pre-and post-mediation litigation and high levels of acrimony.

In the McIntosh study, children were asked about their satisfaction with the shared care arrangements. Children in rigid arrangements were most likely to be dissatisfied and young adolescents in general were likely to want to change the arrangements. The researchers concluded that:[37]

> 'equal or substantial sharing of time may in some circumstances be an arrangement better suited to parents than to children.'

Mediators help parents to consider what their plans will mean in practice and the possible benefits and difficulties for the children concerned. Children have a keen sense of fairness and they want to be fair to both parents. Some children will sacrifice their own needs in order to be loyal to both parents. They can be burdened by arrangements that keep both parents happy at the expense of the child. When children move frequently between two homes, they benefit from close continuing contact with both parents. However, arrangements that work well at one stage may need to be varied as children grow up. Some children want to spend more time with one parent at a particular stage of their development, but fear hurting the other parent by saying so. Circular questions are particularly helpful in asking parents to put themselves in the child's place, without the mediator expressing opinions or giving advice. Parents often assume that their children's needs and feelings coincide with their own, but this may not be the case. Some children who move frequently from one parent to the other manage these transitions very well, whereas others may

---

[36]   McIntosh, Smyth, Kelaher, Wells and Long *Post-separation parenting arrangements and developmental outcomes for infants and children* (Family Court of Australia, Attorney-General's Department, 2010).

[37]   McIntosh, Smyth, Kelaher, Wells and Long *Post-separation parenting arrangements and developmental outcomes for infants and children* (Family Court of Australia, Attorney-General's Department, 2010), p 78.

experience higher rates of anxiety or depression or have significantly higher hyperactivity scores. Steinman found that shared care can work well for children if:[38]

- there is good co-operation and communication between parents and clarity about who is responsible for what;

- both parents are willing to be flexible, within a clear structure;

- travelling time is not too long and tiring for the child;

- the child is free from worries about being fair to both parents;

- practicalities are sorted out: having duplicates of some things in each home avoids the child having to carry everything to and fro all the time;

- the child's friendships and activities are respected – this becomes increasingly important as the child gets older;

- parents listen to the child and can hear when the arrangements need adjusting.

Smart identified three factors that distinguish successful from unsuccessful shared care arrangements:[39]

(1) whether children's needs are prioritised, or whether the arrangement is based on the needs and wishes of the parents;

(2) whether the arrangements are flexible rather than rigid;

(3) whether the children feel equally 'at home' with both parents.

For many parents, shared care of children is impracticable because of work, accommodation, and the time and cost of frequent transport and communications between two households. But even where children spend alternate weekends with the non-residential parent in a more traditional arrangement, the three factors identified by Smart are still important for the well being of the child.

---

[38] Steinman 'The Experience of Children in a Joint Custody Arrangement' (1981) 51 *American Journal of Orthopsychiatry* 403–414.

[39] Smart 'Equal shares: rights for fathers or recognition for children?' (2004) *Critical Social Policy* 484.

7.12   HELPING PARENTS TO SHIFT FROM CONFLICT TO CO-OPERATION

Many parents have so many problems to deal with when they separate that it is not easy for them to consider what their children may be experiencing. One of the benefits of mediation reported by parents is that they were helped to focus on their children as individuals and to consider their children's feelings and needs, as well as their own.[40] Parents generally want to put their children first and welcome encouragement to do so.

7.12.1   Asking parents for a portrait of each child

Parents tend to bring conflicting versions of events in order to justify their own point of view. A helpful way to start is to ask them to describe each of their children. Parents are proud of their children and like talking about them. Describing each child's personality and interests, with each parent filling in some details, helps to focus on each child as an individual so that they can talk and listen to each other without feeling under attack. This also serves a number of other purposes:

- Sharing information about the children. Often the parent who is involved in the day-to-day care of the children knows more than the other. Asking this parent to start giving the picture can be a means of updating the parent who knows less.

- Seeing how far the parents agree or disagree about the child's personality, temperament and attachments. Often, there is a large measure of agreement even between parents who are in dispute over parenting arrangements. Areas of agreement can be emphasised and used for the next stage of work. Some parents are very surprised to find how far they are in agreement.

- Easing communication in a positive way, encouraging parents to talk about interests they share that are not upsetting or controversial.

- Establishing ground-rules, making it clear that the mediator will ask each parent and allow enough time to listen and respond, without interruptions.

- When conflict is high, mediators can ask focused questions that provide a clear and firm structure.

Gathering information about children may include asking about:

- the child's personality and temperament;

---

[40]   Walker, McCarthy and Timms *Mediation: The Making and Remaking of Co-operative Relationships* (Relate Centre for Family Studies, University of Newcastle, 1994).

- the child's stage of development – physical, emotional, intellectual;

- how the child is getting on at school – schoolwork and friends;

- how the child gets on with siblings;

- the child's health;

- the child's interests and activities;

- any special needs or difficulties;

- how do the parents know when the child is happy?

- how do they know when the child is upset? How do they respond?

Many parents who come to mediation are very concerned about their children and motivated to co-operate. Even if they disagree, the atmosphere usually lightens as they give a portrait of each child. They often smile and look at each other more readily. It is then easier to move on to questions about current and future arrangements. In one case, two parents, who were not speaking to each other and in conflict over their sons' primary residence, relaxed visibly as they talked about each boy's personality and activities.

7.13   TECHNIQUES AND SKILLS IN MEDIATING ABOUT CHILDREN

- **Questioning skills, including past-, present- and future-oriented questions and circular questions**[41]
  Mediators may use future-focused and hypothetical questions for parents to think about before the next meeting. 'If the children are going to live with you (mother) or with you (father), how much time do you think they should spend with the other parent? The children may have one main home or move between two homes, but what part does each of you want to have in their upbringing and general development – what do you see as your strengths and contribution as a parent? In what ways would you see the other parent having a role in the children's upbringing? What support would you hope for from the other parent? Are there major questions – such as health, education, religion – on which you would agree to consult each other when necessary? What kind of information about the children do you expect to share with each other?'

- **Normalising** – 'Many children show signs of ...', 'Children very often ...'

---

[41]   See Chapter 6 above.

When parents blame each other for a child's reactions, the mediator may be able to comment that this is normal or a commonly experienced problem. Toddlers who have tantrums and uncommuni- cative teenagers are found in a great many intact families. Parents tend to blame each other. Instead of looking for cause and effect, the mediator may find that each parent needs more help and support from the other parent. Parents often respond to a request for help and support, once they realise that they are not being blamed for causing the problem. It is important to acknowledge parents' efforts and the support they need, without suggesting that they are failing to meet their children's needs. Criticism, whether overt or implied, increases defensiveness and resistance. When parents constantly blame and find fault with each other, the child's reactions may be reinforced and the parents may turn to experts, having lost confidence in their ability to help their children. One of the difficulties is that children's behaviour may be ambiguous and capable of being interpreted in different ways. Conflict increases when parents interpret the child's reactions differently. To help them realise that they could both be right and that there could be other possible explanations, mediators need to understand how children may hide their feelings or act them out.

- **Acknowledging and mutualising** – 'You both care a great deal about the children ...'

- **Anger and concerns can be acknowledged while keeping the focus on the present and future** – 'So you are both concerned to work out arrangements for ... (names of the children) that would help them manage these changes as well as possible?'

- **Reframing** – 'So you are both looking for reliable arrangements?'

- **Prioritising** – 'What do you think is most important for the children right now?'

- **Structuring** – 'Shall we decide the order in which we are going to discuss these questions?'

- **Information** – 'The courts prefer parents to reach their own agreements', 'Have you come across these books for children?' It is not the mediator's role to instruct parents on what is best for their children. Many parents are however in need of information and guidance on how to help their children cope with the separation. There are helpful books, DVDs and websites for parents and also helpful books for children that parents can read with young children or give to an older child. Mediators should have a selection of books and other materials to show parents who are interested and copies of a list to give to them.

7.13.1   Using the flipchart, drawing an ecogram

The flipchart is very useful for highlighting key questions, providing a common focus and prioritising. Listing parents' issues and options helps to show which areas of parental responsibility are agreed, such as residence, education and health care, and which areas are not agreed, such as contact arrangements and financial support. It may be very helpful to draw a calendar on the flipchart showing a five-week (or any other) period, with each day divided between am and pm. Parents may be invited to explain their current arrangements and the arrangements they are looking for. Marking these on the flipchart, possibly with different colours, helps to highlight how much time the children are spending with, or could spend with, each parent. The contrast between two or three Saturdays a month with their father, compared with twenty-eight days with their mother, is shown much more clearly on the flipchart than in discussion.

7.13.2   Timing and structure in mediation sessions concerning children

Mediators need to focus on the main issues and keep an eye on the clock. Discussions about children can take a long time and mediation is not therapy. Questions and comments need to be focused and the pace of discussion needs to be managed. If the priority is next weekend, it is important to allow time to deal with this, rather than embarking on a wide-ranging discussion which leaves no time to sort out next weekend's arrangements. Sensitivity and skills are needed in deciding how many questions to ask about the children, and at what stage. Questions about what each parent has said – or allegedly said – to the children are often highly sensitive and may be a subject to come back to at another meeting, after they have worked out contact arrangements. 'Have you talked together with the children, or do you talk to them separately?' Or 'Have you told the children that you are coming to mediation?' Generally, children seem to welcome being told that their parents are meeting together to work out arrangements. Many children are able to understand the idea of mediation and even young children can understand the need for a person who does not take sides.

7.14   CHILDREN SAID OR CONSIDERED TO BE AT RISK

When parents express worries about a child, it is important to establish the level of concern and urgency. If priority is to be given to this concern at the next meeting, questions may be put to parents in advance, to help them focus on and consider possible ways of solving the problem. If there is urgency, then clearly the concern must be given immediate priority. Referral for medical, therapeutic or other help may be needed and parents may need information about the services available. If a parent expresses concern that a child is or may be at risk, then clearly this must be explored immediately to clarify the grounds for concern. Is the concern a subject of dispute between the parents? What advice has each of them sought and has any action been taken? Are other agencies involved? What action needs to be taken now? Should the mediator contact the appropriate agency immediately?[42]

7.15   CHILDREN'S ROLES AND STRATEGIES IN RELATION TO PARENTAL CONFLICT

Sometimes children are passive bystanders who are kept out of their parents' disputes. But the greater the conflict, the more likely it is that children are drawn into it. The child may become caught in an emotional triangle in which the parents' unresolved conflicts are channelled through the 'triangulated child.' Children who are distressed by their parents' separation may react in ways that seem attention seeking or manipulative. To describe this behaviour as the child's 'strategies' suggests that it is conscious and premeditated, whereas it is often an intuitive response to a combination of personal needs and parental pressures. Children try to make things all right, according to their own needs and understanding. They may try to protect their parents, as well as themselves. In some circumstances children resort to behaviour that is the only means they can find of showing needs they cannot express in words.

Five Elements of Family Mediation

	Child's role	Role of mediator
1.	Messenger, go-between	Helps parents talk with each other directly, instead of communicating via the children
2.	Reconciler (tries to bring parents together)	Helps parents agree what needs to be explained; helps parents discuss how to reassure the child
3.	Peace-maker (tells each parent what s/he wants to hear)	Helps parents resolve conflicts
4.	Ally enlisted by one parent to give support	Helps parents reach agreements and resolve conflicts to free the child
5.	Decision-taker	Helps parents take responsibility for difficult decisions
6.	Scapegoat (tests out, fears being abandoned by both parents)	Helps parents give reassurance and agree necessary limits, define rules etc.

---

[42]   See FMC Code of Practice 2010, Section 5; set out in Appendix A below.

	Child's role	Role of mediator
7.	Confidante	Helps parents consider how to avoid burdening the child
8.	Substitute partner (replacing spouse who has left)	Helps parents feel more secure so that they depend less on the child
9.	Substitute parent or carer (looking after a parent or younger siblings)	Encourages parent/s to look for other souces of help. Help parent/s to understand the child's needs
10.	Judge (encouraged to blame a parent)	Discusses with parents how they can help children understand, without condemning either parent
11.	Fugitive (truancy, delinquency)	Discusses risks and concerns with parents. Seeks greater parental involvement
12.	Mourner for lost family. Shows grief that parents are repressing	Helps parents to recognise and share sadness as well as anger

It is normal for children of all ages to dream that their parents will get back together. The desire to reunite separated parents is often intense and of long duration. Children may develop physical symptoms associated with emotional stress. They may also fantasise that both parents will come together again to care for a child who is ill.

Example

Sarah, aged six, complains of feeling unwell whenever she is due to visit her father.

Mother's interpretation: *the visits are distressing Sarah – especially as her ex-husband has a new partner. It is in Sarah's interests to reduce the visits or stop them altogether for a while.*

Father's interpretation: *his ex-wife is turning Sarah against him, because she is jealous of his new girlfriend. If his ex-wife is blocking his relationship with his daughter, maybe it would be better for Sarah to come and live with him. His girlfriend has children too and she is an excellent mother.*

Possible outcomes if the dispute is not resolved:

• *Sarah may lose contact with her father.*

• *The family doctor, teachers, child psychologist and solicitors may all become involved.*

- *A social welfare report may be called for.*

- *If a court order is made, contact may not work in practice if Sarah continues to resist it.*

- *The dispute over contact may escalate into a dispute over residence.*

Mediation may help the parents to:

- *Focus on Sarah: how do they describe her? Do they have other children? If Sarah is an only child, the pressures on her may be particularly intense.*

- *Clarify the present situation and the main questions.*

- *Consider whether and how Sarah can keep her relationship with both parents.*

- *Consider how this can be managed in a way that gives Sarah as much support and reassurance as possible. What are the options and practical possibilities? Might Sarah need some time alone with her father? What about the length of time and frequency of visits? If the parents argue when they meet, could contact take place without them coming face to face, at least for a time? Could grandparents help?*

- *Explore what is troubling Sarah: could it be that she loves both her parents and does not understand why they cannot stay together? Maybe she hopes her father will come and help her mother look after her so that they can all go on living together? Maybe Sarah is trying to protect both her parents by avoiding them coming into contact with each other?*

- *A step-by-step agreement may lead to a gradual increase in contact so that Sarah does not have to cope with too many changes too quickly. This might help to reassure Sarah's mother of the need to give her stability, while also reassuring her father that agreed contact arrangements are a step towards more flexible contact.*

- *Can Sarah be reassured that her mother supports her having contact with her father? And that she need not worry about her mother while she is away? Can her mother give her this reassurance?*

- *Helping Sarah be clear when the contact visits are happening. Suggesting that her mother marks the dates on a calendar may be helpful.*

- *Particularly where there is reluctance to make any firm commitment to specific contact arrangements, planning another mediation meeting to review how the arrangements are working, after a few visits.*

- *Consider what has been said to Sarah so far? What may she need to hear from both parents? How can she be helped to understand and come to terms with their separation?*

- *Are there any other changes which would make things easier? Can Sarah's father keep in contact with regular phone calls?*

Mediators should be careful not to reject a parent's interpretation of a child's behaviour or to claim to know better than the parents. An idea may be offered as a possibility, not as a solution. Parents can take an idea on board and think about it, if they wish. If it opens up a fresh perspective, it may help them work together in a problem-solving way, rather than in a confrontational way.

7.15.1 Acting-out strategies to test parents' love and commitment to the child

Example

Jake, aged 13, was caught stealing DVDs from a local shop.

Mother's interpretation: *Jake is in need of more discipline and control. He is rude, sullen and goes out all the time. She cannot cope with him – she has tried and she has had enough. She cannot make him go to school. At this rate he will end up a criminal. It's time his father took responsibility for him. He can go and live at his father's.*

Father's interpretation: *Jake is getting out of control. His mother never did handle him very well. Maybe she is right about Jake needing to live with him instead of with his mother – only it's no good expecting him to be at home when Jake comes out of school. The lad will have to do as he is told and stay out of trouble. Otherwise, he'll end up in care. He'd better be aware that's what will happen if he carries on stealing.*

Possible outcomes if Jake does not get the help he needs:

- *Further arguments between the parents about whose fault it is that Jake is in trouble.*

- *Neither parent makes Jake feel loved and wanted.*

- *Jake re-offends.*

- *Social Services become involved.*

- *Jake ends up in care.*

Mediation could help the parents to:

- *Focus on Jake: What was he like as a small boy? And now? Do his parents think he is unhappy? Angry? Worried? Do they have other children?*

- *Discuss Jake's needs. What are the present arrangements for Jake? Can they co-operate in meeting his needs? If he lives with his mother, can she rely on his father backing her up over questions of 'boundaries' (staying out late) and discipline?*

- *Settle other related issues including financial issues. Might these be affecting Jake? Does he get pocket money?*

- *Consider whether Jake is angry with both his parents. Maybe he imagines they don't care what happens to him? Maybe he is hoping that if he is in trouble, they will get together somehow and sort it out?*

- *Is it possible for the parents to talk with Jake together? Do they think it would be helpful for him to be involved in the mediation? If so, how might this be done?*

7.15.2 Children's protective strategies

Children become very anxious when they realise that one parent is unable to cope or that it is not safe for their parents to meet. They may engage in protective strategies to make things safer for all concerned and to try to protect one or both parents from hurting each other.

> 'Everything is all right as long as I don't let Mum and Dad speak to each other.'[43]

One way in which children seek to protect their parents and themselves is by refusing to see the other parent – even if, deep down, they long to do so. Some children try to help their parents by telling each parent what that parent needs to hear.

Example

Daniel, aged 9, did not want to hurt either parent by choosing one and rejecting the other. He told each of them what he thought they wanted to hear from him. He told his father he would like to live with him. He told his mother the same. Daniel was unsure if his mother would manage without him. He knew she depended on him.

---

[43] Cockett and Tripp *The Exeter Family Study: Family Breakdown and its impact on children* (University of Exeter Press, 1994), p 43.

Mother's interpretation: *Of course Daniel wants to live with her. She has always looked after him and they are very close. His father is putting words in Daniel's mouth and pressurising him. This is irresponsible and wrong.*

Father's interpretation: *Daniel is a boy and it is understandable that he has reached an age where he wants to live with his father. Unfortunately his mother cannot see this. She is over-protective. Daniel should be allowed to decide and then it will be clear where he wants to be.*

Possible outcome if the parents cannot agree: *If their dispute continues following an application to the court, the possibility of a Cafcass report saying that either parent could provide a good and caring home for Daniel. The judge may have to decide issues of sole or shared residence and contact.*

Mediation could help these parents to:

- *Focus on Daniel and his needs, through use of present-focused, past-focused and future-focused questions. When Daniel was a baby, did both parents share in looking after him? How did this work? Did they contribute to looking after him in similar or different ways? Did they each value the other parent's support? Or did they wish the other parent had done more? How could both of them be involved now?*

- *Think about their particular qualities as parents (as mother/father, with their different personalities, interests and abilities) and what each of them can give to or share with Daniel in complementary ways.*

- *Identify and consider options for shared parenting and how these would work in practice.*

- *Consider immediate issues in the context of longer-term needs.*

- *Consider how Daniel himself can be helped to express his feelings and needs, without being caught up in conflicts of loyalty.*

Parents often recognise in mediation that what they both care about most is their continuing love for their child, and their child's love for both of them. They may need an acknowledgement that it is extremely difficult to continue to be co-parents, while also dealing with the ending of their couple relationship.[44] Mediators can help parents to separate the endings that need to be made – the changes involved in ending their couple relationship – from the continuity of connections and ongoing relationships between parents and children, in the present and the future.

---

[44] See Chapter 2 at **2.7** above.

Rachel's Poem[45]

My Mum and my Dad are inside who I am
They are part of me wherever I go
When they divorced, they hated each other
And that was like they hated me.
And when they hurt each other they hurt me.
When Mum did not want me to see Dad she wasn't seeing me
When Dad didn't want me to love Mum he wasn't loving me
Now that's stopped and they get on OK
So I can be who I am, with my Mum and Dad inside me.

---

[45] Reprinted with permission from McIntosh *Because it's for the Kids – Building a Secure Base Parenting Base after Separation* (2006).

CHAPTER 8

CHILD-INCLUSIVE FAMILY MEDIATION

'Why can't you grow up and put the past behind you? It's so disappointing. You may not like each other but you've got to think about me. Grow up and talk to each other!'[1]

'I think there should be some kind of agreement between the children and the parents as to what should happen. I think the people who are involved should get to decide, not by themselves, but by helping each other to reach some kind of agreement as to what would be best.'[2]

CONTENTS

---

[1] Message from 11-year-old child to her parents in child-inclusive mediation (The Mediation Centre, Stafford, January 2011).

[2] Jake, aged 11, quoted in Neale and Wade *Parent Problems – children's views on life when parents split up* (Young Voice, 2000), p 32.

8.1   CHILDREN WHO WANT TO HAVE A SAY

Many children want to have a say in family arrangements. They want their parents to listen to them and take account of their views and feelings.[3] Very often, however, children are left in the dark when their parents separate. They may not be told what is happening and rarely feel that their views are taken into account. A quarter of children whose parents had separated said that no one had talked to them about the separation when it happened. Only 5% said they had been given full explanations and a chance to ask questions.[4] It was left to the mother in over 70% of families to tell the children and some mothers told them only that their father had left, without giving any explanation.[5] One girl said about her mother: 'She didn't understand how I felt. She was too busy being angry'.[6] A boy remarked: 'You're the first person who's ever bothered to ask me how I felt'.[7] Morrow found that most children wanted to have a say in matters affecting them.[8] Even young children could understand and talk about the notion of being listened to. Some wanted to be heard and involved in decision-making, whereas others wanted to be consulted but did not want any responsibility for decisions.

> 'We needed to know what was going on, what was happening, how things would work out ... We needed help from outside but there just didn't seem to be the right person to turn to. No one seemed to be there to help us, especially us, the children. Mum and Dad had the lawyers but we had no one.'[9]

Older children, in particular, think they ought to be included in decision-making that will have a profound impact on their lives. One 15-year-old girl pointed out:[10]

> 'We are people too and shouldn't be treated like low-lifes just because we are younger. I think kids deserve the same kind of respect that we are expected to give so-called adults.'

---

[3]   Smart and Neale 'It's My Life Too – Children's Perspectives on Post-Divorce Parenting' [2000] Fam Law 163–169.

[4]   Dunn and Deater-Deckard 'Children's Views of their Changing Families' (2001) *Joseph Rowntree Research Findings* 931.

[5]   Cockett and Tripp *The Exeter Family Study: Family Breakdown and its impact on children* (University of Exeter Press, 1994).

[6]   Mitchell *Children in the Middle* (Tavistock, 1985), p 94.

[7]   Ibid, p 81.

[8]   Morrow 'Children's Perspectives on Families' (1998) *Rowntree Research Findings* 798.

[9]   Child quoted by O'Quigley in *Listening to children's views: the findings and recommendations of recent research* (Joseph Rowntree Foundation, 2000), p 10.

[10]   Quoted by O'Quigley ibid, p 30.

8.2 THE VOICE OF THE CHILD

Until the middle of the nineteenth century, children were treated as small adults who were put to work at an early age, without consideration of their needs as children. Child welfare campaigns and public concern led to laws being passed to protect children from exploitation or other harm and to provide them with education. However, it was not until the later part of the twentieth century that children were recognised as having the right to be heard, as well as having needs for care and protection. Under section 1(3) of the Children Act 1989, in any proceedings concerning a child the court is required to have regard to 'the ascertainable wishes and feelings of the child concerned (considered in the light of his age and understanding).' In public law proceedings, the child automatically becomes a party to the proceedings and in private law proceedings the child can become a party, represented by a guardian ad litem. The Children (Scotland) Act 1995 requires all those with parental responsibility to have regard, so far as practicable, to the views of the child concerned. A child aged twelve or over is assumed in Scotland to be of sufficient age and maturity to form a view. Internationally, Article 12(1) of the United Nations Convention on the Rights of the Child 1989, adopted by the UK in 1991, says that in any matter or procedure affecting the child, the views of the child are to be given due weight, in accordance with the child's age and maturity. Children who are capable of forming opinions should be assured 'the right to express their views freely.' Article 12(2) says children should be given the opportunity to express their views 'either directly or through a representative or an appropriate body'.

The Brussels II revised Regulation (27 November 2003), concerning jurisdiction and the recognition and enforcement of judgments in matrimonial matters and matters of parental responsibility, likewise recognises the right of the child to be heard, in accordance with his or her age and maturity, on matters relating to parental responsibility over the child (Article 4).

Seeing children as individuals with rights of their own means that decisions concerning children need to be approached in a different way. Adults need to consider whether, and if so, how, a child or young person should be consulted about decisions that affect their lives. The need to hear the voice of the child in family proceedings under the provisions of the Children Act 1989 was upheld in the House of Lords by Baroness Hale of Richmond:[11]

> 'There is a growing understanding of the importance of listening to the children involved in children's cases. It is the child, more than anyone else, who will have to live with what the court decides. Those who do listen to children understand that they often have a view that is quite distinct from

---

[11]   *Re D (A Child) (Abduction: Rights of Custody)* [2006] UKHL 51, [2007] 1 AC 619.

that of the person looking after them. They are quite capable of being moral actors in their own right. Just as the adults may have to do what the court decides whether they like it or not, so may the child. But that is no more reason for failing to hear what the child has to say than it is for refusing to hear the parents' views.'

8.3   SHOULD JUDGES SEE CHILDREN?

Judges in England and Wales are being encouraged to listen more to the voice of the child. The then President of the Family Division gave strong reasons in favour of judges seeing a child who is at the centre of a dispute.[12] Some judges, however, are concerned that they do not have the necessary training and expertise to meet with children involved in private law proceedings and are troubled by the potential dilemma of explaining a judicial decision to parents without betraying a confidence from a child. Judges may therefore be reluctant to see a child:[13]

> 'preferring that the voice of the child in private law proceedings is heard either through a Cafcass report or through a r.9.5 guardian. However, circumstances do arise where it is not just appropriate but actually necessary for the judge to hear the voice of a child before making his decision.'

One of the problems is that Cafcass is so overloaded with work that children are seen only briefly. Hunt found that 60% of children seen by Cafcass were reported as having been seen for half an hour or less.[14] Judges who see a child in chambers are encouraged:[15]

> 'to enable children to feel more involved and connected with proceedings in which important decisions are made in their lives.'

However, if a child talks directly to the judge, there is a risk of the child being coached by one or both parents. The court is an intimidating environment for children and meeting with the judge may put great pressure on the child. For these reasons and wherever there is an acceptable alternative, judges may still prefer other professionals to carry out the skilled task of listening to children and ascertaining their needs, feelings and wishes. In Australia, 'interviews by other professionals have long since replaced judicial interviews as the normal means of

---

[12]   Potter [2008] IFL 140.

[13]   Bellamy, Platt and Crichton 'Talking to Children: the Judicial Perspective' [2010] Fam Law 647.

[14]   Hunt *Parental Perspectives on the Family Justice System in England and Wales: a review of research* (Report for the Family Justice Council, December 2009).

[15]   *Guidelines for Judges Meeting Children who are subject to Family Proceedings*, produced by the Family Justice Council and approved by the President of the Family Division [2010] Fam Law 654.

ascertaining the views of children'.[16] Research in Australia suggests that the focus should be not only on how children are heard in legal proceedings, but also on how they can be better heard in families who resolve their conflicts without going to court. Child-focused mediation and child-inclusive mediation are two of the ways in which parents and children can be helped to listen to each other and communicate more easily during and following parental separation, in order to reach agreed decisions about arrangements for the children. In child-focused mediation, parents are helped to consider their children's needs and feelings and to talk with their children at home, without including them directly in mediation.[17] In child-inclusive mediation, children and young people are offered opportunities to meet with a specially trained professional within the mediation process – family mediator or child counsellor – either on their own, or with siblings and possibly also with the family together. Given the principle of least intervention, Direct Child Consultation (DCC), also known as Child-Inclusive Mediation, offers opportunities for children and young people to have a say and be listened to, when decisions are being made about arrangements affecting the child.

8.4 CHILD-FOCUSED MEDIATION

Separated parents often need some help to explain their decisions and new arrangements to their children. A parent's inability or unwillingness to explain a painful situation to a child may combine with children's tendencies to suppress their feelings. A collusive wall of silence may be erected around the parent who has left. The longer this wall remains, the harder it becomes to dismantle it. It is understandable that many parents feel unable to talk about the separation with their children. They are already overwhelmed by their own pain and worry. When children are asked what would have helped them, they nearly always say that they needed more information, explanation and reassurance from their parents than they actually received. Family mediators can help parents to discuss the difficult questions of what should be explained to the children, by whom and at what stage. Many parents who come to mediation have reassured the children that the separation is not their fault, but they may not have been able to tell the children whether they will go on living in the same home or how much time they will spend with each parent. When parents blame each other for the separation or divorce, children are liable to be given conflicting accounts. Mediators help parents to work out agreed explanations, appropriate to the age of the child, that they can give separately or together without contradicting or denigrating each other to the children.

---

[16] Parkinson and Cashmore 'Judicial Conversations with children in parenting disputes: the views of Australian judges' (2007) 21 *International Journal of Law, Policy and the Family* 160.

[17] See Chapter 7 above.

8.5 REASSURANCES THAT PARENTS NEED TO GIVE TO CHILDREN

- Both parents still love the children and will go on loving them.

- Both parents (or otherwise one parent) will continue to look after the children.

- They will go on living in the same home (or, if a move may be necessary, their needs will be considered in planning new arrangements).

- They will continue to see the parent they no longer live with. Children need to know where this parent is or will be living.

- The children are in no way to blame for the separation.

- Even if the parents divorce, there is no divorce between children and parents.

- Both parents are sad about the separation (rather than angry with each other).

- They decided to separate because they were making each other unhappy (or some variation that fits the parents' situation. Telling children that their parents are splitting up because they no longer love each other can make young children fear that their parents might stop loving them too).

- They will tell the children about any new arrangements that affect them.

- They are working out new arrangements for the family with a mediator: explaining to the children what this means. Even young children can understand the idea of mediation very well (sometimes better than adults do).

- The children's views and feelings are important and they will be listened to. Their parents will work out decisions that take the children's views into account, as far as possible.

- The parents understand that the changes are profoundly upsetting for children and that the children may feel angry or sad or both; that these feelings are natural and understandable and that it is safe to talk about them.

- If something is worrying the child, they hope the child will feel able to tell one or both of them about it, so that they can help.

Most parents prefer to talk with the children in their own home, but they may be unsure how to go about it. Mediators can help them plan the timing and content of a joint discussion with children and also to agree what should *not* be discussed with the children. Parents need to be aware that children can react in very different ways. Some cry and show distress, whereas others may appear unconcerned, barely listening and then asking: 'What's for supper tonight?' Even if children appear not to be listening, they are usually taking in what is said. They may need to hear it more than once, especially the reassurances, in order to absorb them fully. Mediators can help parents anticipate how a particular child might react ('what if ...?'), by asking how they would respond to an angry outburst directed at one parent in particular. Parents who are well prepared are more able to cope with their feelings and back each other up in front of the children. Sometimes parents are at a loss to know what they can say to a child to help the child understand. One way to help them is for the mediator to place an empty chair and ask them to imagine that the child is sitting there and needs some explanation from them. Although this sounds highly artificial, parents may start to talk to their imaginary child with great emotion and intensity and think about the child's reactions. What matters is not so much what the parents want to say as what the children need to hear. Parents can be asked to imagine their child in, say, five years' time, and the questions the child might ask then. A mother who thinks that a child under three will not miss her father may be asked to imagine the child at twelve or fifteen, asking why her father did not love her enough to keep in touch.

8.6 CHILD-INCLUSIVE MEDIATION

Studies have shown that in the UK, the direct involvement of children in mediation is rare.[18] Most mediators see their role as facilitating adult negotiations and assisting parents to reach decisions. They may be opposed to children's direct involvement on the grounds that this would undermine the parents' authority, thus 'disempowering' parents instead of 'empowering' them. However, experience in the UK and Australia suggests that there can be significant benefits for children in including them directly, provided there is careful planning with both parents and agreement as to the objectives of including the children, the pre-conditions for involving them and the approach to the child.[19] Pre-requisites include parental agreement, clarity about the role of the family mediator or other professional, the principles and limits of confidentiality for (a) parents, and (b) the child, and the need to seek the child's informed consent.

---

[18]   Hayes 'Family Mediators in the UK – A Survey of Practice' [2002] Fam Law 760; Murch 'The Voice of the Child in Private Family Law Proceedings in England and Wales' [2005] IFL 8.

[19]   Parkinson 'Child-Inclusive Family Mediation' [2006] Fam Law 483–488; Pendlebury 'Divorce and separation: listening to children and young people in mediation' [2008] Fam Law 1255.

8.7   DIFFERENT WAYS OF INCLUDING CHILDREN IN MEDIATION

Family mediation services that have a positive policy of including children have noted the benefits reported by children of feeling heard and contributing to decisions. Mediation in Divorce (MID), based in Richmond, has a project called *Listening to Young People* designed to give a voice to the children of separating or divorcing parents. MID now routinely invites young people to have a say about family change and arrangements affecting them.

> 'Previously, it was always possible to involve children directly in mediation, but in practice it rarely used to happen. We were cautious about undermining the authority of parents in mediation and we tended to think that the best people to talk to children were usually their parents. Several factors caused us to review our policy, including the emphasis given in the European Convention of Human Rights to children's rights to have their views heard, and more importantly, the research findings resulting from interviews with children whose parents had separated/divorced. Offering children a more direct voice in the mediation process is not so much a change of policy, more a change of emphasis. We present the idea to parents in a more positive way, and at an earlier stage. We don't consider children's participation as an exceptional option, but rather as something we actively encourage because we see that most children appreciate the opportunity to be heard directly.'[20]

Even with this policy of encouraging the direct involvement of children, children are actually involved in only a minority of cases, for a variety of reasons. A Scottish study by Garwood found that although the family mediation service in Edinburgh had a policy of considering children's involvement in every case, children were actually involved in only 36 out of 186 cases (19% of cases).[21] The main reason for not involving children was that they were too young (average age 3 and ½ years). The most frequent reason given by parents (42 out of 84 cases) was that they did not think it necessary for the children to see the mediator, because they felt able to talk with their children at home. Other reasons given by parents were that the issues did not involve the children (14 cases) or one parent was not in favour (9 cases). Devon Family Mediators Agency (DFMA) uses a different approach in offering the opportunity for children whose parents are taking part in mediation to meet with an independent Children's Resource Worker. When parents request an appointment for their children, this is usually arranged to coincide with a mediation meeting with the parents. Children are seen by at the request of their parents and children are involved in the decision to attend the appointment. Attendance is voluntary. The content of the meeting is

---

[20]   Pendlebury, quoted in Parkinson 'Child-Inclusive Family Mediation' [2006] Fam Law 484.

[21]   Garwood *Children in Conciliation* (Scottish Association of Family Conciliation Services, 1989).

confidential between the child/children and the worker and the same rules of confidentiality apply as in adult mediation. The child/children decide what information, if any, they would like to be taken back to the adult mediation process. No written documentation is produced from the meeting unless agreed by the participants. Children's Resource Workers adhere to the strict Code of Practice of their own particular profession in accordance with the Code of Practice of the Family Mediators Association and the requirements of the Legal Services Commission. Cockett explains the DFMA service in this way:[22]

> 'Children's Resource Workers are attached to the Agency ... they are the most experienced of the children's psychologists in the area and totally supportive of the mediation process. With the permission of both parents the children of the family can be offered a confidential appointment. Children are usually seen together ... and separately. Nothing comes out of the meeting unless the Resource Worker and the child decide that it should. The report is always prepared from the viewpoint of the Resource Worker, e g "I have spoken with the child and in my view these are the matters that both parents may wish to consider ..." This is very important, as the child should never be put in the firing line. Children can be seen more than once. If the Resource Worker considers that the child/family might need more ongoing help, they will be referred to the children's services, so that they are not left high and dry. Last but not least, the confidentiality of the child is respected with the usual exceptions regarding child protection issues, and the mediator's position is not compromised.'

Before any decision is reached concerning the inclusion of children, it is important to consider with parents the potential advantages and disadvantages, primarily from the child's point of view.[23]

8.8 POTENTIAL PROBLEMS IN CONSULTING CHILDREN WITHIN THE MEDIATION PROCESS

- Children are not responsible and they should not be drawn into parental disputes.

- Involving children increases their distress and confusion.

- Children will be upset if they become more aware of parental conflict.

- Children should not be involved in what are properly adult negotiations.

---

[22] Personal communication quoted in Parkinson 'Child-Inclusive Family Mediation' [2006] Fam Law 485.

[23] See also Cantwell 'The Emotional Safeguarding of Children in Private Law' [2010] Fam Law 84–90.

- Power imbalances between parents and children lie outside the boundaries of mediation.

- Empowering children risks 'disempowering' one or both parents.

- Parents' decision-making authority is undermined if the mediator is seen as the expert.

- The mediator's role may be confused with the role of counsellor or child advocate.

- Involving children may create expectations that things will be made better for them.

- Children may feel under pressure to express their views and feelings.

- Children may fear being asked to make a choice.

- Children may not be reliable judges of their own long-term interests.

- The mediator may get triangulated between parents and child.

- The mediator could be left holding secrets or confidences from a child that the child does not want shared with parents: this would be an untenable position for the mediator.

- The child's conflicts of loyalty may be heightened.

- Parents may be unable to manage their distress in front of the children.

- Parents may pressurise and brief the child on what to say to the mediator.

- Feedback to parents afterwards may result in them being angry with the child.

- Young children who see their parents talking in a friendly way may think their parents are going to get back together again – feeding hopes of reconciliation.

8.9   POTENTIAL BENEFITS OF INCLUDING CHILDREN IN THE MEDIATION PROCESS

- The majority of children who have been involved say that this helped them a great deal.

- Explanations and reassurance can be given to children.

- Children adjust more easily if they understand their parents' decisions more clearly.

- Involving children shows them that their wishes, views and feelings matter and that they are treated with respect.

- Listening to children is a way of showing care.

- A way of helping both parents to listen to their children.

- Parents may choose to explain their decisions and arrangements to their children in a family meeting (some parents need the mediator's support to do this).

- Dispelling misunderstandings: for example, that a child does not want to see a parent when the child actually wants to do so.

- Enabling children to ask questions, comment and contribute their ideas.

- Enabling children to express a worry or concern, such as where the family's pets will live.

- Easing communication and reducing tensions in parent-child relationships.

- Giving children an opportunity to see the mediator alone and talk about their feelings and concerns, without being anxious about how the parents will hear them.

- Helping children to work out the messages they may want to give to their parents (or other people involved) and to feel able to give these messages.

- Enabling a child to receive a message from a parent who cannot give it directly, for some reason.

- With the child's agreement, to give feedback to parents to help them understand the child's concerns and feelings, so that these can be taken into account in the parents' decisions.

Positive reasons for including children need to be weighed against potential risks and disadvantages. When both parents agree that their child should be included in some way in order to help the child, there are different options and considerations to work through. The flipchart is a helpful tool in considering each option. Some parents would like to include the children in a family meeting with the mediator present, to help them explain things to the children with the mediator's help. Alternatively, depending on the age of the child and the particular circumstances, parents may ask if a child counsellor or the mediator could see a child alone. Adolescents, in particular, may be willing to talk alone with a third person who knows both parents but who is not emotionally involved in the situation. Some adolescents need a space to talk through their feelings and decisions, especially when they are old enough to take decisions themselves. Occasionally there are direct requests from children who ask to meet the mediator, because they know that the mediator already knows their family situation, whereas a school counsellor may not have this knowledge and is not in contact with both parents. Many children are anxious not to be labelled as having problems and needing counselling. Even young children are able to understand that mediation is not the same as counselling or therapy and that the mediator is not a social worker or investigator. If both parents want a counsellor or mediator to meet with children on their own, will siblings be seen together or separately? Will feedback be given to the parents afterward? There are so many questions to consider that it is helpful to have a checklist to work through, although obviously not in a rigid or bureaucratic way.

8.10 PRE-REQUISITES AND CHECK-LIST FOR CHILD-INCLUSIVE MEDIATION

• Suitable rooms and facilities for meetings with children.

• Before meeting with children, family mediators and child counsellors must have a Criminal Records Bureau check, training in child consultation/child-inclusive mediation and a professional practice consultant with this training.

• Risk assessment – both parents confirm that there are no child protection issues.

• Are any professionals involved with the child – currently or previously?

• Understanding of the family's situation, culture and current issues.

• A picture of the child from the parents – personality, stage of development, activities, relationships, etc.

• Asking what each parent has said to the child so far.

• Considering whether the child is of sufficient age and maturity to take part directly.

- Considering with parents possible options for child-inclusive mediation and the pros and cons.

- Objectives and the role of a child counsellor/mediator to be clarified and agreed with both parents.

- Nature and limits of confidentiality in child consultation (a) for the parents, (b) for the child.

- Whether parents are willing to receive feedback, including a negative message from a child, and also able to accept that a child may not want any feedback to be given.

- Parents' agreement on the stage and timing of child-inclusive mediation.

- Parents' written acceptance of any charges, or confirmation of public funding.

- Agreement on the structure of the meeting – for example, children and both parents initially for introductions, then children seen alone? Siblings together or separately? Will children be asked to choose?

- Date for a subsequent mediation meeting, when agreed feedback may be given.

- Agreement as to whether one or both parents will explain to the children what is proposed.

- Agreement as to whether the mediator should also write directly to the child.

- Can the child being offered a follow-up meeting, if the child wishes to come again?

- Parents sign a Parental Consent Form for child consultation in mediation.[24]

- The child also needs to give consent and show willingness.

8.11 AGREEING ARRANGEMENTS WITH BOTH PARENTS AND WITH THE CHILD

It is important for parents to consider the boundaries of discussions with children in or alongside mediation. Confidentiality cannot be absolute

---

[24] See Appendix F below.

and child protection procedures must be followed where a child is said or believed to be at risk of serious harm. This must be made clear to all concerned, including the child, and parents must give their written consent. It also needs to be clear whether, with the child's consent, feedback may be given to parents following a meeting with a child. As a child may not want feedback to be given, the parents need to accept that they might not be given feedback, but this does not mean that the meeting with the child was a wasted effort. Many children feel confident enough, after talking things through, to be able to say to each parent what they want to say, without needing to use the mediator as intermediary. Younger children may need more help, however. In practice, assuring children that what they say to the mediator or child counsellor will be held in confidence, unless someone is in need of protection, has not been found to leave child counsellors or mediators burdened with confidences from children that cannot be shared with their parents. Often, children decide on a message that they want to give one or both parents themselves, either at home or with the mediator's help. Very often, these are positive messages about how the child has been trying to help the parents, or about the kind of help the child would like from a parent. If a child asks the counsellor or mediator to explain something to the parents on the child's behalf, the content of this feedback should be written down and checked with the child.

8.12   THE APPROACH TO THE CHILD AND THE CHILD'S CONSENT

Parents need to explain to children why they would like them to take part, to allay their anxieties and encourage a positive response. It is usually helpful for the mediator to write a personal letter of invitation to the child as well. Children need to understand what is being offered and to be reassured that they can decline the invitation. They need to know that they will not be cross-questioned. If they wish to talk, they will be listened to, but they are not being asked to make choices or given responsibility for difficult decisions. Parents need to agree that they will not brief the child beforehand, nor question the child afterwards about anything the child may or may not have said. Children need reassurance that they can speak freely, without fearing that they will get into trouble or hurt their parents in some way. Parents need to accept that the purpose of involving the child is to help the child, not to use the child as judge or arbitrator. Great care must be taken at all stages – before, during and afterwards – to avoid causing further distress to children.

Children are usually anxious about talking to an outsider and may fear saying something that will upset one or both parents. They are usually very protective of both parents, or may be aligned with a vulnerable or 'wronged' parent. They also worry about adding to their parents' worries. Children may however be worrying about things that their parents can deal with, once the parents understand what these things are. Mediators can help children explain their worries to their parents and this can free children from some of their anxieties. Mediators also need to be aware that children may not be able to put their fears into words – and have the humility to recognise that they cannot alleviate a child's pain. There are family situations in which a great deal of loss has already occurred and where a child feels deeply estranged from one parent. There are also situations in which a child needs a parent to apologise for saying or doing something that has hurt the child. If the parent concerned is able to say to the child that he is she is genuinely sorry (sometimes there has been a misunderstanding between a parent and a child), considerable healing may take place.

Involving children in mediation can help them to feel clearer and more confident about what they want to say to their parents, as well as what they need to hear from their parents. There are occasions, however, when the child wants help to explain something to the parents. This needs to be planned first with the child and then with the parents. There can be considerable relief if parents understand that sending messages to each other via the child is distressing the child. Even a limited agreement on a small step may be valuable in helping parents and children to talk and listen to each other. In talking with children, it is important not to see it as a one-way process of seeking their views and feelings. It is equally important to give explanations that are appropriate to their age and to convey reassuring messages, especially when communication between a child and a parent has broken down. The feelings and views children may express – or be unable to express – depend on the child's perceptions. These perceptions are liable to change as they gain a better understanding of their parents' positions and feelings. A child's rejection of a parent is often a reaction to feeling rejected by that parent. The main benefit of involving children directly is to re-open channels of communication between the child and both parents, so that they can all talk with each other with more empathy and understanding.

In a case referred to The Mediation Centre in Stafford after three years of court proceedings, a final, tightly defined, shared residence order broke down immediately because the twelve-year-old boy did not consider that the order met his recorded wishes and feelings. He flatly refused to see his mother at all, who took this to be yet more evidence of manipulation by his father. The mother's solicitor referred the matter to mediation rather than seeking enforcement of the order. The parents, however, refused to meet together, and even in shuttled sessions refused to consider any co-operation, the father stating he was following his son's wishes and the mother re-asserting her belief in his manipulation and bullying by the father. In a separate session, the boy told the mediator that he wished to see his mother, but on a more limited basis than as set out in the Court Order. He had withdrawn from contact because he was angry that the Court had not listened to him. Whilst not expressing any judgment, the mediator found no evidence of current manipulation. In the two following sessions, the mediator invited the active participation of the parents' solicitors, who:

(1)   supported their clients in these highly emotive and distressing circumstances;

(2)   with the parents' agreement, met with the mediator to plan process and consider permutations;

(3)   gave independent advice about the difficult question of returning the matter to Court or re-involving experts;

(4)   supported interim arrangements so that the boy's relationship with his mother could be rebuilt; and

(5)   worked with the mediator and the parents to draw up a binding agreement that would supersede the Court Order, so as to avoid the necessity of return to Court.

8.13   CHILDREN'S EXPERIENCE OF CHILD-INCLUSIVE MEDIATION

An early project on child-inclusive mediation in Edinburgh used a similar approach to Mediation in Divorce in Richmond, offering parents the opportunity for their children to meet with the mediator on their own. Despite their initial uncertainty, almost all the children who met with the mediator spoke very positively about their experience.[25] Benefits they reported included:

• Feeling 'relieved', 'much easier', less anxious about being caught between parents.

• Better communication: opening up channels of communication.

• Better contact arrangements, feeling happier about contact visits.

• More understanding of their situation ('we like going to dad's now that we understand more' said an eight-year-old girl, speaking for herself and her sister).

• Having the opportunity to express their own feelings. One teenager said she had not spoken to anyone before about what she was feeling, and she now felt that she and her parents understood each other better.

---

[25]   Garwood *Children in Conciliation* (Scottish Association of Family Conciliation Services, 1989).

- Realising they were not alone in having these feelings.

- Asking the mediator's help to convey a message to their parents or to make requests, such as making phone calls to an absent parent.

- Borrowing books to help them understand what was happening.

- Being able to keep out of issues between parents that did not concern them.

Nearly all the children interviewed (24 out of 28) felt they had definitely benefited from seeing the mediator. The other four said everything was all right for them anyway, so it had not made much difference. The findings suggested that:

- There can be considerable benefits for children in being involved in mediation.

- Parents and children agree about the benefits.

- Children would come more readily if they understood the purpose better.

- Confidentiality should be clear: there should be a code of practice on involving children in mediation.

- Parents should be willing to accept feedback, if the child wants them to have it.

- Mediators should have additional training before involving children in mediation, to equip them with the necessary understanding and skills.

- Experience and skills in working with children should be shared more.

- More children could be helped in this way, if mediators are clear about the benefits for children and more confident in discussing these benefits with parents.

Devon Family Mediators Agency likewise finds that their service works well, taking into account the following:[26]

(1) Just offering the appointment can encourage parents to review their arrangements for their children.

(2) There is a focus on the children's issues in mediation.

---

[26] See n 22 above.

(3) The children really value the opportunity and often do not need any other intervention.

(4) The children always emerge more relaxed and happier than when they went in.

(5) A member of the mediation team is always there when the appointment takes place, to receive the family and to support the process, but do not take part. They are there to act as receptionists and to make everyone feel comfortable before and after the meeting.

McIntosh reported on a pilot project in Australia in which parents were offered the opportunity for their child to have a one-off meeting with a trained child counsellor.[27] If all concerned accepted the invitation and the child consented to feedback being given, the child counsellor joined in a subsequent mediation session and discussed the feedback with the parents and the mediator. The use of a child counsellor alongside the mediation process was generally found to have many positive benefits for the children and their parents. A later study compared child-focused mediation, in which children did not take part directly, with child-inclusive mediation in which children met with a child counsellor.[28] In both groups in the year following mediation, the researchers found lasting reductions in levels of conflict and improved management of disputes, as reported by the parents and the children. The child-inclusive group showed more significant improvements in parental and child-parent relationships, particularly between fathers and children, and more noticeable benefits in children's developmental recovery from high-conflict separation. Child-inclusive mediation:[29]

> 'offered children a safe, specialist avenue for their views and needs to be considered and indeed to impact significantly upon the way in which their parents were able to resolve their parenting disputes.'

Research in Britain[30] and Australia[31] suggests that children are more competent to take part in family decision-making than adults generally believe. It is important to take time and trouble to listen to what children tell us and to understand how they feel. The challenges of consulting with children and young people concerning changes in their family life are considerable for all concerned. Adults need sensitivity and awareness, non-judgmental attitudes and a good sense of humour. With these qualities and good professional training, mediators are likely to find

---

[27] McIntosh 'Child-Inclusive Mediation' (2000) 18(1) *Mediation Quarterly*.

[28] McIntosh, Wells, Smyth and Long 'Child-Focused and Child-Inclusive Divorce Mediation: Comparative Outcomes' (2008) 46(1) *Family Court Review* (Association of Family and Conciliation Courts).

[29] Ibid, p 22.

[30] Smart and Neale 'It's My Life Too – Children's Perspectives on Post-Divorce Parenting' [2000] Fam Law 163–169.

[31] McIntosh 'Child-Inclusive Mediation' (2000) 18(1) *Mediation Quarterly*.

conversations with children illuminating and life-enhancing, despite the sadness and anger felt by many children when they lose the security of living with both parents in an intact family. Children understand far more than adults generally imagine. Insights and practical suggestions from children can often help parents to resolve problems in ways that will make life easier for the family as a whole. In a child-inclusive mediation undertaken at Gilbert Stephens Family Mediation Service in Exeter, an 11-year-old boy had chosen to remain with his father in the family home because, as he explained, he and his dad were both keen on football, while his 13-year-old sister had decided to leave the home with her mother. The parents were locked in intractable disputes over residence and contact, each of them convinced that their solution was the right one. Both parents agreed that the children should be involved in the decision-making process, recognising that no arrangement would work if the children were not prepared to go along with it. The mediator met with the brother and sister together and although the 13-year-old girl was initially unresponsive, both children became interested when the mediator sketched possible plans on the flipchart. The children then wanted to contribute their own ideas. With their consent, the children's suggestions were put forward at the next mediation meeting. The children's suggestions had not occurred to the parents, who had been caught up in fighting each other. The parents agreed with the arrangements proposed by the children and a further application to the court was averted. In another child-inclusive mediation, two young brothers commented with regard to their parents: 'We knew they could not do it without our help.'

8.14 APTITUDE, KNOWLEDGE AND SKILLS FOR CHILD-INCLUSIVE MEDIATION

However experienced they may be in other professional fields, family mediators need personal aptitude, knowledge and skills to discuss with parents possible ways of including their children in the mediation process, and secondly, to take this forward in an appropriate and well-planned way. Lead bodies affiliated to the Family Mediation Council offer advanced training courses in Direct Child Consultation (DCC) for experienced mediators. This training extends specialist areas of knowledge and develops special understanding and skills.[32]

Contextual knowledge needs to include knowledge of:

• Private family and child law.

• Child and adolescent development.

---

[32] See also *Children, Young People and Family Mediation* (UK College of Family Mediators, 2000).

- Children's reactions to parental separation and divorce, at different ages and stages.

- Family systems theory: family structure and communication.

- Ways of helping children cope with parental separation or divorce.

- Stepfamilies, especially adjustment to new roles and different family structures.

- Cultural differences, diversity of family patterns and family values.

- Services for children, where further referral may be indicated.

Understanding needs to include:

- Understanding of the mediator's role in facilitating communication between children and parents.

- Understanding children's needs.

- Understanding children's responses to parental separation, conflict and loss.

- Understanding that children may be unable to say what they want or feel.

- Imaginative understanding to enter into children's fantasies and wish for magic.

- Capacity to help children understand and accept that some things cannot be changed, however much one wants them to change.

- Different ways of including children in mediation.

- The mediator's self-awareness and ability to be pro-active without taking a directive stance.

Mediation skills for child-inclusive mediation:

- Engaging both parents equally in planning whether, and if so, how their children could be included.

- Agreeing the approach to the child, whether it should include a letter of invitation from the mediator to the child.

- Engaging with children, putting them at ease.

- Explaining who you are, what your role is and how you are trying to help.

- Explaining the reasons for the meeting and the nature and extent of confidentiality.

- Listening to children, 'third ear' listening.

- Communicating clearly – use of language – not talking down to children.

- Acknowledging and normalising a child's feelings.

- Giving a message from a parent to a child (where a parent is unable or not yet able to communicate directly with the child).

- Tuning in to what is important from the child's perspective.

- Helping children to feel safer and clearer about talking with their parents.

- Giving agreed feedback from children to parents and helping parents to take the feedback on board.

- Using humour appropriately and sensitively.

- Using images, anecdotes, books and other materials for children and parents.

8.14.1 Two examples of involving children in mediation

Anna (aged 11) and James (aged 7)

Carl and Tricia both felt it would help their children – Anna, aged 11 and James, aged 7 – to talk with the mediator without their parents being present. Anna was showing reluctance to visit her father and neither parent wanted to force her. They thought she might talk more easily to someone outside the family. All the pre-conditions for involving Anna and James were discussed and agreed. Tricia would invite them to come and explain the arrangements to them. Anna and James accepted the invitation.

It was agreed with the parents that, after initial introductions, Anna and James would be seen together, while Carl and Tricia waited in the reception area. Carl and Tricia would then rejoin the meeting. If the children wanted to share anything with them, the mediator would help them do so, but they would not be pressed to say anything, if they did not want to. The parents said they would listen to what the children wanted to say, without getting angry or upset with them. They accepted that (subject to the usual limits on confidentiality regarding child protection) Anna and James should decide whether they wanted anything shared with their parents afterwards. Tricia and Carl thought this freedom would help the children to feel less worried about hurting either of them and that giving them an opportunity to talk, without pressure, would be helpful for them.

The following extracts recalled more or less verbatim may help illustrate the content and style of a short discussion with Anna and James. Both children talked readily and showed great insight and sensitivity to their parents' difficulties. They also made suggestions, increasingly with a strong sense of humour:

> '**Mediator:** *James, do you have any friends at school whose parents don't live together?*
>
> **James:** *Yes, I do – I have a friend called Gary and his parents ... (etc)*
>
> **Mediator:** *How do you think Gary is getting on – is it O.K. for him?*
>
> **James:** *Well, Gary says the thing to do is to tell your parents jokes, to stop them arguing. I tried that ... I tried to tell my Mum and Dad a joke about a monkey but they didn't listen. They went on arguing. Anyway I hadn't finished making up the joke.*
>
> **Mediator:** *You really are trying hard to help your parents. I think they'd like to know the way you are trying to help them. Could you tell them about it?*
>
> **James:** *Yes, I will ...*
>
> **Mediator:** *Anna, you said just now that it was just small things you don't like about going to your Dad's at weekends and that you didn't think they were worth bothering about. But sometimes small things can hurt a lot.*
>
> **James:** *Yes, that's right. Sometimes I have a scratch that really hurts and other times when I fall off my bike I've got a real gash I hadn't noticed ...*
>
> **Anna:** *What I don't like is when Dad picks me up from school he is talking all the time on his mobile and I've told him I don't like it and my friends tease me about it. But he still does it ...*
>
> **Mediator:** *So you'd like your father to listen and take more notice of what you say?*
>
> **Anna:** *Yes, he doesn't listen properly ...*
>
> **Mediator:** *What kind of things do you like doing when you go to your Dad?*
>
> **Anna:** *Well, I quite like playing on his computer but the thing is, when I tell him I've got stuck, he just comes and takes over.*

Mediator: *You mean, you'd like him to show you what to do to get unstuck?*

Anna: *Yes, he just does it all himself.*

Mediator: *I think he would show you, if he understands you'd like him to show you.*

James: *Yes, and I want him to show me too.'*

Carl and Tricia looked extremely apprehensive when they joined the meeting. They listened very attentively to what the children explained to them with great liveliness and spontaneity. Their eyes filled with tears when James told them he had tried to tell them jokes to stop them arguing. But they also smiled. The atmosphere relaxed and lightened, as both parents understood that they had not 'failed' as parents and that the children were not judging or blaming them. The meeting helped them realise, however, the great importance of listening carefully to their children. Things that the parents had not noticed, or which they had dismissed as unimportant, were extremely important from the children's perspective. Anna's withdrawal, which had troubled them both, turned out to be her way of showing resentment that when she did tell them something, they usually forgot about it. Tricia and Carl might not have realised the significance of these apparently small things in talking with the children at home, because they were looking for 'something bigger', through the other end of the telescope. The children might also have felt more inhibited in talking with the mediator in front of both parents. Feedback from the children and the parents after the meeting was extremely positive: 'We can talk more easily now.'

Tom (aged 15)

Tom's mother, Jenny, was leaving her second husband, Wilf, to live with a new partner, Harry. Jenny wanted Tom to come to live with her and Harry, while Wilf thought Tom should stay with him, as he had helped to bring Tom up since he was small and Tom had no contact with his natural father. Both parents were concerned that Tom was staying out late in the evenings, not bothering with his schoolwork and becoming increasingly aggressive or uncommunicative. They could not get a response from him about where he wanted to live and were worried that if the situation continued, he might get involved in drugs and petty crime. They were not sure if he would come to see the mediator but thought it was worth a try.

Tom came. Initially silent, he listened to the positive message from his mother that Jenny had asked the mediator to give him. Jenny's anger and frustration – and possibly guilt feelings – had led to a barrier between her and Tom. Their discussions invariably turned into arguments. Tom began to talk with the mediator, whom he accepted as impartial and not making judgments. He explained that he was angry with everyone in his family and very upset. At the end of the discussion, he told the mediator that he felt he could handle talking with his mother, provided she was willing to try too. He thought it would help if the mediator would also explain to his mother and stepfather how he was feeling, so that they would understand better when he talked to them. He particularly asked the mediator's help in conveying a request to his mother not to keep pressing him to live with her and Harry. He needed more time and he did not want to have to choose between his parents. His mother was receptive to the feedback from the mediator, which the mediator had checked through with Tom. Jenny and Tom then found they could talk more easily on their own, without arguing as they had done before. Tom also said he would be willing to go out for a walk with his stepfather, which he had previously refused to do. The trouble had been that his stepfather had always asked him too early in the morning. Mornings were not his best time ...

The notion of *consulting* with children and young people in order to understand their views, feelings and needs, is too limited if it implies that the sole purpose is to seek views and feelings *from* the child. Communication needs to be two-way, not one-way. It is often important to convey reassuring messages *to* children, especially when communication between a child and a parent has broken down. A child counsellor or mediator can acknowledge and normalise how children often feel, without a child feeling interrogated. The feelings and views that a child expresses – or is unable to express – depend to a large extent on the child's perceptions. These perceptions may change, as the child gains more understanding. A child needs to understand the reasons for a parent not being in touch for some time, sometimes for a very long time, and in some cases the child may need an apology from a parent before being willing to have contact. Child-inclusive mediation means having conversations with children, not plying them with questions and extracting answers for the benefit of adults who 'need to know'. The main value of these conversations with children is often to unblock channels of communication between children and parents so that they can listen to each other and talk together with more understanding. The mediator's role can be a catalyst, but it is not directive or controlling. Sensitive 'micro-interventions' by mediators can help parents to work out practical arrangements and consider how to help their children adjust to these arrangements. Mediators' questions and observations need to draw on their understanding of attachment and systems theory, crisis and chaos theory, family interactions and communications. All these are relevant to mediating with parents, children and young people and other family members.

8.15   PARENT-CHILD MEDIATION

Even in the most stable families, conflicts between adolescents and their parents is a normal part of growing up. In many families, these are normal quarrels that do not threaten the core of the parent-child relationship. But in others, frequent arguments may escalate into a painful, exhausting and at times life-threatening battle in which anger, depression and self-doubt erode the love and affection that children sorely need. Some children and teenagers leave home following bitter arguments with parents and/or stepparents. An ADR process for children and parents, for example to explore whether a child who has run away from home is willing to return under conditions acceptable to the child and the parent (or other carer) may involve child protection issues that would not be suitable for a standard model of family mediation but which might be made available in an adapted model.[33] As children become more aware of their rights and able to make their own applications – for example, for contact with a parent – they also need to know that there are ways of making their needs and feelings heard, so that solutions can be worked out with the agreement of all concerned. Good practice stresses the importance of involving children in decisions about themselves and respecting their point of view. Schools and colleges need to be able to give children, young people and parents information about mediation (using websites) and consider having a mediator available at certain times.

8.16 MEDIATION WITH CHILDREN, PARENTS AND TEACHERS

In the year 2008–09, an average of 511 pupils per day were excluded from primary, secondary and special needs schools in England.[34] Most were temporary exclusions (503) for verbal abuse (412) but some (91) were for assaulting an adult. Disputes over exclusion or discipline in school may flare up between children and teachers and may escalate if irate parents become involved as well. Children need encouragement to discuss learning or discipline difficulties and may be directly involved in working out a contract with parents and the school that all concerned can accept. There are of course major power imbalances between children, parents and education authorities. Mediation will not always be appropriate or possible, but it should be considered at an early stage before problems accumulate and positions harden. Family mediators with expertise and experience in working with children, as well as with adults, could offer mediation to schools – for children, parents and teachers – through a special sector of the family mediators' register. Mediators should have additional training for membership of this sector.

8.17 DISCUSSION GROUPS FOR CHILDREN

Discussion groups for children of separated parents, catering for children of different ages, are scarce. In the 1980s, when the divorce court welfare service was under the wing of the Probation Service, some teams of divorce court welfare officers used to organise discussion groups for children, based on American models. In France and Quebec there are

---

[33] See Chapter 4 at **4.14.3**.
[34] (2010) *Guardian Weekly*, 31 December.

'Groupes de Paroles' for children and in Italy, 'Gruppi di Parola'. These groups are led by family mediators and consist of four sessions, each lasting two hours. The children share their experiences and realise that they are not alone in having these experiences. They are helped to express their feelings and to develop ideas for 'coping strategies' through talking, drawing pictures and writing individual or group letters to their parents, explaining what they would like the parents to understand better. These letters are very moving and can have a powerful effect on parents. A research study in Milan studied videotapes (made with the written consent of parents and children) of twenty groups involving 113 children aged from 6–12. The researchers found that these groups offered a private place where children could 'give voice' to their experiences of parental separation and divorce, share ideas on how to cope better and help their parents as well.[35]

8.18   TRAINING CHILDREN AS PEER MEDIATORS

Children are intrigued by conflict. They watch how adults react and may get satisfaction from acting out aggressive and violent scenes. Children understand more about the nature of relationships at an earlier age than many adults realise. They can learn to manage their own anger and non-violent ways of dealing with conflict. Instead of arguing with parents, teachers, siblings or classmates, children can learn about mediation and be trained in mediation skills. Drama groups in schools may be used to explore ways of expressing and managing conflict. One method of teaching children conflict management skills has been developed from drama exercises with adults created by the Brazilian theatre director, Augusto Boal.[36] Boal was nominated for the Nobel Peace Prize in 2008 and in 2009, shortly before his death, UNESCO awarded him the title of World Theatre Ambassador. In drama groups for children, children as young as seven can take part in role-plays led by a skilled trainer and/or mediator. A quarrel or fight may be acted out. It is then acted out a second time and this time any child in the group can shout 'stop' at any point and take over one of the roles, showing how the conflict could be managed differently. Constructive ways of managing conflict are discussed and tried out. Following this training, class teachers have reported that relationships between children are greatly improved and disagreements sorted out more easily. There has been a steady growth in the use of peer support, buddy groups, anti-bullying strategies and mediation.[37] These schemes have high rates of success. In Scotland also, many schools have peer mediation programme. The Scottish Mediation Network provides training and runs conferences on mediation in schools.[38]

---

[35]   Marzotto (ed) *Gruppi di parola per figli di genitori separati* (Vita e Pensiero, 2010).
[36]   Boal *Games for Actors and Non-Actors* (Routledge, 1992).
[37]   See www.peersupportworks.co.uk.
[38]   See www.scottishmediation.org.uk.

8.19   A HOLISTIC APPROACH TO FAMILY MEDIATION

The word holistic comes from the Greek word *holos*, meaning whole or entire. Holism is defined[39] as:

> 'a theory or principle of a tendency in nature to produce an organised whole which is more than the mere sum of its component parts.'

Holistic medicine treats the whole person, not just the symptom. A doctor treating pain in the stomach needs to consider whether grief and pain in the heart are causing pain in the stomach. Mediators do not treat people as patients: the analogy is between holistic medicine and mediators' concern for the family as a whole. Mediators mediate between family members and groups who are in conflict and often vulnerable and in pain. A family system is more than a collection of individuals. Children need to be respected as subjects of rights and as family members who need to be listened to, rather than as objects of welfare with no voice of their own. There are then greater possibilities of resolving conflicts that affect the family as a whole.

On Children

Your children are not your children.
They are the sons and daughters of Life's longing for itself.
They come through you, but not from you,
And though they are with you yet they belong not to you.
You may give them your love but not your thoughts,
For they have their own thoughts.
You may house their bodies but not their souls,
For their souls dwell in the house of tomorrow,
which you cannot visit, not even in your dreams.
You may strive to be like them, but seek not to make them like you.
For life goes not backward nor tarries with yesterday.

Kahlil Gibran 'The Prophet' (1926)

---

[39]   New Shorter Oxford English Dictionary.

CHAPTER 9

MEDIATING ON MONEY MATTERS

'The world is too much with us; late and soon,
Getting and spending, we lay waste our powers'[1]

'The sadness of lives and the comfort of things'[2]

CONTENTS

---

[1]   William Wordsworth *Sonnet*.
[2]   Miller *The Comfort of Things* (Polity Press, 2008).

9.1   RELATIONSHIP BREAKDOWN AND POVERTY

Financial worries and problems over debts contribute to the breakdown
of relationships that are already under strain. The economic recession is
taking a heavy toll on families facing unemployment, cuts in welfare
benefits and rising fuel bills. Couples with mortgages or rent they can no
longer afford may find themselves going further into debt. Far from
solving their financial problems, separation and divorce generally
compound them, since two households cost more than one and the
break-up itself generates further costs. Dual-income couples who
previously enjoyed a relatively good standard of living may find on
separation that they have little capital and inadequate incomes. A father
who leaves the home may find the cost of renting even a small flat leaves
him close to the breadline, while a mother who remains in the family
home (or vice versa) may be shocked to realise that the roof over her head
is no longer secure. The future may be bleak. Householders who can no
longer pay their mortgage may be faced with repossession of their
property. Some parents who face being homeless as a result of
relationship breakdown are obliged to move back to live with their own
parents, renewing an unwanted dependency and losing their privacy and
autonomy. Having adequate accommodation for children to stay
overnight in reasonable comfort requires considerable resources. Children
in separated families tend to grow up in households with lower incomes,
poorer housing and greater financial hardship than intact families,
especially those headed by lone mothers.[3] Child poverty is associated with
children's lower educational achievements.

9.2   THE MEANING OF MONEY AND PROPERTY

Money means security and, for many people, it means owning your own
home and being able to buy the things you need or want. Having access to
money is both a source of power and a means of control.[4] When a couple
decide to live together and buy a property, their investment is far more
than a purely financial one. It is also an investment in their relationship
and future happiness, in building a nest for bringing up their children and
the hard work and fun of furnishing and decorating their home to their
mutual satisfaction. If, later on, the couple's relationship breaks down, the
occupation or sale of the family home is likely to be a highly emotive issue
for them both. Even asking for a valuation in mediation can cause great
distress if it suggests that the home will inevitably be sold. The idea of
becoming homeless may instil a paralysing fear. The home provides
security – having a roof over your head – and privacy, a refuge to retreat
to from the hurly-burly of life, where you are free to live as you wish,
without unwanted intruders. Living in your own home also means having

---

[3]   Rodgers and Prior *Divorce and separation: the outcomes for children* (Joseph Rowntree
       Foundation, 1998).
[4]   See Chapter 10 below.

social status and being part of a community, with neighbours, friends and maybe relatives nearby or within reach. In emotional terms, the home contains memories of the past, the challenges of daily life and dreams for the future. Memories include the hard work put into maintaining and improving the property. If there are children, it is the children's home too. Parents have memories of their children being born and growing up and the joys and trials of each stage. But the home may have unhappy associations, as well as pleasant ones. There may have been cracks in the couple's relationship long before the actual break-up. If the atmosphere in the home has become very strained, with parents not speaking to each other or constantly arguing, or if there has been domestic violence and/or relentless psychological abuse, the home is no longer a refuge. It may be a prison where violence continues unchecked and unheard. In mediation, it is very important, therefore, to understand not only the legal ownership and financial value of property, but also the meanings it holds for both partners, in emotional and symbolic terms.

9.3   INTERRELATED ISSUES – CHILDREN AND FINANCIAL MATTERS

Discussions about children often need to be combined with discussions about financial issues, because of the linkages between them. If parents do not own property and both of them are dependent on welfare benefits, their dispute may be on the single issue of the children's contact with the non-residential parent. More often, arrangements for children are entangled with other questions, such as whether the family home will be retained or sold and where the non-residential parent will live. Mortgage payments on the family home, the cost of renting alternative accommodation, loans, debts and the payment of maintenance are relevant factors to be taken into account in working out whether the family home can be retained or whether it has to be sold. Some fathers question why they should pay child support, if the mother is refusing to let them have contact with the children. Some mothers argue that the father has no right to see the children if he is not supporting them. Arguments and worries about money spill over into arguments about children. Many parents regard paying child support and keeping a roof over the children's heads as essential components of parental responsibility, inseparable from day-to-day responsibilities for the children. Yet the law deals with financial and property issues in separate proceedings from child residence and contact. The close connections between these issues in emotional and practical terms are not addressed in the legal system. For parents, however, it may be impossible to agree arrangements for children until they know where they will be living and how they will pay their bills. Mediation on all issues provides a forum in which these interrelated issues can be addressed in conjunction with each other, instead of being artificially fragmented.

9.4   THE LACK OF A STATUTORY FORMULA FOR FINANCIAL SETTLEMENTS

In some countries, standard principles make it easier to settle financial issues because a statutory formula determines the level of child support to be paid. In Norway, each partner keeps what he or she brought into the marriage and they divide equally what they have acquired during the marriage.[5] Norway has guidelines for determining the level of spousal maintenance or child support, based on gross income. A continuing criticism of the English system is that the guidelines enshrined in section 25 of the Matrimonial Causes Act 1973 (MCA 1973) provide so much scope for uncertainty. However, this uncertainty in the court system may be seen as an *opportunity* for mediators. Parents in child-focused mediation are often reminded in mediation that they know their children's needs better than anyone else. In the same way, they are likely to be best placed to make informed decisions about their financial resources and needs. Mediation encourages them to use their own judgment in finding a workable solution, instead of asking a judge to decide on their behalf. Recent case law on the division of (admittedly exceptional) assets and income on divorce may be equally bewildering for lawyers and clients, in attempting to predict the likely outcome of an ancillary relief application. Mediators, on the other hand, can explain the parameters to participants jointly, without advising them on the likely outcome if they take their dispute to court, but identifying questions that they need to put to their legal advisors. In this way, participants are helped to make an informed evaluation of the options available to them and encouraged to use their own yardsticks and creativity in working out what they think is fair.

9.5   UNMARRIED COUPLES

Opportunities for mediation created by the discretionary and sometimes unclear application of divorce law rules and precedents are even greater in financial disputes arising from the separation of unmarried couples. In contrast to considerations of fairness in ancillary relief proceedings, fairness is *not* the guiding principle in litigation between former cohabitants. Cohabitants unable to resolve their respective interests in a home legally owned by only one of them, but contributed to by both, face lengthy and costly litigation in the *civil* jurisdiction under the Trusts of Land and Appointment of Trustees Act 1996. If dependent children are involved and Schedule 1 to the Children Act 1989 is also invoked, matters become even more complex. It is estimated that one sixth of couples living together in England and Wales are unmarried, a proportion predicted to rise to one in four by 2031, while 25% of children are born to unmarried parents. Many cohabitants believe that they have legal rights as 'common law' spouses and are shocked to find on separation that this is not the

---

[5]   Tjersland 'Mediation in Norway' (1995) 12(4) *Mediation Quarterly* 339–351.

case. This is an area of law urgently in need of reform. The President of the Family Division said in February 2011:[6]

> 'I am in favour of cohabitees having rights because of the injustices of the present system. Women cohabitees, in particular, are severely disadvantaged by being unable to claim maintenance and having their property rights determined by the conventional laws of trusts.'

The President's views will strengthen the case for legislative reform in this area, a reform for which Resolution has long been pressing. In the future, the courts would then have the same discretion to award maintenance payments, a lump sum or a share of the property. Meanwhile, as current law fails to provide the remedies they need, many more unmarried couples may choose to come to mediation to reach financial settlements that they both regard as fair in their particular circumstances (see example of mediation with an unmarried couple at **9.17** below). Mediators need to be familiar with the principles set out in *Stack v Dowden*[7] and *Kernott and Jones*.[8] With up-to-date knowledge of the law, mediators (often dual-trained) can provide a forum where needs, resources and 'fairness' can be balanced and where the history of contributions can be explored as part of a collaborative information-sharing exercise rather than in destructive and adversarial ways.[9] This is an area ripe for further development, both in mediation and in collaborative law.

9.6 MEDIATION COMPARED WITH THE DISPUTE RESOLUTION ELEMENTS OF ANCILLARY RELIEF LITIGATION

It is often argued that, particularly once proceedings have started, judge-led Dispute Resolution offered by the First Directions Appointment (FDA) and Financial Dispute Resolution (FDR) appointments is likely to be more effective than mediation. Whilst this may be true for the few truly entrenched cases that exercise the courts up to a contested final hearing, many clients who have experienced the pressures of in-court negotiations may have different views. Negotiation 'at the court door' led by counsel may produce a forced settlement without genuine agreement. It can be demonstrated that mediation provides a sound basis for comprehensive financial disclosure that may be more effective than interlocutory court orders – before even beginning to consider the comparative costs! Essentially, those engaged in mediation or collaborative law invest in a co-operative exercise to share information and explore options, whereas court-led Dispute Resolution remains grafted on to an adversarial process. There are of course many cases where the authority of a judge is still required to guide progress and direct co-operation. In these

---

[6] (2011) *The Times*, 3 February.
[7] [2007] UKHL 17, [2007] 2 AC 432, HL.
[8] [2010] EWCA Civ 578, [2010] 2 FLR 1631.
[9] See Robinson [2009] Fam Law 253.

cases, ways can still be found to combine the strengths of court proceedings and mediation in an inquisitorial process, rather than an adversarial one.

9.7   FINANCIAL DISCLOSURE IN MEDIATION

9.7.1   Gathering information

Mediators explain at the initial information and assessment meeting that if there are financial issues that need to be settled, full financial information, supported by the necessary documents, will be needed from both parties in order to achieve a final settlement in divorce that the court can be asked to approve and ratify in a consent order. Mediators use standard financial questionnaires similar to those used by family lawyers and the courts (Form E). Factual financial information is provided in mediation on an 'open' basis, unlike discussions in mediation that are legally privileged and not reportable to the court. The information gathered in mediation is shared and considered with both partners. At their request, the mediator may produce an Open Financial Statement (OFS) that participants take to their lawyers for advice.[10] The information may also be considered in court, if necessary, since there would be wasteful duplication in collecting the same information all over again.

It is important for participants to understand that if the level of disclosure is not satisfactory and does not meet Form E requirements, their legal advisors, and subsequently the court, will be less likely to sanction a proposed settlement. The district judge has discretion to refuse a settlement if he or she is not satisfied that it falls within the MCA 1973 'band of reasonableness'. Mediators therefore need to be able to provide legal information in a neutral and comprehensible way, explaining section 25 of the MCA 1973 and the 'band of reasonableness', so that participants are clear about what the district judge would look for, when they ask for a consent order. Giving this information in mediation is particularly useful, as clients may have received a different level or quality of information from their lawyers (or none at all). The lack of a standard formula in the MCA 1973 means that mediation clients have the advantage of being able to come to their own decision (ie empowered) whilst being aware of the MCA 1973 requirements. The same level of legal information in mediation is useful for ToLATA and Schedule 1 applications too. In terms of obtaining financial disclosure, it is easier to obtain the cooperation of reluctant clients to provide disclosure if they understand the benefits of agreement and the criteria applicable.

The first step, generally, is to help couples plan how they will gather full information about their financial circumstances, as a basis for exploring their financial needs and options for settlement. Just as shared knowledge

---

[10]   See Appendix C below.

of children's needs informs the debate about how to meet those needs, so couples cannot negotiate usefully on financial matters until they know the values of their assets and extent of their liabilities. Some individuals come to their first mediation meeting with spreadsheets already prepared. Others, when asked, have no idea what assets there are or what the other partner earns. Helping both partners equally to determine the value of their assets and the level of their incomes and liabilities is more important in the first instance than explaining section 25 criteria.

Different ways of obtaining professional valuations may need to be considered. The cost of obtaining expert valuations can be more than the asset is worth. Participants may wish to consider instructing a single joint expert (SJE) who has not previously acted for either of them individually. The clients' solicitors should be involved in the selection of the SJE. There may need to be correspondence on this issue with possible approval of a joint letter of instruction drafted by the mediator on a 'without prejudice basis' until agreement has been reached as to whom is to be instructed.

Where pensions are concerned, unless the fund is very limited, a professional pension report is essential. The clients should consult their lawyers, as their lawyers need to approve the pension report provider and the letter of instruction that is prepared prior to the clients commissioning the report. There may need to be consideration as to which fund should be split and how that is to be achieved with the necessary court order: such considerations can make a significant difference. Some pensions are underfunded and some CETVs (Cash Equivalent Transfer Value) do not reflect the real value of that pension. Service pensions are particularly complex. With the clients' solicitors' approval, a pension report can be commissioned during the mediation process and a copy of the report may be attached to the MOU (not to the OFS, as the report may contain recommendations that are not agreed). The same applies if clients have business interests and a forensic valuation of a company is required. In these circumstances, the approval and involvement of the lawyers in the commissioning of the report is equally essential and the report can be annexed to the MOU. Another possibility for difficult valuation work is the use of dual experts working together in a cost-effective way.[11]

Mediators need to use process management skills, as well as interpersonal and problem-solving skills[12] when they discuss the completion of financial questionnaires and the valuations that will be needed. Apart from the practical aspects, there are other considerations. Filling in a form is very daunting for some people. The mediator needs to watch for signs of anxiety or resistance and make sure that both partners are willing to fill in their form and feel able to manage it. Some people are anxious that they will not be able to fill it in, because they do not all have the information.

---

[11] Adam-Cairns 'Why Instruct a Single Joint Expert Valuer?' [2010] Fam Law 656–657.
[12] See Chapter 5 above.

The mediator can reassure them by explaining that if they do not have the information, the other participant may have it:

> 'Don't worry if you do not know the current mortgage balance as Brenda says that she has the mortgage statement and she will bring it. Put down all you can and we will go through both forms next time and see if the information from both of you gives a complete picture.'

The mediator should make it clear that each participant should fill in their own form, even if they know little about the family finances. Sometimes one partner offers to fill in the other one's form, but normally this should be discouraged even if it is a genuinely helpful offer and not an attempt to take control. If each partner fills in their own form the mediator can see how much information is available to each of them and how far they agree about figures and valuations. Some couples, especially those who are still living together, might get into arguments if they discuss on their own the figures they are putting down on their forms. It may be sensible to discourage them from comparing notes and discussing figures on their own and to suggest that going through their forms and looking at differences can be done in mediation, when the mediator is there to help them. Couples generally see the sense of avoiding arguments that would be premature, at this stage. On the other hand, there is no need to discourage co-operative couples from discussing financial matters together. The amount of time that people need to complete their questionnaires and obtain supporting documents needs to be discussed with them. If their circumstances are straightforward, three weeks may suffice, but it can take much longer to obtain pension statements. It may be possible to start working on income and outgoings while information on pensions is being obtained, if the participants have collected other necessary information.

Anxious or confused people need reassurance and step-by-step guidance. Mediators can explain how to obtain the surrender value of an endowment policy and discuss with them how they will organise getting valuations. Some couples come to mediation wanting a settlement that they have already worked out together in broad terms. Others do not know where to begin. The pace of mediation needs to be adjusted for couples at varying stages of separation and for partners who are generally at a different stage from each other in adjusting to the separation or divorce. Often, one of them is much more knowledgeable about financial matters than the other, creating a power imbalance that needs to be managed.[13] It is important to encourage participants to find Independent Financial Advisors (IFAs) specifically trained in divorce and pensions, because not all IFAs have the necessary knowledge and skills.

---

[13] See Chapter 10 below.

9.7.2   Supporting documents

It is important to discuss the supporting documents that are needed and to plan who will provide them. Co-operation is sought by asking, for example, 'It would be useful if we could have ...' *or* 'Do you think you could help us by getting hold of ...?' The documents each partner is asked to produce should be listed and recapped at the end of the session. The quantity of supporting documents varies according to the financial circumstances. Mediators need to consider the amount of documentation that participants will need to inform their discussion, and that legal advisors will need in order to advise. The key is proportionality. The level of trust, or mistrust, between partners also needs to be taken into account in considering how much verification will be needed to satisfy both of them. Gathering and considering full financial information in mediation can take considerable time, but it should still be much quicker than correspondence between lawyers, because the information is clarified with both partners together. A time-scale should be agreed for the completion of forms and obtaining valuations and documents, as the following mediation meeting would need to be rescheduled if the information is not available.

9.7.3   Setting manageable tasks

A task that is easily manageable for one person may be overwhelming for another. Some people have all the financial information at their fingertips, whereas for another, it may be the first time that they phone a bank or building society. Proposing manageable tasks that need to be undertaken before the next session helps to build confidence, as well as gathering information. 'Homework' tasks should be recapped at the end of the meeting and both parties should have a written note to refer to. Some people need the mediator's help to understand the questions that need to be asked, before they can begin to look for answers.

9.7.4   Considering expenditure

When there are issues involving spousal maintenance and/or child support, the mediator needs to discuss how each participant will provide details of current monthly expenditure and budgets of estimated future expenditure. Some people do not know how they spend their money, only that they spend it. The mediator helps them to plan how they will record their current expenditure, as a basis for working out future needs. Detailed monthly budgets help to work out future housing needs and child support payments. A monthly budget form lists all items of expenditure – housing costs, insurance, gas, electricity and other essential utilities. Expenditure on food, housekeeping, clothing, health, cars, travel to work etc needs to be itemised. There should be a special section on costs connected with the children – shoes and clothing, education, school trips, pocket money and presents. The mediator may need to explain that while some expenditure can be put in a separate category for the children, child support payments by the non-residential parent should include an element of housing and general costs to maintain a home for them.

'Monthly' needs to be defined as a calendar month – not as four weeks. Mediators need to be sensitive to the embarrassment felt by a person who is unable to work out monthly figures and who needs some help to do so. Discussion of monthly incomes and expenditure can be productive if there are clear objectives and if discussions are managed carefully by the mediator. If they are managed well, predictable arguments can often be pre-empted and avoided. Mediators also need to ask whether participants are claiming the welfare benefits to which they may be entitled. Many single parents do not claim the benefits to which they are entitled, because they do not know about them.

Arguments flare up quickly if the mediator is passive and allows each parent to attack the other's expenditure: 'Do you really spend that much on clothes every month?' 'Are you telling me you can afford to have all those meals out? Lucky you!' Arguments about 'needs' can take a long time without getting anywhere. Expenditure generally exceeds income and shortfalls need to be highlighted in red on the flipchart. Both parents may be asked to think of possible ways of reducing their own expenditure and/or increasing their income and to come back next time with revised figures. If one parent's monthly budget is for that parent alone, whereas the other budget is for the other parent and the children, this needs to be shown clearly on the flipchart. It is helpful to total the figures and combine the totals under the headings of 'Family Income' and 'Family Outgoings'. A parent bringing up children on a low income may be unable to cut a tight budget any further. There is understandable anger and resentment if further cutbacks are expected. The mediator's sensitive use of language is therefore very important. Parents may accept the notion of a temporary 'survival budget', as a means of working out immediate and essential needs, while also assessing their needs for the longer-term. Prioritising essential outgoings is more useful than a laborious examination of what each party spends or claims to spend on every item, including holidays and leisure activities.

Parents quite often come up with their own ideas and may respond to suggestions. Some parents decide to open a bank account for the children to which they will each contribute an agreed amount per month in proportion to their income. This account will be used by either of them to purchase clothes or other items for the children. The purpose of this account needs to be agreed and the level of expenditure that would require joint consent. These kinds of arrangements can work well for dual-career parents who are committed to sharing their parenting responsibilities.

9.7.5 Debts and liabilities

People are sometimes so worried about debts that they are reluctant to admit how much money they owe, but this is clearly necessary in order to obtain a complete picture of their financial position and potential risks. If arrears are accumulating, mediators can help people to prioritise and encourage them to take reliable advice on debt management, such as negotiating an arrangement with their lenders. If mortgage payments are overdue, there may be ways of avoiding the repossession of the family home. If lenders have difficulty making contact with the borrower and the borrower makes no effort to explain their difficulty, the lender is more likely to start repossession proceedings. A person who is in debt may need to write a letter or arrange an appointment with the bank or other lender, explaining their problems and asking for a break or reduction in their repayments until their financial affairs are in order again.

Clients are often able also to arrange a freeze on credit card interest payments and may be able to negotiate manageable reduced payments of outstanding debts. Again, communication with lenders is the key. Other 'money management' suggestions for those on very tight budgets may include using a price comparisons website for changes to utility, phone and insurance costs. Advice agencies such as the CAB may help with checking ongoing reliance on credit cards rather than switching to debit card usage where credit card expenditure continues to mount.

9.7.6 Filling in the gaps

There are often omissions and errors that are not deliberate. Mediators need to look out for errors and double accounting, accepting that it is easy to make a mistake but watching for any sign of dishonesty and bad faith. Some omissions are easy to deal with. Mediators need knowledge and experience to analyse financial information and spot the gaps or inconsistencies. Although participants generally accept the need for disclosure, there are some who see mediation as an easy option and who hope to pull the wool over the mediator's eyes, as well as over their partner's eyes. Deceiving an experienced mediator and their former partner at the same time may, however, turn out to be harder than expected. Mediators need to watch for any sign that a person is being less than frank, such as a life-style not explained by the income declared. A probing question from the mediator may be picked up by the other party: 'But, Archie, I distinctly remember your mentioning that account we had in Switzerland'. The mediator needs to be alive to power imbalances in relation to each participant's understanding of financial information and the management of their income and assets. Where one of them is more informed and/or astute than the other, as is often the case, mediators need to use power-balancing techniques in addition to other mediation skills.

9.7.7   Anticipating and pre-empting

It is not easy either for mediators or for participants to think ahead to the next stage, when they are in the midst of managing the present stage. However, it is very helpful if mediators foresee difficulties that may arise before or in the next session, helping participants to anticipate and avoid them by putting 'what if?' questions: 'You mentioned earlier, David, that you have a big tax bill to pay soon. If this demand comes in, would it help to discuss ...?' Or 'I know this sounds rather pessimistic, but what would you do if ...?'

Clients who are determined to stay in the family/former matrimonial home, despite their inability to meet the outgoings, may be inclined to switch to an interest only mortgage. Before taking out an interest only mortgage or converting an existing repayment mortgage to interest only, they should be strongly encouraged to consult an IFA, so that they understand that they will have to plan for a sale at the end of the mortgage term, unless they have some other potential repayment vehicle in place. Where it is necessary to agree a reduced budget, mediators can help participants to explore options for changes in the future, such as working more hours when a child moves to secondary school and finding out what this would produce in terms of increased income. Those contemplating a further training course would need to know what income they could expect after the qualification is achieved. Sometimes an IFA can assist with cash flow forecasting that alleviates fears preventing settlement and gives clients a window on future changes that allow for planning and more control of their finances.

9.7.8   Achieving finality

It is important to clarify whether a full and final settlement is looked for and to distinguish a final settlement on financial matters from arrangements for children that need to be kept under review. Arrangements for children change as they get older or because family circumstances change, whereas once a consent order has been made in divorce, a former partner cannot ask for a bigger share. It is very important for mediators to explain the difference between realisable assets and unrealisable ones such as pensions, so that participants understand why these forms of assets should be treated differently. These differences should be shown clearly on the flipchart.

9.8   MEDIATING ON FINANCIAL MATTERS – COMBINING DIFFERENT APPROACHES

An example of an eclectic mediation model, combining elements of settlement-seeking, transformative and narrative mediation, involved a separated couple called Matt and Rachel. There were no children of their marriage. Matt had been married previously and had a son from his first marriage. Matt and Rachel explained that they were coming to mediation because they were divorcing and needed to reach a settlement on the division of property and other assets. Following separate information and assessment meetings, they came to their first mediation meeting. They behaved very politely towards each other, with no visible anger or raised voices. Feelings were kept under tight control. In a typology of separated couples they would belong to the *suppressed conflict* or *non-communicating* group. Matt and Rachel each seemed to feel hurt and rejected by the other, but could not say so. They had both been relieved to know that mediation was not marital counselling and that the mediator would not explore the breakdown of their relationship. However, there were some elements from the past that had a direct bearing on the present and the future. Matt's son lived with his mother and needed to be provided for. Some pieces of narrative were needed to clarify how past relationships were affecting present ones.

Matt and Rachel needed a structured mediation process to identify issues and agree an agenda. Their shared aim was to reach a fair and balanced financial settlement, as quickly and cheaply as possible. After gathering and sharing financial information and supporting documents, they were invited to explain their priorities and needs, to consider possible options and the implications of each option. The structure offered emotional security in analysing their financial assets without fear of attack or blame. Logical reasoning was important. On the surface, the negotiations were about the share of financial assets that each of them would receive. However, when underlying feelings were acknowledged in a mutualising way, Matt and Rachel began to express their positive feelings towards each other and to explain what they needed emotionally, as well as financially. Each of them then found words to express their appreciation of the contribution that the other had made to their relationship and to recognise the positives that were not all lost. Instead of being drawn apart through legal proceedings, Matt and Rachel remained friends. They said that if they had come to mediation a few years earlier, they might not have separated at all. Although they felt it was too late to get back together, mediation helped them to preserve links of mutual respect and affection, good communication and a shared sense of humour. They laughed in mediation in a way that they would never have laughed in court.

This mediation combined different theoretical models and methods. In the structured settlement-seeking model, mediators process financial information efficiently, often using a flipchart to analyse financial information. Technical skills are needed to compute figures, explain possible claims and explore a range of settlement options, converting figures into percentages and vice versa. Family mediators need to be efficient and numerate information-processors, but equally importantly, they need to acknowledge strong feelings and manage intense emotions. Matt and Rachel wanted a concrete settlement and they achieved it. The mediation process was not therapy, but it had therapeutic effects in facilitating communication, transforming perceptions and enhancing their post-divorce relationship.

9.9   SHARING AND CONSIDERING FINANCIAL INFORMATION – THE FLIPCHART

A flipchart provides a very effective method of collating and displaying the information gathered from financial forms and documents. It can be used to highlight key issues and to explore options systematically.[14] The flipchart can be updated as the mediation progresses, with adjustment of previously estimated figures once valuations have been obtained and agreed. The summary of finances set out on the flipchart is generally transcribed into the OFS.[15]

There are, however, potential pitfalls and disadvantages in using the flipchart, as well as advantages. Realisable and unrealisable assets, such as pension funds, should not be totalled together as this would give a misleading picture of capital available to fund property purchase.

9.9.1   Disadvantages of using a flipchart

- The mediator who remains standing at the flipchart can seem like a lecturer talking down to the participants. However, the height of many flipcharts is adjustable. If it can be set at chair level, the mediator may not have to jump up and down like a jack-in-a-box.

- When the mediator writes on the flipchart, eye contact and dialogue with participants are easily lost, especially if the mediator's back is turned.

- Participants may fear that what is written is 'tablets of stone' that cannot be changed. They may be alarmed to see the value of the family home written up, fearing this means that their home is going to be sold.

- Listing assets that one participant regards as their own personal possession – such as a savings account or jewellery – can cause intense anger and distress if it gives the impression that a treasured possession is to be disposed of or shared with the ex-partner. Mediators need to reassure participants that what is written up for consideration does *not* imply any assumptions or decisions.

- Flipchart pages used in mediation need to be stored safely.

---

[14]   See also Chapter 7 at **7.13** above.
[15]   See Appendix C below.

- Participants may take offence if facts and figures are written in an untidy scrawl. Professional presentation of flipchart information is very important. Figures need to be neat and legible and lines need to be straight.

9.9.2 Advantages of using a flipchart

- Financial information is collated and considered in a clear and systematic way.

- A visual overview that enables participants to consider the information together.

- Participants and mediators look at the same figures at the same time.

- The mediator keeps eye contact and notices changes in facial expression, whereas if participants keep heads lowered, in going through forms, it is difficult to see reactions.

- Errors or differences in values can be spotted quickly.

- Where there are differences about estimated values, these can be shown as a range, avoiding unhelpful arguments. For example, one partner may exclaim:

  'That's a ridiculous figure. It's worth far more than that.'

  The mediator can clarify each partner's valuations (how recent, by whom):

  'So you both think your property is worth between x and y? Shall we use x and y as the range for now and then come back to how you agree an actual figure?'

- Symbols can record queries or issues needing further attention – question marks, asterisks, arrows.

- Different colours can distinguish assets held in sole names from those held in joint names.

- A visual display can be very powerful, showing the reality that participants need to grasp.

- A flipchart is preferable to a whiteboard because information generally needs to be referred to and updated at the next meeting. It is a working document that encourages movement and focused thinking. Several flipchart pages can be displayed alongside each other, so that capital assets and incomes/outgoings can be considered in conjunction with each other.

- Flipchart figures can be copied onto a spreadsheet, interim or final OFS sent to participants to help them consider options and take professional advice.

Flipchart skills hardly figure in mediation literature, but they are very important. As a visual aid, the flipchart can be used creatively as well as efficiently, to gather and share information and explore options. Some mediators use a spreadsheet on their computer during the session, but the computer screen may be too small for participants to read the figures easily. In studying the information transferred from their Form Es to the flipchart, one partner may propose spontaneously that a particular asset should remain in, or be transferred to, the other partner's name, because this makes good sense. Provisional proposals can be shown on the flipchart in colour or marked in some way.

9.10   MEDIATING ON FINANCIAL MATTERS – SUMMARY OF TASKS

- Explain process and objectives.

- Identify issues and time frames – interim, long-term or both?

- Discuss completion of Form E, valuations, CETVs, supporting documents.

- Plan and prioritise, consider degree of urgency.

- Maintain balance in gathering/giving information.

- Display information on flipchart for focus and clarity.

- Analyse figures, any gaps or discrepancies?

- Set tasks – enquire about borrowing capacity, cost of alternative accommodation.

- Current income and anticipated changes, adjustments in tax credits, benefit entitlements.

- Income needed to fund borrowing, loan payments, essential outgoings.

- Identify need for professional advice – legal and financial, pensions.

- Identify and explore options.

- Discuss factors to take into account – children, earning capacity, health ...

- Reality-testing – viability and effects of each option.

- Spousal maintenance?

- Child support – formula, budgets for children, additional contributions, sport and leisure activities, birthday and Christmas presents.

- Recap on any proposals and outstanding issues.

- Identify range in which settlement may be reached – convert figures into percentages and vice versa, BATNA and WATNA questions.[16]

- Consider alternative routes to final settlement, if necessary.

- Produce accurate interim/final OFS.

9.11 MEDIATION SKILLS

- Acknowledge feelings – anger, fear, confusion – and concerns.

- Motivate participants to undertake manageable tasks.

- Mutualise concerns (for security) and needs as far as possible.

- Give clear and verifiable information in a balanced way.

- Crisis management.

- Prioritise and plan.

- Manage conflict in gathering and sharing financial information.

- Recognise gaps and discrepancies.

- Use of flipchart.

- Facilitate communication, awareness of non-verbal communication.

- Combine hard financial calculations with 'soft' mediation skills (process, people and problem-solving skills).

---

[16] See Chapter 11 at **11.11** below.

- Build trust and seek reassurances.

- Manage power imbalances – money as a source of power and means of control.

- Manage time well.

- Understand emotional values of financial assets.

- Encourage a constructive approach.

- Facilitate negotiations.

- Encourage co-operation in relating children's needs to financial means.

- Impasse strategies.

- Maintain notes and records.

- Presentation of OFS.

9.11.1 Planning and prioritising

High levels of conflict may be manageable if a plan is agreed for addressing and working on issues. Priorities need to be identified. The agenda for each meeting needs to be reviewed at the start, as circumstances may change between meetings. At the end of each meeting, matters for discussion at the next meeting may be identified and tasks agreed, so that participants can make further enquiries, take advice and consider possible options. Time for reflection between mediation sessions may be very beneficial.

9.11.2 Exploring options

Mediation itself is an option and exploring options is one of the main elements of the mediation process. After gathering and understanding all the information, the next stage is to identify and explore possible options, looking at what would be possible and examining advantages or disadvantages from the point of view of each participant and the children. Broad options may be divided into sub-options. Future housing needs are usually a dominant concern and the starting-point for identifying possible options. Housing options can be listed under broad headings. A preferred option or options can then be examined in more detail in terms of capital needs, income needs, priorities for the children – such as staying at the same school – and priorities for the parents – such as the area they would prefer to live in. Exploring housing needs provides a framework for considering both parties' monthly income and expenditure. After working through income, expenditure and future budgets, housing plans may need to be looked at again and scaled down. Some options may be rejected, but it is better not to cross them out. A previously rejected option may need re-examining. Mediators should not dismiss what seems an unrealistic idea, as it may not be as crazy as it first sounds. If participants seem to have got stuck, suggesting unlikely options may encourage brainstorming and help them to broaden their thinking. This exploration can be done graphically on the flipchart. Idiosyncratic and tailor-made arrangements are worked out more easily in mediation than in the courts.

9.12   MEDIATION EXAMPLE

A married couple in their thirties, Richard and Joanna, came to mediation to settle the issues arising from their separation. Richard, an accountant, had left the family home three months previously. He was renting a one-bedroom flat. Joanna was a teacher, teaching two mornings per week. Their children, Adam and Lucy, aged seven and five, were living with her in the 3-bedroom family home. The property was owned in joint names with a part repayment/part endowment mortgage. Richard wanted to sell the family home and buy a property of his own where the children could come to stay. Joanna objected strongly to the sale of the family home and argued that this would upset the children even more. After assets and liabilities had been listed and estimated values accepted, incomes and pensions were noted and discussed. The next step was to explore available housing options and test the viability of each option. The options were listed on the flipchart, showing the advantages and disadvantages that Richard and Joanna identified from their own points of view and for the children.

	OPTION 1 **Sell the family home**		**OPTION 2** **Joanna and children to remain in the family home**	
	Advantages	*Disadvantages*	*Advantages*	*Disadvantages*
Richard	Would be able to buy own home	None	None	Unable to buy a home of his own
Joanna	None – wants to stay where she is	Would have to move to a smaller property, away from friends	Many	Financial cost of maintaining the family home

	OPTION 1 Sell the family home		OPTION 2 Joanna and children to remain in the family home	
	Advantages	*Disadvantages*	*Advantages*	*Disadvantages*
Adam & Lucy	Would be able to stay overnight with their father	Loss of the home they know. Change of school? Further away from grandparents?	Many	Unable to stay overnight with their father in small rented flat

Further questions included:

(1) If the family home were to be retained, could the mortgage be transferred to Joanna's sole name?

(2) How would mortgage payments be maintained?

(3) The monthly income that Joanna would need to remain in the family home, with child support payments from Richard.

(4) Whether Joanna could increase her working hours.

(5) If the home were to be sold, the asking price and costs of sale.

(6) Price ranges of suitable new properties and how a purchase could be funded.

(7) How other assets, including pensions, would be taken into account.

(8) Responsibility for debts.

(9) If Richard took a charge-back on the family home, the level of the charge.

Richard thought the obvious solution was for Joanna to return to full-time work so that she could take out a bigger mortgage. Joanna felt the children had suffered a great deal of upset and said that she was not willing to work full-time until Lucy was older.

9.12.1 Preliminary proposals

Joanna said she did not want to make a direct claim on Richard's inheritance from his father, which he had invested. Richard responded by proposing that Joanna should keep a savings account into which she had been paying her earnings, as Richard earned enough to support the family. These assets were provisionally allocated as proposed on the flipchart as a worksheet visible to all participants. Richard and Joanna then decided to split a joint savings account on a 25/75% basis, in Joanna's favour. This proposed division was added in as well.

9.12.2 Working towards solutions

At the beginning of the third meeting, the mediator recapped areas of provisional agreement. Joanna and Richard both wanted a full and final settlement in divorce and were in agreement that the children should continue to live with Joanna and spend alternate weekends and part of their holidays with Richard. Richard said he would continue to pay the mortgage for at least the next six months and make child support payments to Joanna. Options were worked on intensively in two further meetings, with Richard and Joanna each taking interim advice from their lawyers. Their joint preference, finally, was for Richard to take a deferred charge on the family home, payable to him on the earliest of the usual 'trigger' events. Joanna took on more teaching hours and this entitled her to working tax credit. As her income increased, she became able to pay more of the outgoings on the family home so that Richard could afford to rent a bigger flat where the children could stay with him. Having taken advice, they remortgaged their property, surrendering the endowment to provide a deposit for Richard towards his future house purchase and reducing the size of his charge-back on the family home. In the longer term, Joanna envisaged being able to buy Richard out of his share of the home long before Lucy reached the age of 18. Joanna and Richard arrived in mediation as embattled antagonists. They gradually became joint problem-solvers who, in pooling their ideas and using their resources and energies for the benefit of the family as a whole, found that they could reach their own solutions and keep their legal costs to a minimum.

9.13 PENSION PROVISIONS IN DIVORCE SETTLEMENTS

In some countries, such as Germany, there are fixed principles and mechanisms for pension splitting on divorce. However, in England and Wales pensions come to be considered within the general discretion provided by section 25 of the MCA 1973 and the court's powers under the Welfare Reform and Pensions Act 1999. There are no formulae, and indeed attempts to impose general principles have been frowned upon by the courts. Within mediation, as in litigation, the choice is between 'offsetting' against other assets, or by pension sharing ('splitting') or pension attachment ('ear-marking'). Over the ten years of availability of the pension sharing option, it has not been as popular as might have been expected, but nevertheless around 11% of all ancillary relief orders now include a pension sharing provision.[17] It should be borne in mind that:

---

[17] Salter 'A Decade of Pension Sharing' [2010] Fam Law 1294–1298.

(1)   pension sharing is only available by way of order on divorce;

(2)   pension sharing or attachment will have significant administrative
       costs;

(3)   consideration of pensions, including in mediation, is a highly
       technical matter and requires expert assistance.

This does not mean that mediators should fight shy of dealing with
pensions; indeed they must deal with them and must equip themselves to
do so. Mediators need to be able to explain available pension options in
broad terms, to help participants understand the possible advantages and
disadvantages of each option. Mediators need enough knowledge to
understand different kinds of pension schemes and to enquire about
additional voluntary contributions and benefits payable on death in
service or when retirement age is reached. However, there are questions
relating to pensions on which expert advice is needed and participants
must be encouraged to take this advice. The value of the mediator's
knowledge of pensions may therefore be to acknowledge the importance
of what s/he does *not* know. Expert advice may be made available within
mediation much as an IFA is used within Collaborative Law. The MOU
needs to record the extent to which pension options were considered in
mediation and that the participants were encouraged to seek independent
legal and financial advice.

9.14   THE EMOTIONAL AND SYMBOLIC VALUE OF
POSSESSIONS

It is fashionable today to deride consumerism and the preoccupation with
material possessions, 'but the paradox is that as more and more of our
lives are mediated by screens and keyboards, and the virtual world of
word and image dominates, the enchantment of things intensifies'.[18] A
loved object has a familiar touch and may have a voice, speaking of past
owners and generations and thus providing a link in the construction of
identity.

Possessions may thus be heavily charged with emotional value. Furniture,
pictures and jewellery may have emotional or symbolic values that bear
no relation to their financial worth. Participants become very upset if
their savings and treasured possessions are valued in mediation solely in
monetary terms. With one couple, a carpet they had bought on their
honeymoon was wanted desperately by both of them, because it
symbolised the marriage and their hopes they had had for their happiness.
If there are children, couples may agree that a treasured possession will be
held by one of them in trust for a child. If there is more than one child, it
is obviously helpful if there is more than one possession in this special

---

[18]   Bunting 'Our history told in just 100 objects' (2011) *Guardian Weekly*, 7 January, p 24.

category. Emotional attachments to possessions need to be understood and acknowledged whenever questions of valuing them are raised. A question put hypothetically, in a sensitive way, is less disturbing than a closed, factual question. Mediators need to facilitate the *recognition* and *empowerment* that are central elements in transformative and family-focused mediation. A mediator using a settlement-seeking approach may concentrate too exclusively on the figures and may not give enough attention to the feelings that, for one or both participants, may be flooding the figures.

9.15   EXAMPLE OF MEDIATING ON INTERRELATED ISSUES

Gemma, aged 29 was unemployed and in receipt of income support, child benefit and child tax credit. Martin aged 31, was a transport manager earning just on £2,000 net per month. They had recently separated after an 11-year marriage. No third parties were involved. Gemma and Martin had two children, Rose aged 11 and Samantha aged 9. Both the children were said to be in good health and doing well at school. Gemma and the children were living in the family home and Martin had moved into rented accommodation. Gemma's solicitor was preparing a divorce petition. Martin had also taken legal advice. Both parents understood that they would continue to share parental responsibility for their children, who would be based with Gemma and see their father often. Their arrangements for the children were agreed before they came to mediation. The children were staying Friday and Saturday nights with their father on alternate weekends and would also spend part of their school holidays with him. If either parent wanted to change their arrangements for a particular weekend, they agreed to give each other as much notice as possible and to schedule a regular meeting to review how the arrangements were working for the children and to discuss any minor problem at an early stage. Martin was paying the mortgage and £400 per month for the children.

Valuations of the family home were around £155,000–160,000 and it was decided to take the lower value of £155,000. The mortgage balance was around £95,000. Allowing for costs of sale at 3%, the notional net proceeds of sale were worked out. Martin was willing for Gemma and the girls to remain living in the family home until the earliest of the usual 'trigger' events:

(1)   Gemma remarrying or cohabiting for more than six months;

(2)   Samantha reaching the age of 18;

(3)   Gemma's death.

On this basis Martin was willing to take a charge on the property registered in his name equivalent to 11.6% of its gross value. His name would remain on the mortgage and Gemma would use her best endeavours to have his name removed from the mortgage as soon as she was able to do so. Gemma and Martin had three joint bank accounts, with an overdraft of around £600 on one of them. Martin was paying £100 per month into this account and as soon the overdraft was cleared, this joint account would be closed and the other two split equally and closed. They had cars of roughly comparable value. Martin was willing for Gemma to keep the contents of the family home, apart from some items in the garage that he was arranging to collect.

9.16   EXAMPLE OF MEDIATION WITH A RETIRED COUPLE

There are many couples like Gemma and Martin who are caring parents, committed to maintaining their co-operation. Other couples come to mediation after years of wrangling and with no goodwill towards each other at all. Edward and Vera were in their early seventies and drawing their pensions. They were living separately under the same roof and barely speaking to each other. Their marriage had broken down eight years previously but they could not agree financial matters and the divorce proceedings had stalled. Edward had refused an earlier offer of a mediation information and assessment meeting. Six months later, he decided to accept it. He had not taken legal advice because he did not want to incur legal costs and was afraid the allegations in Vera's 'unreasonable behaviour' petition would prejudice his position on financial matters. Once this misapprehension was cleared up through the mediation information meeting and an initial half hour with a solicitor, Edward was ready to negotiate a settlement with Vera. Communications between them in two mediation meetings were civilised, although not amicable. As neither could afford to buy the other out, they decided, having taken further legal advice, to sell the matrimonial home and split the proceeds equally on the basis that Edward would pay spousal maintenance to Vera to equalise their pensions. There was apparently a history to the marital breakdown that had caused great bitterness between them and rifts in the extended family as well, but Vera and Edward concurred that the past was the past and that they wanted to get on with the rest of their lives. Once they had worked out how to do so, the hostility between them lessened. When Vera mislaid her house keys and car keys, Edward helped her to find them, whereas previously, as they both acknowledged, they would have had another unpleasant argument.

9.17 EXAMPLE OF MEDIATION WITH AN UNMARRIED COUPLE

Claire aged 30 is a sales representative currently off work with depression. She is receiving her basic salary of £1,300 per month net and hopes to return to work soon, but this will be on a no-commission basis for the first six months. Graham, age 31, is a director of the family firm, Bennett and Steel, and a beneficiary of two discretionary Trusts (see Open Financial Statement).

Claire owned her own home before moving in 2003 to live with Graham in the home that he owned, agreed now to have equity of around £160,000. Claire rented out her property to tenants and following the breakdown of the relationship in 2010 she incurred legal costs in regaining occupation of her property so that she could move back into it. In addition to the cost of living temporarily in rented accommodation, Claire incurred costs of about £12,500 in restoring her property to its previous condition and replacing equipment. From Graham's standpoint, he had been largely responsible for the mortgage and outgoings on the home in which they had been living up to the separation. Claire and Graham have been endeavouring for some time to reach a settlement through solicitors and have been told that the next step is for Claire to commence civil proceedings to claim a share of the equity in Graham's home. Neither of them wishes to be involved in litigation.

Claire considers that her financial position has worsened considerably as a result of the cohabitation. While accepting Graham's view that she bears partial responsibility for her financial difficulties, Claire is seeking some compensation for her losses, enabling her to regain the financial independence that she enjoyed prior to the cohabitation. The mediators helped Graham and Claire to articulate their concerns over fairness, the monies they had each contributed and lost, and their anxieties for the future. Their analysis of the balance between these issues was informed by a mediator-led discussion of the current legal background and their different views of 'fairness', leading to an exploration of options in a problem-solving forum. After considerable discussion in the course of three privately paid mediation sessions, proposals were arrived at whereby Graham offered to pay Claire £23,500 to clear the debts she incurred in regaining and restoring her property, with an additional sum to help her regain her financial security. Their agreement was formalised through their solicitors.

9.18 CAN MEDIATION DEAL WITH COMPLEX FINANCES?

Mediating on complex financial issues and high-value assets requires mediators to have the necessary levels of expertise and experience. This being so, mediation offers a means of reducing or avoiding lengthy and costly correspondence between legal advisors and extremely expensive litigation. The question of valuing assets has been touched on earlier. In mediating with a couple who owned six properties in sole or joint names, valuations were particularly difficult because two of the properties were overseas and one was half-built. The couple discussed in mediation how realistic valuations could be obtained and agreed. The wife recognised that the half-built property was not worth as much as their original investment and that it would be sensible to agree a value pragmatically, based on a single valuation, without incurring even more expense. Collaborative ways of working,[19] in which mediation is combined with independent legal and financial advice provided to participants outside – or inside – the mediation process and drawn on by them in mediation meetings, can be harnessed in a problem-solving approach instead of an adversarial one. In complex cases, as in straightforward ones, the motivation of participants is the key factor. Mediators offer space, time, positive energy – and knowledge and skills – to help people find the keys that will turn a set of locks in their own particular gateway to conflict resolution.

9.19   PRE-NUPTIAL AGREEMENTS

The Supreme Court ruled in *Radmacher v Granatino*[20] that:

> 'the court should give effect to a nuptial agreement that is freely entered into by each party with a full appreciation of its implications, unless in the circumstances prevailing it would not be fair to hold the parties to their agreement.'

Nevertheless, the parties cannot by agreement oust the jurisdiction of the court and in ancillary relief proceedings the court is not obliged to give effect to nuptial agreements. The court must, however, give appropriate weight to such agreements. Robinson[21] suggests that:

> 'mediators should approach pre- and post-nuptial agreements with caution and with sufficient understanding of the law. There is then no reason why a similar forensic information gathering exercise could not take place as, for example, when considering the history of contributions in a cohabitation case.'

Negotiations in mediation involving a pre- or post-nuptial agreement or separation agreement should involve their lawyers directly. This is another way in which legal advisors and mediators can work with a consensual settlement-seeking focus, but keeping their different roles distinct and clear. Cases involving pre-nuptial agreements often involve high and

---

[19]   See Chapter 4 above.
[20]   [2010] UKSC 42.
[21]   [2011] Fam Law forthcoming.

complex assets and are likely to lie beyond the expertise of the average family mediator. However, 'the crux of the matter is a proper exploration of process options. Just as in any other complex cases that come for mediation assessment, the expertise available and relative cost-effectiveness will decide what form of hybrid and collaborative ADR process would be most appropriate'.[22]

9.20 CIVIL PARTNERSHIP DISPUTES

Since 1989, when Denmark became the first country to recognise civil partnerships, the legal recognition of same-sex relationships has been accepted in many countries. Half the Member States of the EU have now introduced legislation on the recognition of same-sex relationships. A civil partnership is a legal marriage between a gay or lesbian couple, giving them responsibilities and rights comparable to those of heterosexual married couples. The Civil Partnership Act 2004 came into force on 5 December 2005 in England and Wales. Civil partners have the same property rights as heterosexual married couples and acquire joint parental responsibility for the children of one partner. To dissolve a civil partnership, the couple must have been in a civil partnership for at least a year and a petition must be filed on the same basis as a divorce petition, citing similar 'facts', together with a Statement of Arrangements for any child residing with the couple.

If their relationship breaks down, more civil partners and same-sex couples might come to mediation if they were better informed of its availability and reassured that family mediators offer the same help and empathy to same-sex couples as they do to any couple. A lesbian couple referred themselves to mediation because they wanted to resolve property matters privately through mediation, without going to court. The dynamics of 'the leaver' and the 'left' and their turmoil of anger, grief and continuing attachment were no different from those of male/female partners. In this particular case, the couple had two dogs that they loved like children. Working out contact arrangements with the dogs was a more pressing issue for them both than financial matters. Mediation provides a forum for issues that the court would not consider, as well as for those that could take up a great deal of court time.

9.21 MEDIATION IN INHERITANCE DISPUTES

Disputes over the terms of a Will (or in the absence thereof), for example, between the family and cohabitant of the deceased, or between adult children, can be fuelled by similar feelings to those experienced in separation and divorce – bitterness, grief, rejection, loss, anger and resentment. Mediation gives opportunities to recognise and express these

---

[22] [2011] Fam Law forthcoming.

emotions in negotiating over the terms of a disputed Will, whereas these painful feelings risk being further enflamed by court proceedings. Litigation in inheritance disputes also carries high risks of the value of the estate being consumed by legal costs and culminating in the permanent breakdown of relationships between siblings.

Henry Brown has written (personal communication):

> 'It is certainly a common experience that inheritance disputes may disguise other emotional issues between the parties. An underlying and unstated issue may for example be "Who did daddy – or mummy – love best?" In addition to these emotional aspects, mediating inheritance disputes may be very practical, for example relating to claims for provision and redistribution under the Inheritance (Provision for Families and Dependants) Act 1975, where the process may involve discussion and businesslike negotiation between the parties, or organising the allocation and management of inherited assets and beneficial interests.'

The dual trained family and civil/commercial mediator may offer a model of mediation in inheritance disputes that is sensitive and responsive to the intense emotions between estranged family members, while also providing the lawyer-assisted financial negotiation characteristic of civil mediation.

9.22   CHOOSING THE APPROPRIATE DISPUTE RESOLUTION PROCESS FOR FINANCIAL DISPUTES

Mediation offers one form of ADR for the resolution of disputes on financial and property matters. Lawyers may consider that collaborative law, possibly involving a family mediator to assist with child-related issues, offers a 'better' process, but these different forms of ADR should not be seen as competing with one other. They each have their own strengths and limitations. Mediation, especially interdisciplinary co-mediation, or the 'hybrid' models that fall outside the scope of this book, can help family members to resolve an increasingly wide range of financial and property matters in conjunction with related issues concerning children and other family matters.

CHAPTER 10

MANAGING POWER IMBALANCES IN MEDIATION

'Among unequals, what society can sort ... Which must be mutual, in proportion due giv'n and received'[1]

'One's cruelty is one's power, and when one parts with one's cruelty, one parts with one's power, and when one has parted with that, I fancy one's old and ugly'[2]

CONTENTS

10.1   DIFFERENT FRAMES FOR VIEWING POWER

The word 'power' tends to have negative associations associated with dominance and control. When power is used aggressively to control other people or seize a bigger share of available goods or territory, this involves an *abuse of power* by one person or group. However, when seen in a positive frame, power can have positive values in terms of *capacity, competence and responsibility*. It can be used in consensual and democratic ways to serve collective or mutual needs. Mediators need to recognise that with a positive frame, power can mean positive capacity or strength. In a negative frame, power is used to dominate, manipulate or abuse other people.[3]

---

[1]   Milton *Paradise Lost* (1667), Book VIII.
[2]   Congreve *The Way of the World*.
[3]   'All power is a trust, we are all accountable for its exercise': Benjamin Disraeli.

Equality of power may be an unattainable ideal. Power imbalances are often found in relationships that work well. It is rare for partners who live together to have equal power in all areas of their relationship. Different capacities and resources may be used in complementary ways to the benefit of the whole family. Inequalities need not cause envy and competition, if different strengths are valued. When one partner or parent has greater resources, strengths or responsibilities in certain areas, these can be used to mutual benefit. One of the mediator's main functions is to help participants identify their resources as well as their needs, so that they can consider how these resources can be used most effectively for the maximum common benefit.

10.2   POWER AND GENDER

Concerns about power imbalances in family mediation are often associated with gender issues. Men tend to be in a stronger position financially than women who have stayed at home or worked part-time while looking after children. Men may also be more knowledgeable about financial matters, although this varies a great deal. Sometimes the female partner has managed the family finances. Mediators need to be on the alert for individuals who come to mediation aiming to bulldoze an unsuspecting partner into a quick financial settlement, or a parent who dictates the conditions on which contact may take place.

Issues often arise about the different economic positions of fathers and mothers and expectations of their roles and responsibilities, before and after separation. These issues stir up powerful cross-currents in mediation. There may be significant disparities of income and earning power when one parent has stayed at home to look after the children while the other has built up a successful career. Power imbalances in mediation are also increased by one party's ignorance of their financial circumstances. Often, one partner – not always the husband – has had control of the finances and the other one does not know what to ask for, not knowing what there is. Disparities of income tend to become wider in divorce, with many one-parent families falling into poverty. In general, women earn less than men and have poorer career prospects, even if equally qualified. In some cultures, women are taught to be subservient to men. It may be very difficult for a woman to put her case strongly in mediation, if this is contrary to her cultural upbringing, religion and beliefs about how a woman should behave. An Asian woman brought up in a traditional Asian culture would consider it wrong to assert herself.[4]

Although women are often at a disadvantage economically, most divorce petitioners are women. Men who face losing their marriage, the family home and daily contact with their children tend to feel the loser on all counts. Apart from gender issues in domestic violence, assumptions that

---

[4]   See 'cross-cultural mediation' in Chapter 3 above.

men have power whereas women are powerless are not confirmed in mediation experience. It is more helpful to think in terms of personality traits than gender stereotypes. Traits of gentleness and caring that may be thought of as typically female are also shown by men. Gilligan suggests that those who function in a 'female mode' – whether biologically male or female – are willing to negotiate because they value co-operation highly.[5] Individuals with more forceful, aggressive personalities – whether men or women – tend to value co-operation less highly. In mediation, they may be ready to exploit their partner's concerns about relationships and greater willingness to settle.

Research studies have been carried out to study whether women are inherently disadvantaged in mediation. The findings have not shown this to be the case.[6] Provided there is systematic screening for all forms of violence and abuse so that situations unsuitable for mediation are screened out,[7] women report as many benefits as men. There is no simple dichotomy based on gender alone. Although one partner may be more powerful than the other, it often emerges in mediation that each has significant power or influence in certain areas. It is important for mediators not to assess too quickly who has more power and where the power lies. Research findings underline the importance of mediators' training and experience in enabling them to recognise and manage different power imbalances, including their own use of authority and power.[8] Power is a fluid, rather than a solid, entity. It can be observed shifting and fluctuating during a mediation session and often from one session to the next. Fluctuating power is often seen in mediation, because power relationships tend to change during marriage breakdown and divorce. Although some patterns remain the same, one partner's decision to leave the other may alter the previous balance of power, sometimes dramatically. Other factors may come into play for the first time.

10.3   COUPLES WHO SHARE THE DRIVING

The essence of a good partnership is that it functions well. In many relationships that work well, it suits both partners for each of them to be in the driving-seat at different times. One may look after the children full-time, while the other goes out to work. Other couples choose to share both kinds of driving – childcare and careers – more or less equally, changing drivers when convenient. Either parent may take over from the other by arrangement, following a general direction that is agreed between them. The wheels go on turning, whichever partner is driving, because they are both competent and trust each other. However, when partners

---

[5]   Gilligan *In a Different Voice: psychological theory and women's development* (Harvard University Press, 1982).

[6]   See Chapters 3 and 13.

[7]   Ibid.

[8]   Kelly 'Power Imbalance in Divorce and Interpersonal Mediation: assessment and intervention' (1995) 13(2) *Mediation Quarterly* 85–98.

disagree as to who should drive or about the direction they ought to take, both may struggle to grab the wheel from the other. They may then find themselves stuck and unable to move in any direction at all.

The diagram below illustrates different kinds of capacity, resource or power that are frequently encountered in mediation. The diagram is itself constructed in the form of a wheel, each segment representing an area in which one partner may have more power or strength than the other. One partner may be more powerful in having greater social prestige and influence, higher earnings and better career prospects. In relation to children, however, it is the parent who has day-to-day contact and close emotional bonds with the children who is in the stronger position, compared with a parent who is distant from the children, geographically or emotionally, or both.

The partners' internal and external resources usually differ. The outer segments of the wheel represent external resources that may not be equally available to both partners, such as support from family and friends, work opportunities and access to legal advice. The segments are clearly interrelated and need to be looked at as a whole. However, when there is conflict, attention is drawn to the particular area or areas in which dispute is evident. Power imbalances in these areas are like spokes protruding through the rim of the wheel, upsetting its balance and impeding its movement. The diagram suggests some of the 'spokes' which impede balanced negotiations and make forward movement difficult.

Aspects of Power

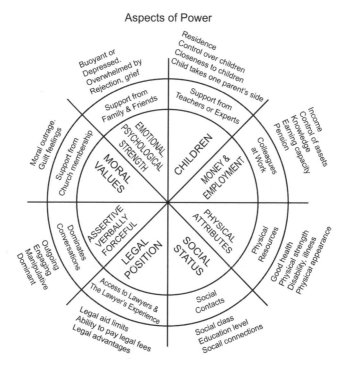

Differences that were previously managed may become prominent and 'stick out', like jagged spokes in the wheel. A partner who feels abandoned, without any say in the ending of the relationship, generally feels powerless. On the other hand, family and friends may rally round to give support and it may be the parent who has left the home who is ostracised, even, on occasion, by his or her own family.

10.4 POWER IMBALANCES IN FAMILY MEDIATION

There are many different kinds of power imbalance that affect the dynamics in mediation. These include:

(i)   power to end the marriage or relationship;

(ii)   power to resist or block change;

(iii) gender;

(iv)   knowledge, control of finances, income, earning power;

(v)   emotional pressure;

(vi)   personal characteristics;

(vii) verbal domination, education, social status;

(viii) physical and/or emotional closeness to children;

(ix)   new partners, family support, support from friends and colleagues;

(x)   cultural factors, moral power, religion, support from religious leaders;

(xi)   legal advantages, eligibility for legal aid.

A few comments about some of these power imbalances and their impact in mediation may be helpful, before considering techniques that mediators can use to manage imbalances without taking control and disempowering participants.

10.4.1 Power to end the marriage or relationship

The decision to end the marriage or relationship is not usually a mutual decision. A unilateral decision to end the marriage, taken by one partner without the other's acquiescence, is associated with anger, bitterness and lengthy disputes. Mediators see many couples whose decision to separate or divorce is not a mutual one. The partner who initiates the break-up starts a train of change that the other partner does not want to happen. Although initiators also suffer loss and grief, they are stronger because they have commenced the process of adjustment earlier, often after considerable time thinking through their decisions and future intentions.

It is difficult for mediators to maintain a balance so that they give equal support to two partners who are facing in opposite directions and reacting in entirely different ways. The difficulties of bridging these deep divisions were referred to in Chapter 3.

10.4.2   Power to resist or block a settlement

It is important to be aware that an apparently powerless and passive partner may be able to exercise power through blocking and resisting. Delaying tactics may be used to postpone decisions and settlements. It is naïve to imagine that both parties who accept referral to mediation are necessarily seeking a settlement. Their motives vary. One party's apparent acquiescence with the referral may disguise a profound determination to resist agreeing to anything at all. Accepting mediation may be a delaying tactic in itself. Mediators need to watch out for delaying tactics and recognise the advantages for one party in prolonging the status quo. Both the duration and the pace of mediation need to be kept under review.

A parent who blocks the other parent's contact with the children or who resists a financial settlement may be objecting to the non-mutuality of the separation. If these underlying objections are not acknowledged and addressed in some way, disputes over children or finance will be hard to settle. Mediation may be accepted by a resistant partner, not in order to settle, but as a means of prolonging contact and emotional involvement, instead of letting it go. Mediators need to be careful not to be drawn into one party's hanging-on tactics, believing that they are working towards settlement but actually enabling one party to delay settlement as long as possible. The effect of prolonging a status quo needs to be borne in mind, when considering requests for more time and further sessions, despite little sign of movement.

10.4.3   Gender

See **10.2** above.

10.4.4   Knowledge is power, financial control

> 'As a general rule, the most successful man in life is the man who has the best information.'[9]

---

[9]   Benjamin Disraeli.

Knowledge is a major source of power. Lack of financial information or unfamiliarity with financial documents and business accounts are major disadvantages in financial negotiations. Although there are traditional marriages in which the wife has stayed at home and left financial matters to her husband, there are also many marriages in which it is the wife who manages the family finances. Sharing knowledge reduces feelings of powerlessness. One of the mediator's main tasks is to identify and piece together the information that needs to be shared. Participants are helped to gather and share full information. The mediator also helps them gain information which both may be lacking. Often both partners are encouraged to seek legal advice before the next mediation meeting, so that they can discuss matters on an equally informed basis.

A useful technique is to put words into the mouth of one party's lawyer:

> 'I'm sure Julie's lawyer will want to know about this loan. Is there a limit on the borrowing?'

Mediators need enough financial knowledge themselves to know how much probing is needed and what supporting documents they should ask for. They also need to be careful not to engage in a long dialogue with one partner that leaves the other excluded or bemused. Discussions need to involve both partners, without cross-questioning either of them or talking down to a less informed party. Knowledge about finances often goes together with control of assets and with higher income and earning capacity. These are clearly major power imbalances whenever there are financial matters to settle. The information that the mediator gathers from both partners and also provides to them both (see chapter 9), combined with advice to each of them from their legal advisors, are all major elements in enabling a couple to negotiate on financial matters on a more equal level.

10.4.5   Emotional pressure

Sometimes one partner seeks to manipulate the other one by playing on fears or guilt feelings. An over-generous offer prompted by guilt feelings may be regretted later on, when there has been more time for thought or advice and the consequences are clearer. Mediators should acknowledge offers and concessions but they should also ask 'what if?' questions, applying the brakes to reduce the risks of premature or ill-considered agreements. Both parties need to be in possession of all the relevant information and have time to consider their positions carefully, before an agreement is reached. Showing extreme distress can also be a way of putting pressure on the partner who has decided to leave. The grief of the 'left' partner may be entirely genuine, but it can be used to manipulate the other one. It may be impossible – and inappropriate – to continue a mediation session when one partner continues to weep. Tearfulness in mediation is common and may be a much needed release of feelings that brings some relief. Sometimes both partners are upset and both cry, but one partner's persistent weeping makes it impossible to discuss any issues. If mediation is abandoned or postponed, possibly to allow for counselling or psychotherapy, this can have the effect of stopping the other partner from moving in any direction. Ending or shelving mediation so that a distraught partner can seek help may be necessary, but it can shackle the other one indefinitely. When there is great distress, it is still worth asking both partners what could help them in some way, given the existing situation, and whether easing stress on a relatively small area or issue could alleviate some distress.

In some cases, one partner's dominating behaviour and the other's submissiveness may be a long-established pattern. One partner may also suffer an acute loss of self-esteem, having discovered that a relationship of love and trust has fallen apart. Mediators need to combine personal warmth and sensitivity with sufficient firmness in holding back one partner while encouraging the other one to come forward. This is part of the art of mediating. The disadvantages of low morale and feelings of inferiority may be only temporary. Mediation can help restore self-esteem, by giving careful and balanced attention to both partners. Changes in dress and posture are often noticeable from one mediation session to the next and these may be signs of a gradual recovery of self-esteem. If, however, despite the mediator's efforts, a participant shows no sense of self-worth and no ability to express a need or point of view, mediation is inappropriate and should be carefully terminated. The personal support of a legal advisor is likely to be needed in these situations and probably therapeutic help as well. Suicide threats may be real and medical referral may be needed urgently. Mediators should not underestimate the risks. The experience of losing a partner through death or divorce is known to be a precipitating factor in suicide. The individual concerned may request the mediator to telephone their GP in their presence and make an appointment that the individual promises to keep (this can be checked, if necessary). In some cases, however, suicide threats are a form of emotional blackmail that put enormous pressure on the other partner to return home, or not to leave at all. Sources of professional help may be discussed in mediation, if both partners accept that there is a need for help. The mediator may need to seek both partners' permission before giving or sending information to one of them, after the mediation session. This permission is usually given very readily. Departing from the usual rules of equal contact may be warranted, if it is necessary in the circumstances and the mediator does not take on a counselling role. Suicide and homicide risks may be high during separation and divorce. Any concerns that a mediator has about a high-risk situation should be discussed without delay with a consultant or supervisor. Normal rules of confidentiality may be breached when medical help is needed urgently. The Agreement to Mediate allows mediators to breach confidentiality in a life-threatening situation.

10.4.6   Personal characteristics

Sometimes there is a significant age difference or one partner suffers from chronic illness or disability. There may be differences between them in force of personality, stamina, assertiveness, or physical attractiveness. Mediators need to be aware not only of the existence of any such differences but also the impact they have on both partners and on any relevant legal considerations. If either party has a learning disability, serious speech impediment or is deaf, mediation may be considered inappropriate. However, before ruling out mediation, it is worth considering the nature and severity of the disability or impairment. In some situations, it may be possible to bring in specialist help so that the mediation can be balanced and workable.

10.4.7   Verbal domination, education, social status

Sometimes one party tries to take control of the mediation by talking at length and preventing the other one from speaking. The quieter party may be less articulate, ill at ease and generally less able to put needs and feelings into words. Being articulate involves some command of language but this does not correlate with intelligence and education. Highly intelligent people may be unable to discuss emotional issues, or may be traumatised and overwhelmed by stress. Silences are very important in mediation. They may be a space in which strong feelings are conveyed between the couple, without words. Mediators should respect these silences and be careful not to intervene too quickly. At other times, a refusal to answer may be a sign of assumed superiority, intended to frustrate or intimidate. Quite often, it is the decibel level and tone of voice that one partner uses which results in the other one staying silent. The louder the harangue, the more stubborn the silence. The mediator needs to intervene in this kind of angry silence, putting a question to the silent partner in a quiet voice that is not emotionally charged. The silent partner usually responds to a thoughtful and considerate question from the mediator.

Participants need sufficient intelligence and reasoning abilities: they need to be able to provide information coherently and able to comprehend the information that is given. If one partner is more highly educated or has higher social status and uses this to belittle the other partner, overtly or more subtly, the mediator needs to use techniques to manage bullying behaviour without losing impartiality.

10.4.8   Physical and/or emotional closeness to children

Often one parent has more financial knowledge, while the parent with day-to-day care knows more about the children. Mediators can help parents share knowledge about their children, as well as information about their finances. The parent who is currently looking after the children needs to share their knowledge and understanding with the parent who sees the children only occasionally or who may have lost contact with them. Fathers often have higher earnings, better pension provision and more control of financial assets, while mothers typically have more influence in relation to the children. A mother who has always looked after the children is in a strong position to say what the children want or need. Fathers who work long hours or whose work often takes them away from home inevitably have less contact and involvement with their children. They may have had little opportunity to build a close relationship, particularly with a baby or toddler who might not cope well with overnight visits.

Many fathers fear that they will lose their children altogether. In mediation, the mother may be more supportive of the children's relationship with their father than he had imagined. Fear of the other parent taking the children away may be a very real fear and may need direct reassurance that this would never happen. When this reassurance is given directly by one parent to the other, the impact can be considerable and positions on other issues often shift. Separation can provide a second chance for the non-resident parent to forge a closer relationship with the children. Even then, it is hard to manage the pain of goodbyes and absences from the children. There are also some parents who wield power through the children by manipulating them and telling them what they must say or do. If children have become caught up in alliances or power battles between parents, the conflict in the family may be very hard to resolve.[10]

10.4.9   New partners, support from family, friends and colleagues

New partners are likely to wield considerable influence. The stance they take varies a great deal, ranging from extreme hostility towards the new partner's ex-partner to a helpful and conciliatory approach and even taking on the role of mediator. When a new relationship is formed after separation, the ex-partner may accept the new partner more easily, but not necessarily so. The new partner may be thrown into the discussion like a hand grenade – 'your boyfriend is not coming anywhere near my children …'. When arguments rage over who is dictating what to whom, the mediator needs to intervene. There are questions to be asked, such as 'do the children already know Sophie?' It is particularly difficult when Sophie was formerly the mother's best friend or next-door neighbour. On the other hand, 'Sophie' or 'George' may be a complete stranger to the children and the other parent, who may need reassurance about the children's gradual introduction to the newcomer and when and how he or she will be introduced to them. If a new partner is peripheral as far as the children are concerned, the mediator may need to focus both parents' attention on what their children are currently feeling and needing from

---

[10]   See Chapters 7 and 8 above.

them, as parents. The battle between the parents may be more 'marital' than parental. Focusing on what both parents see as their children's primary needs may help them to work out arrangements they can both accept, possibly on a step-by-step basis. Sometimes there is a stepparent on one or both sides and adjustments may be difficult and painful. Research studies have shown widely differing reactions from children, especially in the early stages.[11] Many children form good relationships with stepfathers as well as keeping a good relationship with their father. It may be important to draw parents' attention to the findings from research that, generally speaking, children do not regard a stepparent as a replacement or substitute for their mother or father. Dunne and Deater-Deckard (2001) found that although a large proportion of children did not feel emotionally close to a resident stepparent, 91% of children thought a stepparent should be a parent or a friend or both.[12] Only 9% of children thought a stepparent should not be accepted as a parent or as a friend.

Families, especially grandparents, give crucial support following separation, and their opinions and attitudes may carry great weight. The American researcher, Judith Wallerstein, compared the circle of relatives, friends and advisors who line up behind the divorcing couple to the chorus in a Greek tragedy.[13] The surrounding chorus laments the breakdown and gives much-needed support. Stoking the flames of conflict may serve other people's emotional needs. If there is a bigger or more forceful family clan on one side, this creates a further imbalance and may tip the scales, if one parent has more practical support with childcare than the other.

10.4.10   Cultural factors, moral power, religion, support from religious leaders

When a couple's cultural or ethnic background differs from the mediator's, there may be religious or social traditions affecting the relative strength of their positions. Mediators' questions encourage participants to explain their values to each other, as well as to the mediator. This is very important, especially when moral values and religious precepts are a dominant influence. In mediations with members of some religions or communities, such as Muslim couples, it may be necessary to involve family members and community or religious leaders.[14]

---

[11]   FF Furstenberg 'The new extended family' (1987) in Pasley and Tallman (eds) *Remarriage and Step-parenting* (Guildford Press); Ferri and Smith *Step-parenting in the 1990s* (Family Policy Studies Centre, 1998).

[12]   Dunn and Deater-Deckard 'Children's Views of their Changing Families' (2001) *Joseph Rowntree Research Findings* 931.

[13]   Wallerstein and Blakeslee *Second Chances – Men, Women and Children a Decade After Divorce* (Bantam Press, 1989).

[14]   See Chapter 2 at **2.11** and Chapter 3 at **3.6** above.

Where one or both partners speak English as a second language, the mediator needs to clarify and summarise frequently, checking assumptions and whether nuances of language are understood. Actually, this is not very different from mediating between couples whose first language is English. Their inability to comprehend each other is sometimes so great that they might just as well be speaking two different languages. Where English is a second language or where there is some form of language disadvantage, mediation may not be appropriate. If both partners want to mediate, attention needs to be given to checking their understanding of what has been said, clarifying meanings and giving information as clearly as possible. In a mediation with a middle-aged English father and a young Thai mother concerning their 3-year-old daughter, the Thai mother confirmed that despite her limited English she could understand well, provided the mediator spoke slowly and used clear language. The mother stressed that she definitely wished to continue with mediation rather than go to court. She and the father worked out a shared care arrangement (the mother was working and the father unemployed) and after a few practical problems had been sorted out (such as delay in text messages coming through on the father's mobile), the parents were able to work together very well. The mediator may be able to act as a translator for the couple[15] but in some circumstances a co-mediator or interpreter with specialist language skills may be needed.

10.4.11   Legal advantage

Couples often work out arrangements in mediation that are different from those the court would order. However, as Mnookin and Kornhauser pointed out in a seminal article,[16] there are 'bargaining chips' that would apply in court and which influence negotiations in mediation. Furthermore, one partner may not qualify for legal aid or be able to afford to pay for legal advice. The imbalance is increased if the mediator lacks legal knowledge and fails to spot the tactics that the more astute partner has been coached to use. The stance taken by each party's legal advisor is an important factor. When both legal advisors have had mediation training and understand the process, they are likely to give their clients legal advice that balances and complements mediation, without undermining it.

10.5   EMPOWERING PARTICIPANTS IN MEDIATION

In mediation, each participant frequently perceives the other as more powerful. These perceptions can be very strong and are not necessarily rational. The more each partner fears losing something they need or value, the more they ascribe power to the other and take up defensive

---

[15]   See Chapter 4 and Chapter 6 at **6.19**.
[16]   Mnookin and Kornhauser 'Bargaining in the shadow of the law: the case of divorce' (1979) 88 *Yale Law Journal* 950–997.

positions. An aggressive or threatening stance may disguise feelings of powerlessness and fear. The aim of mediation is to 'empower' participants to reach their own informed and balanced decisions through helping them to consider relevant information, possible options and the needs of those involved. When participants have comparable resources in emotional, financial and other terms, they can negotiate with each other on a level playing field. In the real world, however, their resources are rarely equal. The negotiating table is often tipped in one partner's favour. Sometimes one holds all the cards and the other has none. More often, each partner has some cards that the other one wants. One parent may hold the financial cards while the other parent holds cards relating to the children. Stalemate may result if neither parent is prepared to share their cards and reach a fair deal.

Mediators do not have power to shuffle the pack and deal out the cards more fairly. Yet mediation claims to provide fair and balanced outcomes. If mediators are impartial and do not accept responsibility for ensuring the fairness of the outcome, how are the interests of the more vulnerable party protected in mediation? Could a weaker partner be put under pressure to give way, in the interest of getting an agreement? Assisting participants to recognise that their different areas of power and control can be negotiated over, 'balanced' and shared differently is an important mediator skill.

10.6   HOW INTERVENTIONIST SHOULD MEDIATORS BE?

There is an inherent tension between impartiality and empowerment, both of which are key principles in mediators' code of ethics. Remaining strictly impartial at all times would limit interventions by the mediator to assist one participant at a particular juncture. Pro-active mediators are likely to:

- acknowledge emotions and respond to the dynamics in the room;

- intervene more frequently to manage open conflict;

- apply ground rules to prevent one partner taking control of the mediation;

- raise questions that neither partner has raised;

- help participants recognise that a certain manner of speaking or acting may be counter-productive;

- use caucusing to give individual attention and support;

- offer suggestions, without putting them forward as solutions.

Pro-active mediators have been found to be more effective than passive facilitators,[17] provided the mediator's impartiality is not called into question. Agility and empathy are both important in attending to individual needs while maintaining a balance in the process as a whole.

10.7 MANAGING POWER IMBALANCES IN MEDIATION

Mediators' training should develop awareness of power imbalances and skills in managing imbalances at each stage:

(1) Initial meetings – assessing whether mediation is appropriate and acceptable to both parties.

(2) Terminating mediation, if despite the initial assessment the situation turns out to be inappropriate for mediation. Mediators need to watch for signs of intimidation by one partner and submissiveness from the other, terminating mediation if the imbalance is extreme and not responsive to mediation.

(3) Mediators should show respect themselves and look for respect and civility between participants. They should take active steps to control abusive language or threatening behaviour.

(4) Mediation involves equal participation. If a participant constantly interrupts the other and tries to dominate, the mediator should not allow this to continue.

(5) The mediator has an active role in creating space for both to speak and be heard. A partner who may have felt oppressed or depressed may be able to speak for the first time, feeling safe to speak in the mediator's presence.

(6) The mediator should control the documents that are brought into mediation, explaining that the only documents that can be accepted in mediation are those that both participants and the mediator agree to be relevant.

(7) Sharing information. Obtaining information and sharing it openly are fundamental elements of mediation that can greatly reduce knowledge imbalance.

(8) Identifying and understanding needs, both present and future needs. The process of identifying and exploring each party's needs and the

---

[17] See Chapter 13 below.

needs of the children must be done thoroughly and systematically. This helps to balance negotiating positions.

(9) Information provided by the mediator may affect the parties' expectations and positions. Mediators should not shy away from giving information that both parties need to have. The information should be factual, given in a neutral way and able to be double-checked. For example, information about what the court would consider a joint asset may stop one party claiming that this asset does not come into the reckoning.

(10) Legal advice. A basic principle of mediation is that both parties should seek independent legal advice before committing themselves to an agreement that will be legally binding. Independent advice to each party provides a check and a balance.

(11) All available options need to be explored – not just one party's solution. Mediators may prevent one party forcing 'the obvious answer' on the other by ensuring that other possible options are identified and considered fully.

(12) Impartiality is not immobility. The small moves mediators make in the course of a mediation session should maintain rapport with both parties and an overall balance.

(13) Awareness of those who may be exercising power outside the mediation. Children, new partners, grandparents may be very powerful. Mediators help parents consider who has or who should share in decision-making power and whose co-operation is needed, if their decisions are to work in practice.

(14) Written summaries of mediation. Summaries should explain the proposals for settlement and the extent to which other options have been considered. Attention should be drawn to points on which legal advice is needed.

(15) Quality control of mediation. National standards on the selection and training of mediators, supervision, accreditation and monitoring of practice help to provide safeguards for mediation clients and for mediators.

(16) Follow-up consumer studies are important to gather clients' experience of mediation and what can be learnt from it, to improve mediators' practice and develop their skills.

10.8 AGREEING GROUND RULES IN MEDIATION

> 'Oh there's no need to bother with filling in this form. We've already got an agreement and we just want you to draw it up for us. Can you do that today so that we can both sign it?'

Some people want a quick agreement without providing any information. Mediators need to explain as clearly and diplomatically as possible that providing the necessary information is an essential part of reaching a full and final settlement. Participants can choose the forum in which they provide the information, but not whether they provide it. If the court forum is used, the court will require the information. Many participants prefer to provide information in mediation, rather than in court. A reluctance to provide information may be acknowledged as concern to maintain privacy (reframing refusal to co-operate as concern about privacy). However, mediators should beware allowing mediation to continue without obtaining supporting documents. A wily participant may promise to provide documents but avoid doing so. In such cases, a deadline should be set and if it is still not met, the mediation should be terminated. If there is genuine difficulty rather than unwillingness, for example in obtaining pension information, both participants may decide to extend the time-scale for mediation. It should not be extended indefinitely, however, where one partner appears to be playing for time to gain an advantage or maintain the status quo:

> 'Mediators will always try to ensure that the process of mediation is not being used as a delaying tactic.'[18]

Most participants accept and respect ground-rules,[19] but when the emotional temperature is high, ground-rules may need to be emphasised to control interruptions and disrespectful language and asking participants to speak for themselves and not for each other. The mediator's ability to remain calm and respond firmly helps to reassure individuals who fear being controlled or losing control. Sometimes, particularly where litigation has been suspended while mediation takes place, it is important to emphasise ground-rules and even to write them on the flipchart and provide them in a handout. These ground-rules may list principles that separated parents want to apply to their communications outside the mediation room. An example of such ground-rules is attached as Appendix E.

10.9 THE MEDIATOR'S USE OF POWER

The more mediation becomes institutionalised, the greater power mediators may acquire and be expected to use. Mediators carry authority

---

[18] *Independent Mediation – Information for Judges, Magistrates and Legal Advisors* (FJC and FMC, 2011), p 3.
[19] See Chapter 5 at **5.3** above.

in having knowledge, experience and familiarity with the problems of separation and divorce. They often have professional qualifications and are likely to impress their clients as confident and articulate people. They may also have strong personalities. Diffident people may find mediators with all these qualities decidedly intimidating. Mediators may also be perceived as invested with some of the court's authority when they take part in In-Court Mediation or take referrals from the court. The court may expect them to exert authority over clients and if they do not press unwilling parents into mediation or 'bang heads together' they may be seen as not doing their job properly. Mediators must resist this pressure from judges and others, since they derive their power from the very fact that they empower others. The four core principles of family mediation are voluntary participation, confidentiality, impartiality and empowering participants to reach their own decisions.[20]

> 'It is the preservation of these principles which has enabled mediation to provide a highly effective Out of Court Resolution process. The advantage to this is that, where mediation succeeds, there is far less likelihood of a return to the court process.'[21]

In adhering to these principles, mediators resist pressure from participants, fellow professionals and, on some occasions, their own inclinations to act in directive ways. Mediators are sometimes perceived as having a 'child-saving' agenda that leads them to prioritise what they believe to be in the best interests of the child over parents' views and needs. This ought not to happen if listening to individual needs and exploring what would benefit personal and family well being is differentiated from protecting the welfare of a child. Mediators refer child protection concerns to the appropriate agency for investigation. In mediation, children's well being and the well being of each parent are closely interconnected. The children quoted in Chapter 8 have clear ideas about how children and parents can reach agreements through listening and talking with each other. The mediator's role is to support this process, neither imposing a 'child welfare discourse' on parents nor ignoring the fact that some children's views may differ from those of one or both parents. Abel argues that informal institutions 'claim to render parties more autonomous when they actually engage in more subtle manipulation'.[22] Turning a multi-faceted sculpture around so that different facets catch the light is not manipulation, if manipulation means persuading participants to accept how the sculpture ought to be viewed. Looking at a sculpture from different angles increases vision and encourages reflection, in both senses of the word.

---

[20] See Chapter 1 above.

[21] *Independent Mediation – Information for Judges, Magistrates and Legal Advisors* (FJC and FMC, 2011).

[22] Abel *The Politics of Informal Justice* (Academic Press, 1982), Vol 1, p 9.

Some participants invite the mediator to say what is right or wrong, reasonable or unreasonable, but mediators have to resist making judgments or giving opinions. They need to be aware of their personal values and conditioning, so that their attitudes and responses are not coloured by their own family history and culture, personal experience and professional influences. Faced with wavering or tediously argumentative clients, mediators would not be human if they did not sometimes feel sorely tempted to tell them what to do. Participants may expect the mediator to express an opinion, perceiving the mediator as an expert who is expected to know the answers. There are real possibilities of mediators expressing opinions, making diagnoses and exerting influence. A directive mediator controls the process vertically from a superior position, conveying recommendations, explicitly or implicitly, from the apex of the mediation triangle to the participants on the base line, as shown in Figure 1 below.

Figure 1

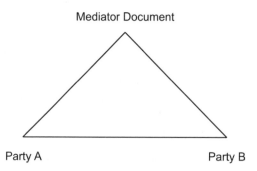

A passive mediator, on the other hand, may not intervene sufficiently to prevent one partner from dominating the other one and the mediator as well. The dominant partner may then exercise control from the apex of the triangle, while the mediator gives ineffectual support to the other on the base-line, as shown in Figure 2 below.

Figure 2

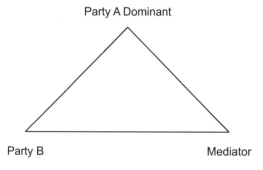

There are also possibilities of a mediator becoming aligned with one partner, consciously or unconsciously. One partner may make an apparently reasonable proposal for settlement and the mediator may be anxious to secure an agreement. The triangle could then turn upside down, with the mediator and the stronger party aligned along the top and the weaker one left alone at the bottom, as shown in Figure 3 below.

Figure 3

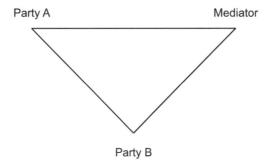

Party A   Mediator

Party B

Shattuck undertook a study of mandatory mediation on child-related issues in the United States, exploring differences between mediators who intervened too much, those who intervened too little and those who kept the balance about right.[23] The study group included recently separated parents who had problems communicating with each other; parents with particularly difficult issues and parents with a long history of conflict and entrenched attitudes. Each group contained parents who looked to the mediator for personal support, sympathy and opinions in their favour. These parents wanted the mediator to exercise authority and were loath to take any responsibility for finding solutions themselves. Shattuck found that that when mediators used five elements of their role in appropriate and balanced proportions, many high-conflict parents managed to reach agreements concerning their children. Mediators who used one or more elements to excess, exerting too much authority and control, tended to steer parents towards the mediator's favoured outcome and these forced agreements were unlikely to last. In contrast, when mediators did not intervene enough and failed to maintain adequate control over the process, parents continued to battle and no agreements were reached. Trinder et al made similar findings in their studies of in-court conciliation by Cafcass.[24] Mediators need a range of techniques, models and skills that help participants to work out their own, mutually acceptable solutions.

---

[23] Shattuck 'Mandatory Mediation' in Folberg and Milne (eds) *Divorce Mediation – Theory and Practice* (Guilford Press, 1988).

[24] Trinder, Connolly, Kellett, Notley and Swift 'Making Contact happen or making contact work? The process and outcomes of in-court conciliation' (2006) *DCA Research Series* 3/06; Trinder and Kellett *The Longer Term Outcomes of In-Court Conciliation* (Ministry of Justice 2007); Trinder 'Conciliation, the Private Law Programme and Children's Well-being' [2008] Fam Law 338–342. See also Chapter 13 at **13.2** below.

The table below, adapted from Shattuck, is relevant to all issues mediation, as well as to child-focused mediation.

Five Elements of Family Mediation

	Element	Purpose	Results of Overuse	Results of Underuse
1.	Use of rules and procedures to draw people into mediation	To encourage settlement of disputes	Mediation used inappropriately. Parties put under pressure	Mediation easily bypassed, parties turn to the court
2.	Conflict management	To define issues, reduce conflict, set boundaries	Parties not given enough time to explain concerns	Parties get bogged down in repetitive arguments
3.	Focus on children	To help parents consider their children's needs and position	Parents may feel their own concerns and needs have not been heard	Parents may make decisions which suit them, without considering their children
4.	Giving information about children	To help parents understand how to help their children adjust	Parents may be lectured and may feel guilty and disempowered	Parents deny impact of their separation on the children
5.	Seeking agreement	To help parties reach mutually acceptable arrangements	Mediator too directive, imposes solutions	Parties continue their power battles

10.10   FLEXIBLE BALANCE IN MEDIATION

Mediating can be rather like standing in the middle of a seesaw. If the mediator stands passively in the middle, the seesaw is likely to remain tipped one way, in the position it was in at the start. If, on the other hand, the mediator shifts weight towards the participant at the lower end of the seesaw, the seesaw may be more level, but the mediator's perceived or actual impartiality may be lost. Skilled mediators manage to make small moves in either direction in managing power imbalances in the room. Whether working singly or in pairs, they may make frequent small shifts of position. Temporary shifts from a midway position include actively seeking and sharing information, enabling a less articulate party to speak and encouraging one who seems overwhelmed. As mediation continues, the seesaw that was initially tipped one way may gradually settle in a more level position. The levelling out depends on each participant and on the circumstances, as well as on the skills of the mediator or co-mediators.

Even when the seesaw seems very unbalanced, effective mediators can help participants explore where the balance could or should lie. Different positions may be considered and tried out, before any position is firmed up. In financial terms, different sets of figures may be run through on the flipchart, to see what they would produce for each partner, before there is any notion of settlement. A male-female co-mediating team is very helpful in managing gender issues and power imbalances.[25] Male-female co-mediators provide a visible balance that reassures participants. There are also increased opportunities of bringing in different perspectives and managing power imbalances strategically. Many mediators believe that co-mediation is the most effective model, because there are always some kinds of power imbalance. There are certainly strong arguments for requiring all mediators to have experience of co-mediating as a stage in their training and to be able to bring in a co-mediator.

The emphasis so far has been on power imbalances that are potentially manageable in mediation. It must be recognised, however, that there are forms and degrees of power imbalance in which referral to mediation or the continuation of mediation would be inappropriate. Circumstances unsuitable for mediation, such as those involving intimidation, violence or abuse, mental incapacity or psychotic illness, should normally have been screened out at the initial assessment stage, but there are some forms of abuse or mental illness that may only become apparent during mediation. Problems or issues impeding settlement may only surface during mediation. Mediators need to demonstrate a combination of empathy and toughness in managing power imbalances in mediation. Pre-occupation with balance may seem a modern concern, but the ancient instrument known as the balance was used in many early societies, both as a practical tool and as a guiding metaphor. *Al-Mizan*, the Arabic word for balance, was applied both to the *spirit level* used by surveyors and builders and to the metaphorical pursuit of justice and harmony in human endeavours. The balance became the focus of a science in the medieval Islamic world, the science of weights. Dozens of treatises on the theory, construction and use of the balance dealt not only with weighing scales with equal arms, but also with the steelyard which had *unequal arms and a sliding counter-weight* (such as mediators sometimes need!). A major text on the science of weights, completed in 1121, placed the balance as an artefact within a larger moral framework.

---

[25] See Chapter 4 above.

CHAPTER 11

DEALING WITH DEADLOCKS

'We had the experience but missed the meaning,
And approach to the meaning restores the experience
In a different form'[1]

CONTENTS

11.1   CONFLICT CYCLES AND TRAPS

The concept of a struggle between two opposing forces, the force of Love, which attracts, and the force of Discord, which separates, goes back to Aristotle and even earlier to Empedocles in the fifth-century BC. Empedocles was a philosopher and scientist who posited the idea of the twin forces of love and discord interacting with each other in a cycle of construction, destruction and reconstruction. The struggle between these two opposing forces is often seen in mediation, where discord usually dominates over love, but love sometimes reasserts itself. Ending a couple relationship is very difficult and painful. Some degree of conflict may be an inevitable part of the emotional and psychological transitions of separation and divorce. Although the adversarial system is often accused of causing and prolonging conflict, the origins of divorce conflict lie between and within the protagonists, rather than being solely a product of the adversarial system. Deep-rooted conflict is not resolved by denying its

---

[1]   TS Eliot *The Dry Salvages.*

existence or by suppressing it, nor by stigmatising it as pathological. Separated couples need to find ways of integrating their disillusionment and negative emotions with their positive feelings and memories, as each partner traverses the difficult path from 'breaking up' as a couple to achieving a new identity as a separate, whole and autonomous self.

Although mediators do not provide therapy, it is helpful if they have some understanding of the psychological processes that drive or resist change. Mediators need to accept that negative emotions, as well as positive ones, are involved in the reconstruction of families and selves. Some separated couples find it very hard to let go of their discord and move on. These couples are hard to work with. If they take a small step forwards, a negative comment from one of them is enough to throw them both back into the vortex of accusing and blaming. The vortex spirals downwards and threatens to suck the mediator down as well. Mediators need to resist the 'downward gravitational tug of antagonisms'[2] and encourage movement upwards and forwards. Systems theory helps us to think about family circles and family processes whose function is to maintain existing systems and resist change. The circle – or dance – which some couples display in mediation may be part of a long-established pattern. Mediators who intervene for a brief period may not understand the family's patterns and dynamics. Should we try to change a revolving cycle without understanding its function? Change that has not been thought through can be dangerous for the couple and also for the mediator. Mediation offers opportunities for families to end negative cycles of communication or behaviour, without forcing unwanted change on them. It can open up safer paths of communication and allow new patterns to develop.

Not all conflicts are negotiable and some should not be negotiated. Mnookin identifies two opposing sets of 'traps' surrounding decisions whether to negotiate or not.[3] He suggests that negative 'traps', particularly demonisation of opponents and the need for control, have the effect of fuelling anger and discouraging people from negotiating when they probably should. Positive 'traps' involving religious beliefs and moral values, self-denial and the need for peace at any cost, may encourage people to negotiate when perhaps they should not.

11.2 NLP TECHNIQUES AND MEDIATION

Successful negotiations often take place without third party intervention. Mediation facilitates negotiation between participants who are disposed to negotiate, but more often where face-to-face negotiation is problematic. Many of the concepts and techniques used in mediation have parallels in neuro-linguistic programming (NLP), without being direct borrowings.

---

[2] Cloke 'Mediation and Meditation – the Deeper Middle Way' *Mediate.com Weekly*, No 266 (March 2009).
[3] Mnookin *Bargaining with the Devil – When to Negotiate, When to Fight* (Simon & Schuster, 2010).

NLP teaches patterns, techniques and skills for effective communication, personal development and accelerated learning. These techniques and skills were developed in the early 1970s in collaboration between an American professor of linguistics and a doctoral student of psychology. Their work was strongly influenced by Gregory Bateson.[4] The 'neuro' part of NLP recognises the fundamental reality that all our behaviour stems from neurological processes of sight, hearing, smell, taste, touch and feeling. We experience the world through our senses. We make 'sense' of the information we receive and react to it. NLP is concerned with how we organise our subjective experience and how we edit and filter the outside world through our senses.

Map-making provides an analogy for people's different constructions of reality. People construct maps of their reality as they see it, their representation of the world they live in, which they use to guide their route and condition their responses. Inevitably, these maps are selective. They show certain features and landmarks, but there may be crucial gaps. In mediation, each participant's map depends on the selective filters they use to interpret what they see, the landmarks they pick out and the pathways they want to follow. The filters they use may leave out crucial information and awareness of aspects they may have missed, like a blind spot. Mediators help participants to look at their 'maps' at the same time, comparing what appears on each of them and spotting features that appear on one, but not the other, or which may be missing altogether. Something that appears on one map may be missing on the other map, such as pieces of financial information or reactions a child is showing. In putting the two maps alongside each other, mediators can highlight key features or critical gaps and help participants to create a new 'overlay' that offers them other ways of looking at things, without imposing different views. Mediators' systematic use of questions (corresponding to the Meta Model in NLP) helps to gather additional and more precise information and to gain a fuller understanding shared between all participants. The Meta Model is a series of questions designed to fill gaps in communication, to clarify generalisations, unravel confusions and explore possibilities. Used with sensitivity and rapport, selective questions can elucidate meanings and give choices, without asking blame-inducing 'Why?' questions. Mediators need to be aware that they use maps too. Asking questions that seem irrelevant to participants and outside the 'mediation frame' may create 'Meta Mayhem, Meta Muddle and Meta Misery!'[5]

---

[4]   See Chapter 2 at **2.4** and Chapter 6 at **6.21** above.
[5]   O'Connor and Seymour *Introducing NLP – Neuro-Linguistic Programming* (Thorsons, 1995), p 108.

11.3   STRUCTURE AND PACE

11.3.1   Structure

Unproductive circular arguments can be put on hold if the mediator takes a pro-active and dynamic approach in structuring discussions. It may be necessary to call a halt and suggest a clear structure, with time boundaries for each issue or sub-issue. Participants may accept time boundaries which mean that at the end of each time-span, they leave one issue and move on to the next, whether headway has been made or not. This shows that they will not spend the whole session arguing over the same thing. This is a useful start. The higher the conflict, the more necessary it is for the mediator to ensure that all issues and options are listed systematically – using the flipchart – and examined. The pros and cons of each option can be marked on the flipchart. Often this shows that further information is needed before a particular option can be considered properly. If participants are encouraged to seek this information and bring information and ideas to the next session, they are encouraged to shift from confrontation to problem-solving and mutual recognition. The mediator's encouragement to consider and reality-test all the options conveys optimism that a solution may exist somewhere. This positive belief helps to counteract the couple's depression and may change the direction of the spiral so that it begins to lead them upwards, instead of downwards.

Providing a structure helps to contain and manage strong emotions, but the structure needs to be flexible and adaptable to the complexity of the issues and different levels of conflict. A range of models and structures can be designed for family mediation, including hybrid civil and family cases.[6]

11.3.2   Pace and time

Some couples come to mediation with unrealistic hopes of a solution being produced by the mediator. But the most experienced mediator has no magic wand to wave. Participants' own willingness and motivation to settle are critical factors. Inevitably, there are situations in which mediation is inappropriate. When little movement seems possible, mediators need to consider the use of time more carefully – the use of time in mediation and the length of time between sessions. Allowing ideas to take root gradually, instead of pushing a seedling into the ground and jumping on it, helps delicate plants to grow. Interim arrangements are sometimes like seedlings that need to be allowed some light and air. Time is very helpful in giving these small plants a chance to grow. At a further meeting a few weeks later their 'cultivators' can consider whether the seedling they planted jointly needs to be trimmed back or whether it

---

6   See Chapter 4 and **11.13** below.

should be given more space. Many people are afraid of committing themselves to new arrangements. They may be reassured to know that it is possible to work out interim arrangements, before reaching final decisions on everything.

11.4 TECHNIQUES AND SKILLS

11.4.1 Getting to the nub of the problem

It is natural to try to resolve disputes by getting to the nub of the problem. De Bono points out, however, that this may be unhelpful if the nub is the focus of anger and the source of the bitterest feelings.[7] If protecting this nub is crucial, both parties erect barriers around it that they defend fiercely. Encouraging shared possession may only intensify the battle for control, because conceding the citadel would mean surrender. If focusing on this key issue heightens the conflict, it may be better to work in areas that are not so hotly guarded. Often, there are significant areas where the parties are in full or partial agreement. Mutual concerns – over children, in particular – can be given priority and in some cases the original dispute may fade into the background and lose its importance. Alternatively, after progress has been made on some matters, discussion of outstanding issues can take place in an easier atmosphere.

11.4.2 Dividing problems into smaller parts

When the situation as a whole seems an impossible jumble, like a pile of mismatched bricks, time and energy are needed to take the pile of bricks apart and sort them out in some kind of order. With the mediator's help, participants may decide to put some bricks aside while they concentrate on fitting just a few interlocking bricks together. Spreading them out makes it easier to see which ones may fit. It also helps participants to identify the keystones that provide a firm foundation for a new edifice, such as the continuing co-operation needed to support a new structure of post-divorce parenting. *Chunking* is a term from information technology that means breaking things into smaller bits. *Chunking* (or *stepping down* in NLP) moves from the general to the specific. Chunking or stepping down moves the focus from an overwhelmingly large issue to one aspect of it that can be worked on. The flipchart is a very useful tool for dividing big problems into smaller parts and for seeing how one part relates to the whole.

Inevitably, there are situations where nothing fits, because the parties are too far apart. Mediators are bound to feel tempted sometimes to knock heads together, tell people what they ought to do – or just give up. Instead of succumbing to the depression that may weigh down the participants, mediators need to maintain their psychic energy and ability to ask useful

---

[7] De Bono *Conflicts – A Better Way to Resolve Them* (Penguin, 1991).

questions about immediate next steps. The map that was drawn earlier – verbally or on the flipchart – may need to be looked at again and fresh stock taken of the choice of route – back to lawyers and the court, or staying in mediation? All options should be identified and re-assessed. If participants are willing to continue in mediation a little longer – even for the remainder of the session – it may be worth identifying the block to settlement and asking what would happen if the block no longer existed.

> 'I can't agree to Luke staying for the weekend, because he doesn't want to go'.

> 'What would happen if he said to you one day that he would like to spend a weekend with his father?'

Or:

> 'If you can imagine him changing his mind (even though you think this is very unlikely), would you see this as a good thing, or would you still have concerns about it?'

Co-operation is a two-way street. A deadlock often seems like a dead-end, with no way forward. This may occur in the first mediation meeting or at any stage during the process. Sometimes participants would rather go on fighting than agree with each other. New partners and other family members may need to be involved.

11.4.3 Mediation skills

- Acknowledge participants' feelings – frustration, anger, disappointment – in a balanced way, acknowledge difficulties – and the efforts that are made even in coming to a mediation meeting.

- Summarise and reframe each partner's position frequently, so that they both feel heard and understood. This also helps to clarify the nature of the problem.

- Anticipate and pre-empt, or put an issue aside for a while.

- If there are children, the children's needs and parental concerns need to be distinguished from issues over ending the couple relationship. It is hard to separate the different roles and feelings as partners and as parents as these often get entangled.

- Brainstorm. The mediator should avoid taking responsibility for solving an impasse. 'Can we spend five minutes thinking of any way forward that any of us thinks could help?' Mediators can contribute suggestions and options themselves, provided these are not presented as the solution. Write all the ideas on the flipchart.

- Use humour – sensitively and when appropriate.

- How significant is this problem? Does a particular sticking point have to be dealt with now, or at all? If it is not urgent, or if it is minor in terms of the overall situation, it may be possible simply to note it and move on. This can be a relief to both participants.

- Occasionally think of telling a short anecdote. An anecdote can be effective if it is well chosen and non-judgmental.

- If there is time, suggest a break – a cup of coffee? Loosening up physically and shifting physical positions can help.

- Ask about underlying fears – 'What is the worst thing that could happen?' If both parties name their fears they may turn out to have mutual fears and mutual reassurance is sometimes possible, once they understand each other's worst fear.

- If the mediator feels exasperated or alienated by one party, this may be a signal that the mediator is becoming more aligned with the other party. Examine these reactions and discuss them with a supervisor or consultant. Are negative reactions linked with the mediator's difficulty with a certain kind of personality?

- Discuss difficulties with a supervisor or consultant. Consider involving a co-mediator.

- Discuss whether third parties should be consulted or involved in some way.

- Don't see a deadlock negatively. It may be better than a bad solution.

- Discuss other routes to settlement – and a do-nothing option. Which is worse?

- Summarise the options that have been considered. Sometimes people come back later to an option they had ruled out, having given it further thought.

- Don't assume that a mediation that ends without a basis for agreement has 'failed', or that the mediator has failed personally. Some couples re-refer themselves to mediation after a period of time, saying they now feel ready to work at it.

11.5   A TYPOLOGY OF IMPASSES

Johnston and Campbell developed a typology of impasses in divorce to distinguish three different levels of impasse: external, interpersonal and 'intrapersonal'.[8] The diagram illustrates these levels and shows that they are interconnected. The word 'block' is used here, instead of 'impasse' because an impasse implies that there is no way forward, whereas a block may be shifted or surmounted. Mediation is a process in which possibilities of getting over, under, through, or around barriers and blocks can be explored and tried out.

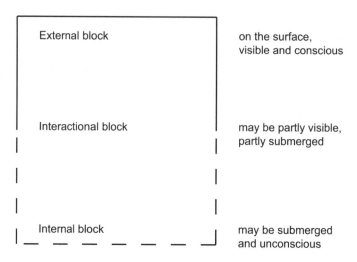

11.6   WHERE DOES THE BLOCK LIE?

When there seems to be a block somewhere, it is useful to have a conceptual map to work out where the block may lie. Although the aim is to work as openly as possible, mediators do not share all their thinking with participants. In planning for each session, the mediator should do some thinking beforehand about the structure of the session, possible ways forward and whether other forms of help are needed. If there seems to be a deep internal block, one party or both may need counselling, psychotherapy or family therapy to reach the roots of the conflict, rather than working to no avail on the surface of the dispute. Systemic treatment may be needed, rather than repeated application of ineffective solutions.

Sometimes other family members – children, new partners, grandparents – have become closely involved in the conflict and may be fuelling the flames for reasons of their own. Other family members may have a stake in keeping the conflict going. Family feuds may prevent a couple reaching a settlement they actually want to reach. Sometimes a child has become caught up in a conflict that cannot be settled without some way of including the child. It is useful to ask parents who should be involved in reaching the necessary decisions. Would it help to involve new partners?

---

8   Johnston and Campbell *Impasses of Divorce – the Dynamics and Resolution of Family Conflict* (Free Press, 1988).

Some new partners act as mediators between the ex-partners. In other situations, their direct involvement might be counter-productive.

Level 1 – External blocks

These are difficulties beyond the control of the participants, such as an inability to sell their home because of the housing market. Recognising these problems does not solve them, but it can help to stop couples blaming each other. There may be problems associated with unemployment or redundancy. One participant may need assurances that the other is actually looking for work. Although it may not be possible to shift an external block through mediation, it may be worth spending time considering how to cope with it.

- **Brain-storming**
  When the obstacles seem insurmountable, the mediator may suggest brain-storming, to see how many ideas all the participants, including the mediator, can come up with, however crazy they may first appear. All the ideas can be written up on the flipchart. A crazy suggestion may make people laugh. Feeling more relaxed may unfreeze thinking that has become firmly set.
  A divorcing couple who could see no solution to their housing problems were invited to brain-storm. After some minutes, one of them came up with an original idea that took the other's breath away, because it was both ingenious and practical. This breakthrough would probably not have happened without encouragement to brainstorm and the emotional intensity of the process. Building rapport with participants and focusing their energy can produce unexpected and positive results.

Level 2 – Interpersonal or interactional blocks

An interpersonal block lies *between* the participants. Many of these blocks involve difficulties in communication between them. The main focus of this book is the role mediation can play in easing communications and managing interpersonal conflict.

Different kinds of interpersonal blocks

(1) **Lack of knowledge**
  Lack of knowledge is a very common problem in mediation. One partner often lacks knowledge of the other's finances. Mediators help participants to identify what they need to know and to share this information. Mediators also provide information, without giving solutions. A couple who disagree on the valuation of an asset or contribution, in financial and emotional terms, may need the

mediator to suggest ways of obtaining a valuation. This can encourage them to suggest ideas of their own.

(2) **Incorrect information**

Sometimes wrong information or misunderstandings have given rise to unrealistic expectations. If participants are relying on mistaken information or advice that seems to be incorrect, the mediator can question and encourage them to check further. If, however, the incorrect or misleading information is attributed to a legal advisor, this is more delicate, as mediators need to be careful not to destroy clients' trust in their legal advisors.

Anxious clients may have misunderstood their lawyer's advice or have heard only what they wanted to hear. Mediators can formulate checking-out questions for them to take back to their lawyers, encouraging them to write down the questions so that they remember them exactly and to ask for a written reply from their lawyer. If a client continues to be given information that is clearly wrong, perhaps by a lawyer who does little family law, the mediator should express doubts and consider whether seeking a second opinion is an option available to the client. Sometimes clients are seriously dissatisfied with the advice they have been given and want to change their legal advisor. Mediators need to be careful not to advise clients to change their lawyer or to use one particular lawyer. If a mediator is asked to recommend a lawyer, a list should be given of lawyers in the area who are known to subscribe to Resolution's Code of Practice and The Law Society's Family Law Protocol, with reference where necessary to those undertaking publicly funded work.

(3) **Different notions of fairness**

Participants often have different notions of what is fair. One may define fairness as a 50/50 split while the other argues that 50/50 would be completely unfair. It is useful to convert percentages into the amount of money they represent and vice versa. The difference may be relatively small when converted into figures. However big the gap, it is important to quantify it. When parents disagree about a concept or principle of fairness, such as children dividing their time equally between the two parents, it is useful to focus on the child as an individual and what may work in relation to the particular child's age and needs. In focusing on the child's actual experience, rather than on fairness, parents may come to see that fairness is not the most appropriate criterion where children are concerned. Some parents may agree arrangements that may be unfair to one of them but are nonetheless accepted by both of them as better for the child. Mediators are often asked what is 'fair'. A short commentary from the mediator about different criteria for deciding fairness may be helpful:

'There is a question of principle here. You each have an idea of fairness that makes sense – but it is based on different standards of fairness, so naturally you don't agree. There are different ways of defining what is fair. There is fairness at a personal level, based on what each of you feels is your due. Then there is the court's approach in which the factors the court considers relevant are taken into account and the court seeks to strike the right balance. But even when the court does this, an order may be made which neither party finds fair. I can explain the factors the court considers relevant, if you would like me to. But would it be useful, first, to look at your resources and then list what each of you needs to live on and see how big the gap is between what is available and what you each need?'

(4) **Mistrust**

When a close relationship breaks down, trust usually breaks down as well. If mediation were considered suitable only where there is complete trust, there would be very little mediation. It is neither realistic nor necessary to look for complete trust at the outset. The question is whether there is sufficient trust for mediation to be possible. For example, although couples have often lost trust in each other as partners, there is often a good level of trust between them as parents. There may be no doubts about the other parent's reliability where the children are concerned and therefore good reason to mediate on issues relating to the children.

If, on the other hand, one parent mistrusts the other *as a parent,* the mediator needs to enquire into the fears and suspicions. At one end of the scale it could be about child abuse or at the other end it could be giving a child a fizzy drink before travelling. How a mediator responds must depend on the type of mistrust expressed. If it is of such a serious nature that mediation cannot continue, the mediator should refer to the Agreement to Mediate explaining that confidentiality cannot be absolute, in all circumstances.[9] In many – but not all – cases where doubts are expressed on financial questions, these doubts may reflect lack of information. They do not necessarily mean that the other party will give unreliable information or deliberately withhold information. In explaining and following through each stage of mediation, mediators should always emphasise the need for complete information and for verification, before participants are asked to consider proposals for settlement.

Mediators need to be alert for any expression of mistrust and quick to acknowledge it. If it is ignored, the mistrust will grow. It is important to acknowledge the difficulties of trusting the other person when the relationship breaks down ('normalising'). If one partner suggests that the other is untrustworthy or accuses the other of dishonesty, the mediator can identify mistrust without identifying with it and losing impartiality. One way is to reframe the mistrust as a need to be fully satisfied, convinced or reassured:[10]

---

[9]   See Chapter 3 above.
[10]   See Chapter 4 above on reframing.

'So, Wendy, in order to feel completely clear [about the value of these shares] ... reassured that [this payment has been made], you would like to see a document showing ... Jim, do you think you could satisfy Wendy by bringing [this document] to our next meeting?'

Sometimes one partner has resisted providing financial information and then surprises the other by producing it. Whereas angry demands or a formal request letters from a lawyer may increase resistance, the mediator may lower it by putting the request in a different way:

'Jim, Wendy says she feels insecure because she does not know enough about ... It would be really helpful if you could bring ... to our next meeting. Would that be possible?'

If there is still resistance, it can be pointed out that in court proceedings there is not a choice between providing financial information and not providing it. The choice is the forum in which it will be provided – in mediation or in court.

(5) Bad faith in mediation

It would be naïve to believe that everyone who comes to mediation will co-operate fully and honestly just because they are asked nicely. Some see mediation as a soft option and may try to pull the wool over the mediator's eyes, as well as their partner's eyes. Mediators need to watch for signs of bad faith indicated by:

- lack of punctuality or failure to keep appointment;
- refusal to sign the terms of the mediation;
- body language;
- delaying tactics or, alternatively, pressure to get a quick agreement with as few questions asked as possible;
- delay or reluctance in providing financial information and supporting documents;
- evasive answers to probing questions from the mediator or the partner;
- figures which do not add up: income not tallying with expenditure;
- Sabotaging or failing to keep to arrangements or interim agreements;
- offering plausible excuses in order to continue negotiations;
- posturing and playing for time, with no real evidence of motivation;
- evidence of ulterior motives, such as making a bid for residence or more contact to strengthen a position on financial or property issues;
- if paying for private mediation, forgetting to bring the cheque-book.

11.7 TESTING COMMITMENT TO MEDIATION

Mediators can test participants' commitment to mediation by:

- Demonstrating their own commitment to absolute transparency and balance in all dealings with participants.

- Making sure any ground-rules are clear and accepted.

- Applying these ground-rules firmly, explaining that mediation can continue only if they are kept.

- Being persistent in asking probing questions, but avoiding interrogation.

- Being firm in relation to mediation procedures. If excuses are accepted for non-production of information, being clear whether there is a deadline.

- Asking whether participants trusted each other before the break-up.

- Assisting them to give each other concrete and verifiable information.

- Structuring mediation sessions, agreeing time-scales and deadlines.

- Discussing particular sanctions that could be used for non-compliance – such as how long one parent would wait, if the other is more than x minutes late.

- Explaining the documents that the court will need, the questions that legal advisors may ask and the documents they will need to see.

- Summarising frequently and recording interim arrangements or proposals clearly.

- Considering terminating the mediation if, having given a person the benefit of the doubt, he or she continues to give evidence of abusing the mediation process.

- Warning of possible termination and explaining the reason if possible, rather than saying as one mediator did in a training role-play: *'Right, that's it. Obviously we can't go on',* leaving both parties open-mouthed.

- Drafting written summaries carefully.

11.7.1   Confronting and challenging

Mediators have different views about confronting and challenging a
participant who seems to be procrastinating, withholding information or
possibly giving false information. A direct challenge is a high-risk strategy.
There are risks if mediators assert authority, since one of their main
strengths is not having authority. Too direct a challenge may also
jeopardise the mediator's impartiality. Alternative strategies to a direct
challenge include:

Being puzzled

If there is a factual discrepancy, the mediator may say in a puzzled, rather
than inquisitorial tone:

> 'I'm sorry, I don't quite understand how what you just said ties in with the
> figures on page x of your financial form. Could you help me understand
> how ...?'

Asking for supporting documents is another means of clarifying and
verifying information, without aggressive questioning. Ask people to help:
'Could you bring ...? ... it would be useful to have ...'

Acknowledging difficulties

Where there is a contradiction between words and actions, it may be
necessary to point out the contradiction, but only if there is enough
rapport. Another way would be to suggest that the person concerned may
be finding it very difficult to do something, when it actually comes to the
point. Acknowledgement and empathy may make it easier for a person to
admit a difficulty or to recognise ambivalent feelings.

Reversing roles

Sometimes it helps to ask partners to take each other's position, even
swopping chairs for the purpose of the exercise. Alex could be asked to
imagine himself in Katie's place and say what he thinks her main concerns
are and what might be acceptable to her. Then Katie could be asked to
imagine herself in Alex's place. Looking at a situation through the other's
eyes can sometimes change the way they both see it.

Setting tasks and time-limits

Where there are doubts about commitment and motivation to finding any
solution, it often helps to identify small tasks that participants agree to
undertake before the next session. This can be a useful test of motivation.
Letting each other down is more difficult if they know the mediator will
be monitoring that these tasks have been carried out. Each parent may be

asked to suggest something they could do personally which might help. Questions may be put forward for further reflection, or interim arrangements worked out in the very short term. Time limits need to be emphasised. If one parent seems to be wasting time during a session, look at the clock and comment on the amount of time left. The last part of the session can be used to recap, prioritise and discuss next steps.

11.8   HIGH CONFLICT IN MEDIATION

Some couples seem determined to combine forces to defeat the mediator. They may belong to the category of implacably hostile and 'enmeshed' couples described in the typology of divorcing couples.[11] There may indeed be an unconscious collusion between them to prevent any professional intervention being 'successful'. If settlement is reached and the arguments ended, what would take their place? When mediation is deadlocked, it is often useful to consider, not what would be gained from settlement but what would be lost from it, and by whom? For some people, an empty void is far more frightening than a continuing battle. With battles, there is a chance of winning and the triumph of inflicting defeat. Settlement may bring utter loneliness and depression. Couples with an emotional need to fight are addicted to fighting and sometimes referred to as 'hostility junkies'. They seem to get high on the adrenalin of fighting and have a greater investment in keeping the conflict going than in ending it. They have a strong emotional need to keep their fight going and know exactly which button to press to raise the temperature and renew the battle. Mediators are increasingly mediating with couples referred by the court as a last resort, because litigation has not ended the battle.

Raging tirades can have a galvanising function for individuals who are otherwise close to despair. But these couples are liable to annihilate each other. The virulence of their onslaughts may paralyse the mediator, who may feel like a rabbit caught in the glare of oncoming headlights. Couples who are addicted to fighting usually have a well-rehearsed pattern of argument. They may get perverse satisfaction in acting their script. They like having an audience and the mediator is another audience, even if the actors have to pay. They may combine forces to keep the fight going. The mediator's usual techniques of setting rules, agreeing structure, exploring options are unlikely to have an effect because this is what the couple expect. It is worth trying to make them forget their script, by doing something unexpected. Techniques that may help include:

- Brainstorming, putting all the ideas on the flipchart using different symbols and colours. Involve both parties in selecting and prioritising from the ideas that are written up. Suggest they copy the

---

[11]   See Chapter 3 above.

list of ideas on the flipchart and think about them at home. At the
next meeting the flipchart can be looked at again.

- If you are co-mediating, debate the issues with your co-mediator in
  front of the couple. Then invite their comments. It is particularly
  useful if co-mediators take up different positions and engage in a
  genuine debate, with one mediator saying for example to the other:

  > 'Jim, I don't think I see this in the same way as you do. I am not clear
  > why Roy (husband) needs to be satisfied that Barbara (wife) is
  > choosing suitable housing for herself. Surely that is for her to decide?'

  A debate between co-mediators can rehearse the arguments and in
  this way change the dynamics in the room. It models a way of
  disagreeing without fighting, often using humour.

- List the things each party needs to find out about or think about
  before the next meeting. Ask practical questions such as 'What
  would make it possible for you to ...?' Also ask questions such as
  'What do you fear most? What is the worst thing that could happen
  to you now?'

- Change the mood dramatically if necessary. When couples are
  arguing endlessly over rights and wrongs, it can be useful to enquire
  what would happen in an emergency? Questions about emergencies
  involving sudden illness can have a very sobering effect. The need to
  draw up fresh Wills may need to be considered, in any case. Help
  people to think about what matters most to them.

- If the arguments are raging so loudly that the mediator cannot be
  heard, stand up and say what a pity it is you cannot help. The sudden
  movement tends to stop the couple in mid-flow. Use the momentary
  lull. The mediator can regain control by summarising issues quickly.
  If the couple quieten down, it may be possible to focus on a limited,
  short-term issue.

- Surprise people! Instead of responding in the way the couple expect,
  do the opposite! Some mediators ask questions that take people by
  surprise. These need to be used with care – and with empathy.
  Examples are:

  > 'Maybe it is safer for you not to reach an agreement at the moment.
  > Would it be better to leave things as they are?'

  > 'Would you rather have this argument outside? Then it would not cost
  > you so much!'

  > 'If Jodi (daughter) is asked by her friends whether the two of you are
  > getting things sorted out, what do you think she will say?'

'What would you like her to be able to say?'

The conscious use of surprise in mediation is worth thinking about and cultivating.

11.8.1   Anticipating a walk-out

When one party is on the verge of walking out, their body language usually gives clues before they get up to leave. If the mediator notices signs of fidgeting, staring out of the window or mounting anger or distress, a walk-out may be prevented by the mediator saying something like:

> 'Karen, you are looking very upset (fed up). People often feel so desperate at times that they just want to give up and get out of here. Is that how you are feeling at the moment? ... Do you think you could manage just another five/ten minutes? If you could, maybe we can concentrate on immediate steps to make things slightly easier for you both?'

It may be possible to pre-empt a walk-out by offering a short caucus,[12] but if a person leaves the mediation room, the mediator needs to consider whether to let them go – sometimes they come back again – or whether the person is acutely distressed and the mediator should try to catch them before they leave the building. Participants have the right to leave if they want to, but careful attention to body language and eye contact helps to recognise that someone is very distressed or frustrated, before they actually leave the room. An additional room should always be available where one party can wait and recover in safety, leaving only after the other one has left.

11.9   INTERNAL BLOCKS WITHIN INDIVIDUALS

Blocks which are external to the couple or which lie between them are generally evident and visible, whereas internal blocks within individuals may not be so evident and may be unrecognised by them. Blocks in thinking or perception may be unconscious, especially if they come from childhood experience. Deeply rooted blocks are unlikely to be reached or addressed directly in mediation. However, as the different levels are interconnected, even small changes on the surface[13] can have the effect of reducing fears or easing resistance at a deeper level.

11.9.1   Acute grief

Mediators need to be aware of reactions to grief and different stages of grieving, in considering whether a partner who is deeply bereft is ready

---

[12]   See Chapter 5 above.
[13]   See Chapter 1 'surface tension effects' above.

and strong enough to take part in mediation. There is a great deal of literature by psychologists and psychiatrists about attachment, bereavement and loss.[14] Different stages in the grieving process have been described as an initial phase of numbness and shock, then yearning and searching for the lost person, followed by a phase of disorganisation and despair leading, usually, to gradual recovery and reorganisation. People who come to mediation in the initial phase of numbness and shock are unlikely to be in an emotional state to reach decisions or negotiate on financial issues.

Comparisons have been made between grieving following death and grieving in separation and divorce. A study of widows and divorced wives showed that both groups experienced similar feelings of loss and grief and had similar difficulties in adjusting to the loss, reconstructing their lives and coping with economic problems. Despite these similarities, grieving in separation and divorce differs significantly from grieving the death of a partner. A partner who leaves the marriage has exercised a choice. The voluntary nature of the decision causes deeper hurt and rejection and more anger than where the loss occurs involuntarily through death. Death involves funerals and 'rites of passage' that help to establish the reality and finality of death, whereas a partner who has been left may refuse to accept the breakdown as a final one. Maintaining contact through the children may prolong and intensify pain, with its constant reminders of the former partner's continuing existence and refusal to return.

11.9.2   Understanding different stages of grieving and adjustment

Mediators need an ability to recognise and understand the stage each partner has reached, especially in the common situation where they are at different stages. The partner who initiated the separation may have spent a long time thinking about it and preparing for it. The one who is left may be stunned, unable to accept the fact of the separation or to see any justification for it. The wider the gulf between them in seeing that their relationship is over, the harder it is to mediate on the issues that need to be settled. Acknowledging this gap explicitly may help a little. The gulf between the partner wanting separation or divorce and the partner who wants to continue the relationship is a very common problem in mediation. Mediation can be tried, to see whether the partner who has made the break is willing to slow down and allow the other one to 'catch up' emotionally. The second partner may become more able to acknowledge the reality of the breakdown of their relationship. In other words, mediation may be able to bridge the gap between them.

Mediation may be suspended while counselling takes place. The difficulty about this is that there are often urgent issues regarding the children and immediate financial matters. Discussion of these issues is extremely

---

[14]   See also Chapter 2 above.

difficult and may not be appropriate, when one partner is very distressed. On the other hand, it may not be possible to put urgent questions on hold, while counselling takes place over a period of months. Mediation may take place concurrently with counselling, but this also has its problems. There has to be enough clarity about the different focus of work in each process. Otherwise, clients can get confused about what they are supposed to be doing with whom. There may be overlap and duplication of effort.

There are situations in which the grief and loss are so intense that it is inappropriate or impossible to mediate. Mediators need to take account of:

- how recently the separation took place;

- whether there are multiple losses occurring simultaneously;

- the extent to which decisions are being taken unilaterally by one partner;

- the degree of distress shown;

- the capacity to engage in mediation.

When one partner cannot let go of the relationship, this may be shown in the following ways:

- inability to contemplate the future or to discuss ways of settling issues;

- inability to express any needs apart from the need for the partner's return;

- great distress, continuous weeping during mediation;

- repeated assertions that the other partner will soon 'come to his (or her) senses' and return home;

- strong moral judgments, especially if the other partner has a new relationship;

- denial of the breakdown coupled with refusal to acknowledge having contributed in any way to the other partner's decision to leave;

- blocking and delaying tactics, refusal to fill in forms etc;

- lack of co-operation over the children, possibly as a means of punishing the other parent or putting pressure on him/her to return home;

- emotional threats or blackmail, such as suicide threats;

- attempts to manipulate others, including children and mediators, into seeing the abandoned partner as the innocent victim.

11.9.3   Acknowledging acute shock, distress and grief

Mediation cannot resolve the profound loss and grief of separation and divorce. The grieving process may take years for some people and may never be fully resolved. Mediators are not therapists, either for both partners or for the more wounded partner, but they need to be aware of people's pain. Understanding can be conveyed non-verbally, in attentiveness and eye contact and in verbal acknowledgements to both participants, without taking sides or making judgments. Mediators often need to make mutualising statements such as 'You are both under enormous stress ... It's frightening when one isn't sure what is happening next week, let alone next month ... I can see that you are both desperately worried.' People seem appreciative of these comments. There must be eye contact with both partners and the words need to be said with real warmth and sincerity. When one partner becomes very distressed, the other partner may be very distressed too, but may show it less. It is important not to acknowledge the distress of one partner in a way that suggests the other one is not distressed. It is safer to include both in acknowledgements of distress. The partner who assumes that he or she is suffering far more than the other one can be stunned to realise the suffering of the other. These moments are very powerful and must not be hurried. Acknowledgement through illustrating positions on the 'loss cycle', perhaps by use of a pre-prepared sheet or the flipchart, can mutualise loss and grief in powerful ways.

Small practical details may seem trivial, but it is essential to have a box of tissues, to avoid having to go out to look for them. When people break down in tears, as they quite often do, it is important to ask, after a few moments, whether they want to continue the meeting or whether it would be better to stop. Usually they want to continue. As well as reassuring a person who is crying that it is normal to be upset in these situations, offering more tea or coffee may be helpful.

Short-term focus

When the level of distress is very high, a short-term focus on how to manage the next week or month is more helpful than looking for long-term or final solutions. Dividing a future that seems like an endless desert into 'chunks' of weeks or months helps people to cope with one chunk at a time.

Enabling a grieving person to express anger

Those who seem overwhelmed by grief often find it difficult to express their anger. It may help to say that feeling angry, as well as sad, is normal. Anger needs to be expressed, but kept under enough control. It is an energising force, which can protect against depression and despair. Referring to anger in an accepting, normalising way can help both the partner who is showing anger and the one who is suppressing anger. Accepting anger as normal can also reduce people's need to show it in their behaviour towards each other. Allowing some safe expression of anger can be combined with stressing that this does not mean acceptance of physical or verbal violence.

Making connections between anger and grief

The rejected partner usually experiences and shows the most acute grief, whereas the initiator of the separation commonly experiences grief also but may have greater difficulty in showing it. It is safer for the initiator to express anger than grief, because grief might be interpreted as regret and a change of mind. If one partner expresses all the grief and the other expresses all the anger, they may each remain stuck in these emotions until both can share in the grief and the anger. When one or both partners are locked in anger and unable to express grief, it may help to speak of the sadness that often underlies anger, saying how hard it can be to show sadness when one is extremely angry. The timing of such a comment is important, as well as its sensitivity. One partner, sometimes both, may cry. When anger turns into sadness, the pain may be acute but may be mitigated by awareness that it is shared. Some exceptionally bitter divorces involve the death of a child. If the parents have been unable to grieve their child's death together, their unresolved grief can turn into bitter anger against each other. These situations are deeply tragic and indicate a need for counselling or therapy.

Even where counselling or psychotherapy is sought, there are often practical issues that still need to be settled. Settlement can be helped by the realisation that anger is often linked with grief. The distinction between the roles of mediator and that of therapist is that the mediator is not exploring grief and anger in depth and offering therapeutic help. The mediator acknowledges feelings and helps to make connections. The aim is to ease communication, rather than working with individuals on emotional problems.

Valuing dreams and aspirations

When there is a tendency to idealise the other partner and the marriage that has been lost, it may be possible to recognise the deep disappointment of recognising that there were expectations that may not have been fulfilled. People need to value their dreams and aspirations, yet also acknowledge that a dream is over:

> 'It must be a profound disappointment for both of you that the marriage you invested so much in hasn't worked out in the way you hoped. People often feel that they have failed. But there hasn't necessarily been a failure. It may be a question of different needs and expectations not matching up any more, despite real efforts.'

Using metaphors and analogies

The use of metaphors in mediation and analogies was mentioned in Chapter 6. Sometimes it helps to say something on these lines: 'It seems it feels like being in the middle of a black tunnel' (observe both participants and see if there is a non-verbal or verbal response):

> 'This is probably the hardest stage of all, right now. But it is surprising how often people find after a year or so that their situation has changed in ways they had not expected to happen. It's impossible to know how things will change or maybe to believe that they can change. But over time things do change. They can get better.'

Optimistic comments may be received with disbelief, but they can bring a smile. As already stressed, empathy must be shown equally to both partners, keeping eye contact with both and showing warmth to both. Metaphors need to be chosen with care, to tune in with clients' language and feelings.

Referral to counselling or psychotherapy

Those whose grief is particularly acute and prolonged or who show pathological reactions linked to earlier unresolved loss need therapeutic help. Many people seek help from their doctor for symptoms associated with the distress of separation. Although some doctors just write out a prescription for drugs, many recognise the value of other kinds of therapy and some employ a counsellor in their practice. Experienced mediators may be able to manage situations of high conflict and difficulty, but however skilled and experienced the mediator, there must be discretion to terminate a mediation which is inappropriate or unworkable, making suggestions of other sources of help. Referrals to counselling must be made with care, however. A recommendation to go elsewhere could be interpreted as a Pontius Pilate kind of gesture, increasing the sense of rejection felt by a person already abandoned by their partner.

Deciding when and how to suggest counselling or therapy needs to be done carefully. A suggestion that counselling might be helpful should be made to both partners equally, without appearing to suggest that one needs counselling, whereas the other does not. Counselling to repair the marriage is only one form of counselling. Counselling to cope with relationship breakdown, or divorce counselling, may help both the initiator and the non-initiator of the separation to understand what has happened between them so that they can move forward with less pain or self-blame. People often want to know what help others have found useful in similar situations. Information about local services may encourage individuals to seek help, without feeling stigmatised. A list of counselling agencies and private therapists can be given to those who want it or posted to them afterwards. Some situations are not suitable for mediation because there are problems of individual psychopathology, a history of mental illness, alcoholism or drug abuse. Mediators cannot and should not be expected to mediate in such cases.

Meeting obduracy and resistance

- Acknowledge concerns.

- Be positive, patient and encouraging.

- Use focused or closed questions.

- Cut short rambling or irrelevant answers. Bring people back to the question asked.

- Interrupt pleasantly but firmly, to maintain control of the discussion.

- Do not lecture parents on their responsibilities towards their children. This is not the mediator's role. It alienates a parent who feels criticised and allies the mediator with the other parent. Try to help parents focus on children's needs, hopes and fears.

- When, despite failing to turn up for previous contact visits, a parent maintains that he or she is committed to the children and wants to see them, ask this parent to demonstrate to the other parent that the arrangements made in mediation will be kept. If one party undertakes to provide a financial document and fails to do so, explore the reasons and put the commitment to mediation to the test by giving another chance, with a deadline.

- Ask 'what if?' questions. Ask both parties if they would agree to telephone each other within an agreed time, if anything should occur to prevent either of them keeping an arrangement. Ask a mother who complains of the father's unpunctuality to say how many minutes she would be prepared to wait for him to call for the children, beyond the agreed time. Ask the father what could delay him. What would they do if the arrangement does not work? If it breaks down, would they be willing to come to a further mediation session?

- Stress that you will be really glad to hear that the arrangements are working. Show that you are genuinely concerned and monitoring the outcome.

- If there is to be a further mediation appointment, allow enough time to agree the date and time of this appointment. Note the date of any interim contact or other arrangement and the next mediation meeting.

- Make it clear that the mediation will end if it does not seem to be serving a useful purpose. Do not wait passively for a party who has been let down countless times to be let down again. If you do, you will lose the trust and confidence of both parties.

- When an interim arrangement has been worked out, it can be written down with both parents. If possible, they should have a copy to take away with them. An interim agreement – for example on contact arrangements – may not require legal advice.

11.10   BLOCKS WITHIN THE MEDIATOR

Mediators need to be able to accept that getting stuck is not confined to participants. It may be the mediator who gets stuck. A mediator may fail to grasp an important point or have difficulty relating to one of the participants. Feelings of irritation or frustration – or plain dislike – may impede the mediator's ability to hold a balance and think creatively. Mediators need to tune into their own feelings and examine their own subjective reactions, in order to understand what is happening in the room. The mediator may have become triangulated into the couple's conflict. Something may have been said that resonates with the mediator's personal history, consciously or unconsciously. A parent's attitudes or the couple's values may be so alien to the mediator that a negative reaction blocks the mediation. Whenever there are difficulties like this, the mediator should seek to discuss them with a supervisor or consultant, before deciding that no progress can be made. Reflecting with a consultant or supervisor may lead to a different perspective and generate new ideas.

11.11   BATNAS AND WATNAS

BATNAs and WATNAs[15] are useful tools when there is stalemate in mediation. The mediator might say:

---

[15]   See Chapter 2 at **2.2** above.

'You are both in a very difficult situation and it looks as though you might need the court to decide for you. Before you start court proceedings, there are some questions you may need to put to your lawyers. Would it help to make a list of these questions?'

Questions for participants to take to their legal advisors may include:

- If the judge has to decide, what do you think I should get, in terms of the best outcome I can look for? (= BATNA, the Best Alternative to a Negotiated Agreement)

- What do you think, realistically, I probably would get? Could you guarantee that I would get this? (Obviously, not)

- If things go against me, what is the worst outcome I might get? (=WATNA, the Worst Alternative to a Negotiated Agreement)

- Can you give me the range between 'best' and 'worst' likely outcomes, in terms of percentages?

- How long would it take to get a final court order?

- How much could the court proceedings cost me in total, if they are strongly contested by 'the other side'?

- Do judges vary in the view they take and the decisions they make?

- How much uncertainty would there be about the final court outcome?

- Could there be other consequences of going to court that I ought to think about?

The mediator helps the participants to identify these and any other relevant questions and can provide a written list of them, if needed, or encourages the participants to write them down. The lawyers' answers should provide them with an outcome range. The participants can discuss this range at a subsequent mediation meeting and consider a basis for settlement within this range, without pressure from the mediator. Even where there is agreement, participants should be encouraged to put these BATNA and WATNA questions to their lawyers, to check that their proposed settlement falls within the range of outcomes that the court would endorse. Clients should also be warned that their lawyers' comment on a mediated agreement might be: 'Oh, you would do better if you went to court'. If this is said, clients should be encouraged to ask further questions to test their lawyer's advice. Few lawyers will guarantee that the client will get a better deal in court, especially after the costs have been taken into account. Clients should ask their lawyers to put their advice in writing. Encouraging clients to formulate questions to ask their lawyers does not imply that lawyers give poor advice. On the contrary, clients are encouraged to seek advice and to use it as a basis for well-informed and well-considered decisions. There are risks of premature agreements being reached in mediation. Participants may be anxious to reach a settlement without realising the risks of premature or ill-informed agreements. One party may try to pressurise the other into an unbalanced agreement. There are risks for all concerned if participants do not understand the full consequences of their decisions and if mediators without adequate legal knowledge do not recognise the pitfalls. Suggesting that they take questions back to their lawyers is not a sign of failure on the mediator's part, but rather a way of assisting the lawyer to 'invest in' the process of settlement. If BATNA and WATNA questions are used, participants may return to mediation with renewed willingness to settle. In keeping with the *confidentiality* of mediation and *openness* within the process, questions for lawyers should be defined and responded to on a 'without prejudice' basis, in the expectation that the responses will be shared in mediation.

11.12   SOME DEADLOCKS REMAIN DEADLOCKED

'I deserve it
because I have it.
You have not got it
therefore you do not deserve it.
You do not deserve it
because you have not got it
You have not got it
because you do not deserve it ... etc.'[16]

Some disputes remain intractable and the knots remain knotted, no matter what the mediator tries. When preparing their portfolio for competence assessment and also in consultancy or supervision, mediators are encouraged to consider whether, with the benefit of hindsight, they might have handled a particular mediation differently. In a case referred to mediation by the court, the unmarried parents had been in dispute over contact throughout the life of their five-year-old daughter, Maya. They appeared to make some headway in the first co-mediated meeting. Contact arrangements for the next six weeks, including Christmas, were written up in an interim MOU. However, the father, Kieran, was insisting on staying contact and Melanie, the mother was adamantly refusing it, based on a number of objections and concerns that needed to be worked through, one by one. Kieran and Melanie had never lived together in an established partnership. Melanie had lived for a short time with Kieran in his parents' home, when she was expecting Maya. She left Kieran before Maya was born. Kieran was not present at Maya's birth and he had seen very little of her when she was a baby. His name was on her birth certificate and he had parental responsibility and a court order defining

---

[16]   RD Laing *Knots.*

contact. He had made a further application to the court claiming that Melanie had breached the contact order and seeking staying contact. Melanie counter-claimed that Kieran had breached the contact order himself by not returning Maya after a contact visit, keeping her for three days without Melanie's consent. There were other difficulties that contributed to the deadlock:

(1)   Kieran and Melanie lived forty miles apart.

(2)   As Kieran did not drive, he needed members of his family to provide transport.

(3)   Kieran's mother and other members of his family were involved in his feud with Melanie.

(4)   Kieran worked in a retail store with a constantly changing work schedule. He usually worked on Saturdays and Sundays with two weekdays off in lieu, but in spite of requesting his schedule as far in advance as possible, he generally received it only about a week ahead. Melanie argued that she could not be expected to change her arrangements at such short notice and also that Maya was too tired at the end of her school day to go out with her father for a couple of hours.

Melanie cancelled the second mediation meeting at twenty-four hours' notice and asked for it to be rearranged. Kieran had already booked a day's leave for the meeting, to be followed by a short outing with Maya. He was incensed. The rearranged second meeting was shuttled, as the level of hostility was too high for a face-to-face meeting. It emerged from talking with Melanie on her own that her concerns about staying contact were as strong as ever and that Maya was being used in the power battle between her parents. At the end of the second meeting, the deadlock over staying contact continued and Kieran said he would try to bring forward the date of the next court hearing. What could be learnt from this 'failed mediation'? If mediation information and assessment is carried out at court, it may be too brief. Fuller assessment may be needed to design a tailor-made model. Although Maya was only five, both parents described her as bright and articulate for her age. If an experienced child counsellor had been available for child-inclusive mediation, this counsellor, with the agreement of all concerned, might have met with Maya and might, in therapeutic play with her, have elicited messages that she needed her parents to hear, or a painting she wanted them to see. Children's paintings and messages can have a very powerful effect on warring parents. They may then be able to reach agreements that rest with them, not with the child, and which are informed by mutual understanding of their child's needs and feelings.

11.13   KNOT THEORY AND MEDIATION

Knot theory – the study of surfaces and interconnections – is a branch of science. Without attempting to understand the mind-boggling mathematics involved, mediators may find parallels between getting stuck in mediation and the invariance of knots – that is, knots which cannot be untied. Knot theory studies linkages and interconnections. In a similar way, mediators disentangle communications between family members whose relationships have changed or which are in the process of changing. Mediation helps people to gain information, better understanding, time to think and fresh perspectives. Although problems may be insoluble, participants may perceive a means of survival and the tangle may loosen when the mutual benefits of agreement and co-operation become clearer.

Neil Robinson suggests (personal communication) that another way to approach the challenge of deadlocks and impasses in mediation is to build an alternative structure, using experience from other fields such as civil mediation or litigation. Such models are beyond the scope of this book, but:

> 'the key will often lie in the balance of creativity and boundary, of improvisation and form. The mediators at The Mediation Centre at Stafford and their colleagues use annual training events to develop new structures to address these new challenges. In so doing, they are like musicians who improvise and create new dialogues over a ground – a set pattern of notes or harmonic progression – with examples ranging from Henry Purcell's "Dido's Lament" to Tord Gustavson's "The Ground".'

Coping with change, like coping with a crisis,[17] needs courage, because it involves danger as well as opportunity. Twenty-five centuries ago, Empedocles sought to reconcile changing phenomena with the concept of an underlying unchanging existence. Those who resist the profound and sometimes life-threatening changes involved in disassociating from a broken relationship need to discover the continuity of their own identity and the potential for reconstructing relationships:[18]

> 'We shrink from change, yet is there anything that can come into being without it?'

---

[17]   See Chapter 3 at **3.3** above.
[18]   Marcus Aurelius *Meditations Book Seven*, 18.

CHAPTER 12

THE MEMORANDUM OF UNDERSTANDING AND OPEN FINANCIAL STATEMENT

'Sir, I have found you an argument; but I am not obliged to find you an understanding'[1]

'In giving and taking it is easy mistaking'[2]

CONTENTS

12.1 INTRODUCTION: WHY DO WE NEED A STANDARD FORMAT FOR MEDIATION SUMMARIES?

The 'empowerment' of the mediation process derives from its flexibility and from the creativity of all participants, including the mediator. A written summary of the outcome of mediation seeks to provide a tailor-made Alternative (ADR) to court-imposed settlements that may, with their constraints and legal language, sometimes seem more like a straitjacket than a well-designed garment. Yet it is important that any written summary of a mediation outcome is comprehensive, intellectually rigorous and accurate. For this reason, all Mediation Lead Bodies and many individual services have their own standard templates for the documents that are prepared at the end of the process. What follows in this chapter is but one way of undertaking this task, modelled on the precedents of the Family Mediators Association. It is not intended to be

---

[1]   Samuel Johnson *Letter to Lord Chesterfield* (1784).
[2]   Proverb.

prescriptive or to limit invention, but may be particularly helpful in the early stages of development as a mediator. For the mediator, developing a personal (but not too personal) style is important, but it is essential above all for participants to feel that the contents of the written summary *and* the way in which it is written accurately convey their concerns, objectives and concrete proposals. For example, many mediators end the summary with a note of encouragement, but this might seem patronising to some participants or might strike a jarring note. Feedback from lawyers and participants will help in the continuing evolution of a mediator's style in writing up mediation outcomes, as well as in face-to-face meetings.

12.2   THE MEMORANDUM OF UNDERSTANDING (MOU)

The Agreement to Mediate that participants sign before beginning mediation explains that at the end of the mediation (and if needed also during the process), the mediator offers to prepare a confidential Memorandum of Understanding (MOU, often also called a 'Summary of Proposals') summarising the outcome of mediation and their proposals for settlement. Depending on the issues brought to mediation, the MOU sets out parents' arrangements for their children and proposals for settlement of financial and property matters, thus providing the basis for a Consent Order in ancillary relief proceedings. Proposed agreements on family matters other than separation and divorce should be similarly summarised in an MOU. Copies of correspondence and records should have been kept in the case file throughout the mediation, recording dates of sessions, issues considered and a brief summary of each session. Participants sometimes ask for an interim summary or Note of Meeting to help them obtain legal advice, consider options and prepare for the next session.

The objectives of the MOU are:

- To explain proposals and identify questions on which legal advice is needed, so that participants are fully informed and clear about the likely consequences, before they enter into a legally binding agreement.

- To provide a clear summary of proposed terms of agreement that participants accept as an accurate summary. Otherwise, if each of them gives their own version to their legal advisors, further work will be needed by their lawyers to clarify the outcome of the mediation.

- To explain the rationale for proposed terms of agreement, to help legal advisors understand the reasons for their clients deciding on one particular option over other possible options that they have also considered in mediation.

- To reinforce co-operation between participants, especially where children are involved, by emphasising their mutual concerns and joint objectives as parents.

- To explain not only the issues and aspects that have been covered in the mediation but also issues or aspects that have not been considered – possibly because of lack of time.

- Where there are outstanding issues, to explain each participant's position in neutral terms, clarifying the issues, narrowing areas of dispute and reducing misunderstandings.

- To maintain a written record on file. This is needed in any event and especially if further mediation takes place after an interval.

- To protect the mediator in the case of complaint. The use of correct standard wording is essential for the mediator's professional indemnity insurance.

- To fulfil the mediator's contractual obligation to participants (see Chapter 5 and Appendix B).

- In legally aided mediations, to meet LSC requirements and enable a claim to be submitted for the work done.

Separating and divorcing couples need a solid structure on which to build their post-separation lives. The MOU lays foundations and provides scaffolding. If the scaffolding needs adjustment with the help of legal advisors, adjustments can be made without dismantling the whole framework. In an early study of pilot projects on all-issues mediation, the researchers found that 'most clients felt that the Memorandum of Understanding represented a fairly accurate record of what had been agreed.' There was 'no evidence of clients being persuaded to change agreements with which they were satisfied'.[3]

Participants are often anxious to know whether understandings and terms of agreement reached in mediation will be legally binding. When there is little trust and no love lost between them, they may have little confidence that arrangements worked out in mediation will survive, once they leave the mediation room. Especially where there is a history of intractable conflict, contact arrangements may be fragile. Parents who do not trust each other to adhere to a contact schedule need the security of an agreement that is legally binding and reportable to the court in the event of it being breached. A binding agreement can be achieved in a number of ways. The MOU may be taken to legal advisors with a request to confirm it in an 'open' exchange of letters, without the need for a court order, or it

---

[3] Walker, McCarthy and Timms *Mediation: The Making and Remaking of Co-operative Relationships* (Relate Centre for Family Studies, University of Newcastle, 1994), p 136.

may be used as the basis for a consent order providing a full and final settlement in divorce proceedings. The confidentiality covering the MOU in relation to the court is referred to in Chapter 1. In some cases, clients may wish, and be so advised by their lawyers, to waive the legal privilege attaching to the MOU to help the court understand the rationale for the proposed agreements and the options considered in mediation. Their joint consent to waive confidentiality should be given in writing. Particularly in court-referred mediations, it may be helpful for confidentiality to be waived in order to facilitate orders being made with consent. Usually, legal advisors have advised their clients in the course of mediation on their legal position and terms of settlement. Experience suggests that lawyers rarely set the MOU aside. There have been a few, but very few, unrecorded cases in which a client's solicitor sought to use the content of mediation in court to gain an advantage for the client, but in these cases the confidentiality of the mediation process was upheld by the court.

12.3   OPEN STATEMENT OF FINANCIAL INFORMATION (OFS)

In concluding mediation on all issues or solely on financial and property matters, there should be an Open Statement of Financial Information (OFS) setting out the financial information provided by participants, including a schedule of accompanying supporting documents. A format for the OFS is given in Appendix C. The legal status of the OFS and MOU is not the same. Whereas the MOU is confidential and not reportable to the court, except with the joint written consent of both parties, the Financial Statement and factual financial information provided in mediation are 'open', meaning that they may be referred to in ancillary relief proceedings or to support a consent order. This saves unnecessary duplication in gathering financial information both with lawyers and mediators. As the legal status of the two documents is different, the OFS should not be stapled or otherwise attached to the MOU.

A common error is to mix the contents of the MOU and OFS. It follows from its open status that it is vital that the OFS contains no information that forms part of the proposals reached between the participants. Similarly, but with less risk, it is also unhelpful to slavishly repeat all the financial information in the MOU.

Again, Lead Bodies have their own precedents for the OFS. Usually, it is helpful to have short explanatory notes and an overview of the finances in tabular form (which can be transcribed from the flipchart).[4]

The opening paragraphs of the OFS should use approved standard wording, stating that both parties agreed in writing at the outset to

---

[4]   See Chapter 9 at **9.8** and Appendix C.

provide full financial information. It should state that while certain supporting documents have been obtained (copies listed and attached), the mediator did not undertake to verify the information supplied. The OFS should also record whether both parties have confirmed that full disclosure has been made and have signed the OFS to this effect. They need to be aware that, having signed to confirm that full disclosure has been made, any subsequent agreement based on information provided in mediation could be set aside, if it emerged later that the information had been inaccurate or incomplete. In cases where mediation has ended inconclusively, the OFS should state that it records *the information disclosed so far*. Clients and their solicitors can then take matters forward to amplify the information gathered in mediation, without needing to go back to square one.

12.4   PROFESSIONAL DRAFTING AND CHARGES

The MOU should provide a clear summary of arrangements and proposed terms of settlement, reinforcing co-operation by emphasising mutual concerns and objectives. Relevant considerations should be explained concisely, impartially and positively, without conveying any opinion or value judgment on the part of the mediator. Both the MOU and the OFS should be well drafted and presented to a high standard, as they are the main product on which mediators' professional standards are judged by legal advisors, as well as by participants themselves. The style should be neither legalistic nor overly informal. It is better to avoid using the first person as this could give the mediator an intrusive presence. The passive tense is preferable ('Various options have been considered') and headings should be used, to make the MOU easier to follow.

The preparation of these documents takes time. When one or both participants are publicly funded, a claim for preparing the MOU may be made to the Legal Services Commission and paid at a standard rate. Charges to private clients need to be discussed and agreed with them in advance. Sometimes clients do not see a need for an MOU and do not wish to pay for one. If the mediation file does not contain adequate case notes, a mediator could have difficulty constructing an MOU and OFS at a later stage.

For those with access to the Internet, online communications are mostly instant and cheap. Although correspondence by e-mail is not an adequate substitute for meeting face-to-face, it offers a practical way of sending out mediation forms and fast-forwarding negotiations, where both partners are equally comfortable using email and have reasons for needing to expedite the mediation process. The same rules on confidentiality should apply as in caucusing.[5] Settlement proposals can be clarified through exchanges of emails. If there is a scheduled court hearing and time is

---

[5]   See Chapter 4 above.

short, a draft Memorandum of Understanding can be emailed to participants for them to check, before hard copies are sent for them to take to their legal advisors. Mediators may choose to use tools such as 'track changes' in Microsoft Word, in order to engage participants further in the drafting process.

12.5 WHAT DO PARTICIPANTS NEED IN THEIR MEMORANDUM OF UNDERSTANDING?

- A document that explains proposals and priorities accurately and clearly.

- Clear and comprehensible language, with a minimum of legal terminology.

- Impartial wording, no opinions or value judgments on the part of the mediator.

- Accurately recorded facts, figures and details of actual or proposed arrangements.

- Precise drafting that does not give scope for different interpretations.

- Sufficient focus on the children, usually with more details about parenting plans and arrangements than would be found in a Statement of Arrangements or court order.

- Proposals that participants feel they own.

- A document that will facilitate the legal process, reducing legal costs and avoiding delay.

- Sufficient explanation of reasons for selecting a particular course of action.

- In some cases, reference to concerns that have emotional rather than legal significance.

- Positive and sensitive phrasing that strikes a balance between formality and informality.

- Reference to points on which legal or other expert advice is needed, in terms the participants understand.

- A summary that will assist them to achieve a lasting and, where needed, legally binding, settlement.

12.6   WHAT DO LEGAL ADVISORS LOOK FOR IN THE MEMORANDUM OF UNDERSTANDING?

- A heading and standard wording explaining the function and legal status of the document.

- The name/s of the mediator and the mediator's practice or agency, information about the duration of the mediation and approach used (eg single or co-mediation).

- Background information about the participants: names, addresses, date of marriage or cohabitation, names of children and dates of birth, whether the parents are separated, with whom the children are living, date of separation and so on. The background information should be provided in a short preamble to the main body of the summary.

- The issues brought to mediation, with a concise summary of proposals or positions on each issue, set out in a clear structure with sub-headings.

- The legal framework for settlement explaining whether the couple have separated and (in the case of married couples) whether a divorce petition has been filed and whether the timing and grounds for divorce are accepted.

- Financial disclosure: lawyers need to know whether a separate OFS has been produced and signed by both parties confirming that full financial disclosure has been made and information agreed, with supporting documents.

- Clarity: a professionally presented document, well organised and easy to follow.

- Precise drafting: proposals should state for example the amount of monthly child support payments, the date on which payment will be made and how it will be made, provision for review and so on.

- Explanation: lawyers need sufficient explanation of the rationale for the proposals so that they can understand the reasons for preferring a particular option among a range of possible options.

- Comprehensiveness: lawyers need to see whether the issues brought to mediation have been covered fully and that all relevant questions arising from these issues have been addressed. If some matters have not been addressed in mediation, the reason for not addressing them, such as lack of time, should be explained.

- Concise drafting: lawyers do not want lengthy explanations of each party's feelings or concerns and details of their discussions. They may however like to have an indication that there are still high levels of stress, anxiety, uncertainty or conflict. Mediators can give such indications in wording agreed with both parties.

- Specific points on which legal advice is needed.

- Proposals, not agreements – unless an interim agreement, for example on contact arrangements, is appropriate and does not need legal advice.

- An action plan setting out the next steps: are solicitors being asked to liaise in order to finalise the proposed settlement?

- Whether mediation has ended.

12.7   STRUCTURE OF THE MEMORANDUM OF UNDERSTANDING

12.7.1   Cover page

As the MOU is intended as a permanent document for the participants and as a good advertisement for the Mediation Service, it needs to look professional. A standard cover page setting out the status of the document (e g Interim/Final), the participants' names and the name of the service is advisable.

12.7.2   Required introductory paragraphs

The required introductory wording[6] should be used, so that there is no ambiguity as to the purpose and legal status of the MOU. The participants' full names should be given at the beginning. Most mediators then proceed to refer to them by their first names, if first names have been used in the mediation.

Background Information

A paragraph of background information is intended to assist legal advisors by providing brief details – names and dates of birth, date of marriage/or length of cohabitation and where applicable, date of separation or divorce. Names, ages and dates of birth of the children of the family should be given, also the address and living arrangements for each parent and the children. Each party's occupation and approximate net monthly or annual earnings should be given.

---

[6]   See example at **12.9** below.

Issues brought to mediation

The number of mediation sessions should be stated with their dates, to show the time-scale of the mediation. The main issues brought to mediation should be listed, so that the range of the mediation can be grasped quickly.

Proposals for settlement

Proposals need to stand out clearly, preferably in bold type. Otherwise, a key proposal may get buried in explanations. There is no need to record the whole content of discussions. The words 'agreement' or 'agree' should be avoided, because proposals for settlement worked out in mediation are subject to legal advice to each party.[7] If the words 'agree' and 'agreement' are used, they cause confusion and may increase conflict, where there is need for amendment or further negotiation following legal advice from solicitors. Many mediators set out the specific proposals as a separate section at the end of the document.

Separation/Divorce

Usually this major issue needs to be addressed first, so that it is clear whether there is mutual acceptance of the need for separation or divorce and if so, in what time-scale. The Memorandum should record whether some general information has been given about divorce and divorce procedure. It is important that couples understand and consider their options in relation to separation and divorce. When there is continuing dispute about separation or divorce, each partner's position needs to be explained sensitively, without reopening wounds. It may be important to acknowledge strong feelings on separation, divorce or other issues, without any implication of blame or causing further hurt. Information concerning actual or intended co-habitation or remarriage should also be given.

Parents' arrangements for their children

Where parents have emphasised in mediation that their children are their first priority, this section should underline their commitment to their children and mutual wish to give their children as much support as possible and/or concern to help their children adjust to the separation (provided these statements emphasise the parents' expressed wishes and objectives, not the mediator's personal ideals).

When parents have agreed their arrangements for their children before coming to mediation on financial issues only, the arrangements should still be explained briefly. Rather than referring to participants by their

---

[7]   See Chapter 1 at **1.11.4** above.

first names throughout, it is helpful to emphasise parent-child relationships – 'will live mainly with their mother/father', 'both parents are concerned that ...', as well as referring to each child by name. Legal terms such as 'contact' and 'residence' should be avoided if possible, because parents tend to imbue these labels with meanings that fuel dispute.[8]

> 'Both parents accept that Jessica and Richard will continue to live with their mother and spend substantial periods of time with their father, on a regular basis.'

Details should be given as far as necessary of the times or periods that the children will spend with their father/mother, including weekdays and weekends, school holidays, Christmas and other festivals, birthdays. Both parents' involvement in other areas of the children's upbringing and development, such as education and school events, should also be mentioned. It is helpful to record whether the parents will communicate directly with each other on day-to-day matters and review their arrangements for the children periodically. If the parents have talked with their children and explained new arrangements to them, this should be mentioned to show that the children have been consulted. Often it is helpful to append a Parenting Plan, for which many mediation services have a precedent.

The Family Home

Brief information should be given of the address, date of purchase, how financed, in whose name and loans outstanding. The MOU should explain to what extent possible options have been considered and the main reason/s for the preferred option, if there is one. Proposals for the continuing occupation of the family home (eg by one parent and the children) and/or purchase of a new property by one or both parties should be explained clearly, with sufficient detail. Is either party seeking to maintain an interest either in the family home or in a new property to be purchased by the other? What would be the triggers for repayment of a charge? What level of borrowing would be needed? Have enquiries been made?

Schedules of projected future monthly income and outgoings for each parent (as opposed to actual monthly income and outgoings summarised in the OFS) may be attached to the MOU, so that participants and their legal advisors can check that their housing proposals are financially viable.

---

[8]   See Chapter 7 at **7.11** above.

Proposals for division of capital and other assets

A schedule should be provided, so that the proposed 'package' can be read easily at a glance. It is not necessary to replicate all the detailed information contained in the OFS. It may be more useful to record in succinct terms the considerations and discussions that led to a particular plan being preferred. Many mediators will set out the 'net effects' of a series of options, explaining for the benefit of participants and their legal advisors how a set of proposals was arrived at.

Child Support

The Memorandum should state the level of proposed child support payments and method of payment, the day of the month on which the payment will be made and over what period of time. Even where there is no intention to make an application to CMEC (Child Maintenance and Enforcement Commission), the MOU should state that relevant information has been given. Participants who are insisting on an application to CMEC need to be aware that CMEC specifically encourages private ordering of disputes.

Spousal Maintenance

Is either party seeking spousal maintenance from the other or are claims to be mutually dismissed? If there is a proposal for spousal maintenance, is it intended to be time limited and should there be index linking? It may be helpful to note that the borderline between clean break and nominal spousal maintenance where there are children is controversial and may require further legal advice.

Welfare Benefits

The Memorandum should state whether information has been given about possible entitlement to welfare benefits, especially those that would automatically trigger CMEC becoming involved. If an estimate of the Child Support calculation been obtained by either parent, this should be given.

Pensions

Full details and supporting documents should be given in the OFS. The MOU should state whether the mediator has provided basic information regarding pension options and whether options have been considered. The MOU should record that both parties have been encouraged to seek legal/financial advice regarding pension provisions and potential claims.

Inheritance

The MOU should record whether either party has recently received an inheritance or has immediate prospects of receiving an inheritance that would have a bearing on the division of matrimonial assets. The MOU should also record that both parties have been encouraged to seek legal advice on inheritance matters.

Wills

The MOU should record that information has been given about the effect of divorce on Wills and the need to take legal advice on drawing up new Wills. They will need their lawyers' advice as to any interim arrangements that should be put in place.

Tax

The Memorandum should record whether the tax implications of proposals have been considered and that the parties have been encouraged to take tax advice.

House contents/personal possessions

Brief details should be given of proposals and/or intentions to agree the division of house contents and possessions without the need for detailed discussion in mediation.

Outstanding Issues

The MOU should list issues that were not dealt with in the mediation – either because of lack of time or because participants did not wish to discuss them. Questions raised by the mediator should be summarised: eg 'Questions were raised as to whether ... and ... were encouraged to consider these questions and take further legal advice on them.' Where some or all issues remain unresolved, the MOU should give a concise and impartially worded statement of each participant's position, to facilitate movement towards settlement, with advice from solicitors.

Questions on which legal or financial advice is needed

The main points on which legal and/or financial advice is needed should be summarised. Even where there appears to be full agreement between participants, it is useful to anticipate legal advisors' responses to the proposals ('Well, you could do better than that') by framing neutrally worded questions for participants to put to their legal advisors in order to reach or confirm agreements.

Action Plan and Time-Scale for Action

The MOU should set out the next steps that participants intend to take, such as seeking legal advice and clarifying which partner's solicitor will be asked to draw up a consent order. Time-scales should be given if possible and, if needed, the date for a further mediation meeting.

Ending

The MOU often ends on a positive note that underlines participants' stated intentions to maintain their co-operation, especially with regard to their children. A review or further meeting may be offered, after legal advice has been taken or at some future stage, for example if parents need to discuss changes in their arrangements for their children, because the children are older and/or because of changes in family circumstances.

The MOU should be signed and dated by the mediator and not by the participants. The mediator's address and contact details should be given on the document.

12.8   INTERIM ARRANGEMENTS, INCLUDING AGREEMENTS INTENDED TO BE LEGALLY BINDING

Every mediation session has some form of outcome, even if it is disagreement. It is usually desirable to provide a written note of the session for participants, even where it simply confirms their agreement to meet again and to provide certain information (a 'task list'.) This is another area of evolving practice, with some services always providing a 'session record', whereas others provide an interim agreement or Outcome Note (this may be particularly important where there are parallel Court proceedings). Other services may summarise the outcome of a meeting in a personalised letter. Clarity and rigour are as essential in recording interim arrangements as in the formulation of the final MOU – clarity of purpose, clarity as to what is proposed or actually agreed and, perhaps most of all, clarity as to the extent that any understanding is 'open'.

Parents often make their own contact arrangements without involving lawyers or mediators, but if they do not communicate easily they may need a written agreement to avoid confusion or arguments over dates or times of visits. If details are recollected differently, each parent may complain that the other parent broke the agreement or got it wrong. When parents need an interim agreement on contact, a signed agreement gives it force and formality. Sometimes they want to have a document that they can show to new partners or other third parties, as evidence of their agreement. Depending on the ages of their children, parents may also show it to the children themselves.

If understandings are verbal only, there can be muddle and misunderstandings. Mediators do not only help participants to work out proposals for settlement: they also help them to reach agreements that can be recorded in legally binding terms, according to need. They should be cautious, however, in recording an agreement that is not subject to legal advice and intended to be legally binding. A written agreement should be considered with care and provided only in limited circumstances, such as:

- **Interim agreement on contact arrangements**
  Where there is urgency to confirm short-term arrangements, such as times of picking up and returning a child the following weekend, the mediator may draw up an Interim Agreement recording the arrangements on an 'open' basis, ie not confidential and legally privileged. Parents do not need legal advice as to whether their child is to be picked up from a swimming lesson or from Aunty Sue's home: they can agree these practical details and sign an Interim Agreement that reduces scope for confusion or argument.

- **Agreement on the use or disposal of a minor asset, in relation to total assets**
  Participants sometimes wish to record an agreement on the sale or disposal of a minor asset in circumstances where they do not require legal advice. In one case, a couple wanted to clear a debt by selling a china vase. Their total assets were such that neither partner's position would be prejudiced by the sale of the china vase for their joint benefit. In another mediation, the couple owned three cars and they decided to sell one of them and split the proceeds 50/50. They also owned two properties in joint names. Their interim agreement on the sale of the third car recorded that the division of sale proceeds on a 50/50 basis was to be taken into account in any future division of matrimonial assets. Mediators need to have enough legal knowledge and expertise to deal safely with an agreement involving the use or disposal of a financial asset, even if it appears to be a minor one. They need to be able to recognise when independent legal advice should be sought.

In all cases, mediators should take care to conclude mediation with positively worded closing letters and, where appropriate, written summaries. When mediation ends without any basis for agreement, closing letters should conclude the mediation clearly, with encouragement to return to mediation at any stage if participants think it would be worthwhile. Research shows that personal commitment is the key factor in lasting agreements. Many parents still have sufficient trust in each other to believe in the commitments they make to each other where their children are concerned.

12.9   SAMPLE MEMORANDUM OF UNDERSTANDING

(Privileged Summary of Proposals)

This Memorandum is a summary of the outcome of mediation and proposals for settlement reached by Sandra M [...] (Sandra) and James M [...] (James).

This Memorandum is legally privileged and 'without prejudice'. It does not record or create a legally binding agreement between Sandra and James and the proposals have not been set out with the intention of creating legal relations by the creation of this document. It is intended to assist Sandra and James in obtaining independent professional advice, as the mediators have recommended them to do before they take steps to enter into an agreement whether through solicitors or informally between themselves. Unless and until Sandra and James decide to enter into a binding agreement, no such binding agreement exists between them.

Sandra and James understand that the financial information they have given may be produced to the Court (unlike this Memorandum) and they have had the necessity for full and complete disclosure explained to them and recorded to them in writing. The Memorandum may of course, be produced to legal advisors upon the basis that it is and remains a legally privileged document.

The mediation was carried out in accordance with the professional requirements and the Code of Practice of the Solicitors Regulation Authority, the Family Mediation Council and the Family Mediators Association.

Sandra and James attended two mediation meetings on [...] and [...] 201[...] They were referred to mediation by Sandra's solicitors under the Funding Code. Sandra is publicly funded and James is paying privately for mediation

1.   Background information

Sandra, age [...] dob [...] is an administrator with [...]. Her monthly income is £[...] net. Sandra expects to earn £[...] gross in this financial year.

James, age [...], dob [...] is a foreman with [...] Building Ltd. He earns £[...] net per month and expects to earn £[...] gross in this financial year.

James also receives child benefit and tax credits of £[...] per month.

Sandra and James married on [...] and separated on [...].

They have two children:

Fiona aged 13 dob [...].

Tobias (Toby) aged 11 d.o.b. [...].

Both children are in good health. They live with their father in the family home at [...].

Sandra is lodging with her brother at [...] until she is able to purchase a property.

2. Separation

Sandra and James wish to have their settlement made legally binding in a Deed of Separation that provides the terms for a 'clean break' settlement in divorce after two years' separation with consent. Subject to further legal advice, Sandra will ask her solicitor to draw up a Deed of Separation based on this Memorandum. James is willing to share the legal costs with Sandra.

3. Shared parental responsibility

Sandra and James understand that they will continue to share parental responsibility for Fiona and Toby after they divorce. They are in agreement on all the main areas of parental responsibility and usually attend school functions together.

Fiona and Toby see their mother regularly, usually every Saturday or Sunday. Sandra and James are able to make arrangements directly with each other and as soon as Sandra has her own property, the children will stay overnight and spend part of each holiday with her.

Sandra and James describe Toby as a sensitive boy who is feeling the impact of their separation keenly. As Sandra finishes work early some days, she calls in at the family home to see Toby and Fiona after school. James has no objection to Sandra keeping a key and calling in to see the children, whether he (James) is there or not. James will also arrange with Sandra that on certain evenings by prior arrangement Sandra would stay longer in the home with the children so that he can go out.

4. The Family Home

Sandra and James bought the family home in joint names in [...] for £[...] with a repayment mortgage of £[...]. Based on three recent valuations ranging from £[...] to [...], Sandra and James decided to take the value as £[...] for their negotiations. There is a repayment mortgage with a balance of around £[...], leaving equity of £[...] James will provide Sandra with a copy of the latest mortgage statement.

5. Loans and credit cards

Sandra and James have a joint loan of £[...] for their two cars and joint debts on two credit cards (£[...] on Sandra's card and £[...] on James' card) making a total of £[...]. Sandra and James wish to share these debts equally and to clear them by agreement as part of their settlement.

There is also a joint bank account with [...] that is currently £[...] overdrawn. Sandra will take her name off this account. Arrangements to clear the overdraft will be made between Sandra and James direct.

6. Flat in Italy

Sandra and James are co-owners with members of James' family of a flat in Italy. The value is estimated at [...] euros and there are bills needing payment. Sandra and James are in agreement that their share of this property should not form part of their financial settlement. They will deal with their share of any bills and decide on the future use or sale of the property with James' family.

7. Pensions

James has a frozen pension with Scottish Equitable with a CETV dated of £[...]. He is contributing to a pension with Abbey Life. There is a small fund value of £[...]. James will provide Sandra with copies of both pension statements to take to her solicitor, together with any other pension details.

Sandra has a frozen pension with Scottish Equitable with a CETV of £[...]. Since [...] Sandra has contributed £[...] to a pension with [...].

Subject to the advice they receive, Sandra and James wish to leave pensions out of account in their settlement and to have pension claims waived in their eventual divorce.

8. Proposals for settlement

Sandra wishes to purchase a 2–3 bed property and she has ascertained that she can borrow up to £[...] on her income.

James wishes to remain in the family home with Fiona and Toby. He has made enquiries about the cost of further borrowing on a repayment mortgage.

Sandra and James propose that:

(i)   James will arrange further borrowing in his own name that will enable them in the first place to clear their joint debts of £[...], this to be deducted from the equity of £[...] in the family home, leaving £[...] for division between them;

(ii)   notional costs of sale should not be deducted so that some allowance can be made for Sandra's costs in furnishing and equipping her new property;

(iii)   the balance of £[...] be split 55/45 in James's favour, as he is maintaining the family home for Fiona and Toby;

Sandra and James have considered the option of Sandra having a charge registered on the property and splitting the equity 50/50 in three years' time. Sandra's preferred option is to receive 45% now so that she can purchase a property and clear her credit card debt.

(iv)   James is willing to raise the sum of £[...] to pay Sandra in full and final settlement after clearance of joint loans and debts [...], (property) to be transferred to James' sole name and Sandra's name to be taken off the mortgage. Depending on the level of mortgage she decides to raise, Sandra could have nearly £[...] available for house purchase.

(v)   Sandra to pay 20% of her net monthly income (£[...] per month) to James for Fiona and Toby by standing order on the 15th day of each month starting from the date of the capital settlement.

(vi)   Sandra's name to be taken off the life insurance policies in joint names. There are two policies assigned to James. James to decide which of these policies he wishes to continue paying into.

(vii)   Bank accounts and credit cards in joint names to be separated.

(viii) Sandra and James will each keep their own cars.

(ix)   Contents: when Sandra has bought her property, she will arrange with James to collect some furniture and possessions from the family home including the following—

        (a)   The smaller leather sofa

        (b)   Stereo and a TV

        (c)   Garden furniture

        (d)   A bookcase and some books

        (e)   Some other items from the attic

        Sandra and James do not expect to have any difficulty over Sandra collecting items from the family home when she is ready to do so.

(x)   A further discussion will take place as to where Toby's rabbit is to live when Sandra has her own property, as Toby is concerned about maintaining his relationship with his rabbit.

(xi)   Summary of settlement proposals setting out proposed division of assets.

9. Inheritance

Neither Sandra nor James has a prospect of receiving an inheritance in the foreseeable future.

10. Wills

When they divorce, Sandra and James will need to draw up fresh Wills to be effective after their divorce. They will need their lawyers' advice as to any interim arrangements that should be put in place.

11. Next Steps

Sandra and James are concerned to maintain their co-operation, especially where Fiona and Toby are concerned. They will take legal advice from their solicitors on their proposals for settlement. Subject to this advice, Sandra will ask her solicitor to draw up a Deed of Separation incorporating their proposals, to be sent to James for his signature.

No further mediation meetings have been arranged, but Sandra and James are welcome to return to mediation if they should encounter any difficulty.

Dated: _____

Signed: _____

Family Mediator
(Name and address of mediation service)

CHAPTER 13

RESEARCH ON FAMILY MEDIATION

'Can you know what is emerging, yet keep your peace while others discover it for themselves? You can do this if you remain unbiased, clear and down to earth'[1]

CONTENTS

13.1   TESTING THE BENEFITS OF MEDIATION

Mediation is widely believed to benefit participants and their children through resolving conflict and reducing stress. Disputants are encouraged to take a good dose of mediation before following the signpost marked 'To the Court'. When Alice (in Lewis Carroll's *Alice's Adventures in Wonderland*) fell down the rabbit-hole, she came upon a table with a small bottle on it:[2]

> 'and tied round the neck of the bottle was a paper label with the words "DRINK ME" beautifully printed on it in large letters. It was all very well to say "Drink Me", but wise little Alice was not going to do *that* in a hurry. "No, I'll look first", she said, "and see whether it's marked 'poison' or not" ... However, the bottle was not marked "poison", so Alice ventured to taste it.'

---

[1]   Lao Tzu *Tao Te Ching*.
[2]   Carroll *Alice's Adventures in Wonderland* (First published 1865, Folio 1961), p 7.

Public information about mediation does not list all the ingredients of the mediation process. Like Alice, once people feel satisfied that mediation is not a dangerous remedy, many of them decide to accept it without knowing its exact ingredients, even though the main elements are explained. As described in Chapter 2, family mediation offers mixtures of different ingredients, all carrying the same label.

Family mediation is not a universal panacea and mediators bring to it their different professional backgrounds and experience and their own style of working. Claims about mediation's benefits need to be substantiated to justify its place in the family justice system. Efforts to persuade policy-makers and members of other professions of the benefits of mediation may encourage unrealistic claims and expectations of what mediation can actually achieve. Social scientists need to cut through the rhetoric of mediation in examining practice and outcomes. But this is no simple task. Lines of inquiry do not always produce reliable results. Investigators do not always get the answers they were hoping for, as the schools inspector found when he asked a small boy in a primary school how many sheep he could see in the field and got the answer 'All o' them'.

Research literature on family mediation has developed in many countries over the last three decades, growing both in volume and sophistication. The results need to be interpreted with caution, however. Comparability across studies is low, because research has been undertaken with disparate client groups using different types of mediation process over varying periods of time. Irving and Benjamin (1995) reviewed fifty research studies on family mediation and found that:[3]

> 'although two services might look the same on paper, they may provide very different services to different client groups using very different service models and differently trained mediators ....'

Interpretations of findings are complicated further if experiences and outcomes from brief, court-referred conciliation are generalised to out-of-court mediation. In both settings, there are variations in the timing of interventions, the types and levels of dispute referred to conciliation or mediation and the approaches used by conciliators and mediators. A criticism levelled at some studies is that they were not objective, because the researchers were mediators themselves. The methodology and findings were therefore liable be skewed by the desire to prove the benefits of mediation. Maintaining impartiality presents challenges for mediators. Researchers, too, need to demonstrate that they have neither an inherent bias towards mediation, because they happen to be mediators as well, nor a bias against it. Sometimes there seems be a wish to deflate confidence in mediation, rather than present the evidence objectively. For example,

---

[3]   Irving and Benjamin 'Research in Family Mediation – an Integrative Review' in Irving and Benjamin (eds) *Family Mediation – Contemporary Issues* (Sage, 1995), p 408.

Dingwall's assertion[4] that 'mediation fared little better in the Davis evaluation' overlooked findings in the Davis study[5] reported below. Dingwall noted low conversion rates from mediation information meetings to mediation, but 'non-conversions' include couples who attend a joint information meeting and go on to work things out between themselves, without needing further help from mediators or lawyers. Mediators tend to be accused of over-egging the mediation cake, but a researcher might cut into one slice of a fruitcake and analyse it as though it were the whole cake.

13.2 PARENTS' EXPERIENCE OF IN-COURT CONCILIATION

Before considering studies of the mediation process and participants' experiences of mediation, it is useful to look at experience and outcomes of court proceedings and in-court conciliation schemes. The Private Law Programme introduced in 2004 encouraged early dispute resolution for parents involved in proceedings relating to children. This Programme was found to be very successful in enabling the majority of disputes to be settled by consent at the First Dispute Resolution Hearing (FDRHA). The amount of time spent by Cafcass on in-court conciliation increased and the number of reports reduced.[6] The Revised Private Law Programme implemented by the Practice Direction of 1 April 2010 builds on the earlier programme and takes account of recent developments in law and practice. In-court conciliation at the FDRHA aims to settle disputes and help parents reach agreement. Hunt found evidence from a number of studies that it is now relatively unusual for a family case to end in a fully contested hearing.[7] In-court conciliation appears to be very effective in avoiding further litigation. 72% of parents in Trinder's study[8] reached full (45%) or partial agreement (27%). 62% of these parents said they were satisfied with their agreements, demonstrating that a single, brief session was instrumental in 45% of conflicted parents reaching an agreement with which at least one of them was satisfied. Many of these agreements did not last, but a quarter of them were later renegotiated by the parents concerned, without further professional intervention. Only a minority of

---

4   Dingwall 'Divorce mediation: should we change our mind?' (2010) 32 *Journal of Social Welfare & Family Law* 109.
5   Davis G et al *Monitoring Publicly Funded Family Mediation – Report to the Legal Services Commission* (Legal Services Commission, 2000).
6   Cafcass Annual Report 2006–07.
7   Hunt *Parental Perspectives on the Family Justice System in England and Wales: a review of research* (Report for the Family Justice Council, December 2009).
8   Trinder, Connolly, Kellett, Notley and Swift 'Making Contact happen or making contact work? The process and outcomes of in-court conciliation' (2006) *DCA Research Series* 3/06.

parents had re-litigated to arrive at a new arrangement. Overall, only 21% of agreements were judged to have failed.[9] The main benefit reported by parents was:[10]

> 'having a structured, managed, and fair opportunity to establish communication and reach agreement. Other themes were the value of having an unbiased person dedicated to achieving a workable set of agreed arrangements and the role of conciliation in encouraging the parties to focus on the child's interests.'

58% of parents had felt anxious, however, before the conciliation meeting and 61% said the meeting had been tense and unpleasant.[11] Resident parents were significantly more likely than non-resident to report feeling under pressure, both from the conciliator and from their ex-partner. Analysis of cases where data was available from both parents showed that there were twice as many 'father win, mother lose' cases as vice versa (35% compared to 16%). Resident parents reported 'less choice about entering the process, more anxiety beforehand, more tension in the meeting, felt more dissatisfied with the amount of time available, less able to say all they wanted to, less likely to see the Cafcass officer and district judge as helpful; more likely to feel their concerns were not understood, dismissed or marginalised and to report being pressurised into agreement by their ex-partner'.[12] 40% of women expressed feelings of anxiety and worries about intimidation, increasing their sense of confrontation and being at risk. Parents who had sat next to their ex-partner had all felt uncomfortable. Mantle suggests a triangular arrangement might be more acceptable.[13] This arrangement is normally used in out-of-court mediation.[14] Perry and Rainey reported that some parents felt obliged to accept arrangements that they did not feel were appropriate or which fell far short of what they wanted.[15] They could be disconcerted by finding the judge more focused on getting them to find a solution themselves than on adjudicating for them. Some parents were not happy with this approach. Fathers, in particular:[16]

---

9   Hunt *Parental Perspectives on the Family Justice System in England and Wales: a review of research* (Report for the Family Justice Council, December 2009), p 89.
10 Ibid, p 83.
11 Trinder, Connolly, Kellett, Notley and Swift 'Making Contact happen or making contact work? The process and outcomes of in-court conciliation' (2006) *DCA Research Series* 3/06.
12 Hunt *Parental Perspectives on the Family Justice System in England and Wales: a review of research* (Report for the Family Justice Council, December 2009), p 83.
13 Mantle *A Consumer Survey of Agreements reached in county court dispute resolution (mediation)* (Essex Probation Occasional Paper 2, 2001).
14 See Chapter 4 at **4.3** above.
15 Perry and Rainey *Supervised, supported and indirect contact: orders and their implications* (Report to the Nuffield Foundation, University of Wales, Swansea, 2006).
16 Smart, May, Wade and Furness *Residence and Contact Disputes in Court* (Dept of Constitutional Affairs, London, 2005), Vol 2; quoted in Hunt *Parental Perspectives on the Family Justice System in England and Wales: a review of research* (Report for the Family Justice Council, December 2009), p 27.

'became angry when the courts seemed to imply that parents themselves should be able to find a solution. It was as if they did not go to court to be told to try harder themselves; rather they went to court to have the right solution imposed upon the recalcitrant spouse.'

Where children themselves were concerned, 61% of parents in Trinder's study said that the session had focused on children's needs, but of those who reached agreement, less than half (48%) thought the agreement was in their child's best interests.[17] At the time the studies were undertaken:[18]

'it was rare for children to take part in conciliation directly. Hence the child's views would typically be presented through one or both parents.'

Conciliation is a very brief intervention, typically involving one meeting lasting no more than an hour and often less. While most parents seem to accept the limited time, a substantial minority would have preferred to have more time with the conciliator.[19] A two-year follow-up study found that:[20]

'hammering out a deal and getting contact going does not in itself repair relationships or address the underlying or embedded conflict that probably gave rise to the contact dispute in the first place.'

Hunt reported that 'parents find the whole experience of going to court traumatic and alienating'.[21]

13.3 IN-COURT MEDIATION

Some pilot schemes have involved family mediators from independent services attending court to assist the judge and Cafcass with in-court conciliation and/or to explore the possibility of mediation taking place out of court. The Good Practice Guidelines for In-Court Mediation (Family Mediation Council 2010) state that:[22]

'the Mediator is to take an active role with CAFCASS and the gatekeeper for the day (District Judge or Legal Advisor) in case triage (ie reviewing the cases in the list for the day and determining which may be suitable for

---

[17] Trinder, Connolly, Kellett, Notley and Swift 'Making Contact happen or making contact work? The process and outcomes of in-court conciliation' (2006) *DCA Research Series* 3/06.

[18] Hunt *Parental Perspectives on the Family Justice System in England and Wales: a review of research* (Report for the Family Justice Council, December 2009), p 89.

[19] Hunt *Parental Perspectives on the Family Justice System in England and Wales: a review of research* (Report for the Family Justice Council, December 2009).

[20] Trinder 'Conciliation, the Private Law Programme and Children's Well-being' [2008] Fam Law 338 at 341.

[21] Hunt *Parental Perspectives on the Family Justice System in England and Wales: a review of research* (Report for the Family Justice Council, December 2009), p 121.

[22] Family Mediation Council 2010, pp 1–2.

mediation) at the beginning of each list. CAFCASS safeguarding information must be available at this stage.'

The Guidelines go on to say that mediators must establish clearly with parties whether they wish their agreements, reached as a result of in-court or court-referred mediation, to be converted into consent orders and whether they wish to waive the legal privilege and confidentiality of mediation so that mediators may provide feedback on the outcomes of mediation to legal advisors, district judge and Cafcass. Mediators must not however enter into dialogue when giving this feedback, orally or in writing. Data collected in a pilot project at Milton Keynes County Court (1 April 2007–31 March 2008) indicated that in-court mediation assessment by mediators attending court on a rota system led to acceptance of mediation by 85.5% of those assessed, with 79% of these cases reaching settlement.[23]

The Evaluation Report of the In-Court Mediation Trial[24] found that where mediation took place, 71% of parties reached full agreement or were able to narrow some of the main issues in dispute. 73% of parties who were referred to an information and assessment meeting accepted the offer of mediation. In 43% of cases, they had not previously considered mediation. This suggests that there may be a considerable number of people who would accept mediation if they know about it, thus highlighting the importance of increasing awareness of mediation prior to proceedings. In-court mediation offers a pathway for disputants who are prepared to consider or reconsider mediation at a later set of crossroads. Experience and consumer research indicate, however, that it is preferable for mediation itself to take place out of court[25] to allow parents more time for discussion and consideration of children's needs and feelings, and to deal more fully with embedded conflicts. Consideration of mediation at the pre-court stage is designed to enable more parents to resolve matters at an early stage before conflict becomes 'embedded', and in many cases to avoid court proceedings.

13.4   EVALUATING MEDIATION

One of many problems in evaluating mediation is deciding the criteria to be used and applying 'technically robust' indicators. A small historical digression may illustrate the point. In 1982 the government set up an Interdepartmental Committee on Conciliation (known as the 'Robinson Committee', after its Chairman) to review existing arrangements for conciliation (by which they meant 'mediation'), to report on its functioning and results and to make recommendations on any changes that should be made in matrimonial law and procedure. Conciliation (mediation) was evaluated by matching conciliation files with divorce

---

[23]   Banham-Hall 'Children Act First Appointment Scheme' [2008] Fam Law 1054–1055.
[24]   Legal Services Commission (August 2010), 5.
[25]   See also Chapter 3 above.

court files, to identify the proportion of cases in which consent orders on ancillary matters confirmed agreements reached through mediation. In many mediation cases, there was no divorce file because the couple was unmarried, or they had reached a separation agreement with a view to divorcing with consent after two years' separation, or they had sought marital counselling. A few had reconciled. All these were counted as 'failed conciliations'. The Committee concluded (in a 1983 Report) that conciliation might best be developed by court-based services and adapting court procedures. In response to criticism, the Committee acknowledged that it was difficult to assess the effectiveness of conciliation. They recommended that further research should be commissioned before any policy decisions were taken. A senior official in the Lord Chancellor's Department remarked that the cost of setting up the Interdepartmental Committee on Conciliation and commissioning its evaluative study would have funded family mediation services for a considerable time.

Researchers face methodological difficulties in obtaining a representative sample and establishing a control group with whom valid comparisons can be made. Research studies with samples of varying sizes, with or without control groups, have been conducted on different aspects including:

- the take-up of mediation and settlement rates;

- follow-up studies of consumer experience and satisfaction;

- follow-up to see whether mediated agreements last over time;

- analysis of mediators' methods and techniques;

- comparison of mediation costs with legal costs;

- comparisons between mediators and lawyers;

- consideration of what makes one mediator more effective than another.

In the 1980s, researchers evaluated mediation mainly in terms of settlement rates and client satisfaction. More attention is now given to outcomes over longer periods of time and to different aspects of the mediator's role – the input as well as the output. Some researchers recommended that mediation should 'consider a longer-term horizon for adults rather than concentrating on short-term dispute resolution'.[26] Mediators face many challenges if they are expected not only to settle disputes but also to improve relationships between separated parents and between children and parents in the longer term.

---

[26] Walker and Hornick *Communication in Marriage and Divorce* (The BT Forum, 1996), p 65.

13.5 RESEARCH ON THE FAMILY MEDIATION PILOT PROJECT 1996–2000

A study of the first family mediation service in the UK supported measures to encourage mediation at the pre-court stage. The researchers recommended that 'prior to legal aid being granted, the possibility of reaching agreement … should be fully explored'.[27] Before Part III of the Family Law Act 1996 was implemented nationally, the Legal Services Commission funded a four-year research study on publicly funded family mediation.[28] The researchers analysed 4,593 case monitoring forms supplied by 33 mediation providers. These included 'mediation intakes' attended by one party only. The main study focused on data from five services providing all-issues mediation (102 cases) and child-focused mediation (298 cases). 70% of the referrals to mediation came from lawyers, 18% were self-referred and 12% were court-referred. 148 mediations sessions were recorded with clients' permission and follow-up interviews were conducted with 47 clients. Of the parents who took part in mediation in child-related issues, 82% considered the mediator had been impartial, 70% had found mediation either very or fairly helpful and 78% thought the mediator had understood their situation either very well (51%) or fairly well (27%). 71% said they would recommend mediation to others in a similar situation. Experience of mediation on financial matters was also positive. Most participants thought it had been helpful and said they would recommend it to others experiencing similar problems. The researchers concluded that the mediation process had its own distinctive and positive features and should be supported as a separate system running in parallel to the court system.

Once the requirement to consider mediation before legal aid could be granted was introduced nationally, the number of family mediations rose sharply. In 2002/03, 13,841 mediations were started in which one or both parties was publicly funded, an increase of 12% over the previous year. In 2002/03, 21,146 participants qualified for legally aided mediation and received it free of charge, an increase of 14% over the previous year. A year later, in 2004/05, 14,355 family mediations were started in which one or both parties received mediation free of charge, equivalent to approximately 10% of the divorcing population, although mediation is also used by unmarried and married couples who separate without divorcing.

---

[27]   Davis and Lees *A Study of Conciliation – its Impact on Legal Aid Costs and Place in the Resolution of Disputes arising out of Divorce* (Dept of Social Administration, University of Bristol, 1981), p 164.

[28]   Davis et al *Monitoring Publicly Funded Family Mediation – Report to the Legal Services Commission* (Legal Services Commission, 2000).

13.6 MEDIATION AND GENDER ISSUES

Researchers have been concerned to establish whether mediation provides fair and balanced outcomes for men and women equally. Attempts have been made to compare men's and women's experiences of going to court with their experiences of going to mediation. One study found that mediation seemed to produce greater benefits for men than for women,[29] but this was later explained as reflecting men's greater dissatisfaction with their experience in court, rather than women's dissatisfaction with mediation.[30] Despite concerns that women would inevitably be disadvantaged in mediation by gender inequalities and lack of bargaining power, Davis et al found that 'women's responses were, on the whole, slightly more positive than those of men'.[31] Irving and Benjamin reviewed feminist objections to mediation and concluded from their survey of research findings in several countries that mediation does not systematically disadvantage women.[32] Most women have reported that they found the process balanced and helpful. However, where there were financial issues and conflict or distress was high, a single, inexperienced mediator sometimes failed to manage the process adequately.

Research by Hester et al found limitations in mediators' handling of domestic violence issues.[33] Mediators who took part in this survey had considered mediation suitable in many cases despite concerns about domestic violence. There were no national requirements at that time for the specialist training, supervision and monitoring now provided by mediation Lead Bodies. Ten years later, concerns about adequate safeguarding by judges, lawyers and Cafcass were not replicated in relation to mediators.[34] Researchers both in the UK and the United States have found that abused women did not feel adequately protected in the court system.[35] In consequence, cases involving domestic violence are no longer exempted from referral for mediation assessment. Systematic screening by mediators also avoids the stigmatising effects of routine safeguarding checks by Cafcass for all parents who take a private quarrel

---

[29] Emery and Wyer 'Child Custody Mediation' (1987) 55 *Journal of Consulting and Clinical Psychology* 179–186.

[30] Emery and Jackson 'The Charlottesville Mediation Project: mediated and litigated child custody disputes' (1989) 24(3) *Mediation Quarterly* 1.

[31] Davis et al *Monitoring Publicly Funded Family Mediation – Report to the Legal Services Commission* (Legal Services Commission, 2000), para 17.2.

[32] Irving and Benjamin 'Research in Family Mediation – an Integrative Review' in Irving and Benjamin (eds) *Family Mediation – Contemporary Issues* (Sage, 1995).

[33] Hester, Pearson, Radford 'Family Court Welfare and Voluntary Sector Mediation in Relation to Domestic Violence' (1997) 117 *Rowntree Social Policy Research Findings*.

[34] Craig 'Everybody's Business: Application for contact orders with consent' [2007] Fam Law 261. See also Chapter 3 at **3.13** above.

[35] Corcoran and Melamed 'From coercion to empowerment: spousal abuse and mediation' (1990) 7(4) *Mediation Quarterly* 303–316; Erickson and McKnight 'Mediating spousal abuse divorces' (1990) *Mediation Quarterly* 7 (4), 377–388; Hunt *Parental Perspectives on the Family Justice System in England and Wales: a review of research* (Report for the Family Justice Council, December 2009).

to court. Where either the applicant or respondent requests a separate information and assessment meeting because of concerns, the initial meeting with one party alone is likely to take an hour of careful exploration and assessment. The other party is not contacted by the mediation service, if this would increase risks. Assessment by a mediator using mediation skills to listen, ask questions and observe reactions is likely to be more thorough than a purely legal triage. When both parties are seen separately, the composite picture that emerges from separate assessment with each of them is likely to have more depth and detail than information given by one of them to a legal advisor, or a routine check by Cafcass. An Australian study[36] found that women who had suffered domestic violence and abuse generally experienced less pre-mediation anxiety, a more positive experience of the mediation process and a higher level of satisfaction with agreements where the woman:

- had been subject to emotional abuse, one-off physical threats, or threats only;

- had been separated from their ex-partner for a considerable time;

- had received personal counselling (as opposed to relationship counselling);

- reported that she no longer felt intimidated by her ex-partner; and

- felt confident in her legal advice and knew what she could reasonably expect from the settlement;

and where mediators:

- asked specific questions about violence and abuse, including non-physical abuse;

- offered specific guidance in considering the possible impact of violence and abuse on the mediation process;

- offered separate time with the mediator before, during and after sessions;

- worked as a gender-balanced co-mediation team;

- demonstrated that they understood fears and concerns both within and outside the mediation session by implementing specific strategies to deal with these concerns;

---

[36] Keys Young Social Research Consultants *Research Evaluation of Family Mediation Practice and the Issue of Violence* (Legal Aid and Family Services, Commonwealth of Australia, 1996).

- demonstrated that they could control abusive behaviour within the session; and

- assisted a vulnerable individual to deal with any harassment and intimidation which occurred outside the actual mediation session itself.[37]

There is no recent research in the UK on mediators' screening for domestic abuse and child protection concerns, but the criteria used in assessing whether mediation is suitable are similar in many respects to the Australian ones. Mediation is considered unsuitable where there are child protection issues and/or a history of violence and/or a person is in fear of continuing violence and intimidation.[38] The use of shuttle mediation and gender balanced co-mediation teams may enable some issues to be mediated that would not be suitable for face-to-face mediation in the same room.[39] Rather than opposing mediation altogether, feminist mediators in the United States such as Girdner and Neumann have argued for 'feminist informed' models of mediation that address the needs and rights of those experiencing and/or fearing violence and abuse.[40] Further research is needed in this difficult area. In the meantime, it is vital that mediators maintain the trust placed in them to screen very carefully. A new system of 'quality control' and accreditation for family mediators is needed to regulate and maintain standards of training and practice.[41]

Few commentators have questioned whether mediation might disadvantage men rather than women. Fathers often complain that the family justice system is heavily weighted towards mothers who have the children, occupation of the family home and child maintenance. Circumstances may put one parent in a much stronger position than the other.[42] There are also some cases, for example where one parent has left the family for a new partner, where guilt feelings could result in financial offers being made in considerable excess of what the court would be likely to order. Parents might make ill-considered concessions if they are too exhausted or depressed to press for a better deal. Mediators strongly encourage participants to take legal advice before finalising a settlement and to return to for a further session if adjustments are needed. Evidence from research does not support the view that either women or men are systematically disadvantaged in mediation.

---

[37] Bagshaw *Disclosure of Domestic Violence in Family Law Disputes: Issues for Family and Child Mediators* (Conflict Management Research Group, University of South Australia, 2001).
[38] See Chapter 3 at **3.14** above.
[39] See Chapter 4 at **4.10** agove.
[40] Girdner 'Mediation triage: screening for spouse abuse in divorce mediation' (1990) 7(4) *Mediation Quarterly* 365–386; Neumann 'How mediation can effectively address the male and female power imbalance in divorce' (1992) 9 *Mediation Quarterly* 227–239.
[41] Roberts 'Quality Standards for Family Mediation Practice' [2010] Fam Law 661–666.
[42] See Chapter 10 above.

With regard to mediators' gender and co-mediation, Hunt's survey[43] found only two studies, both pre-Cafcass, that looked at parental views on the gender or ethnicity of the conciliator and whether having two workers was or might have been helpful. Most of the parents in one study did not think it mattered if there were one or two workers and 91% thought that the gender or race of the worker was immaterial. An earlier study reported more mixed results: 65% of those with a single worker thought a gender balance was not important, whereas 50% of those who had experienced male/female co-working believed that it was:[44]

> 'I think there should be one of each gender in all meetings so that both parties' views can be looked at in different ways plus giving the impression that both are equally represented.'

Irving and Benjamin[45] see significant advantages in using male-female co-mediators, believing that a gender-balanced team helps to give equal attention to male and female perspectives and provides opportunities to model negotiation and clear communication. Irving and Benjamin also consider that interdisciplinary co-mediation, combining a mediator with family law expertise with a mediator experienced in a psychosocial discipline, offers an 'interweaving of divergent sources of expertise' that enhance creativity.[46]

13.7 MEDIATION COSTS COMPARED WITH LEGAL COSTS

One of the main advantages claimed for mediation is that it reduces legal costs. In an early study in Bristol, researchers explored the impact of child-focused mediation on legal aid costs and found that where mediation led to agreement, there was a considerable reduction in legal aid applications. Solicitors considered that mediation had reduced legal costs in 54% of cases.[47] Kelly compared the costs of mediated divorces in California with those of divorces conducted through lawyers.[48] She found that all issues mediation cost considerably less than the use of two lawyers to negotiate or litigate a final settlement. The two groups of mediated and non-mediated divorces were comparable in the complexity of their issues, levels of income, extent of reported marital conflict, initial levels of hostility or co-operation and expected degree of difficulty in reaching settlement. Kelly warned, however, that her results should be viewed with

---

[43] Hunt *Parental Perspectives on the Family Justice System in England and Wales: a review of research* (Report for the Family Justice Council, December 2009).

[44] Ibid, p 82.

[45] Irving and Benjamin (eds) *Family Mediation – Contemporary Issues* (Sage, 1995).

[46] Ibid, p 448.

[47] Davis and Lees *A Study of Conciliation – its Impact on Legal Aid Costs and Place in the Resolution of Disputes arising out of Divorce* (Dept of Social Administration, University of Bristol, 1981).

[48] Kelly 'Is mediation less expensive? Comparison of mediated and adversarial divorce costs' (1990) 8(1) *Mediation Quarterly* 15–26.

caution, since the respondents were self-selected and not representative of the divorcing population as a whole. Another American study conducted by Pearson compared mediated and non-mediated cases.[49] Legal costs were found to be 28–48% higher for those who settled their divorce proceedings through lawyers, compared with those who used mediation. Proving that mediation reduces expenditure on legal proceedings is no easy task, since estimates of savings based on avoidance of litigation assumes that litigation would have taken place without mediation. Variables in clients' circumstances and negotiating strengths, in the model of mediation used and in the experience, knowledge and skills of mediators make it very difficult to draw firm conclusions. Mediation may increase costs in cases where no settlement is reached and court proceedings follow, but may have been of use in obtaining financial disclosure and narrowing the issues in dispute.

In the year 2004/05, the British government spent £14.2 million on publicly funded family mediation, representing 4.2% of public expenditure on private family law.[50] The National Audit Office subsequently examined the cost-effectiveness of public expenditure on family mediation and reported to Parliament that:[51]

> 'mediation is generally cheaper, quicker and less acrimonious than court proceedings and research shows it secures better outcomes, particularly for children ... On average a mediated case takes 100 days and costs £752, compared with 435 days and £1,682 in cases where mediation is not used.'

42% of those who had not been referred to mediation said that they would have accepted it, had they known about it:[52]

> 'Confrontation in court cannot always be avoided, but the alternative of mediation should be pursued wherever possible – to the benefit of disputing individuals and the taxpayer.'

Although the principle of voluntary participation is upheld, Jonathan Djanogly, Parliamentary Under Secretary of State at the Ministry of Justice, has said he does not think the taxpayer should fund court proceedings over arrangements for children unless there are safety issues:[53]

> 'Too often people in family breakdowns are using court as a first answer when they should not. Often it is dealing with contact with children or intimate personal relationships that really shouldn't be going before the courts.'

---

[49] Pearson 'The equity of mediated divorce settlements' (1991) 9 *Mediation Quarterly* 179–197.
[50] Legal Services Commission, 2005.
[51] *National Audit Office Review* (March 2007).
[52] Ibid.
[53] [2010] Fam Law 1235.

In 2009 there were nearly 45,000 private law children cases with legal aid costs totalling £143 million. Greater public awareness and understanding of mediation are of crucial importance, as well as easy access to mediation services without incurring high transport costs. The number of 'quality assured' LSC contracted family mediation services has increased to 210, a 12% increase over the previous level of provision. These 210 services provide information and assessment meetings and mediation in 979 locations across England and Wales, compared with 740 previously, thus 'considerably improving levels of client access to mediation'.[54] Anecdotal evidence suggests that self-referrals to mediation also come from word of mouth recommendations from parents who have taken part in mediation.

13.8   COMPARISONS BETWEEN MEDIATORS AND LAWYERS

The Davis study[55] compared clients' satisfaction with mediators with their satisfaction with lawyers. Lawyers are partisan, even if they are committed to settling cases wherever possible. Many individuals going through separation and divorce need legal advice and partisan support. Mediators do not provide either of these in mediating face-to-face with both parties, whereas, other than in collaborative law, lawyers generally meet with their own client and deal at arm's length with 'the other side'. Davis reported that solicitors scored higher than mediators on most measures of approval, but acknowledged that the researchers might not have been studying 'directly comparable populations'.[56] Listening to and advising one client on a one-to-one basis is a very different matter from mediating between two clients who are in dispute with each other and seeking to help both equally. The roles of lawyers and mediators are different and complementary. One is not a substitute for the other. Well-organised combinations of mediation and legal advice are likely to reduce overall costs, rather than duplicating them. Research both in England and Australia[57] recognises that it is unrealistic to expect mediators to replace lawyers and courts. Various pathways are needed with intersections between them at regular intervals, to cater for different client groups with different levels of dispute needing different kinds of solutions at different points in time.

---

[54]   [2011] Fam Law 102.

[55]   Davis et al *Monitoring Publicly Funded Family Mediation – Report to the Legal Services Commission* (Legal Services Commission, 2000).

[56]   Davis, Finch and Fitzgerald 'Mediation and Legal Services – The Client Speaks' [2001] Fam Law 113.

[57]   Rhoades 'Revising Australia's parenting laws' (2010) *Child and Family Law Quarterly* 172.

13.9   DO MEDIATORS ONLY SETTLE EASY CASES?

It would be reasonable to assume that couples who accept mediation at the pre-court stage are intrinsically more co-operative than those who go to court. It has been argued that mediators settle easy cases that are likely to settle anyway. Davis and Roberts pointed out, however, that:[58]

> 'it might be thought that the parents' decision to take their quarrel to a mediation agency is itself indicative of a willingness to negotiate. But this is not always the case.'

To find out whether parental and child-parent relationships are improved by mediation, it is necessary to compare levels of conflict and co-operation pre-mediation with post-mediation levels. Pearson and Thoennes undertook a large-scale study[59] of court-referred mediation in contested child custody cases to test the hypothesis that parents who reach agreement through mediation are intrinsically more co-operative than those who seek a court decision. Parents were randomly assigned to two groups. The first group was referred to mediation, while the second group was not referred. A third group was formed of couples who went to court having refused the offer of mediation. A conflict scale was used to control for pre-existing characteristics, including the level and duration of dispute. In all three groups there were couples who described their ability to co-operate with each other as 'just about impossible'. Outcomes were then studied in all three categories. Even at the top end of the conflict scale, those who took part in mediation were found to have become more co-operative, compared with those who did not go to mediation. In the third follow-up interview, over 60% of those who reached agreement reported some co-operation with their former partner, twice the rate of co-operation (30%) among those who had not tried mediation.

Kelly et al compared the experience of divorcing couples who used mediation with those who litigated.[60] Co-operation increased significantly in the mediation group, but there was a high dropout rate, explained primarily as due to cost and in some cases to feeling overwhelmed. Withdrawal from mediation did not necessarily mean that participants were unhappy with the process. Half of those who withdrew were found to be either neutral or satisfied. Many had reached some basis for agreement, while some had withdrawn for reasons that had little or nothing to do with mediation. Citing dropout from mediation as evidence of 'failed mediation' would therefore be an over-simplification. Another study[61] used a control group to measure the effects of mediation in the longer term. Parents in dispute over child custody who had been

---

[58]   Davis and Roberts *Access to Agreement* (Open University Press, 1988), p 63.

[59]   Pearson and Thoennes 'Divorce Mediation Research Results' in Folberg and Milne (eds) *Divorce Mediation – Theory and Practice* (Guilford Press, 1988), pp 429–452.

[60]   Kelly 'A Decade of Divorce Mediation Research' (1996) 34 *Family and Conciliation Courts Review* 373–385.

[61]   Emery et al 'Child Custody Mediation and Litigation: Custody, Contact and

randomly assigned to mediation or court proceedings were followed up over a twelve-year period. This study found that, compared with litigating parents, non-residential parents in the mediated group had more contact with their children and were more involved in many areas of their children's lives. Their increased involvement was not found to be associated with increased conflict. The parents who mediated made more changes in their children's living arrangements over the twelve years and generally showed increased flexibility and co-operation.

13.10   SETTLEMENT RATES AND CLIENT SATISFACTION

North American studies, using control groups, found that settlements reached through mediation did not differ significantly from lawyer-negotiated settlements or from litigated settlements. Couples who used mediation were likely to consider that they had reached an outcome fair to them both.[62] Researchers in England and Wales found that mediation participants reported settlement in 45% of child-related cases and 34% of property and finance cases, with about half declaring themselves as 'completely satisfied' with their agreement, while more than half considered it 'completely' in the best interests of their children.[63] Settlement rates have increased since this research was done in the early days of publicly funded mediation.

> 'The full and partial success rate of publicly funded mediations now stands at 70% (with the full resolution of cases accounting for 66% of this).'[64]

Settlement rates reported by family mediation services themselves may be rejected as unreliable on the grounds that mediators are liable to overestimate their own success. However, it may be worth noting that settlement of some or all issues was reported in 83.9% of mediations completed in 2009–2010 by Bristol Family Mediators Association Ltd (2011). Other services have reported similarly high settlement rates.[65] Both the Bristol and Stafford services believe that having the facility to provide interdisciplinary co-mediation enables them to handle more complex and higher-conflict mediations. The Mediation Centre in Stafford found, as other studies have done,[66] that couples may be placed in three categories.

Coparenting 12 years After Initial Dispute Resolution' (2001) 69(2) *Journal of Consulting and Clinical Psychology* 323–332.

[62]   Kelly 'Mediated and Adversarial Divorce: Respondents' Perceptions of their Processes and Outcomes' (1989) 24 *Mediation Quarterly* 71–88; Pearson 'The equity of mediated divorce settlements' (1991) 9 *Mediation Quarterly* 179–197.

[63]   Davis et al 'Mediation and Legal Services – The Client Speaks' [2001] Fam Law 113.

[64]   Green Paper *Legal Aid Reform 2010*, para 4.71.

[65]   Robinson and Brisby 'ADR Professional' [2001] Fam Law 59–64.

[66]   McIntosh et al *Post-separation parenting arrangements and developmental outcomes for infants and children* (Family Court of Australia, Attorney-General's Department, 2010); Trinder 'Shared Residence: A Review of Recent Research Evidence' [2010] Fam Law 1192–1197.

The Stafford categories consist of: Type A – basically co-operative, for whom referral to mediation provides a co-operative form of working that is immediately attractive; Type B – initially antagonistic, but able to see the benefits of agreement on children's needs or shared financial objectives and showing potential for a more amicable relationship; Type C – locked in hostility, but able to understand the pragmatic benefits of mediation for achieving cost-effective solutions and capable of attaining limited objectives through mediation. The Stafford Centre's analysis of a small sample indicated no type As, 11 Bs and 22 Cs.[67]

Experience suggests that there are some divorcing couples who work out arrangements for their children and proposals for financial settlement in mediation and confirm a year later that they have maintained their co-operation, yet neither parent has taken action to apply for the decree absolute and consent order. In one such case, the couple acknowledged ambivalent feelings about ending their marriage, but did not wish to get back together. In contrast, there are some highly antagonistic couples who reach a financial settlement in mediation culminating in a consent order, but their hostility towards each other does not diminish. Savings in legal costs can be demonstrated more easily where a consent order results from mediation, but are harder to prove with semi-divorced couples whose progress in mediation is more ambiguous. Emery et al[68] found that even twelve years after dispute settlement, parents who had taken part in mediation maintained higher levels of child contact and joint parental involvement in their children's lives than those who litigated. The researchers emphasise, however, that their findings may not generalise to mediation and litigation in other courts. Irving and Benjamin's survey[69] of research on mediation in different jurisdictions found in the studies they looked at that 60–80% of mediation participants reported high levels of satisfaction, both with the mediation process and with its outcome.

Clients' experience of and satisfaction with the mediation process has been looked at in some small-scale qualitative studies as well as in large-scale quantitative research. Day Sclater obtained a small sample of thirty participants with the help of local mediators and solicitors and gathered full case-study material from eleven of them.[70] For the remaining nineteen participants, the data gathered was incomplete 'owing to the difficulties ….of maintaining contact with participants and sustaining their commitment to research which is dealing with sensitive and emotionally painful material'.[71]

---

[67] Robinson and Brisby 'ADR Professional' [2001] Fam Law 59–64.
[68] Emery et al 'Child Custody Mediation and Litigation: Custody, Contact and Coparenting 12 years After Initial Dispute Resolution' (2001) 69(2) *Journal of Consulting and Clinical Psychology* 323–332.
[69] Irving and Benjamin 'Research in Family Mediation – an Integrative Review' in Irving and Benjamin (eds) *Family Mediation – Contemporary Issues* (Sage, 1995).
[70] Day Sclater *Divorce: A Psychosocial Study* (Ashgate, 1999).
[71] Ibid, p 121.

In the eleven case studies, four participants who had taken part in mediation went on to instruct solicitors to negotiate on their behalf about property, finances and children. Day Sclater readily acknowledges that her sample was not a random one and makes no claims for the generalisability of her findings. The four participants who had abandoned mediation were perhaps more motivated to maintain contact with the researchers because they had a greater need to recount their grievances than those who had resolved them. Nevertheless, mediators need to listen to the voices of dissatisfied clients just as attentively as to those of satisfied ones.

13.11   THE MEDIATION PROCESS

Early research on family mediation focused on take-up and settlement rates. Other studies focused on the process itself, rather than on its results.[72] These studies analysed mediators' techniques and interventions, their use of authority and factors that contributed to one mediator being more effective than another. One of the main aims of mediation is to 'empower' participants to reach their own decisions. A number of studies showed, however, that it is naïve to believe that 'the mediator controls the process but not the outcome'. Gulliver pointed out that mediators are bound to have their own views,[73] values and interests, while Abel warned that informal processes of dispute resolution are liable to oppress, as well as empower.[74] Greatbatch and Dingwall found in their analysis[75] of audiotaped mediation sessions that mediators influenced the mediation process and outcome by encouraging some proposals and discouraging others. This study was criticised for not seeking participants' perspectives and for not giving 'the whole picture', but the findings nonetheless caused some concern. Could mediators be wolves in sheep's clothing, driving frightened participants into a settlement corner? Piper conducted an empirical study[76] based on observation and tape recordings of mediation with twenty-four couples in a mediation service run by the local divorce court welfare service. Although different approaches and techniques, sometimes stemming from different professional backgrounds, were not found to lead to 'differences of message or outcome',[77] the ethos of the divorce court welfare service may have had some influence. All the

---

[72]   Donahue, Allen and Burrell 'Mediator communicative competence' (1988) 55 *Communication Monographs* 104–119; Greatbatch and Dingwall 'Selective facilitation: some preliminary observations on a strategy used by divorce mediators' (1989) 23 *Law and Society Review* 613–641; Slaikeu, Pearson and Thoennes 'Divorce Mediation Behaviors: A Descriptive System and Analysis' (1988) in Folberg and Milne (eds) *Divorce Mediation – Theory and Practice* (Guilford Press, 1988), pp 475–495.

[73]   Gulliver *Disputes and Negotiations* (Academic Press, 1979).

[74]   Abel *The Politics of Informal Justice* (Academic Press, 1982), Vol 1.

[75]   Greatbatch and Dingwall 'Selective facilitation: some preliminary observations on a strategy used by divorce mediators' (1989) 23 *Law and Society Review* 613–641.

[76]   Piper *The Responsible Parent – A Study in Divorce Mediation* (Harvester Wheatsheaf, 1991).

[77]   Ibid, p 17.

mediators had backgrounds in social and probation work, counselling, family therapy or psychotherapy and the mediations were confined to child-related issues. Piper's finding[78] that outcomes in the cases she studied were often a 'mediator-articulated compromise' should not be generalised to family mediation generally, because mediation on all issues undertaken by independent mediators including lawyer mediators, not run under the wing of a statutory service, might well produce different findings. Most of the British research on independent and probation-based mediation services was undertaken twenty to thirty years ago, before national requirements were introduced with regard to training, supervision and competence assessment. Practice has developed considerably over the last twenty years and fresh studies are needed to analyse mediator 'input and output' today.

13.12 WHAT MAKES ONE MEDIATOR MORE EFFECTIVE THAN ANOTHER?

The findings from studies that have explored this question broadly concur that mediation experience counts. Pearson and Thoennes found major improvements among mediators (lawyers, social workers and counsellors) who had mediated six or more cases.[79] Those who had mediated six to ten cases helped couples reach settlement in 64% of cases, compared with 30% of cases involving inexperienced mediators. In England and Wales, Davis et al found that 'mediators have become more skilled in negotiating settlements than appeared from earlier data collected in the 1980s'.[80] Effective mediators offer relevant knowledge when it is needed and help participants to generate options that draw from the mediator's accumulated experience, without assuming that what worked in one situation will necessarily work in another.

13.12.1 A dynamic, pro-active approach

Pro-active mediators achieve a higher rate of agreement than passive facilitators. It is important to recognise that being proactive is not synonymous with being directive. Pearson and Pearson and Thoennes found in analysing audiotapes of mediation sessions that effective mediators intervened actively, structured the process well and spent time exploring options.[81] In cases where little progress was made, the mediator had focused more on gathering facts and made less headway, especially

---

[78] See n 76 above, p 190.

[79] Pearson and Thoennes 'Divorce Mediation Research Results' in Folberg and Milne (eds) *Divorce Mediation – Theory and Practice* (Guilford Press, 1988), pp 429–452.

[80] Davis et al *Monitoring Publicly Funded Family Mediation – Report to the Legal Services Commission* (Legal Services Commission, 2000), para 18.7.

[81] Pearson *An evaluation of alternatives to court adjudication* (1982) 7 *Justice System Journal* 420–444; Pearson and Thoennes 'Divorce Mediation Research Results' in Folberg and Milne (eds) *Divorce Mediation – Theory and Practice* (Guilford Press, 1988), pp 429–452.

when participants communicated poorly. Audiotapes of mediation
sessions transcribed and analysed by Donohue, Allen and Burrell also
found that mediators who intervened actively during mediation sessions
were more likely to get good results than those who merely facilitated
exchanges between the parties.[82] Positive outcomes were associated with
three particular interventions by mediators:

- laying down and enforcing procedural rules;

- structuring the process to obtain relevant information;

- reframing the parties' statements to identify important issues and
  proposals.

Examination of sessions that ended in deadlock found a tendency among
the more passive mediators 'to let the couples go for a while to see how
they interact'. The researchers found that a non-interventionist approach
by mediators 'may create a runaway freight train that mediators are
unable to stop with tools designed for slower-moving traffic'.[83]

13.12.2   Clear structure and focused questions

Kressel and colleagues[84] found that the techniques mediators used to
gather information were an important component of effectiveness. The
choice of question form was important and the use of structure to gather
information systematically.[85] Kressel et al's analysis[86] of audiotapes and
videotapes of mediation sessions found that mediators tended to be either
settlement-seekers or problem-solvers. Problem-solvers were more flexible
in the way they moved between participants to maintain a balance
between them. They actively encouraged productive exchanges and
discouraged destructive ones. The problem-solving approach was
associated with durable agreements and with greater satisfaction on the
part of participants, compared with a more inflexible, settlement-seeking
approach.

The American Bar Association (ABA 2008) considered factors defining
good quality mediation practice in the context of civil/commercial
mediation, based on interviews with lawyers, mediation users and
mediators. The ABA identified 'good quality' in four categories:

---

[82] Donahue, Allen and Burrell 'Mediator communicative competence' (1988) 55
Communication Monographs 104–119.
[83] Donahue, Lyles and Rogan 'Issue Development in Divorce Mediation' (1989) 24
Mediation Quarterly 19–28.
[84] Kressel, Butler-DeFreitas, Forlenza and Wilcox 'Research in Contested Custody
Mediations' (1989) 24 *Mediation Quarterly* 55–70.
[85] See Chapter 5 above.
[86] Kressel, Frontera, Forlenza, Butler and Fish 'The settlement-oriented versus the
problem-solving style in custody mediation' (1994) 50(1) *Journal of Social Issues* 67–83.

- Good preparation by the mediator, representatives and parties.

- Adapting the mediation process to meet the needs of the individual case/parties.

- 'Analytical' techniques used by the mediator.

- 'Persistence' by the mediator.

Creativity and flexibility, showing an ability to adapt the mediation process to manage different levels of conflict and power imbalance without losing the integrity of the process, are surely among the characteristics of a good mediator.

13.13 PREDICTORS OF POSITIVE MEDIATION OUTCOMES

There are no reliable predictors of positive mediation outcomes. Studies have shown that high initial levels of anger and marital conflict need not be barriers to couples reaching agreement through mediation.[87] In Australia, McIntosh et al[88] identified three different categories of separated parents according to their patterns of co-operation or conflict. The most conflicted parents had high rates of conflict and litigation, both pre- and post-mediation. Some researchers[89] have focused exclusively on client attributes in considering who is most likely to be helped by mediation. Waldron and colleagues[90] concluded that two main factors determine whether couples are likely to benefit from mediation:[91]

> 'The first determinant is a level of personality development that allows the subject to view the world not as black and white but as a gamut of greys ... The capacity for empathy, the ability to see two sides of an issue and the capacity to separate the parenting relationship from the marital relationship are essential.'

The second important determinant is that both partners can let go of their marital/couple relationship sufficiently to be able to work on

---

[87]   Depner, Cannata and Ricci 'Client evaluations of mediation services' (1994) 32(3) *Family and Conciliation Courts Review* 306–325; Kelly and Duryee 'Women's and men's views of mediation in voluntary and mandatory settings' (1992) 30(1) *Family and Conciliation Courts Review* 43–49.

[88]   McIntosh, Smyth, Kelaher, Wells and Long *Post-separation parenting arrangements and developmental outcomes for infants and children* (Family Court of Australia, Attorney-General's Department, 2010).

[89]   Emery and Wyer 'Child Custody Mediation' (1987) 55 *Journal of Consulting and Clinical Psychology* 179–186.

[90]   Waldron, Roth, Fair, Mann and McDermott 'A Therapeutic Mediation Model for Child Custody Dispute Resolution' (1984) 3 *Mediation Quarterly* 5–20.

[91]   Ibid at p 18.

decisions and issues. There needs to be a capacity to face forwards, to listen and to want to solve problems.

Some studies have found that positive outcomes are best predicted by the 'fit' and interaction between the couple's characteristics and dynamics and the mediator's attributes and skills. Pearson and Thoennes found that relevant interrelated factors were client characteristics, the nature of the couple's disputes and the mediator's attributes.[92] Donahue and colleagues[93] also found that agreements reached through mediation were related to the interaction between the parties' attributes and the mediator's communication skills. The interplay of factors in the mediation process illustrates the relevance of chaos theory and ways in which minor variations can help to transform discord into some degree of harmony. Variations of the mediation model and small interventions – relevant questions, acknowledgments, reframing at appropriate moments – may make significant differences during the process and in its outcome.

13.14   CAN ANY CONCLUSIONS BE DRAWN?

While warning of the low comparability between studies, Irving and Benjamin found that mediation generally led to an improvement in co-parental relationships in 60–70% of cases, measured in terms of decreased conflict, improved communication and fewer serious problems.[94] Research in Australia, Canada, the United States and the UK has found indications of increased parental co-operation following mediation.[95]

Mediation is a brief process aimed at improving communication and helping participants to work out agreed decisions. Circumstances and interpersonal dynamics are so variable that it cannot be expected to produce standard outcomes. It offers a pathway towards settlement that may be helpful for many people, but not for all. As two of the most experienced researchers in the United States have pointed out:[96]

---

[92] Pearson and Thoennes 'A preliminary portrait of client reactions to three court mediation programs' (1985) 23(1) *Conciliation Courts Review* 1–14.
[93] Donahue, Allen and Burrell 'Mediator communicative competence' (1988) 55 *Communication Monographs* 104–119.
[94] Irving and Benjamin 'Research in Family Mediation – an Integrative Review' in Irving and Benjamin (eds) *Family Mediation – Contemporary Issues* (Sage, 1995).
[95] Bordow and Gibson *Evaluation of the family court mediation service* (Family Court of Australia Research and Evaluation Unit, 1994); Davis et al *Monitoring Publicly Funded Family Mediation – Report to the Legal Services Commission* (Legal Services Commission, 2000); Emery *The Truth about Children and Divorce* (Viking, 2004); Kelly 'A Decade of Divorce Mediation Research' (1996) 34 *Family and Conciliation Courts Review* 373–385; Pearson and Thoennes 'Divorce Mediation Research Results' in Folberg and Milne (eds) *Divorce Mediation – Theory and Practice* (Guilford Press, 1988), pp 429–452.
[96] Thoennes and Pearson 'Response to Bruch and McIsaac' (1992) 30(1) *Family and Conciliation Courts Review* 142–143.

'the forum in which disputes are resolved is, after all, only a piece in the complex puzzle of couples' divorce experiences. In evaluating the utility of mediation we must consider not only the nature of the mediation intervention and the degree and nature of parents' exposure to adversarial systems, but must also weigh a myriad of factors related to the parties and their marital and separation history.'

The findings from research are capable of different interpretations and may be considered inconclusive. The weight of evidence from a range of studies in different countries would appear, nonetheless, to be positive, supporting mediation's role as an appropriate process of dispute resolution, especially where families are concerned.

CHAPTER 14

INTERNATIONAL FAMILY MEDIATION AND FUTURE DIRECTIONS

'The oneness of human beings is the basic ethical thread that holds us together'[1]

CONTENTS

14.1   FAMILY MEDIATION IN EUROPE – AN OVERVIEW

The ethos of mediation has travelled from east to west and from west to east over many centuries, rather like the acanthus leaf has done in architecture. In Europe, family mediation has developed rapidly over the last thirty years. Many countries have introduced legislation on mediation and international exchanges have multiplied through literature, research reports, conferences and the Internet. However, much remains to be done to increase public awareness and acceptance of mediation. A picture of

---

[1]   Yunus in Kumar and Whitefield (eds) *Visionaries of the 20th Century – a Resurgence Anthology* (Green Books, 2006).

family mediation in Europe resembles a changing patchwork quilt or mosaic. The pieces making up the patchwork have recurring patterns and colours, but they are not woven uniformly to a single design and there are missing pieces. A variegated patchwork that recognises cultural differences is preferable to uniformity. Northerners may need a different kind of family mediation from Mediterranean people. On the other hand, the expansion of the European Union and the mobility of individuals and families across state boundaries increase the need for universally accepted principles and consistency of approach within an internationally regulated framework. Despite great diversity in the extent to which mediation is used in different jurisdictions – with full public funding, limited public funding or no public funding at all – international exchanges indicate a high level of consensus on the philosophy of mediation, the attributes of a good mediator and the essential elements of the family mediation process. The following overview of mediation in Europe consists of a series of snapshots that are inevitably selective and incomplete, but which may help to illustrate some current trends.

14.1.1 Austria

A pilot project in Austria on family mediation paved the way for the Federal Act on Mediation in Civil Matters that came into force on 1 March 2004. This established the legal framework for mediation in all private law areas, including family law. An earlier Directive on Mediation issued on 1 January 2000 had set out the principles and requirements for family mediation. 'Mediation shall take place only if the participation of the clients is completely voluntary'.[2] A co-mediation model was preferred. 'As far as possible, co-mediation shall take place in a setting with one female and one male co-mediator'.[3] Interdisciplinary teams of co-mediators with qualifications in law and/or psychosocial disciplines fostered 'interdisciplinary cooperation of the mediators involved in order to ensure optimal coverage of the areas [of] law and psychodynamics during divorce and separation'.[4] Austria's model of interdisciplinary co-mediation is very similar to the FMA model.[5]

14.1.2 Denmark

Mediation on child-related issues, administered by regional authorities, is confidential and free of charge. The initial three-hour period may be extended on request. The mediators are child counsellors and lawyers trained in mediation. Private mediation on all issues, including finance and property, is provided on a fee-charging basis by an independent association of family lawyer mediators.[6]

---

[2] See Art 5(4).
[3] See Art 8(2).
[4] See Preamble, p 2.
[5] See Chapter 4 at **4.6** above.
[6] See www.familiemediatorer.dk/english.html.

14.1.3 France

Legislation on civil mediation was introduced in France in 1995 and 1996,[7] but the main legislation providing for court referral to mediation in family matters was contained in the law on joint parental authority of 4 March 2002 and in the reform of divorce law implemented on 1 January 2005. Family court judges are empowered to refer parties in family proceedings to receive information about mediation, but not to order mediation. The family court judge (JAF) may select cases suitable for referral and appoint the mediator. In practice, this provision has been little used. However, in a radically new approach, a draft law[8] under consideration by the French government envisages compulsory referral to mediation in family matters. 'Toutefois, à peine d'irrecevabilité que le juge peut soulever d'office, la saisine du juge par le ou les parents doit être précédée d'une tentative de médiation familiale',[9] ie family mediation must be attempted before an application in family matters will be received by the court. Family mediators in France are concerned that the introduction of compulsory referral to mediation would undermine the principles of voluntary participation and empowerment that they regard as fundamental. There are therefore tensions in France between government policy favouring compulsory mediation and independent family mediation associations represented on the the National Consultative Council on Family Mediation. There are fears that family mediation might be taken over by the State and lose its independence (personal communication from AMORIFE International).

With regard to the training of family mediators, France took its lead from Quebec, the United States and Britain. The first French family mediators were trained in Quebec and in the early 1990s training courses were run in Paris by an international team of French, Canadian and British trainers.[10] A decree of 2 December 2003 created a state diploma in family mediation open to professionals with a minimum of three years' experience in socio-legal or medical disciplines. To qualify as a recognised family mediator, candidates must pass the Diplôme d'Etat de Médiateur Familiale comprising 560 hours of study spread over two years. Credits for some elements may be granted on the basis of previous professional training. The diploma may be extended to 600 hours to obtain a Masters degree. Requirements include a 60-page dissertation, fourteen days of observation and 56 hours of supervised practice in a mediation service. Mediation placements are hard to obtain, since the take-up of family mediation remains low. Although the professional requirements for acceptance for mediation training are very similar in France and Britain, the length of family mediation training in France, leading to an academic qualification with brief practical training, contrasts with shorter

---

[7]   Decree No 96–652.
[8]   No 344.
[9]   See Art 15.
[10] Babu and Bonnoure-Aufière *Guide du médiateur familial* (Editions Erès, 2003).

foundation training in England and Wales followed by a longer period of internship and continuing training. Publicly funded family mediators in England and Wales are required to have recognised training and to complete a detailed portfolio documenting the techniques used in five completed mediations, in order to pass the Assessment of Competence in Family Mediation.[11] The French system demands lengthy academic study, while the English system relies more on evidence-based quality standards. A new Entente Cordiale is needed to develop 'the best of both worlds'! Continuing professional development and professional practice consultancy are requirements for family mediators in both countries.

14.1.4   Germany

After training provided by mediators from the United States, Canada and Israel, the national association of family mediators, BAFM (Bundes-Arbeitsgemeinschaft für Familien-Mediation) was founded in Germany in 1992 with the aim of establishing and maintaining voluntary standards for family mediation training. Members of BAFM must have two years' practice experience in their profession of origin, mediation training of at least 200 hours and practical training under supervision, with documentation of four completed mediations. 50% of BAFM members come from psychosocial professions and 50% from the legal profession. Mediation training must be interdisciplinary, both in the structure of the group (50% psychosocial professionals, 50% lawyers) and in the composition of the training team. Family mediation is offered on all issues in separation and divorce (children and legal and economic matters) and mainly takes the form of interdisciplinary co-mediation. Under a law passed in Germany on 1 September 2009, family court judges can order attendance at an information meeting with a mediator. These information meetings are free of charge but there is no legal aid for mediation itself. Family mediators in Germany generally charge privately for mediation, combined with some pro bono mediation.

14.1.5   Italy

In Italy:[12]

> 'although there have been some proposals for legislation and local authorities to promote mediation, the development of family mediation is very limited. In some pieces of legislation currently in force, there is even some confusion between family mediation, counselling, and other social services aimed at giving support to families.'

There are however a growing number of Italian associations and agencies strongly committed to developing family mediation and building a network to increase public awareness and demand. The Centre for Family

---

[11]   See Chapter 1 at **1.12** above.
[12]   Casals *Divorce Mediation* (European Academy of Law Conference, Trier, March, 2005).

Studies and Research at the Catholic University of Milan publishes seminal research studies and hosts international conferences on families in transition and the use of mediation.[13]

14.1.6 The Netherlands

Since 1 April 2005, family courts in the Netherlands have been able to refer parties to mediation during court proceedings. The statutory framework for divorce mediation is contained in the Post-Divorce Continued Parenthood Act, in force since 1 March 2009. This Act defines parental responsibility and requires parents to submit their parenting plan to the divorce court. Parents may divorce only after they have submitted a parenting plan explaining how they intend to carry out their parenting responsibilities after divorce. Divorce mediation in the Netherlands is mainly concerned with the consequences of divorce for children and maintaining family ties between parents and their children, but may also deal with financial and property matters. Judges in the Netherlands are not permitted to be mediators themselves but all judges receive training in assessing and referring cases to mediation. Legal proceedings are suspended during mediation and can be resumed if the parents are unable to reach agreement. Half the mediations are completed within a month and one-third within 14 days. If agreement is reached, the court proceedings are terminated. Judicial checks on agreements take place only at the request of the parties. Follow-up studies have shown that a large majority of mediation participants were satisfied with the mediation process and with the mediator. Over 80% of participants and their lawyers said that in a similar situation they would choose mediation again and would also recommend it to other people. This was equally the case among parents who did not reach agreement. The mediation referral procedure has been implemented at all district courts and courts of appeal and since 1 April 2005 there have been approximately 10,000 referrals. 'The success rate is currently 61%'.[14]

Under new statutory rules introduced on 1 January 2009, parenting plans must show in what way the parents have involved their children in drawing up the plan. Depending on the age of the child and other circumstances, the mediator may talk with children on their own. Child-inclusive mediation is used in many cases and is likely to become more common. Mediators who undertake to see children without their parents being present must first agree with the parents and explain to the child that what the child says to the mediator will remain confidential (apart from child protection issues). As in child-inclusive mediation in Britain,[15] the mediator checks carefully with the child at the end of their meeting

---

[13]   Scabini and Rossi *Rigenerare I Legami: la mediazione nelle relazione familiare e comunitarie* (V & P, Milan. 2003); Cigoli and Gennari *Close relationships and community psychology: an international perspective* (FrancoAngeli, 2010).

[14]   Pel et al 'Family Mediation in the Netherlands' [2009] IFL 4, 257.

[15]   See Chapter 8 above.

whether the child wants anything fed back to the parents by the mediator and if so, exactly what the mediator should tell the parents. The mediator should also consider whether anything the child has said might get the child into trouble if a parent were to find out about it. (In Britain, child-inclusive mediators seek an undertaking from parents beforehand that they will not brief their children on what they should say to the mediator, nor cross-question them afterwards).

Divorce mediation in the Netherlands takes place both before and during court proceedings. In view of the requirement to submit a parenting plan prior to divorce being granted, there is a view that mediation should logically precede divorce proceedings. No comparable statutory framework exists in the Netherlands for other forms of mediation in family matters, such as children's contact with grandparents, family business and inheritance disputes.

14.1.7   Norway

In Norway, unlike other European countries, mediation is mandatory and confined to issues concerning children. Under a change to the Marriage Act effective from 1993, married couples with children under 16 years of age must attend a mediation meeting before they can obtain a separation or divorce. Mediation is also mandatory before parents can bring a dispute over their children before the County Governor or the court. Family mediation in Norway embodies certain values:

(1)   Families continue, despite separation and divorce.

(2)   Children need to main their relationships with both parents, in the great majority of cases.

(3)   Decisions agreed by parents themselves are more likely to work in practice.

(4)   Mutually acceptable solutions can be reached more quickly through mediation and can be tailored to the needs of individual families.

(5)   The individual claims and interests of each parent need to be understood and addressed in the context of the continuing needs and well being of the family as a whole.[16]

The County Governor in each region is responsible for the provision of family mediation. Couples meet with one mediator, the mediation is free of charge and normally limited to four sessions of one hour each. The first session is used to clarify any issues, exchange information and plan further sessions, if needed. The second session focuses on the children and

---

[16]   Tjersland 'Mediation in Norway' (1995) 12(4) *Mediation Quarterly* 339–351.

the third on finances (regulated more simply in Norway than in many other countries). The fourth session may focus on relationships to family and friends and a fifth session may be used to draw up written agreements and to issue the parents with a certificate showing that they have attended mediation. Agreements reached in mediation are legally binding but not enforceable. Norwegian mediators educate parents about children's needs in separation and divorce and seek to make parents aware of the consequences of their behaviour and decisions for their children. The mediator also has an obligation to inform parents that according to the Norwegian Children Act, children over 12 years of age should be listened to (but not asked to make decisions) before important decisions are taken concerning the child. Children are not usually involved directly, but may meet with the mediator in some circumstances.

14.1.8   Poland

Although victim-offender mediation was introduced in Polish law in 1997, mediation in the family justice system started only in 2005, when an amendment to the Civil Procedure Code made it possible for courts to refer cases to mediation. The court keeps a list of mediators recommended by professional and social organisations to whom the court can refer. Mediation is voluntary in Poland and although parties are not compelled to accept it, many do so. The court can also be requested by the parties to make an adjournment to enable them to go to mediation. Family mediation is also available prior to court proceedings. Family mediators on court lists are members of associations or agencies in different parts of Poland. There are professional standards for training and practice and most mediator associations are represented on a national council advising the Ministry of Justice on ADR. The ADR Council, jointly with the Ministry of Justice, has recently launched a public awareness campaign to make mediation better known (including TV and radio publicity).

Recent developments in district courts include the appointment of mediation co-ordinators (Judges) with responsibility for encouraging the use of in-court and court-referred mediation. In 2009 a further important legislative change increased the number of family mediation cases. The amended Family Code introduced obligatory 'parenting plans' in cases where parents seek joint custody of children after divorce. However, public awareness about children's needs in divorce and other family disputes is still low. Many parents, especially mothers whose chances of getting a sole custody order are over 80%, may not be interested in mediating if they expect to do better in court. Another major deterrent is the cost, as mediation costs must be paid fully by the parties themselves: legal aid is not available for mediation.

14.1.9 Portugal

At the end of the 1990s, the first officially recognised family mediation service in Portugal was set up in a joint initiative taken by the Ministry of Justice and the Order of Lawyers. This court-referred mediation service was restricted to matters concerning parental responsibility and catered only for parents resident in certain districts of Lisbon. Following the establishment of the 'Dirección General de Administración Extrajudicial' in the year 2000, family mediation became more widely available in Portugal, accepting self-referrals from parents in dispute and no longer taking referrals solely from the court. Known as the 'Sistema de Mediação Familiar', family mediation in Portugal continues to be supported and regulated by the Ministry of Justice, providing mediation independently of court proceedings, as well as taking court referrals. Over the last decade, family mediation has developed in Portugal more rapidly than any other field of mediation, in order to comply with European standards and directives in relation to international cross-border mediation in cases of parental child abduction.

14.1.10 Spain

Family mediation is recognised in Spain as essentially multidisciplinary. Just over 50% of services providing publicly funded and private family mediation use a systematic follow up procedure about six months after concluding mediation and have found adherence to mediated agreements in 75% of cases.[17] The Spanish draft federal law on mediation in civil and commercial matters will incorporate the European Directive 2008/52/EC into Spanish law. It will also provide a unifying framework for the regional legislation on mediation introduced over the last two decades by the Autonomous Communities of Spain.[18] The federal law defines mediation as a voluntary, independent and informal process of dispute settlement with important benefits for society and for the administration of justice. Increasing public awareness of these benefits through legislation will encourage further initiatives to build on the progress that has been made through conferences on mediation and training programmes for mediators.

14.1.11 Sweden

In Sweden, qualified social workers in the Family Law Office help separated parents to reach agreement on child-related issues. Parents may refer themselves at any time during or following separation for what are known in Sweden as 'co-operation talks'. Sessions are generally co-mediated, preferably by male-female co-mediators, and on average

---

[17] García and Bolaños *Situación de la Mediación Familiar in España* (Ministerio de Trabajo y Asuntos Sociales, 2007).
[18] García *Paper given at ESFR Conference* (Milan, October 2010).

there are three to five sessions. Municipalities in Sweden provide this help free of charge to parents who request it. Each parent is first seen separately and there is screening for domestic violence, child protection issues or circumstances that would make joint meetings unsuitable. The courts refer disputes over custody or access to the Family Law Office, but parents' participation is voluntary. A government report on Child Custody and Access published in 1997 stated that family mediation was the most cost-effective form of preventive social work. In 1998 the Swedish Parliament amended the law so that parental agreements on custody and access reached through 'co-operation talks' have the same juridical status as a court decision, provided the agreement has been approved by the social worker as being in the best interests of the child. The aim was formerly to assist parents to reach agreements over their children on the basis that parental agreement benefits children. With greater awareness of the impact of domestic abuse on women and children and the continuing risks they may experience, mediators in Norway and Sweden now focus more strongly on ensuring children's safety and well being. Over the last ten years, child-inclusive mediation has become more common. New partners and other family members may also be included.

14.1.12   Switzerland

Conciliation as a method of conflict resolution has a long history and recognised role in civil and criminal procedures in Switzerland, but *mediation* has only recently become part of the legal system. The first unified Federal Code of Civil Procedure introduced on 1 January 2011 abolished the 26 different cantonal codes of civil procedure and gives an important place to mediation.[19] The Federal Code supports ADR and makes conciliation compulsory in most civil matters, whereas family mediation is voluntary, except in international cases. The costs of mediation for child-related issues may be publicly funded in some circumstances. The Code recognises the benefits of family mediation both in reducing litigation and in the quality of outcomes. The regulation of mediation training and practice remains in the hands of private family mediation associations with no active government involvement.

The Federal Code also recognises that mediation has an important preventive role in reducing risks of parental child abduction in international cases. Under the Swiss Federal Act on International Child Abduction of 1 July 2009, mediation is compulsory when application is made for the return of a child abducted into Switzerland from a Hague Convention member state.[20] A central Swiss authority is responsible for establishing a network of experts and institutions that are capable of acting expeditiously in giving advice, undertaking mediation and representing individual children. These Swiss measures could be

---

[19]   See Arts 213–218.
[20]   See Arts 4 and 8.

incorporated in amendments to the Hague Convention and adopted at multilateral level, serving as a model for other States wishing to improve their practice in parental child abduction cases.

14.1.13   Russia

The new Russian law of 27 July 2010 on Alternative Procedure of Dispute Settlement with Participation of Mediator came into effect on 1 January 2011. Under this law, mediation is applicable for the resolution of civil and commercial, industrial relations and family disputes. The law establishes the principles of mediation, including confidentiality and mediator impartiality, and requires an Agreement to Mediate to be signed, setting out the procedures to be followed and the duties of the mediator. A number of family lawyers, psychologists and therapists have taken training in family mediation, hoping that the new law and support from the judiciary will encourage the development of mediation in Russia. Patriarchal traditions are still strong in Russian families, with a tendency to rely on superior authority rather than on personal autonomy and responsibility. Nevertheless, there are signs of changing attitudes and increased migration is producing a growing number of cross-border family disputes. The All-Russian Congress of Judges supports mediation as an extra-judicial method of dispute resolution.[21]

14.2   THE COUNCIL OF EUROPE'S RECOMMENDATIONS ON FAMILY MEDIATION

A study carried out during the 1990s by the Council of Europe's Committee of experts on family law found that:[22]

> 'research in Europe, North America, Australia and New Zealand suggests that family mediation is better suited than more formal legal mechanisms to the settlement of sensitive, emotional issues surrounding family matters. Reaching agreements in mediation has been shown to be a vital component in making and maintaining co-operative relationships between divorcing parents: it reduces conflict and encourages continuing contact between children and both their parents.'

The Committee's recommendations were formally adopted by the Council of Europe in Recommendation No (98)1 of 21 January 1998:

> '9. Realising that a number of States are considering the introduction of family mediation;

---

[21]   Khazova 'Perspectives on international family mediation in the Russian Federation' *Paper given at the Council of Europe's 7th European Conference on Family Law – International Family Mediation* (Strasbourg, March 2009).

[22]   *Report of the Working Party on Mediation and Other Processes to Resolve Family Disputes* (CJ-FA-GT2).

10. Convinced of the need to make greater use of family mediation, a process in which a third party, the mediator, impartial and neutral, assists the parties themselves to negotiate over the issues in dispute and reach their own joint agreements,

11. Recommends the governments of Member States:

    i.   to introduce or promote family mediation or, where necessary, strengthen existing family mediation;

    ii.   to take or reinforce all measures they consider necessary with a view to the implementation of the following principles for the promotion and use of family mediation as an appropriate means of resolving family disputes.'

The Recommendation defines the objectives of mediation as a means of settling family disputes, particularly those arising during separation and divorce, as follows:[23]

    '(a)   to promote consensual approaches, thereby reducing conflict in the interest of all family members;

    (b)   to protect the best interests and welfare of children in particular, by reaching appropriate arrangements concerning custody and access;

    (c)   to minimise the detrimental consequences of family disruption and marital dissolution;

    (d)   to support continuing relationships between family members, especially those between parents and their children;

    (e)   to reduce the economic and social costs of separation and divorce, both to families and to States.'

The Recommendation also points out that family disputes have special characteristics that need to be taken into account in mediation:[24]

    '(a)   there are usually continuing and interdependent relationships. The dispute settlement process should facilitate constructive relationships for the future, in addition to enabling the resolution of current disputes;

    (b)   family disputes usually involve emotional and personal relationships in which feelings can exacerbate the difficulties, or disguise the true nature of the conflicts and disagreements. It is usually considered appropriate for these feelings to be acknowledged and understood by parties and by the mediator;

    (c)   disputes that arise in the process of separation and divorce have an impact on other family members, notably children, who may not be included directly in the mediation process, but whose interests may be considered paramount and therefore relevant to the process.'

In 1996 the Council of Europe established the European Convention on the Exercise of Children's Rights, which came into force on 1 July 2000 with the aim of protecting the best interests of children.[25] Article 3

---

23   At para 5.

24   At para 15 of the Explanatory Memorandum.

25   Council of Europe 2008.

upholds the right of the child to be informed and to express his or her views in proceedings, while under Article 6 (Decision-Making process), the judicial authority shall 'give due weight to the views expressed by the child'.[26]

The Council of Europe's Recommendation 1639 on 'Family mediation and gender equality' (2003) gives family mediation far-reaching objectives, not only to resolve disputes but also as:[27]

> 'a life-building and life-management process between family members in the presence of an independent and impartial third party known as the mediator ... The primary aim of mediation is not to reduce congestion of the courts but to repair a breakdown in communication between the parties with the help of a professional trained in mediation ...
>
> Gender equality in family mediation must be guaranteed [and] individual rights must not be sacrificed to cost-effectiveness or the trend towards alternative conflict resolution methods.'

Where children are concerned, the child:[28]

> 'should also be heard in the mediation process because he or she is recognized as having rights. Children should be allowed their say if a solution is to be found that is genuinely in their best interests.'

14.3   THE EUROPEAN FORUM ON FAMILY MEDIATION TRAINING AND RESEARCH

In a non-official initiative, family mediation trainers from European countries began working together after the first European conference held in Caen, France in November 1990. The Association pour la Promotion de la Médiation Familiale (APMF), based in Paris, invited a group of trainers to work together to define standards of training for family mediation based on common principles and objectives. This group, comprising trainers from Belgium, France, Germany, Italy, Switzerland and the UK, set up a voluntary association, the European Forum on Family Mediation Training and Research. Multilingual discussions, sometimes requiring impromptu simultaneous translation ('no, wrong language!') led to the publication in French and English of a European Charter on Training Standards for family mediation (APMF 1992). These Standards (updated in 2001) set criteria for the content of training (knowledge and skills), qualifications of trainers and trainees, length of training and accreditation. The Standards emphasised that:

---

26   See Art 6c.
27   See paras 1, 5 and 7 of the Recommendation.
28   See para 6 of the Recommendation.

'family mediation training provides an interdisciplinary approach and co-operation between family mediation trainers from different professional backgrounds in training family mediators to high professional standards. It is important to make a clear distinction between mediation awareness training and a full course of training lasting at least 180 hours leading to a recognised qualification to practise as a family mediator. Mediation awareness training provides an introduction to mediation but does not equip participants to undertake the role of mediator.'

Some countries, including France and the UK were meanwhile setting their own national, State-regulated standards for family mediation (see France, above). In the field of civil and commercial mediation, a group of stakeholders from different countries worked together, with the assistance of the European Commission, to develop the European Code of Conduct for Mediators, published on 2 July 2004.

14.4   THE EUROPEAN DIRECTIVE ON MEDIATION (2008/52/EC)

The European Directive on Certain Aspects of Mediation in Civil and Commercial Matters issued by the European Parliament and the Council of the European Union on 21 May 2008[29] recognises that:[30]

'agreements resulting from mediation are more likely to be complied with voluntarily and are more likely to preserve an amicable and sustainable relationship between the parties. These benefits become even more pronounced in situations displaying cross-border elements.'

The provisions of this Directive apply:[31]

'only to mediation in cross-border disputes, but nothing should prevent Member States from applying such provisions also to internal mediation processes.'

Mediation is recognised as first and foremost a voluntary process:[32]

'in the sense that the parties are themselves in charge of the process and may organise it as they wish and terminate it at any time. However, it should be possible under national law for the courts to set time-limits for a mediation process. Moreover, the courts should be able to draw the parties' attention to the possibility of mediation whenever this is appropriate.'

The Directive was to have been made binding on Member States in 2011, but the period for implementation has been extended.

---

[29]   See Chapter 1 at **1.3** above.
[30]   See Preamble, para 6.
[31]   See Preamble, para 8.
[32]   See Preamble, para 13.

14.5 HARMONISATION OF LEGAL SYSTEMS IN EUROPE

The harmonisation of legal systems in Europe is of great importance because disputes involving a cross-border element may be complicated by the simultaneous involvement of two or more jurisdictions following different sets of legal principles and presumptions. To reduce competition between different jurisdictions, significant moves have been made to harmonise civil and family law in Europe. The Regulation known as 'Brussels I' (1968) regulated the Jurisdiction and Enforcement of Judgments in Civil and Commercial Matters. This regulation may be used to enforce orders or judgments in matrimonial maintenance claims, but not matrimonial property rights. The Regulation known as 'Brussels II' (the Regulation on Jurisdiction in Matrimonial Matters and Matters of Parental Responsibility), which entered into force on 1 March 2001, introduced uniform jurisdictional rules throughout the EU (with the exception of Denmark), providing for almost automatic recognition of all matrimonial judgments granted by the courts of Member States. With effect from 1 March 2005, Brussels II Revised (also known as 'Brussels II bis') extended the recognition still further to cover legal proceedings over children, irrespective of whether divorce proceedings are issued. Brussels II Revised aims to ensure the creation of a common judicial area within the European Union and to ensure a stronger consideration of the interests of the child. This Regulation provides uniform recognition of decisions by family courts in EU Member States on parental responsibility for children of married or unmarried parents, including stepchildren. The court in the originating State is entitled to make the final ruling.

In December 2010 the EU Justice Ministers approved a draft EU Council Regulation as to which country's laws should be applied on divorce and legal separation. Although the UK is not a party, the proposed regulation would have an impact for UK citizens in cross-border cases. Couples would be able to agree which law will apply to their divorce and the new rules would control 'forum shopping' by participating Member States. This regulation is likely to come into force in June 2012. The European Convention on Children's Rights and EU legislation thus provide an overarching framework of European law. Global law is of even greater significance, particularly where child protection and child welfare are concerned.

14.6 THE HAGUE CONFERENCE ON PRIVATE INTERNATIONAL LAW

Child protection and child welfare lie at the heart of the 1989 United Nations Convention on the Rights of the Child and the Hague Conventions dealing with child welfare and child protection: the 1980

Hague Child Abduction Convention, the 1996 Hague Child Protection Convention and the Intercountry Adoption Convention 2002. As of November 2009, 194 countries have ratified the United Nations Convention on the Rights of the Child, including every member of the United Nations apart from Somalia and the United States of America. To date, 84 Contracting States have ratified the 1980 Hague Child Abduction Convention and 30 States have ratified the 1996 Child Protection Convention. Recent Hague Conventions encourage the use of mediation and ADR as a means of achieving agreed solutions in cross-border disputes over children. In April 2006 the Permanent Bureau of the Hague Conference on Private International Law was asked by its Members to 'prepare a feasibility study on cross-border mediation in family matters, including the possible development of an instrument on the subject'. After consideration of this study[33] by the Hague Council, the Permanent Bureau was asked to prepare a Guide to Good Practice on Mediation in the context of the 1980 Child Abduction Convention. Work on this Guide commenced in 2009, with assistance from a small advisory group of independent experts in international family mediation. A meeting of this advisory group was held in The Hague in February 2011 to discuss the Draft Guide.

Following the recommendations of the Third Malta Conference in 2009, the Hague Conference also set up a Working Party 'to promote the development of mediation structures to help resolve cross-border disputes concerning custody of or contact with children. The Working Party would comprise experts from a number of States involved in the Malta Process, including both States Parties to the 1980 Child Abduction Convention and non-States Parties. It would also include independent experts'. The 'Malta process' consists of a series of discussions between judges and senior government officials from a number of Hague Convention States and Shariah law-based 'non-Convention' States, with the objective of developing solutions to cross-border disputes over children that are particularly difficult to resolve because relevant international legal frameworks are not applicable. Experts from twelve States were invited to join the Working Party. Six of these States are Contracting States to the Hague Child Abduction Convention, namely Australia, Canada, France, Germany, the United Kingdom and the United States of America. The remaining six are non-Contracting States, namely Egypt, India, Jordan, Malaysia, Morocco and Pakistan.

14.7 JUDICIAL CO-OPERATION IN INTERNATIONAL CROSS-BORDER CASES

The Council of Europe's Recommendation on Family Mediation (1998) recognised the increasing number of disputes involving children in which

---

[33] Vigers *Feasibility Study on Cross-Border Mediation in Family Matters* (Permanent Bureau, Hague Conference on Private International Law, March 2007).

there is a cross-border element. Disputes over child residence and contact are very difficult to resolve when a parent removes a child to another country without the other parent's agreement, especially where there is more than one judicial or competent authority. Religious law and cultural factors bring additional complications to these relocation cases. In Jewish communities, family disputes have historically been referred to the rabbinical courts and are still referred to them, even where there are secular courts with parallel jurisdiction. In cases involving cross-border conflict, if either or both jurisdictions refer the case to the local religious court, problems of jurisdiction and enforcement become even more complex. Apart from South Africa and Morocco, no African countries are contracting members of the Hague Conventions and in the Middle East, only Israel. Nigeria has three different legal systems that operate concurrently: customary law, Shariah law and the common law. Customary law is further complicated by the fact that 350 different ethnic groups in Nigeria all have their own, slightly different versions of customary law. This multiplicity of legal systems makes accession to the Hague Conventions even more difficult. There is need for an International Family Court to provide global jurisdiction and to encourage international co-operation between lawyers and judges dealing with cross-border cases.

In August 2009, judges from twenty-three jurisdictions (Hague and non-Hague members) took part in the second International Family Justice Judicial Conference for Common Law and Commonwealth Jurisdictions. Lord Justice Thorpe, Head of International Family Justice in England and Wales, opened the conference by describing the work of the Office of International Family Law in London and the steep increase in demand for its services since its creation in 2005. In 2007 the Office reported a 333% increase in the number of cases handled. The majority of these cases are at European level but the Office also facilitates judicial co-operation in international cross-border cases involving countries outside Europe. A senior judge from the Supreme Court of Pakistan suggested that international family law offices should be opened in non-Hague countries to assist with facilitating cross-border judicial co-operation in international family law cases. Judges learn from each other in developing more effective systems of family justice. The Family Court of Trinidad and Tobago has introduced procedural reforms drawn from New Zealand that encourage referral to mediation and counselling services. The Conclusions and Recommendations of the 2009 International Family Justice Judicial Conference include the recommendation that mediation in cross-border child abduction cases should be recognised and supported, using mediators trained in this specialist field. A register of trained and competent mediators should be compiled and made readily available to the judiciary in each participating state.[34]

---

34   Baker 'The International Family Law Judicial Conference for Common Law and Commonwealth Jurisdictions' [2009] IFL 250–254.

14.8 INTERNATIONAL CROSS-BORDER FAMILY MEDIATION

In the Feasibility Study prepared for the Hague Conference,[35] cross-border family mediation was defined as 'mediation in family disputes (concerning maintenance, family assets or matters of parent responsibility) where the parties have or are about to have their normal residences in different countries. This working definition includes cross-border mediation in the literal sense of being conducted across borders (for example bi-national mediation involving parties and mediators located in two countries), as well as mediation occurring in one country, but involving parties and/or mediators from two countries. The definition also covers the situation in which two parties resident in the same country enter mediation in order to resolve the problems surrounding the intended relocation by one party with a child to another country'.[36]

In April 2007 the European Academy of Law in Trier, Germany organised a conference to consider the practice and experience of mediation in international cross-border disputes over children. It was recognised that specialised training for mediators should be developed and a central register set up of family mediators with specialist training for international cross-border mediation. The Council of Europe's 7th Conference on Family Law held in Strasbourg in 2009 focused on international family mediation throughout the world. Speakers reported on experience of family mediation in Europe and the Caribbean, Latin America and Ismaili Muslim communities. Judge Winter from Austria (Conference Conclusions 2009) welcomed this worldwide, rather than Eurocentric focus. Child welfare is as fundamental in Shariah Law as it is in other jurisdictions. In line with 1400 years of Islamic tradition, the 49th Imam, Aga Khan IV, established National and International Conciliation and Arbitration Boards to encourage amicable resolution of conflicts through impartial conciliation, mediation and arbitration. Some 800 Ismaili mediators in over 15 countries of Asia, Africa, Europe, North America and the Middle East have been trained in modern techniques of mediation both in the family and commercial fields. In Portugal, Ismaili trainers run a training programme on mediation for the Ministry of Justice, designed for professionals in the family justice field. In Syria in 2006, seven High Court judges from outside the Ismaili community participated in a mediation training programme conducted in Salamieh. In India in the same year, three High Court judges attended the training programme, and one, a female judge, participated as a trainer.[37] These

---

[35] See **14.6** above.

[36] Vigers *Feasibility Study on Cross-Border Mediation in Family Matters* (Permanent Bureau, Hague Conference on Private International Law, March 2007), 5.1.

[37] Keshavjee 'Family mediation in Ismaili Muslim communities throughout the world' *Paper given at the Council of Europe's 7th European Conference on Family Law – International Family Mediation* (Strasbourg, March 2009).

training programmes report unanimous agreement on the need to harmonise systems for international family mediation, to specify qualifications and agree equivalences, and to create a central register to assist individuals and authorities to identify and contact qualified family mediators with specialist training for international cross-border mediation.

However, opportunities for referral to mediation are often missed for a number of reasons:

(i)   lack of awareness of mediation;

(ii)   lack of a central register to facilitate access to suitably qualified mediators in different countries;

(iii) costs of mediation – fees, travel, interpreters if needed;

(iv)   disparities in laws regulating mediation practice, such as limits of confidentiality;

(v)   fears that mediation will cause delay (although *reunite*, the leading British agency in this field, found that mediation does not generally delay the final hearing under the Hague Convention, Pilot Project Report, October 2006);

(vi)   the shortage of mediation models adaptable to non-European as well as European family disputes.

14.9   SPECIALIST SERVICES PROVIDING INTERNATIONAL FAMILY MEDIATION IN CROSS-BORDER CASES

reunite, the leading UK charity specialising in international parental child abduction, was formed in 1986 and registered as a charity in 1990. *reunite* provides advice, information and support to parents, family members and guardians who have had a child abducted or who fear being abducted; advice to parents who may have abducted their children; and advice on international contact issues. The primary focus is the best interests of the child, with the aim of facilitating the child's return with minimum disturbance and trauma. A research study based on feedback from parents in 30 cases found that 86% were either highly satisfied or satisfied with the outcome of mediation, while 95% said they would recommend mediation to others. Key findings showed that these cases of international parental child abduction should always be co-mediated in a specially designed model of mediation practice. From the parents' perspective, it was not necessary to have mediators of mixed gender. The key requirements were the expertise, professionalism and impartiality of the mediators. The study found that although relocation cases focused on issues of residence and contact, children who were removed to a different country did not only lose their relationship with the left-behind parent. Wider family relationships were often lost as well. Many children experienced profound dislocation at every level. *reunite* is undertaking further research on factors that significantly affect the impact of abduction on the child, such as the length of the abduction period, and on the legal complexities when one of the countries concerned is a Muslim State. *reunite* is working in co-operation with over 40 Muslim States.[38]

In 1998 the Ministers of Justice in France and Germany set up a Franco-German Parliamentary Mediation Commission leading to a bi-national mediation scheme that ran from February 2003 until 1 March 2006. In this pilot scheme, a French mediator co-mediated with a German mediator in cross-border disputes over children.[39] In France, a court dealing with a Hague Convention case formerly referred parents to the French agency MAMIF (Mission d'aide à la médiation internationale pour les familles). MAMIF, created in 2001 within the French Ministry of Justice, intervened in international child abduction and contact disputes either under the Hague Convention or outside its scope. MAMIF undertook single State mediations in Convention cases and also bi-national mediations involving a MAMIF mediator and a mediator from the other State.[40] Although MAMIF has closed, the Groupement Européen des Magistrats pour la Médiation (GEMME) is pursuing further initiatives in this field.

As well as *reunite* and the International Family Law Group in the UK, the Dutch Centre for International Child Abduction and MiKK in Berlin (Mediation bei internationalen Kindschaftskonflikten), there is a partnership of French, Italian and Swiss agencies.[41] Paul and Walker report[42] that conflict is high in cross-border cases and many parents feel helpless and despairing. The left-behind parent fears losing contact with the child even if a contact order is made, while abducting parents fear they will not receive fair treatment in the country of abduction, because they are often not citizens of that country. Young children are likely to forget the language of the left-behind parent or never to have learnt it: communication as well as contact then becomes hard or impossible to sustain. International cross-border mediation needs to be readily available, quickly accessible and used more widely. If both parents are willing and able to come to a meeting or series of meetings, mediation

---

[38] Carter 'Das englische *reunite*-Projekt (2009)' in Paul and Kiesewetter (eds) *Mediation bei internationalen Kinderschaftskonflikten* (Verlag Beck), 135–145.

[39] Carl, Copin and Ripke 'Le projet pilote franco-allemand de médiation familiale professionnelle, un modèle de collaboration internationale dans le cadre de conflits familiaux' in *Kind-Prax Special* 2004, pp 25–28.

[40] D Ganancia *La Médiation Familiale Internationale* (Ed Eres, 2007).

[41] See www.amorifeinternational.com.

[42] Paul and Walker 'Family Mediation in International Child Custody Conflicts' (2008) 22(1) *American Journal of Family Law* 42–45.

offers a quickly organised and child-centred process, whereas legal processes can take months or years, escalating the conflict and risking prolonged trauma and harm for the child. In cases where an abducting parent is unable to return with the child and the left-behind parent is unable to care for the child, a child returned by court order to the country of habitual residence may be removed from *both* parents and placed in a succession of foster-homes until a final court order is made.[43] The psychological harm to a small child, and indeed to older children, of being separated from both parents for months, even years, is so serious that 'institutionalised child abuse' may not be too strong a term. In considering parents' rights to be granted child custody, residence or contact, the rights and immediate needs of the child should be prioritised. It should be made clear to parents, however, that their willingness or unwillingness to accept mediation will not influence the court's decision regarding the child.[44]

14.10   QUESTIONS TO CONSIDER IN RELATION TO CROSS-BORDER DISPUTES OVER CHILDREN

(1)   Are any or all of the countries concerned partners under The Hague Conventions 1980 or 1996?

(2)   Are both or all countries EU Member States (apart from Denmark)? If so, Regulation Brussels II Revised applies and takes precedence over the Hague Conventions.

(3)   What is the stage of legal proceedings, if any (see below, Stages for Referral to Mediation)?

(4)   Are qualified cross-border family mediators available in, or able to travel to, the country or region concerned? Who would appoint the mediators?

(5)   If mediation is appropriate, which model/s would be appropriate or possible?

(6)   Is there a time limit for mediation under International Conventions and/or set by the court?

(7)   Who would contact the parents to offer mediation and assess suitability?

(8)   Would the mediation be child-focused or child-inclusive?

---

[43]   Bucher 'The New Swiss Federal Act on International Child Abduction' (2008) *Journal of Private International Law* 139–165.

[44]   Vigers *Note on the development of mediation, conciliation and similar means to facilitate agreed solutions* (Permanent Bureau, Hague Conference on Private International Law, October 2006).

(9)   Who would pay for the mediation?

(10) Would the outcome of the mediation be reportable (to whom)?

14.11   DIFFERENT MODELS FOR INTERNATIONAL FAMILY MEDIATION

Various models have been developed for cross-border family mediation, including bi-national mediation, interdisciplinary co-mediation, direct and indirect mediation. The model needs to be adapted for different cultures and circumstances and may consist of:

- A single mediator who mediates with both parents in person (direct, face-to-face mediation).

- Co-mediators (interdisciplinary, gender-balanced, bi-national?) who mediate with both parents together in the same venue, or who use video/teleconferencing facilities for simultaneous meetings with parents in two different States (direct/distance mediation).

- Mediation in which the parents do not meet each other, but the mediator or mediators meet with each parent separately and the mediators liaise with each other. This can take place across two separate States with one mediator and one parent in each State, or in the same State with mediation taking place at different times or at the same time, in different rooms (indirect or shuttle mediation). For further discussion of mediation online, using Skype and video conferencing, see **14.14** below.

- Child-inclusive mediation where appropriate, using any of the above models.

- Co-mediation with the participation of members of the extended family and religious/community leaders, depending on the cultural and religious context.

reunite found in their pilot study that:[45]

> 'allegations of domestic violence do not preclude entering the mediation process and do not affect the ability to reach a Memorandum of Understanding. However, it is important that a risk assessment is undertaken on each case and appropriate measures introduced to ensure that parents feel safe during the mediation process.'

---

[45]   *reunite* 2006, Key Findings.

reunite has also found that where the use of an interpreter is necessary it does not hinder the mediation process and does not affect the ability to reach a Memorandum of Understanding within the allocated time-frame.

MiKK's bi-national cross-border mediation projects are based on the following model:[46]

(1) A gender-balanced team of co-mediators, so that gender issues are understood and both parents feel heard.

(2) Cross-cultural, so that each parent feels able to relate to and be understood by a mediator from the same nationality or culture.

(3) Bilingual mediators, so that each parent can speak freely in their first language.

(4) Interdisciplinary backgrounds, one mediator trained and experienced in a psychosocial discipline while the other mediator must be a lawyer, both with specialist knowledge of international family law and international conventions.

(5) The parents' lawyers need to be readily accessible and involved, although not taking part directly, to advise their clients and to enable agreements to be ratified in legally binding terms in the country with jurisdiction.

14.12   REFERRAL TO CROSS-BORDER MEDIATION

To increase the use of mediation in cross-border cases, referral should be encouraged as early as possible, as well as being considered at later stages.

14.12.1   Stage 1

Before a parent removes a child to another country, to help parents reach agreements that avoid parental child abduction and court proceedings.

Example

A separated couple asked for mediation urgently, six weeks before the wife was due to return to Australia with the couple's two children. Both parents were Australian and had been living in England for several years. The mother was acutely aware of the children's attachment to their father, but felt her own psychological survival was also critical and that she needed her family's support. Her husband had left a few months previously to live with a new partner. Three mediation meetings took place during the six weeks before

---

[46]   Kiesewetter, Paul and Dobiejewska 'Breslauer Erklärung zur bi-nationalen Kindschaftsmediation' (2008) 55(8) FamRZ 753.

the wife left for Australia. Financial information was gathered and, in conjunction with legal advice to each parent interim agreements were reached on child support payments and the ownership and occupation of two jointly owned properties, one in England and one in Australia. Much discussion took place about how to help the children stay in contact with their father. The father bought a computer for his wife to take back to Australia. He and the older child keep in touch by e-mail and with both children by phone, to bridge the long gaps between holiday visits.

14.12.2   Stage 2

Where application has been made for leave to remove a child from the jurisdiction, or pending a court hearing of an application for return of an abducted child.

14.12.3   Stage 3

Where a defence is raised against an order to return a child, on the grounds that return would be harmful to the child, mediation can facilitate communication over the best interests of the child, explore options and look for an agreed outcome.

14.12.4   Stage 4

Following the return of an abducted child under a court order, to facilitate agreements over the child's residence and contact arrangements and also, after the return of the child has been ordered, to help make arrangements for the child's return and arrangements for contact following the return.

14.13   STRUCTURING CROSS-BORDER MEDIATION

PRE-MEDIATION	TASKS AND ACTIONS
Establish the time-limits that apply	Determine whether mediation can be undertaken within these time-limits
Define the framework, principles and network	Define framework and principles, including rules on confidentiality. Appoint mediators? Approach key persons
Screen for suitability of mediation	Offer mediation (direct or indirect), screen for safety and willingness, define process and issues

MEDIATION	TASKS AND ACTIONS
Engage parties in mediation	Confirm informed acceptance of mediation. Consider language needs, clarity of communication, build rapport, define issues and priorities, encourage motivation to find solutions
Gather fuller information	Understand situation, cultural and legal context, family structure, parenting (past and present), issues and concerns, stage of separation, crisis/conflict, fears and aims. Make connections between parents' needs and concerns, culture and ethnic values, relevant legislation
Clarify and consider the child's well-being and needs, including direct consultation with the child if appropriate	Seek further details of child, age and stage of development, the child's experience and reactions, each parent's perceptions of child and the child's present and future needs, the child's relationships, attachments and culture/s
Consider options	Explore possibilities, concerns, common ground, reality-test, preferred options, proposals that take account of the child's wishes, needs and feelings
Liaise with legal advisors	Plan next steps, time-scales, consulting, ways of reaching an enforceable agreement

CONCLUDING MEDIATION	TASKS AND ACTIONS
Reach agreement in conjunction with legal advice	Seek provisional agreement, prepare confidential written summary for parties and lawyers
	Clarify with legal advisors and parties whether a fully concluded agreement has been reached that is to be submitted to the court in a draft consent order

14.14   ENFORCEABILITY OF MEDIATED AGREEMENTS

For mediated agreements to be enforceable in both, or all, the States involved, the contents of a mediated agreement need to be drafted by the parties' legal advisors in a consent order. Once the court has made the consent order, it can be enforced as any other court order.

'Enforceability is a key concern with regard to any decisions made under the Hague Convention and problems have developed in Convention cases where orders made in one State have not been enforced in the other State. For mediation to have a positive effect on Hague Convention applications it is vital that agreements reached are capable of being enforced in both States.'[47]

14.15 TRAINING FOR INTERNATIONAL FAMILY MEDIATION

Rules and procedures are not sufficient on their own. Training for cross-border mediation needs to equip mediators with the necessary combinations of savoir (knowledge), savoir-faire (know-how – skills in communication, mediation and international co-operation), and savoir-être (self-awareness, ethical standards, respect for cultural diversity, the ability to relate to others). A Code of Conduct is needed for international family mediation, covering confidentiality, the range of issues that can be mediated and the legal enforceability of mediated agreements. Training needs to be interactive and experiential, using simulated mediation role-plays that call for legal, psychological and other relevant knowledge and mediation skills applicable to particular situations. For admission to an international register of cross-border mediators, the mediator should have a specified level of experience and have completed a recognised course of training providing accreditation and a system of quality assurance. There should also be requirements for continuing professional development with case analysis or supervision.

MiKK trains mediators in international cross-border mediation and runs bi-national mediation projects (currently Germany/France, Germany/England, Germany/Poland, Germany/United States and Germany/Spain). A French/Italian training programme leading to the Certificat d'Accréditation Européen en Médiation Familiale Internationale (CAE-MFI) is a 180-programme organised during 2011–2012 in different locations in France, Italy and Switzerland and including some distance learning. Child Focus, a Belgian NGO dealing with international child abduction, is leading an EU-funded European project on Training in International Mediation (TIM) in partnership with the Katholieke Universiteit Leuven, MiKK in Berlin and the International Child Abduction Centre (Centrum IKO) in the Netherlands. This project is focusing on mediation in international child abduction cases (usually parental child abduction) and cross-border conflicts involving bi-national couples or couples from the same country living abroad. The objectives are:

(1) To develop and pilot training in international family mediation for mediators and trainers from each EU Member State.

---

[47] Vigers *Feasibility Study on Cross-Border Mediation in Family Matters* (Permanent Bureau, Hague Conference on Private International Law, March 2007), Annex 1, 3.5.

(2)   To create a network of international family mediators in Europe.

The first pilot training is taking place in Brussels in 2011 and the first training for trainers is being organised for 2012. Although the focus is on creating a EU network, many parental child abduction cases involve a child being taken from a EU country to a country outside the EU. The training team includes a Muslim trainer linked to a network of Muslim mediators in India, Pakistan and Middle East countries, and a Spanish trainer linked to networks in the Iberian peninsular and South America.

The structures and histories of families caught up in international, cross-border and cross-cultural disputes over children can be extraordinarily complex. The ecogram below was designed by International Social Service (ISS) Berlin for their 3-day training programme for ISS lawyers and psychologists from eastern European countries in a 'mediation-oriented approach' in cross-border cases. Parents, lawyers and courts frequently seek help from ISS branches and their contacts in different countries for assistance in resolving conflicts in family matters.

Participants in ISS Berlin's 3-day training programme in December 2007 welcomed the suggestion to create an ecogram that could convey a great deal of information in an easily absorbed diagram.[48] They expressed enthusiasm that use of the ecogram by ISS branches would greatly facilitate liaison between professionals in different countries who might have little or no knowledge of each other's languages. They also commented that it would be far quicker for professionals in different countries working on the same cross-border case to be able to email the ecogram to each other, with each of them adding supplementary information to it, rather than sending lengthy case details in different languages.

There is clearly a considerable amount of work involved in gathering and collating all the information to create the kind of ecogram that is needed in relation to international cross-border family mediation. After constructing a picture of the family context and the child's position in this context, the next step is to create a detailed focus on the child who is at the centre of the cross-border dispute. The diagram below is an example of a 'focus on the child' that places the child in the centre, as the child needs to be, with key information concerning the particular child. The child's parents, siblings, other key family members and the child's 'support system' are then displayed around the child, to help consider the child's principal attachments and needs and ways of working out a possible agreement that would meet the child's needs and maintain the child's attachments as well as possible.

---

[48]   Parkinson *A mediation-oriented approach in cross-border cases* (2007, unpublished paper).

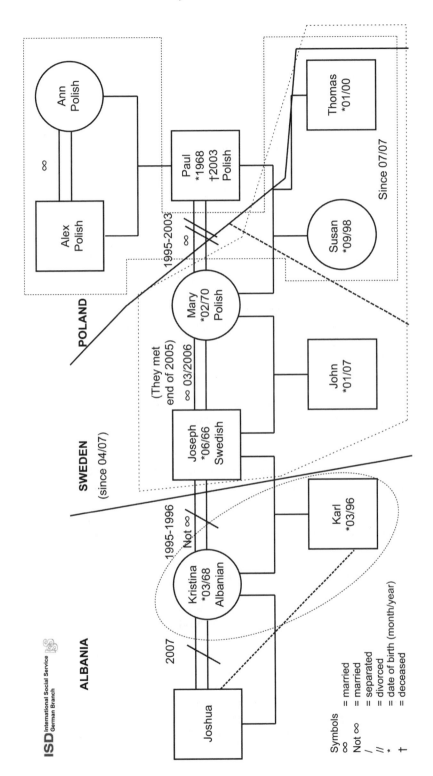

ISD International Social Service
German Branch

ALBANIA

SWEDEN
(since 04/07)

POLAND

Ann
Polish

∞

Alex
Polish

Paul
*1968
†2003
Polish

1995-2003

∞

Thomas
*01/00

Since 07/07

Susan
*09/98

Mary
*02/70
Polish

(They met
end of 2005)

∞ 03/2006

John
*01/07

Joseph
*06/66
Swedish

1995-1996

Not ∞

Karl
*03/96

Kristina
*03/68
Albanian

2007

Joshua

Symbols
∞   = married
Not ∞   = married
/   = separated
//   = divorced
*   = date of birth (month/year)
†   = deceased

Focus on the Child

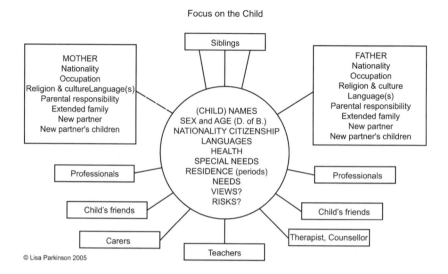

© Lisa Parkinson 2005

To obtain a driving licence, knowledge of the law and the rules of the road are not sufficient. Learner drivers have to take a Driving Test with a qualified instructor to demonstrate competence in driving a car, controlling it in traffic and applying the brakes! An academic qualification in mediation based on a degree or diploma does not ensure competence. International family mediators need to know the rules of the road, such as which driver takes precedence in what circumstances. Learning to ride a motorbike is probably a better analogy than driving a car, because a motorcyclist needs flexibility and good balance, rather than a rigidly erect posture. To negotiate a sharp bend, a motorcyclist needs to lean into the bend. Mediators need similar flexibility to lean in different directions without losing balance or impartiality. Just as motorcyclists take a test to gain a licence, mediators should be required to have professional qualifications, recognised training and evidence of competence for admission to a register of international family mediators.

14.16   MEDIATION ONLINE

Traditionally, mediation involves face-to-face meetings, but geographical distance and travel costs may prohibit face-to-face mediation in international cross-border cases. Online communications can be augmented by the use of VOIP (Voice over internet protocol) services such as Skype that enable telephone conversations over the internet at no additional cost, irrespective of distance. Important life events and negotiations between family members living a long way apart (or even nearby) can be 'buttressed and enhanced by electronic communication'.[49] Mediators with facilities for videoconferencing, Skype and a webcam can offer distance mediation. These facilities enable parents who live a long way apart to communicate without the time and cost of travel. Parents

---

[49]   Melamed 'The Internet and Mediation' (2009) *Mediate.com Weekly* No 298.

can see each other on screen, hear each other's voice and explore options directly with each other. This facility is of obvious value in cross-border cases, enabling parents and mediators in different countries to mediate on screen, if meeting face-to-face is impracticable. Important relationships can be sustained through electronic communications such as emails, Facebook, Twitter and so on. For most young people and many separated parents, texting has become the main means of communication, but texting can bring a fresh set of problems. Text messages and public entries on Facebook can cause misunderstandings and more arguments. However, if communications through mediation are to be relevant to modern families, 'we need to meet people where they are and that is online'.[50]

Family members have access to a range of communication options that mediators need to understand and utilise:[51]

> 'There is a fascinating, ever-evolving relationship between online communication and experience and face-to-face communication and experience. Well-utilized, each wonderfully enhances the other ... The online world is an extension of the physical world and offers new capacities that have not previously existed.'

Melamed goes on to say (personal communication) that family and divorce mediation is evolving to be a 'choreography of communication' in which mediators and other professionals can help participants to identify valuable online information, as well as making progress toward agreement in their own time.

> 'Participants are able to take on more active drafting roles in terms of what will work for them and their family, often by "asynchronous", thoughtful and edited comments, rather than impulsive, often destructive real time declarations. A mediator may act as a buffer and diplomat in supporting these communications. Mediators of the future will be wise to focus on utilizing communication modalities strategically and on tailoring this use to the particular needs and preferences of individual participants.'

14.17   FUTURE DIRECTIONS

In the context of national and international family justice systems, mediators mediate between the private world of families and the public world of institutions. Private decisions and arrangements worked out in mediation need to be congruent with the law. To gain juridical effect, mediated settlements need to be drawn up in unambiguous legal terms and formalised in legally binding orders approved by a judge. Mediators seek to empower people to reach their own decisions in their own way. They have to be careful not to become agents of public policy

---

[50]   Ibid.
[51]   Melamed 'The Internet and Mediation' (2009) *Mediate.com Weekly* No 298.

preoccupied with cutting expenditure on the legal system by diverting cases from the courts to mediation, with quick agreements seen as the hallmark of success. Public funding for family mediation is available in England and Wales on a scale unmatched in most other countries, but legal aid limits impose a tight constraint on the amount of time mediators can offer. Mediators walk a tightrope stretched between individual needs and limitations imposed by the state. Tensions about the proper role of mediation also exist at a higher level. The current Lord Chancellor wishes to move towards:[52]

> 'a simpler justice system, one which is more responsive to public needs, which allows people to resolve their issues out of court, using simpler, more informal remedies where they are appropriate, and which encourages more efficient resolution of contested cases.'

On the other hand, Lord Neuberger, Master of the Rolls, warned in a speech in November 2010 that:

> 'if we expand mediation beyond its proper limits as a complement to justice, we run the risk of depriving persons of their right to equal and impartial treatment under the law ... Mediation can never be a substitute for justice.'

Mediation can never be a substitute for adjudication, but 'justice' in family proceedings may not be experienced as 'just' by the parties concerned, either for themselves or for their children.[53] Mediation, collaborative law and other forms of ADR are part of a new system of family justice that more families may find more just, because of the increased scope it offers them to reach their own decisions.

Counting settlement rates cannot be the sole measure of mediation's effectiveness. There is value in facilitating dialogue that increases mutual understanding, even if no concrete agreement results. The independence of the mediation process would be compromised if the State took it over as a means of restricting access to the courts. Family mediators' primary responsibility is towards those who come to mediation. Mediators are not agents of any moral crusade or political agenda and the personal values of those who come to mediation do not always sit comfortably with state policy or the values of the ruling majority. The process of mediation is a balancing-act. Mediators need good balance to stay on their tightrope, managing the power imbalances and tensions that threaten mediation both internally and externally. A bearable 'lightness of being' helps to resist the downward drag of unremitting disputes. Maintaining buoyancy needs good support and mediators need to nurture each other, as well as other people. Dynamic energy, balance and 'lightness of being' are precious qualities. When they are combined, fragile threads of dialogue can carry a weight of feeling without breaking down. Mediators need to

---

[52]   Green Paper on the Reform of Legal Aid (2010), 1.9.
[53]   See Chapter 13 above.

work within a supportive structure that encourages flexible movement, co-operation and trust. We need practical common sense infused with imagination, holding a balance between the craft of mediation and its creativity. We need to find ways of working together across frontiers – locally, professionally and globally – to encourage peaceful ways of resolving conflicts. The task of the next generation[54] is 'to push towards the widening of the circle of recognition' so that the divisions that cause conflicts – in families, ethnic groups, gender, culture, religion, nations, and between West and East – can be transcended by the common needs and values of our shared humanity. Utopia is a long way off, but if we want to change the world, as well as ourselves, conflict management skills should form part of the core curriculum in all schools and taught to children of all ages, using the experiential methods that children and young people enjoy. In helping children to acquire second order learning so that they can disagree and listen to each other without declaring all-out war, maybe we adults could learn more of it ourselves as well – the innocent teaching the experienced – 'the child as father of the man.' Ideas about 'innocence and experience' in the practice of mediation were explored at an international meeting in Stafford in October 2010 during the Third Weekend of Mediation and the Arts. These 'fragile threads of dialogue' between committed practitioners may help to take forward the evolutionary development of family mediation in the continuing exploration of 'oneness' in our common humanity.

---

[54] Ramsbotham, Woodhouse and Miall *Contemporary Conflict Resolution* (Polity Press, 2nd edn, 2005), p 331.

APPENDICES

APPENDIX A

FAMILY MEDIATION COUNCIL
CODE OF PRACTICE

THE FAMILY MEDIATION COUNCIL
Code of Practice for Family Mediators
Agreed by the Member Organisations

1. DEFINITIONS

1.1   This Code of Practice applies to all family mediation conducted or offered by mediators who are members of the Member Organisations of the Family Mediation Council.

1.2   Family mediation is a process in which those involved in family breakdown, whether or not they are a couple or other family members, appoint an impartial third person to assist them to communicate better with one another and reach their own agreed and informed decisions concerning some, or all, of the issues relating to separation, divorce, children, finance or property by negotiation.

1.3   This Code applies whether or not there are or have been legal proceedings between the participants and whether or not any, or all of them, are legally represented.

1.4   In this Code, 'mediation' means the family mediation to which this Code applies. 'Mediator' means any person offering such mediation. 'Participant' means any family member taking part in mediation.

2. AIMS AND OBJECTIVES

2.1   Mediation aims to assist participants to reach the decisions they consider appropriate to their own particular circumstances.

2.2   Mediation also aims to assist participants to communicate with one another now and in the future and to reduce the scope or intensity of dispute and conflict within the family.

2.3   Where a marriage or relationship has irretrievably broken down, mediation has regard to the principles that the marriage or relationship should be brought to an end in a way that:

   •   minimises distress to the participants and to any children;

   •   promotes as good a relationship between the participants and any children as is possible;

   •   removes or diminishes any risk of abuse to any of the participants or children from the other participants; and

   •   avoids any unnecessary cost to participants.

3. QUALIFICATIONS AND TRAINING

3.1 Mediators must have successfully completed such training as is approved by a Member Organisation and accredited by the Council to qualify them to mediate upon those matters upon which they offer mediation.

3.2 Mediators must be a member of a Member Organisation and must therefore have successfully demonstrated personal aptitude for mediation and competence to mediate.

3.3 Mediators must satisfy their Member Organisation that they have made satisfactory arrangements for regular professional practice consultancy with a professional practice consultant who is a member of and approved for the purpose by a Member Organisation.

3.4 Mediators must agree to maintain and improve their skills through continuing professional development courses approved by a Member Organisation and/or the Council.

3.5 Mediators may only undertake direct consultation with children when they have successfully completed specific training approved by their Member Organisation and/or the Council and have received specific clearance from the Criminal Records Bureau.

3.6 Mediators undertaking publicly funded mediation must have been assessed as competent to do so by a recognised assessment scheme.

3.7 Mediators must not mediate upon any case unless they are covered by adequate professional indemnity insurance.

3.8 Mediators must abide by the complaints and disciplinary procedures laid down by the Member Organisation of which they are a member.

4. SCOPE OF MEDIATION

4.1 Mediation may cover any or all of the following matters:

4.1.1 options for maintaining or ending the marital or other relationship between the adult participants and the consequences of doing so;

4.1.2 arrangements for dependant children: with whom they are to live; what contact they are to have with each parent and other family members; any other aspect of parental responsibility such as, but not exhaustively, schooling, holidays, religious education;

4.1.3 the future of the family home and any other property or assets, including pensions, belonging to the adult participants; issues of child maintenance and spousal maintenance; issues relating to debts;

4.1.4   how adjustments to these arrangements are to be decided upon in the future.

4.2   Participants and mediators may agree that mediation will cover any other matters which it would be helpful to resolve in connection with relationship breakdown between the participants and which the mediators consider suitable for mediation.

5.   GENERAL PRINCIPLES

5.1   **Impartiality and Conflicts of Interest**

5.1.1   It is the duty of the mediator at all times to ensure that he or she acts with impartiality and that that impartiality is not compromised at any time by any conflict of interest, actual or capable of being perceived as such.

5.1.2   Mediators must not have any personal interest in the outcome of the mediation.

5.1.3   Mediators must not mediate in any case in which they have acquired or may acquire relevant information in any private or other professional capacity.

5.1.4   Mediators must not act or continue to act if they or a member of their firm has acted for any of the parties in issues not relating to the mediation.

5.1.5.   Mediators must not accept referrals from any professional practice with whom they are employed, in partnership or contracted, on a full or part-time basis and which is involved in advising one of the participants on matters which relate or are capable of relating to the mediation, even though the practices are separate legal entities.

5.1.6   Mediators must not refer a participant for advice or for any other professional service to a professional practice with whom they are employed, in partnership or contracted, on a full or part-time basis on matters which relate or are capable of relating to the mediation even though the practices are separate legal entities.

5.1.7   Mediation must be conducted as an independent professional activity and must be distinguished from any other professional role in which the mediator may practice.

5.2   **Voluntary Participation**

Participation in mediation is voluntary at all times and participants and the mediator are always free to withdraw. Where mediators consider that a participant is unable or unwilling to take part in the process freely and fully, they must raise the issue and possibly suspend or terminate the mediation.

5.3   **Neutrality**

Mediators must remain neutral as to the outcome of a mediation at all times. Mediators must not seek to impose their preferred outcome on the participants or to influence them to adopt it, whether by attempting to predict the outcome of court proceedings or otherwise. However, if the participants consent, they may inform them that they consider that the resolutions they are considering might fall outside the parameters which a court might approve or order. They may inform participants of possible courses of action, their legal or other implications, and assist them to explore these, but must make it clear that they are not giving advice.

5.4   **Impartiality**

5.4.1   Mediators must at all times remain impartial as between the participants and conduct the mediation process in a fair and even-handed way.

5.4.2   Mediators must seek to prevent manipulative, threatening or intimidating behaviour by any participant. They must conduct the process in such a way as to redress, as far as possible, any imbalance of power between the participants. If such behaviour or any other imbalance seems likely to render the mediation unfair or ineffective, mediators must take appropriate steps to seek to prevent this including terminating the mediation if necessary.

5.5   **Confidentiality**

5.5.1   Subject to paragraphs 5.5.3, 5.5.4 and 5.5.5 below mediators must not disclose any information about, or obtained in the course of, a mediation to anyone, including a court welfare officer or a court, without the express consent of each participant, an order of the court or where the law imposes an overriding obligation of disclosure on mediators.

5.5.2   Mediators must not discuss the mediation or correspond with any participant's legal advisor without the express consent of each participant. Nothing must be said or written to the legal advisor of one party regarding the content of the discussions in mediation which is not also said or written to the legal advisor(s) of the other.

5.5.3.   Where it appears necessary so that a specific allegation that a child has suffered significant harm may be properly investigated or where mediators suspect that a child is suffering or is likely to suffer significant harm, mediators must ensure that the relevant Social Services department is notified.

5.5.4   Mediators may notify the appropriate agency if they consider that other public policy considerations prevail, such as an adult suffering or likely to suffer significant harm.

5.5.5   Where mediators suspect that they may be required to make disclosure to the appropriate government authority under the Proceeds of Crime Act 2002 and/or relevant money laundering regulations, they must stop the mediation immediately without informing the clients of the reason.

5.6   **Privilege and Legal Proceedings**

5.6.1   Subject to paragraph 5.6.2 below, all discussions and negotiations in mediation must be conducted on a legally privileged basis. Before the mediation commences the participants must agree in writing that discussions and negotiations in mediation are not to be referred to in any legal proceedings, and that mediators cannot be required to give evidence or produce any notes or records made in the course of the mediation, unless all participants agree to waive the privilege or the law imposes upon mediators an overriding obligation of disclosure upon the mediator.

5.6.2   Participants must agree that all factual information material to financial issues must be provided on an open basis, so that it can be referred to in legal proceedings.

5.6.3   All information or correspondence provided by either participant should be shared openly and not withheld, except any address or telephone number or as the participants may agree otherwise.

5.6.4   Privilege will not apply in relation to communications indicating that a child or other person is suffering or likely to suffer significant harm, or where other public policy considerations prevail.

5.7   **Welfare of children**

5.7.1   At all times mediators must have special regard to the welfare of any children of the family. They should encourage participants to focus on the needs and interests of the children as well as on their own.

5.7.2   Mediators must encourage participants to consider the children's wishes and feelings. If appropriate they may discuss with them whether and to what extent it is proper to consult the children directly in order to ascertain their wishes and feelings.

5.7.3   Where mediators and both participants agree that it is appropriate to consult any children directly, the consent of the children must first be obtained. Mediators consulting directly with any children must have been specifically trained to do so and have received specific enhanced clearance from the Criminal Records Bureau. Such mediators must provide appropriate facilities for direct consultation.

5.7.4   Where qualified mediators undertake direct consultation with any child, they must offer that child confidentiality as to any disclosure that that child may make to them. This must be explained to the participants before they agree to the direct consultation. Confidentiality in direct consultation with children must always be exercised subject to paragraphs 5.5.3, 5.5.4, 5.5.5, and 5.6.4 above.

5.7.5   Where mediators suspect that any child is suffering or likely to suffer significant harm, they must advise the participants to seek help from the appropriate agency. Mediators must also advise the participants that, in any event, they are obliged to report the matter to the appropriate agency in accordance with paragraph 5.5.3.

5.7.6   Where mediators consider that the participants are or are proposing to act in a manner likely to be seriously detrimental to the welfare of any child of the family or family member, they may withdraw from the mediation. The reason for doing this must be outlined in any further communication.

5.8   **Abuse and power imbalances within the family**

5.8.1   Mediators must be alert to the likelihood of power imbalances existing between the participants.

5.8.2   In all cases, mediators must seek to ensure that participants take part in the mediation willingly and without fear of violence or harm. They must seek to discover through a screening procedure whether or not there is fear of abuse or any other harm and whether or not it is alleged that any participant has been or is likely to be abusive towards another. Where abuse is alleged or suspected mediators must discuss whether a participant wishes to take part in mediation, and information about available support services should be provided.

5.8.3   Where mediation does take place, mediators must uphold throughout the principles of voluntary participation, fairness and safety and must conduct the process in accordance with this section. In addition, steps must be taken to ensure the safety of all participants on arrival and departure.

5.8.4   Mediators must seek to prevent manipulative, threatening or intimidating behaviour by either participant during the mediation.

6.   CONDUCT OF THE MEDIATION

6.1   All assessments for suitability for mediation must be conducted at meetings on a face-to-face basis. Assessment meetings can be conducted jointly or separately depending on client preference, but must include an individual element with each participant to allow mediators to undertake domestic abuse screening.

6.2   Mediators must manage the mediation process. They should consult the participants on management decisions such as the ordering of issues and the agenda for each mediation session but must not relinquish control of the process to the participants.

6.3   Throughout the mediation mediators must keep the possibility of reconciliation of the participants under review.

6.4   Participants must be clearly advised at the outset of the nature and purpose of mediation and how it differs from other services such as marriage or relationship counselling, therapy or legal representation.

6.5   Participants must be informed of all the general principles set out in Section 5 above, including the nature and limits of the principles of confidentiality and privilege and mediators' special concern for the welfare of any children of the family.

6.6   Participants must be informed of the extent of any disclosure which will be required in cases relating to their property and finances.

6.7   Each participant must be supplied with written information covering the main points in this Code and given the opportunity to ask questions about it.

6.8   Mediators must ensure that the participants agree the terms and conditions regulating the mediation before dealing with the substantive issues. This must be in the form of a written agreement which reflects the main principles of this Code. The agreement must also set out the client fees.

6.9   Participants must be requested to notify any legal advisors acting for them of the appointment of a mediator.

6.10   Where during a privately funded mediation, mediators become aware that one or more of the participants may qualify for public funding, they must inform the client of this and, if they do not undertake publicly funded work, of the potential services of a mediation practice with an LSC contract.

6.11   Mediators must assist participants to define the issues, identify areas of agreement, explore the options and seek to reach agreement upon them.

6.12   Mediators must seek to ensure that participants reach their decision upon sufficient information and knowledge. They must inform participants of the need to give full and frank disclosure of all material relevant to the issues being mediated and assist them where necessary in identifying the relevant information and supporting documentation.

6.13   Mediators must ensure each participant is given the opportunity to make enquiries about information disclosed by any other participant and to seek further information and documentation when required. They must promote the participants' equal understanding of such information before any final agreement is reached.

6.14   Mediators must make it clear that they do not themselves make further enquiries to verify the information provided by any participant, that each participant may seek independent legal advice as to the adequacy of the information disclosed before reaching a decision; that in any court proceedings a sworn affidavit, written statement or oral evidence may be required and that authoritative calculations of liability under the Child Support Act 1991 can only be made by the Child Support Agency or may replacement organisation established under the Child Maintenance and Other Payments Act 2008.

6.15   Mediators must inform participants of the advantages of seeking independent legal or other appropriate advice whenever this appears desirable during the course of the mediation. They must advise participants that it is in their own interests to seek independent legal advice before reaching any final agreement and warn them of the risks and disadvantages if they do not do so.

6.16   Mediation meetings are commonly conducted without lawyers present. However, solicitors or counsel acting for the participants may be invited to participate in the mediation process and in any communications if the participants agree and the mediator considers that it would be appropriate.

6.17   When appropriate and with the consent of both participants, arrangements may be made for the attendance of professional third parties other than lawyers, such as interpreters, accountants, actuaries, independent financial advisors, and other advisors.

6.18   When appropriate and with the consent of both parties, arrangements may be made for the attendance of third parties with an interest in the proceedings, such as new partners, parties with a legal or beneficial interest in property that is the subject of dispute, or other family members.

6.19   Mediators must seek to ensure that agreements reached by participants are fully informed and freely made. Participants must have as good an understanding as is practicable of the consequences of their decisions for themselves, their children and other relevant family members.

APPENDIX B

FAMILY MEDIATORS ASSOCIATION
AGREEMENT TO MEDIATE

The following document is the standard Agreement to Mediate currently proposed by FMA to its members on its website. The areas of privilege and confidentiality remain a somewhat grey area and are discussed in Chapter 1 at **1.11**. Family mediation services have their own versions of this document, but the essential clauses must not be altered since they would breach mediation principles and may negate insurance cover. As mediation develops, additional clauses may become necessary. Examples of possible additions based on some of the models discussed in Chapter 4 follow at the end of the document.

AGREEMENT TO MEDIATE
Family Mediators Association

The Principles

1.   Mediation is voluntary. You come to mediation because you want to try to reach resolution of issues in dispute but you have the right to end the mediation if you wish. The mediator also retains the right to end the mediation if he or she judges that it would be appropriate or helpful to do so. In appropriate cases and with the agreement of both parties, the mediator may also seek the assistance of a co-mediator.

2.   As mediators we are impartial and seek to help both parties equally. We do not make judgments or express opinions about who may be right or wrong, and we do not take sides. We help you to reach your own decisions about your futures.

3.   Mediators provide legal and financial information in a neutral way to help you understand the options available to you. We do not provide advice on your 'best interests' and the choices and decisions are yours.

4.   All information including correspondence from either of you will be shared openly with you both. The only exception to this is an address or telephone number which either of you wishes to keep confidential.

The Process

5.   Where relevant we ask you both to provide complete and accurate disclosure of all your financial circumstances, with supporting documents. We do not verify the completeness and accuracy of the information provided, but you will be asked to sign and date a statement confirming you have made full disclosure. If it later emerges that full disclosure has not been made, any agreement based on incomplete information can be set aside and the issues re-opened.

6.   Your financial information is provided on an open basis, which means that it is available to your legal advisers and can be referred to in Court, either in support of an application made with your joint consent or in contested proceedings. This avoids any need for the information to be provided twice.

7.   The actual discussions about possible terms of settlement are understood to be legally privileged. This means that your discussions about the issues between you and proposals for settlement cannot be referred to in Court.

8.   You each agree not to call the mediator(s) to give evidence in Court.

9.   If requested mediators will draw up written summaries of your proposals for settlement (legally privileged) and 'open' summaries of your finances. These summaries help each of you to obtain independent legal advice before entering into a legally binding agreement.

Confidentiality

10. Mediators have a professional duty of confidentiality with exceptions:

(a)   Where any person (particularly a child) is at risk of serious harm we have a duty to contact the appropriate authorities.

(b)   Where we are required to make disclosure to the appropriate government authority under the Proceeds of Crime Act 2002 and/or relevant money laundering regulations. We may also be under a linked obligation to make such disclosure without informing you and may have to discontinue the mediation without further notice.

(c)   Exceptionally, we may disclose personal data in connection with the alleged or established commission of an unlawful act.

(d)   We are 'processors' of personal data for the purposes of the Data Protection Act 1998. You consent to our processing your personal data for the purposes of this Agreement to Mediate. You understand that this includes our retaining and storing your personal data for as long as is necessary in connection with this Agreement. We may retain data for research and statistical purposes but on the understanding that if used it has been stripped of all features from which you could be personally identified.

(e)   Our practice's quality assurance standards require us to monitor our mediation files. Periodically, our practice supervisors and / or the Legal Services Commission may have sight of files, but access is strictly controlled and on a similar confidential basis.

Charges & Payment terms

11.   Full details of fees and refunds will be discussed at the assessment meeting. Fees are charged separately per client. A copy of our Terms and Conditions will be given to fee paying clients. This includes payment and cancellation terms. Please see further details on our website.

Clients eligible for public funding ('legal aid') – all mediation fees will be paid by the Legal Services Commission with no charge to the client.

Concerns and Complaints

12.   Our practice is governed by the Family Mediators Association (FMA) and mediations are conducted in accordance with the FMC Code of Practice (copy available on request). We have a complaints procedure, a copy of which may be obtained from us. Any concern you may have as to our practice should be raised with us in the first instance and thereafter if unresolved in writing to the Family Mediators Association. In this event, you are, by signing this, also agreeing to the release of the file to the complaints adjudicator

13. We shall do our best to help you both. We ask you to show your integrity and commitment to the mediation process and to co-operate as fully as possible in looking for workable solutions.

I have read and understood the above:

Signed: _____

Dated: _____

Additional clauses (only to be inserted where required)

Having taken legal advice, I agree to the limited waiving of privilege so that the Court may be informed of any outcome of mediation.

Signed: _____

Dated: _____

Having taken legal advice, we agree to the amendment of paragraph 4 above so that the mediator may hold confidences about settlement positions revealed in separate meetings.

Signed: _____

Dated: _____

As the legal representatives of the above named participants in mediation, we agree to the principles governing the mediation set out above.

Signed: _____

Dated: _____

© FMA

APPENDIX C

OPEN FINANCIAL STATEMENT

The
Mediation
Specialists

OPEN FINANCIAL STATEMENT

[   ]

and

[   ]

DATE

Prepared by: [   ]: Lawyer/Mediator

The Mediation Specialists

Branksome House

Filmer Grove

Godalming

Surrey

GU7 3AB

Tel No: [   ]

Email: [   ]@themediationspecialists.co.uk

www.themediationspecialists.co.uk

OPEN FINANCIAL STATEMENT

[   ]

and

[   ]

DATE

CONTENTS

SECTION A
Introduction

This Open Statement of Financial Information and its enclosures are furnished on a formal and open basis. It includes amplifying information provided by [   ] and [   ] during the course of the mediation. The Statement reflects the financial information disclosed by [   ] and [   ] to date and which has formed the basis of their discussions within mediation and any proposals, which have resulted from such discussions. The need for full financial disclosure has been explained and supporting documents produced where practical and where requested. It is acknowledged that no independent verification has been undertaken by the mediator as to accuracy or completeness, other than referred to specifically in the Statement.

[   ] and [   ] wished to be referred to as [   ] and [   ] respectively during the mediation process and are referred to as such in this document.

Both [   ] and [   ] confirm that their financial disclosure is complete, save that, [   ].

A separate Memorandum of Understanding relating to the discussions in the mediation, the outcome and any proposals made, which is without prejudice and legally privileged will also be provided at the end of the mediation should [   ] and [   ] wish.

SECTION B
Background Information

[   ] (known as [   ]) (date of birth [   ] – aged [   ]) and [   ] (known as [   ]) (date of birth [   ] – aged xx) were married on [   ] following a period of cohabitation of [   ] years.

[   ] and [   ] have [   ] children namely, [   ] who was born on [   ] and is [   ] years old and [   ] (known as [   ]) who was born on [   ] and is [   ] years old.

[   ] and [   ] report that they are fit and well and neither they, nor [   ] and [   ], have any special needs or disabilities.

[   ] and [   ] continue to reside at the family home at [   ]. This [   ] bedroom property is owned jointly by [   ] and [   ] and is subject to a [   ] repayment mortgage in favour of [   ] Woolwich. [   ] Cottage is currently on the market for sale, but is not under offer.

[   ] and [   ] attend [   ] School, [   ]ford and [   ] and [   ] plan that [   ] will attend either [   ] Secondary School, [   ] South Farnham or [   ] School as from September 2011.

After discussion within the mediation process, [   ] has commenced divorce proceedings. No Decree Nisi date has been obtained as yet. No child support assessment has taken place to date.

[   ] is employed as a [   ] director of [   ] business development and [   ] for an international [   ] Ltd. His national insurance number is [   ].

[   ]'s P60 for tax year ending 5th April 20[   ] indicates a total gross annual income from employment of £[   ] (£[   ] net of tax and national insurance).

[   ] is employed by [   ] County Council as a [   ] secretary at [   ] School, [   ]ford, working [   ] hours per week, and by [   ] Ltd as a [   ] working [   ] hours per week. Her combined gross income is £[   ] per annum (£[   ] net). Her national insurance number is [   ].

SECTION C
Schedule of Assets

[   ] and [   ]

ASSET	DATE/COMMENTS	JOINT	[ ]	[ ]	APPENDIX
Property Address Value £[ ] net of (£[ ]) Mortgage + ([ ]) cos @2.5% Other land/property:		Total:	Total:	Total:	
Bank A/C's		Total:	Total:	Total:	

SECTION C (cont)
Schedule of Assets

[   ] and [   ]

ASSET	DATE/COMMENTS	JOINT	[ ]	[ ]	APPENDIX
Investments		Total:	Total:	Total:	
Policies		Total:	Total:	Total:	
Other Assets Received inheritance Liquid business assets		Total:	Total:	Total:	
Chattels		Total:	Total:	Total:	

SECTION C (cont)
Schedule of Unrealisable Assets

[   ] and [   ]

UNREALISABLE ASSET	DATE/COMMENTS	JOINT	[ ]	[ ]	APPENDIX
Business Interests					
Trust Fund Residuary interest		Total:	Total:	Total:	
Pensions		Total:	Total:	Total:	

SECTION D
Schedule of Liabilities

[   ] and [   ]

LIABILITY	DATE/COMMENTS	JOINT	[ ]	[ ]	APPENDIX
		Total:	Total:	Total:	

SECTION E

Summary of Immediately Realisable Assets after respective Liabilities and Net Total Realisable and Unrealisable Assets disclosed to date

[   ] and [   ]

ASSET	DATE/COMMENTS	JOINT	[ ]	[ ]	TOTAL
PROPERTY Bank Accounts Investments Policies Other Assets Chattels		Total:	Total:	Total:	Total:
LESS LIABILITIES Credit Cards CGT		Total:	Total:	Total:	Total:
NET IMMEDIATELY REALISABLE ASSETS					
UNREALISABLE ASSETS Business Interests Trust Fund Pensions	Shareholding (if any)	Total:	Total:	Total:	Total:
TOTAL NET REALISABLE & UNREALISABLE ASSETS		Total:	Total:	Total:	Total:

SECTION F
Schedule of Income

NAME:

Income from Earnings

Income from Benefits

Child Tax credit   £0,000.00 p.a.

Child Benefit   £0,000.00 p.a.

Income from Property

Rental income net of tax   £0,000.00 p.a.

Total Income   **£00,000.00 p.a.**

NAME:

Income from Earnings

Income from Property

Rental income net of tax   £0,000.00 p.a.

Income from Banks and Building Societies/Investments

Interest received net of tax   £0,000.00 p.a.

Total Income   **£000,000.00 p.a.**

SECTION G
Schedule of documents disclosed by [   ]

As at [*date*] 2011

(Please see Appendix)

Document	Date
Financial Statement	

SECTION H
Schedule of documents disclosed by [   ]

As at [*date*] 2011

(Please see Appendix)

Document	Date
Financial Statement	

SECTION I
Disclosure Declaration

This Open Summary has been prepared by [   ]: Lawyer/Mediator.

Signed: _____

Dated: _____

I, [   ] of [   ] declare that I have made full and complete disclosure of my financial circumstances in this Open Financial Statement.

Signed: _____

Dated: _____

I, [   ] of [   ] declare that I have made full and complete disclosure of my financial circumstances in this Open Financial Statement.

Signed: _____

Dated: _____

APPENDIX D

CO-MEDIATION FILE RECORD

CO-MEDIATION FILE RECORD

Client Name: _____

File number: _____

Please complete as applicable

1.   I have considered that co-mediation/anchor mediation is needed in this matter, after discussion with my Professional Practice Consultant (PPC).

2.   Co-mediation is appropriate by reference to one or more of the following factors:

     (please complete specific reasons and amplify in file note; the following guidance notes may help – refer also to co-mediation protocol of Service or FMA Protocol Nov 2002 as amended on the FMA website)

•   Vulnerability of a participant or relevant child

     _____

•   Vulnerability of a mediator

     _____

•   Significant management issue/shuttle mediation

     _____

•   Requirement of specialist skills

     _____

•   Complexity

     _____

•   Other exceptional circumstance which might prejudice the successful outcome of the mediation if not co-mediated

     _____

     _____

     _____

3.   Co-mediation is appropriate in this case for other reasons, on the understanding that this is a privately funded case or that, if publicly funded, the LSC will not cover the additional costs of the co-mediation, namely:

Guidance Notes

1.   **The LSC Guidance 2010, para 2.23** requires any decision to use Co-mediation to be recorded on the file including, where appropriate, reasons as to the complexity, legal, psychological or otherwise of the case; a risk assessment for the participants and/or Mediator; any reasons as to the requirement of specialist and/or expert skills; any management issues for the Mediation.

2.   **Vulnerability of a participant or relevant child** – current or past domestic violence, drugs or alcohol influence, limited ability of participant, safety issue, allegations of abuse; other 'high risk' issues.

    Vulnerability of a mediator – Complaint about supplier or previous supplier; borderline conflict issue; safety issue; inexperience of mediator; referral of complex case from another service.

    Significant management issue – significant imbalance of perception, understanding, pace, power, experience of participants; significant impasse; shuttle mediation; high conflict; communication management; gender issues; pressure to complete quickly.

    Requirement of specialist skills – Any situation where the complementary skills, competence or experience of a second mediator are appropriate – e g specialist financial/legal knowledge, drugs/alcohol/abuse; therapeutic background/conflict management skills; recognised specialist skills in direct consultation with children.

    Complexity – Legal or psychological complexity; multiplicity of issues; multiplicity of parties to the mediation.

    Other exceptional circumstance which might prejudice the successful outcome of the mediation if not co-mediated – policy of individual service; opportunity to empower the 'victim'.

3.   **Other reasons** may include both the particular circumstances of the case or those of the service or any mediator, such as inexperience.

© FMA

APPENDIX E

ADDITIONAL GROUND RULES FOR COURT-REFERRED MEDIATION

ADDITIONAL GROUND RULES FOR COURT-REFERRED MEDIATION

VOLUNTARY

- Even if you are referred or directed to a mediation assessment appointment, mediation itself is voluntary and requires the continuing agreement of both parties

- We all have a responsibility to be non-abusive, protect safety and provide a safe environment

- We will remain respectful and open-minded, civil, polite and child-centred

- We will not interrupt, and will let everyone speak their turn

IMPARTIAL

- Mediators are impartial

- Unlike the litigation in which you are involved, mediation remains non-judgmental and not finding facts or fault

- Mediators have a special care for children, but we have no investigatory or welfare role; we may work alongside Cafcass, if both are needed

- We will gain information about your children's needs and wishes, not through independent investigation but through your consultation with them, and sometimes by their direct participation in the mediation

- Mediation is non-adversarial, and aimed at bringing an end to litigation

- We look for what can be agreed, not what is in dispute; we solve the problem jointly, not continue fighting the battle

YOUR JOINT DECISION AS PARENTS, NOT ANYONE ELSE'S – MEDIATION IS:

- Positive and optimistic

- Forward facing

- An opportunity for a fresh start

- Focused on you as parents, on your mutual interest in co-operative parenting, and making arrangements run more smoothly

- A real chance to sort things out

- Task centred and time limited

- Your process and your opportunity

CONFIDENTIAL

- Confidential as regards the privileged nature of the proceedings, subject to your agreement otherwise; that is, the mediators will, but only with your joint permission, expect to report in a limited way to the Court about the outcome of mediation

Reproduced with kind permission of The Mediation Centre 12/09

APPENDIX F

DIRECT CONSULTATION WITH CHILDREN PARENTAL CONSENT FORM

DIRECT CONSULTATION WITH CHILDREN PARENTAL CONSENT FORM

Information for parents when parents have requested a Children's Appointment to coincide with parents' attendance at mediation or Collaborative Law

- Children will be seen by a Mediator by agreement of both parents and the Mediator(s).

- Children will be involved in the decision to attend the appointment.

- Attendance at the meeting is voluntary.

- The content of the meeting is confidential between the child/children and the Mediator(s), subject to safety and child protection issues.

- The same rules of confidentiality apply as apply to adult mediation. The discussions within the mediation sessions, with regard to possible terms of settlement or proposals for the future are understood to be 'legally privileged' and cannot therefore be referred to in Court, unless you both agree to waive your privilege. We also ask both of you to agree not to call the mediators to give evidence in Court.

- The child/children will decide, with the Mediator(s), what information, if any, they would like to be taken back to the adult mediation or Collaborative process.

- No written documentation will emerge from the meeting unless the decision to do so is made by the participants.

- Mediators who will be talking to children do so under the strict Code of Practice or in accordance with the Code of Practice of the Family Mediators' Association and the requirements of the Legal Services Commission/Family Mediation Council.

I/We confirm that I am/we are the parent(s) of:

1. _____ dob.

2. _____ dob.

3. _____ dob.

4. _____ dob.

I/we consent to the above named child/children attending an appointment with:

_____ of Family Mediation Manchester Ltd

Mediator/Mediator(s)

_____

Name of Mother: _____

Signed by Mother: _____

Name of Father: _____

Signed by Father: _____

Date: _____

APPENDIX G

BIBLIOGRAPHY

A

R Abel *The Politics of Informal Justice* (Academic Press, 1982), vol 1

R Adam-Cairns 'Why Instruct a Single Joint Expert Valuer?' [2010] Fam Law 656–657

CR Ahrons *The Good Divorce* (Bloomsbury, 1994)

M Ainsworth 'Attachment: Retrospect and Prospect' in Murray Parkes and Stevenson-Hinde (eds) *The Place of Attachment in Human Behaviour* (Tavistock, 1982), pp 3–30

American Bar Association *Final Report – Task Force on Improving Mediation Quality* (2008)

Association pour la Promotion de la Médiation Familiale *European Charter on Training Standards for Family Mediation* (APMF, 1992)

M Aurelius *Meditations* (Penguin Classics, 1964)

Austrian Federal Ministry for Social Security and the Generations *Implementation Directive on Mediation* (1 January 2000)

B

A Babu and P Bonnoure-Aufière *Guide du médiateur familial* (Editions Erès, 2003)

D Bagshaw *Disclosure of Domestic Violence in Family Law Disputes: Issues for Family and Child Mediators* (Conflict Management Research Group, University of South Australia, 2001)

H Baker 'The International Family Law Judicial Conference for Common Law and Commonwealth Jurisdictions' [2009] IFL 250–254

M Banham-Hall 'Children Act First Appointment Scheme' [2008] Fam Law 1054–1055

D Barenboim *Everything is Connected – The Power of Music* (Weidenfeld and Nicolson, 2008)

AE Barsky *Conflict Resolution for the Helping Professions* (Wadsworth, 2000)

G Bateson *Steps to an Ecology of Mind* (Chandler, 1972)

C Bellamy, J Platt and N Crichton 'Talking to Children: the Judicial Perspective' [2010] Fam Law 647-655

R Benjamin *The Constructive Use of Deception: Skills, Strategies and Techniques of the Folkloric Trickster Figure and their Application by Mediators* (1995) 13(1) *Mediation Quarterly*

L Bérubé *Workshop at International Family Mediation Trainers Conference* (Edinburgh, April 2002)

A Boal *Games for Actors and Non-Actors* (Routledge, 1992)

A Bodtker and J Jameson *Mediation as mutual influence: re-examining the use of framing and reframing* (1997) 14(3) *Mediation Quarterly*

P Bohannan *Divorce and After* (Doubleday, 1970)

S Bordow and J Gibson *Evaluation of the family court mediation service* (Family Court of Australia Research and Evaluation Unit, 1994)

M Borkowski, M Murch and V Walker *Marital Violence* (Tavistock, 1983)

J Bowlby 'Loss: Sadness and Depression, Vol 3' in *Attachment and Loss* (Hogarth Press, 1980)

Breslauer Erklärung zur bi-nationalen Kindschaftsmediation (2008) S Kiesewetter, CC Paul and E Dobiejewska FamRZ, 55(8), 753

Bristol Family Mediators Association *Service Performance Review 2009–10* (2011, unpublished)

G Brown 'Early Loss and Depression' in Murray Parkes and Stevenson-Hinde (eds) *The Place of Attachment in Human Behaviour* (Tavistock, 1982), pp 232–268

H Brown and A Marriott *ADR Principles and Practice* (Sweet & Maxwell, 1993)

Brussels II revised Regulation 27 November 2003 (Council Regulation (EC) No 2201/2003)

A Bucher 'The New Swiss Federal Act on International Child Abduction' (2008) *Journal of Private International Law* 139–165

M Bunting 'Our history told in just 100 objects' (2011) *The Guardian Weekly*, 7 January

N Burrell, W Donahue and M Allen 'The impact of disputants' expectations on mediation' (1990) 17 *Human Communication Research* 104–139

RA Bush and JP Folger *The Promise of Mediation* (Jossey-Bass 1994)

C

Cafcass *Annual Report 2006–07*

K Camara and G Resnick 'Marital and parental sub-systems in mother-custody, father-custody and two-parent households: effects on children's social development (1987)' in J Vincent (ed) *Advances in family assessment, intervention and research* (Greenwich), Vol 4, pp 165–196

A Camus *Resistance, Rebellion and Death* (1960)

B Cantwell 'The Emotional Safeguarding of Children in Private Law' [2010] Fam Law 84–90

E Carl, J-P Copin and L Ripke 'Le projet pilote franco-allemand de médiation familiale professionnelle, un modèle de collaboration internationale dans le cadre de conflits familiaux' in *Kind-Prax Special* (2004), pp 25–28

L Carroll *Alice's Adventures in Wonderland* (First published 1865, Folio 1961)

L Carroll *Through the Looking Glass* (First published 1872, Penguin Books, 1948)

D Carter 'Das englische *reunite*-Projekt (2009)' in C Paul and S Kiesewetter (eds) *Mediation bei internationalen Kinderschaftskonflikten* (Verlag Beck), pp 135–145

J Carter *Keeping Faith: Memoirs of a President* (Bantam Books, 1982)

MM Casals *Divorce Mediation* (European Academy of Law Conference, Trier, March 2005)

V Cigoli and M Gennari *Close relationships and community psychology: an international perspective* (FrancoAngeli, 2010)

K Cloke 'Mediation and Meditation – the Deeper Middle Way' (2009) *Mediate.com Weekly* No 266

S Cobb 'A Narrative Perspective on Mediation' in J Folger and T Jones (eds) *New Directions in Mediation – Communication Research and Perspectives* (Sage Publications, 1994)

S Cobb and J Rifkin 'Neutrality as a discursive practice (1991)' in Sarat and Silbey (eds) *Studies in law, politics and society* (JAI Press, USA)

M Cockett and J Tripp *The Exeter Family Study: Family Breakdown and its impact on children* (University of Exeter Press, 1994)

J Coogler *Structured Mediation in Divorce Settlement* (Lexington Books, 1978)

K Corcoran and J Melamed 'From coercion to empowerment: spousal abuse and mediation' (1990) 7(4) *Mediation Quarterly* 303–316

Council of Europe *Recommendation No R (98) 1* (21 January 1998)

Council of Europe *Family Law and the protection of children* (Strasbourg, 1998)

Council of Europe *Conclusions of the 7th European Conference on Family Law – International Family Mediation* (Strasbourg, March 2009)

J Craig 'Everybody's Business: Application for contact orders with consent' [2007] Fam Law 261

Cross on Evidence (Butterworths, 6th edn, 1985)

T Crum *The Magic of Conflict* (Touchstone, 1987)

D

M Dancey 'Contact Activities: Parenting Information Programmes' [2010] Fam Law 1101-1105

G Davis and P Lees *A Study of Conciliation – its Impact on Legal Aid Costs and Place in the Resolution of Disputes arising out of Divorce* (Dept of Social Administration, University of Bristol, 1981)

G Davis et al *Monitoring Publicly Funded Family Mediation – Report to the Legal Services Commission* (Legal Services Commission, 2000)

G Davis, S Finch and R Fitzgerald 'Mediation and Legal Services – The Client Speaks' [2001] Fam Law 110–114

G Davis and M Roberts *Access to Agreement* (Open University Press, 1988)

P Davis 'Special Education Mediation' in DM Kolb and Associates *When Talk Works – Profiles of Mediators* (Jossey-Bass, 1994)

S Day Sclater *Divorce: A Psychosocial Study* (Ashgate, 1999)

E De Bono *Conflicts – A Better Way to Resolve Them* (Penguin, 1991)

C Depner, K Cannata and I Ricci 'Client evaluations of mediation services' (1994) 32(3) *Family and Conciliation Courts Review* 306–325

M Deutsch *The Resolution of Conflict* (Yale University Press, 1973)

R Dingwall 'Divorce mediation: should we change our mind?' (2010) 32 *Journal of Social Welfare & Family Law* 107–117

J Djanogly 'Going into mediation instead of going to court' *Government Gazette* (20 September 2010)

W Donahue, M Allen and N Burrell 'Mediator communicative competence' (1988) 55 *Communication Monographs* 104–119

W Donahue, J Lyles and R Rogan 'Issue Development in Divorce Mediation' (1989) 24 *Mediation Quarterly* 19–28

J Dunn and K Deater-Deckard 'Children's Views of their Changing Families' (2001) *Joseph Rowntree Research Findings* 931

E

F Emery *Systems Thinking: Selected Readings* (Penguin Education, 1969), Vol 1

R Emery et al 'Child Custody Mediation and Litigation: Custody, Contact and Coparenting 12 years After Initial Dispute Resolution' (2001) 69(2) *Journal of Consulting and Clinical Psychology* 323–332

R Emery *The Truth about Children and Divorce* (Viking, 2004)

R Emery and J Jackson *The Charlottesville Mediation Project: mediated and litigated child custody disputes* (1989) 24 *Mediation Quarterly* 3–18

R Emery, D Margola, M Gennari and V Cigoli 'Emotionally Informed Mediation: processing grief and setting boundaries in divorce' in Cigoli and Gennari (eds) *Close relationships and community psychology: an international perspective* (FrancoAngeli, 2010)

R Emery and M Wyer 'Child Custody Mediation' (1987) 55 *Journal of Consulting and Clinical Psychology* 179–186

S Erickson and M McKnight 'Mediating spousal abuse divorces' (1990) 7(4) *Mediation Quarterly* 377–388

European Code of Conduct on Mediation (http://ec.europa.eu/civiljustice/adr/adr_ec_code_conduct_en.htm)

European Forum on Family Mediation Training and Research Training Standards (1992, revised 2003) (www.europeanforum-familymediation.com)

European Parliament *Directive on Certain Aspects of Mediation in Civil and Commercial Matters* (2008/52/EC 21 May 2008)

F

Family Mediators Association (www.thefma.co.uk)

Family Mediation Council *Code of Practice* (2010)

Family Mediation Council *Good Practice Guidelines for In-Court Mediation* (FMC/ap Cynan, 2010)

Family Justice Council and Family Mediation Council *Independent Mediation – Information for Judges, Magistrates and Legal Advisors* (FJC and FMC, 2011)

E Ferri and K Smith *Parenting in the 1990s* (Family Policy Studies Centre, 1996)

E Ferri and K Smith *Step-parenting in the 1990s* (1998) *Rowntree Social Policy Research Findings* No 658

A Fiadjoe 'Family mediation in the Caribbean' *Paper given at the Council of Europe's 7th European Conference on Family Law – International Family Mediation* (Strasbourg, March 2009)

Finer Committee *Report of the Committee on One-Parent Families* Cmnd 5629 (1974)

R Fisher and W Ury *Getting to Yes* (Penguin Books, 1983)

J Folberg and A Taylor *Mediation* (Jossey-Bass, 1984)

J Folger and B Bush 'Transformative Mediation and Third-Party Intervention' (1996) 13(4) *Mediation Quarterly*

FF Furstenberg 'The new extended family (1987)' in Pasley and Tallman (eds) *Remarriage and Step-parenting* (Guildford Press)

G

D Ganancia *La Médiation Familiale Internationale* (Ed Eres, 2007)

LV García and IC Bolaños *Situación de la Mediación Familiar in España* (Ministerio de Trabajo y Asuntos Sociales, 2007)

LV García *Paper given at ESFR Conference* (Milan, October 2010)

F Garwood *Children in Conciliation* (Scottish Association of Family Conciliation Services, 1989)

K Gibran *The Prophet* (Heinemann 1926, Pan Books, 1991)

C Gilligan *In a Different Voice: psychological theory and women's development* (Harvard University Press, 1982)

L Girdner 'Mediation triage: screening for spouse abuse in divorce mediation' (1990) 7(4) *Mediation Quarterly* 365–386

J Gleick *Chaos – Making a New Science* (Abacus, 1993)

A Grand 'Disputes between Parents: Time for a New Order?' [2011] Fam Law 74–75

D Greatbatch and R Dingwall 'Selective facilitation: some preliminary observations on a strategy used by divorce mediators' (1989) 23 *Law and Society Review* 613–641

D Greatbatch and R Dingwall 'The Interactive Construction of Interventions by Divorce Mediators' in J Folger and T Jones (eds) *New Directions in Mediation – Communication Research and Perspectives* (Sage, 1994)

Green Paper *Support for All: the Families and Relationships Green Paper* Cm 7787 (2010)

Green Paper *Proposals for the Reform of Legal Aid in England and Wales* (Ministry of Justice, November 2010)

PH Gulliver *Disputes and Negotiations* (Academic Press, 1979)

H

Baroness Hale of Richmond in *Re D (A Child)* [2006] UKHL 51, [2007] 1 AC 619, [2007] 1 FLR 961

E Hancock 'The dimensions of meaning and belonging in the process of divorce' (1980) 50(1) *American Journal of Orthopsychiatry* 18–27

E Harte and H Howard 'Encouraging positive parental relationships' [2004] Fam Law 456

J Hawthorne, J Jessop, J Pryor and M Richards 'Supporting children through family change' (2003) *Joseph Rowntree Foundation Findings* 323

S Hayes 'Family Mediators in the UK – A Survey of Practice' [2002] Fam Law 760

J Haynes *Divorce Mediation – A Practical Guide* (Springer Publishing, 1981)

J Haynes *Alternative Dispute Resolution – the Fundamentals of Divorce Mediation* (Old Bailey Press, 1993)

BH Herrnstein *Women and mediation: a chance to speak and to be heard* (1996) 13(3) *Mediation Quarterly* 229–241

M Hester and L Radford *Domestic Violence and Child Contact in England and Denmark* (Polity Press, 1996)

M Hester, C Pearson and L Radford 'Family Court Welfare and Voluntary Sector Mediation in Relation to Domestic Violence' (1997) *Rowntree Social Policy Research Findings* 117

EM Hetherington and WG Clingempel et al 'Coping with Marital Transitions – A Family Systems Perspective' (1992) 227 *Society for Research in Child Development* 57

T Holmes and H Rahe 'The social readjustment rating scale' (1967) 11 *Journal of Psychosomatic Research*

Judge C Humphreys *Zen Buddhism* (Unwin Paperbacks, 1984)

J Hunt *Parental Perspectives on the Family Justice System in England and Wales: a review of research* (Report for the Family Justice Council, December 2009)

J

Interdepartmental Committee on Conciliation ('Robinson Committee') *Report* (Lord Chancellor's Department, 1983)

H Irving and R Benjamin 'Research in Family Mediation – an Integrative Review' in Irving and Benjamin (eds) *Family Mediation – Contemporary Issues* (Sage, 1995)

J Johnston and L Campbell *Impasses of Divorce – the Dynamics and Resolution of Family Conflict* (Free Press, 1988)

J Johnston and L Campbell 'A clinical typology of interparental violence in disputed custody divorces' (1993) 63(2) *American Journal of Orthopsychiatry* 190–199

J Johnston and V Roseby *In the Name of the Child: a developmental approach to understanding and helping children of conflicted and violent divorce* (Free Press, 1997)

K

J Kelly 'Mediated and Adversarial Divorce: Respondents' Perceptions of their Processes and Outcomes' (1989) 24 *Mediation Quarterly* 71–88

J Kelly 'Is mediation less expensive? Comparison of mediated and adversarial divorce costs' (1990) 8(1) *Mediation Quarterly* 15–26

J Kelly *Power Imbalance in Divorce and Interpersonal Mediation: assessment and intervention* (1995) 13(2) *Mediation Quarterly* 85–98

J Kelly 'A Decade of Divorce Mediation Research' (1996) 34 *Family and Conciliation Courts Review* 373–385

J Kelly and M Duryee 'Women's and men's views of mediation in voluntary and mandatory settings' (1992) 30(1) *Family and Conciliation Courts Review* 43–49

W Kempe and R Helfer *Helping the Battered Child and his Family* (Lippincott, 1972)

M Keshavjee 'Family mediation in Ismaili Muslim communities throughout the world' *Paper given at the Council of Europe's 7th European Conference on Family Law – International Family Mediation* (Strasbourg, March 2009)

Keys Young Social Research Consultants *Research Evaluation of Family Mediation Practice and the Issue of Violence* (Legal Aid and Family Services, Commonwealth of Australia, 1996)

O Khazova 'Perspectives on international family mediation in the Russian Federation' *Paper given at the Council of Europe's 7th European Conference on Family Law – International Family Mediation* (Strasbourg, March 2009)

J Krementz *How It Feels When Parents Divorce* (Gollancz, 1985)

K Kressel, N Jaffee, B Tuchman, C Watson and MA Deutsch 'Typology of Divorcing Couples' (1980) 19(2) *Family Process* 101–116

K Kressel, F Butler-DeFreitas, S Forlenza and C Wilcox 'Research in Contested Custody Mediations' (1989) 24 *Mediation Quarterly* 55–70

K Kressel, E Frontera, S Forlenza, F Butler and L Fish 'The settlement-oriented versus the problem-solving style in custody mediation' (1994) 50(1) *Journal of Social Issues* 67–83

E Kübler-Ross *On Death and Dying* (Macmillan, 1969)

L

RD Laing *Knots* (Penguin, 1972)

Law Society Family Mediation Code of Practice 1997

Legal Services Commission *Quality Mark Standard for Mediation* (1st edn, December 2002)

Legal Services Commission *Quality Mark Standard for Mediation* (2nd edn, September 2009)

Legal Services Commission *Family Mediation Specification* (December 2009)

Legal Services Commission *Evaluation Report of the In-Court Mediation Trial* (August 2010)

C Lewis, A Papacosta and J Warin 'Cohabitation, separation and fatherhood' (2002) *Joseph Rowntree Foundation Findings* 552

D Lodge *Therapy* (Penguin Books, 1996)

J Loram 'Solicitors in the Mediation Room' [2008] Fam Law 262–266

M Lund 'Research on divorce and children' [1984] 14 Fam Law 198–201

M

P Maida 'Mediating disputes involving people with disabilities' in E Kruk (ed) *Mediation and Conflict Resolution in Social Work and the Human Services* (Nelson-Hall, 1997)

G Mantle *A Consumer Survey of Agreements reached in county court dispute resolution (mediation)* (Essex Probation Occasional Paper 2, 2001)

H Markman, S Stanley and S Blumbers *Fighting For Your Marriage* (Prentice Hall, 1996)

J McIntosh 'Child-Inclusive Mediation' (2000) 18(1) *Mediation Quarterly*

J McIntosh *Because it's for the Kids – Building a Secure Base Parenting Base after Separation* (Children in Focus Program, La Trobe University, Melbourne, for the Commonwealth Attorney General's Department, Canberra, Australia, 2005)

J McIntosh, Y Wells, B Smyth and C Long 'Child-Focused and Child-Inclusive Divorce Mediation: Comparative Outcomes' (2008) 46(1) *Family Court Review* (Association of Family and Conciliation Courts)

J McIntosh, B Smyth, M Kelaher, Y Wells and C Long *Post-separation parenting arrangements and developmental outcomes for infants and children* (Family Court of Australia, Attorney-General's Department, 2010)

C Marzotto (ed) *Gruppi di parola per figli di genitori separati* (Vita e Pensiero, 2010)

A Mehrabian and S Ferris 'Inference of Attitudes from Nonverbal Communication in Two Channels' (1967) 31 *Journal of Counselling Psychology* 248–52

J Melamed 'The Internet and Mediation' (2009) *Mediate.com Weekly* No 298

H Metcalf and L Urwick (ed) *Dynamic Administration: The Collected Papers of Mary Parker Follett* (Harper, 1942)

Midland Courts Judges' Letter (Judiciary of England and Wales, 2010)

D Miller *The Comfort of Things* (Polity Press, 2008)

O Mills 'Effects of Domestic Violence on Children' [2008] Fam Law 165–171

Ministry of Justice *Family Mediation – looking to the future* (November 2010)

A Mitchell *Children in the Middle* (Tavistock, 1985)

R Mnookin *Bargaining with the Devil – When to Negotiate, When to Fight* (Simon & Schuster, 2010)

R Mnookin and L Kornhauser 'Bargaining in the shadow of the law: the case of divorce' (1979) 88 *Yale Law Journal* 950–997

C Moore *The Mediation Process – Practical Strategies for Resolving Conflicts* (Jossey–Bass, 1987)

V Morrow 'Children's Perspectives on Families' (1998) *Rowntree Research Findings* 798

M Murch 'The Voice of the Child in Private Family Law Proceedings in England and Wales' [2005] IFL 8

C Murray Parkes *Bereavement* (Tavistock, 1972)

N

National Alternative Dispute Resolution Advisory Council *Report on Standards* (Australia, 2001)

National Audit Office *Review of Legal Aid and Mediation for people involved in family breakdown* (March 2007)

National Family Mediation *Policy on Domestic Violence* (London, 1996)

B Neale and A Wade *Parent Problems – children's views on life when parents split up* (Young Voice, 2000)

B Neumann 'How mediation can effectively address the male and female power imbalance in divorce' (1992) 9 *Mediation Quarterly* 227–239

O

B Obama *The Audacity of Hope* (Canongate, 2008)

J O'Connor and J Seymour *Introducing NLP – Neuro-Linguistic Programming* (Thorsons, 1995)

A O'Quigley *Listening to children's views: the findings and recommendations of recent research* (Joseph Rowntree Foundation, 2000)

P

B Paolucci et al *Family Decision-Making – an Ecosystem Approach* (Wiley, 1977)

D Parker and L Parkinson *Solicitors and Family Conciliation Services: A Basis for Professional Co-operation* [1985] Fam Law 270–274

L Parkinson 'Bristol Courts Family Conciliation Service' [1982] Fam Law 13–16

L Parkinson 'Conciliation – a new approach to family conflict resolution' (1983) 13 *British Journal of Social Work* 19–38

L Parkinson *Conciliation in Separation and Divorce* (Croom Helm, 1986)

L Parkinson 'Co-mediation with a lawyer mediator' [1989] Fam Law 48–49, 135–139

L Parkinson *Family Mediation* (Sweet and Maxwell, 1997)

L Parkinson 'A family systems approach to mediation with families in transition' *Context, the magazine for family therapy and systemic practice* (October 2002)

L Parkinson 'Child-Inclusive Family Mediation' [2006] Fam Law 483–488

L Parkinson 'Gateways to Mediation' [2010] Fam Law 867–871

L Parkinson 'Family mediation: ideology or new discipline?' [2011] Fam Law 88

P Parkinson and J Cashmore 'Judicial Conversations with children in parenting disputes: the views of Australian judges' (2007) 21 *International Journal of Law, Policy and the Family* 160

C Paul and S Kiesewetter (eds) *Mediation bei internationalen Kinderschaftskonflikten* (Verlag Beck, 2009)

C Paul and J Walker 'Family Mediation in International Child Custody Conflicts' (2008) 22(1) *American Journal of Family Law* 42–45

J Pearson 'An evaluation of alternatives to court adjudication' (1982) 7 *Justice System Journal* 420–444

J Pearson 'The equity of mediated divorce settlements' (1991) 9 *Mediation Quarterly* 179–197

J Pearson and N Thoennes 'A preliminary portrait of client reactions to three court mediation programs' (1985) 23(1) *Conciliation Courts Review* 1–14

J Pearson and N Thoennes 'Divorce Mediation Research Results' in Folberg and Milne (eds) *Divorce Mediation – Theory and Practice* (Guilford Press, 1988), pp 429–452

M Pel et al 'Family Mediation in the Netherlands' [2009] IFL 4, 255–259

M Pendlebury 'Divorce and separation: listening to children and young people in mediation' [2008] Fam Law 1255

A Perry and B Rainey *Supervised, supported and indirect contact: orders and their implications* (Report to the Nuffield Foundation, University of Wales, Swansea, 2006)

C Piper *The Responsible Parent – A Study in Divorce Mediation* (Harvester Wheatsheaf, 1991)

M Potter 'The Voice of the Child: Children's Rights in Family Law Proceedings' [2008] IFL 140

Practice Direction: The Revised Private Law Programme [2010] Fam Law 539–544

Pre-Application Protocol on Family Mediation Information and Assessment Meetings (Ministry of Justice and Her Majesty's Courts Service, February 2011)

D Pruitt and P Carnevale *Negotiation in Social Conflict* (Open University Press, 1993)

R

O Ramsbotham, T Woodhouse and H Miall *Contemporary Conflict Resolution* (Polity Press, 2nd edn, 2005)

A Rapoport *The Origins of Violence* (Paragon House, 1989)

L Rapoport 'The state of crisis – some theoretical considerations' in HJ Parad *Crisis Intervention* (Family Service Association of America, 1965)

Reunite Pilot Project *Mediation in International Parental Child Abduction* (Report, October 2006)

H Rhoades 'Revising Australia's parenting laws' (2010) *Child and Family Law Quarterly* 172

M Roberts *Mediation in Family Disputes* (Ashgate, 2nd edn, 1997)

M Roberts 'Quality Standards for Family Mediation Practice' [2010] Fam Law 661–666

J Robey 'Mediation and the Revised Private Law Programme' [2009] Fam Law 67–70

N Robinson 'Developing Family Mediation' [2008] Fam Law 926–928

N Robinson 'Developing Family Mediation: Innovative Approaches to ADR' [2008] Fam Law 1048–1053

N Robinson 'Developing Family Mediation' [2009] Fam Law 734–744

N Robinson and T Brisby 'ADR Professional' [2001] Fam Law 59–64

B Rodgers and J Prior *Divorce and separation: the outcomes for children* (Joseph Rowntree Foundation, 1998)

J Rothman *Resolving Identity-based Conflict in Nations, Organisations and Communities* (Jossey-Bass, 1997)

M Rutter 'Resilience in the Face of Adversity' (1985) 147 *British Journal of Psychiatry* 598–611

S

D Salter 'A Decade of Pension Sharing' [2010] Fam Law 1294–1298

D Saposnek *Mediating Child Custody Disputes* (Jossey-Bass, 1983)

E Scabini and G Rossi *Rigenerare I Legami: la mediazione nelle relazione familiare e comunitarie* (V & P Milan, 2003)

HR Schaffer *Making Decisions about Children – Psychological Questions and Answers* (Blackwell, 1990)

Scottish Civil Courts Review ('Gill Review') (September 2009)

MT Shattuck 'Mandatory Mediation' in Folberg and Milne (eds) *Divorce Mediation – Theory and Practice* (Guilford Press, 1988)

K Slaikeu, J Pearson and N Thoennes 'Divorce Mediation Behaviors: A Descriptive System and Analysis' in Folberg and Milne (eds) *Divorce Mediation – Theory and Practice* (Guilford Press), pp 475–495

C Smart 'Equal shares: rights for fathers or recognition for children?' (2004) *Critical Social Policy* 484

C Smart and B Neale 'It's My Life Too- Children's Perspectives on Post-Divorce Parenting' [2000] Fam Law 163–169

C Smart, V May, A Wade and C Furness *Residence and Contact Disputes in Court*, Vol 2 (Department of Constitutional Affairs, 2005)

JL Steinberg 'Towards an Interdisciplinary Commitment' (1980) *Journal of Marital and Family Therapy* 259–267

S Steinman 'The Experience of Children in a Joint Custody Arrangement' (1981) 51 *American Journal of Orthopsychiatry* 403–414

V Stirum 'ADR Professional' [2010] Fam Law 1228–1230

T

D Tannen *That's Not What I Meant* (Virago, 1992)

N Thoennes and J Pearson 'Response to Bruch and McIsaac' (1992) 30(1) *Family and Conciliation Courts Review* 142–143

O Tjersland 'Mediation in Norway' (1995) 12(4) *Mediation Quarterly* 339–351

L Trinder 'Conciliation, the Private Law Programme and Children's Well-being' [2008] Fam Law 338–342

L Trinder, M Beek and J Connolly 'Making contact: How parents and children negotiate and experience contact after divorce' (2002) *Joseph Rowntree Foundation Findings* 092

L Trinder, J Connolly, J Kellett, C Notley and L Swift *Making Contact happen or making contact work? The process and outcomes of in-court conciliation* (DCA Research Series 3/06, 2006)

L Trinder and J Kellett *The Longer Term Outcomes of In-Court Conciliation* (Ministry of Justice, 2007)

L Trinder 'Shared Residence: A Review of Recent Research Evidence' [2010] Fam Law 1192–1197

U

UK College of Family Mediators *Children, Young People and Family Mediation – Policy and Practice Guidelines* (2000)

V

S Vigers *Note on the development of mediation, conciliation and similar means to facilitate agreed solutions* (Permanent Bureau, Hague Conference on Private International Law, October 2006)

S Vigers *Feasibility Study on Cross-Border Mediation in Family Matters* (Permanent Bureau, Hague Conference on Private International Law, March 2007)

W

J Waldron, C Roth, P Fair, E Mann and J McDermott 'A Therapeutic Mediation Model for Child Custody Dispute Resolution' (1984) 3 *Mediation Quarterly* 5–20

J Walker and J Hornick *Communication in Marriage and Divorce* (The BT Forum, 1996)

J Walker, P McCarthy and N Timms *Mediation: the Making and Remaking of Co-operative Relationships* (Relate Centre for Family Studies, University of Newcastle, 1994)

J Walker and M Robinson 'Conciliation and Family Therapy' in T. Fisher (ed) *Family Conciliation within the UK* (Family Law, 1990), pp 61–66

Wall LJ *Report to the President of the Family Division on the publication by the Women's Aid Federation of England entitled* 'Twenty-nine Child Homicides: Lessons still to be learnt on domestic violence and child protection'

J Wallerstein 'Children of Divorce – the psychological tasks of the child' (1983) 53(2) *American Journal of Orthopsychiatry* 230–243

J Wallerstein and S Blakeslee *Second Chances – Men, Women and Children a Decade After Divorce* (Bantam Press, 1989)

J Wallerstein and J Kelly *Surviving the Break-up – how children and parents cope with divorce* (Grant McIntyre, 1980)

C Whitaker 'Process Techniques of Family Therapy' (1977) *Family Process*, Vol 1

Y

M Yunus in S Kumar and F Whitefield (eds) *Visionaries of the 20th Century – a Resurgence Anthology* (Green Books, 2006)

INDEX

References are to paragraph numbers.